RHETORIC AND RELIGIOUS IDENTITY
IN LATE ANTIQUITY

Rhetoric and Religious Identity in Late Antiquity

Edited by
RICHARD FLOWER
and
MORWENNA LUDLOW

OXFORD
UNIVERSITY PRESS

Great Clarendon Street, Oxford, OX2 6DP,
United Kingdom

Oxford University Press is a department of the University of Oxford.
It furthers the University's objective of excellence in research, scholarship,
and education by publishing worldwide. Oxford is a registered trade mark of
Oxford University Press in the UK and in certain other countries

© Oxford University Press 2020, Copyright for Chapter 2 Éric Rebillard

The moral rights of the authors have been asserted

First Edition published in 2020

Impression: 1

All rights reserved. No part of this publication may be reproduced, stored in
a retrieval system, or transmitted, in any form or by any means, without the
prior permission in writing of Oxford University Press, or as expressly permitted
by law, by licence or under terms agreed with the appropriate reprographics
rights organization. Enquiries concerning reproduction outside the scope of the
above should be sent to the Rights Department, Oxford University Press, at the
address above

You must not circulate this work in any other form
and you must impose this same condition on any acquirer

Published in the United States of America by Oxford University Press
198 Madison Avenue, New York, NY 10016, United States of America

British Library Cataloguing in Publication Data

Data available

Library of Congress Control Number: 2020941997

ISBN 978–0–19–881319–4

Printed and bound by
CPI Group (UK) Ltd, Croydon, CR0 4YY

Links to third party websites are provided by Oxford in good faith and
for information only. Oxford disclaims any responsibility for the materials
contained in any third party website referenced in this work.

Acknowledgements

This book would not exist without the support and assistance of a number of individuals and organizations. Early versions of most of the chapters were delivered at two conferences held at the University of Exeter: the first, on 24, 25, and 26 July 2015, had the title of *Rhetoric and Religious Identity in Late Antiquity*, while the follow-on event, *Constructing Christians: Rhetorics of Rhetoric in Late Antiquity*, took place on 27 June 2016. Both of these meetings were funded as part of the Early Career Leadership Fellowship awarded to Richard Flower by the UK's Arts and Humanities Research Council for a project entitled *Cataloguing Damnation: The Birth of Scientific Heresiology in Late Antiquity*, with the University of Exeter providing additional financial support. Neither event would have been possible without the fantastic administrative work of Amelia Hurtley and the help of four postgraduate students—Taylor FitzGerald, Giovanni Hermanin De, Maria Kneafsey, Paschalis Gkortsilas, and Reichenfeld—all of whom have now completed excellent doctoral theses. Alongside the scholars whose work appears in the volume, we would also like to thank the other participants at these events for their contributions to some excellent discussions.

Karen Raith at Oxford University Press has been an extremely helpful Commissioning Editor throughout the entire process and the two anonymous readers provided very useful and generous feedback that improved the individual chapters and the volume as a whole. Dr Marcelina Gilka and Dr Helen John both performed extremely important editorial work, for which the University of Exeter and the St Luke's College Foundation provided funding. Jen Hinchliffe, who copy-edited the whole volume for the Press, combined precision and accuracy with good humour. They have all corrected many errors and rectified many problems; responsibility for those that remain lies with us.

Contents

List of Illustrations ix
List of Contributors xi

1. Rhetoric and Religious Identity in Late Antiquity 1
   Richard Flower and Morwenna Ludlow

PART I: THE NATURE OF RELIGIOUS IDENTITIES AND THEIR REPRESENTATION

2. Approaching 'Religious Identity' in Late Antiquity 15
   Éric Rebillard

3. The Rhetoric of Pagan Religious Identities: Porphyry
   and his First Readers 28
   Aaron P. Johnson

4. The Maccabees, 'Apostasy', and Julian's Appropriation of
   Hellenismos as a Reclaimed Epithet in Christian Conversations
   of the Fourth Century CE 48
   Douglas Boin

PART II: AGENTS OF THE REPRESENTATION OF RELIGIOUS IDENTITY

5. Julian the Apologist: Christians and Pagans on the Mother
   of the Gods 67
   Shaun Tougher

6. Bodies, Books, Histories: Augustine of Hippo and the
   Extraordinary (*civ. Dei* 16.8 and Pliny, *HN* 7) 83
   Susanna Elm

7. Classical Decadence or Christian Aesthetics? Libanius, John
   Chrysostom, and Augustine on Rhetoric 99
   Raffaella Cribiore

8. 'Very great are your words': Dialogue as Rhetoric in
   Manichaean Kephalaia 114
   Nicholas Baker-Brian

9. 'A Christian cannot employ magic': Rhetorical Self-fashioning of the Magicless Christianity of Late Antiquity 128
Maijastina Kahlos

PART III: MODES OF THE REPRESENTATION OF RELIGIOUS IDENTITY

10. The Rhetorical Construction of a Christian Empire in the *Theodosian Code* 145
Mark Humphries

11. What Happened after Eusebius? Chronicles and Narrative Identities in the Fourth Century 160
Peter Van Nuffelen

12. The Rhetoric of Heresiological Prefaces 180
Richard Flower

13. Constructing Identity in the Tomb: The Visual Rhetoric of Early Christian Iconography 198
Robin M. Jensen

14. Renunciation and Ascetic Identity in the *Liber ad Renatum* of Asterius Ansedunensis 219
Hajnalka Tamas

15. Christian Literary Identity and Rhetoric about Style 231
Morwenna Ludlow

Bibliography 251
Index 283

List of Illustrations

13.1. Early Christian sarcophagus with scenes from the Old and New Testaments (Sacrifice of Isaac, Jesus healing the blind man, Jesus healing the paralytic, Jesus multiplying loaves and fish, Adam and Eve, Jesus raising the dead). Museo Pio Cristiano, Vatican, early fourth century. Photo credit: Vanni Archive/Art Resource, NY.   199

13.2. Marble sarcophagus with the myth of Endymion and Selene, mid-second-century CE, Rome. Metropolitan Museum of Art, Fletcher Fund, 1924. Photo credit: Open Access for Scholarly Publication.   202

13.3. Sarcophagus of Quinta Flavia Severina, Musei Capitolini, Rome, 230–40. Wikimedia Creative Commons. Photo credit: Jean-Pol Grandmont.   202

13.4. Sarcophagus of C. Junius Euphodus and Metilla Acte, depicted in scenes from the myth of Admetus and Alcestis, 161–70, now in the Museo Chiaramonti, Vatican Museum. Wikimedia Creative Commons. Photo credit: Jastrow.   203

13.5. Sarcophagus with Allegory of the Four Seasons, ca. 280, marble, 24 ¾ × 72 × 25 ¾, Chazen Museum of Art, University of Wisconsin-Madison, Max W. Zabel Fund purchase, 69.13.1, used with permission.   204

13.6. Sarcophagus of Julius Achilleus, Museo Nazionale Romano, ca. 270, found in Rome near the Baths of Caracalla. Photo credit: Vanni Archive/Art Resource, NY.   204

13.7. Sarcophagus said to be of Plotinus, late third to fourth century, Museo Gregoriano Profano, Vatican. Photo credit: Scala/Art Resource.   205

13.8. Sarcophagus of Sta. Maria Antiqua, Rome (Forum), ca. 290–300. Photo credit: Robin M. Jensen.   207

13.9. Early Christian sarcophagus with various biblical scenes, Museo Pio Cristiano, Vatican, first quarter of the fourth century. Photo credit: Scala/Art Resource, NY.   209

13.10. Portrait of Catervius and Severina, now in the Cathedral of San Catervo in Tolentino. Photo credit: Mark D. Ellison, used with permission.   213

13.11. Tree sarcophagus, Proconnesian marble, ca. 375 CE; inv. FAN.92.00.2488, Musée départemental Arles antique © J.-L. Maby, L. Roux.   216

13.12. Strigillated sarcophagus of Catervius and Severina, now in the Cathedral of San Catervo in Tolentino, Italy, ca. 379. Photo credit: Mark D. Ellison, used with permission.   217

List of Contributors

Nicholas Baker-Brian is Reader in Ancient Religions at Cardiff University's School of History, Archaeology, and Religion. He has published extensively on religion in Late Antiquity, and on emperorship in the later Roman Empire.

Douglas Boin is Associate Professor of History at Saint Louis University and the author of four books, including the forthcoming *Alaric the Goth: An Outsider's History of the Fall of Rome* (New York).

Raffaella Cribiore is Professor of Classics at New York University. She is a papyrologist and has written several books on ancient education and rhetoric in late antiquity.

Susanna Elm is Sidney H. Ehrman Professor of History and Classics and specializes in the social history of the later Roman Empire. She is author of *Sons of Hellenism, Fathers of the Church: Emperor Julian, Gregory of Nazianzus, and the Vision of Rome* (Berkeley 2012), and co-editor, with Barbara Vinken, of *Braut Christi. Familienformen im Zeichen der sponsa*, (Munich 2016).

Richard Flower is Associate Professor in Classics and Late Antiquity at the University of Exeter. He specializes in the construction of imperial and ecclesiastical authority, particularly in late-antique invective and heresiology. His publications include *Emperors and Bishops in Late Roman Invective* (Cambridge 2013) and *Imperial Invectives against Constantius II* (Liverpool 2016). He is also editing *The Cambridge Companion to Christian Heresy*.

Mark Humphries is Professor of Ancient History and Head of the Department of Classics, Ancient History, and Egyptology at Swansea University. He has published widely on the political, religious, and cultural history of late antiquity, and is one of the general editors of the book series *Translated Texts for Historians* (Liverpool University Press).

Robin M. Jensen is the Patrick O'Brien Professor of Theology at the University of Notre Dame (USA). Her teaching and published works span the intersection of early Christian art, architecture, ritual practice, and theology.

Aaron P. Johnson is Associate Professor of Classics and Humanities at Lee University. His work has focused on key figures who contributed to the intellectual cultures of Late Antiquity. He is the author of *Religion and Identity in Porphyry of Tyre* (Cambridge 2013) and *Eusebius* (London 2014).

Maijastina Kahlos is Research Fellow at the at the Helsinki Collegium for Advanced Studies, University of Helsinki. She is the author of *Debate and*

Dialogue: Christian and Pagan Cultures, c. 360–430 (Aldershot 2007), *Forbearance and Compulsion: The Rhetoric of Tolerance and Intolerance in Late Antiquity* (London 2009), and *Religious Dissent in Late Antiquity* (Oxford 2020), and editor of *The Faces of the Other: Religious Rivalry and Ethnic Encounters in the Later Roman World* (Turnhout 2012) and *Emperors and the Divine—Rome and its Influence* (Helsinki 2016).

Morwenna Ludlow is Professor of Christian History and Theology at the University of Exeter. She is author of *The Early Church* (London 2009), co-editor with Scot Douglass of *Reading the Church Fathers* (London 2011) and has written widely on Gregory of Nyssa. Her most recent book is *Art, Craft and Theology in Fourth Century Christian Authors*, also published with Oxford University Press (2020).

Éric Rebillard is the Avalon Foundation Professor in the Humanities and Professor of Classics and History at Cornell University. His research focuses on the transformations of religious practices in Late Antiquity. He is the author of *Christians and Their Many Identities in Late Antiquity, North Africa, 200–450 CE* (Ithaca, NY 2012).

Hajnalka Tamas is Research Associate in Late-Antique Christianity at the Faculty of Theology and Religious Studies, KU Leuven (Belgium). In 2016 she concluded a research project funded by the Fritz Thyssen Stiftung, entitled 'The Monk in Society: Late-Antique Asceticism and Social Relations'. In 2016–2018 she was a Marie Curie Research Fellow at the University of Exeter (Grant no. 650265, 'Christian Diversity in Late Antique Sirmium (ca. 350 – ca. 450 AD): A Historical, Literary and Theological Study').

Shaun Tougher is Professor of Late Roman and Byzantine History at Cardiff University. He has published extensively on Julian the Apostate and eunuchs. His publications include *Julian the Apostate* (Edinburgh 2007), *The Eunuch in Byzantine History and Society* (London 2008), and (co-edited with Nicholas Baker-Brian) *Emperor and Author: The Writings of Julian the Apostate* (Swansea 2012). He is currently completing a monograph on eunuchs in the Roman Empire.

Peter Van Nuffelen is Professor of Ancient History at Ghent University. His most recent publications are *Penser la tolerance durant l'Antiquité tardive* (Paris 2018) and, with L. Van Hoof, *The Latin Fragmentary Histories of Late Antiquity* (Cambridge 2020).

1

Rhetoric and Religious Identity in Late Antiquity

Richard Flower and Morwenna Ludlow

The topic of religious identity in late antiquity is highly contentious, with a recent upsurge of interest in this issue, partly driven by a growth in interdisciplinary research between classics, ancient and medieval history, philosophy, religion, patristics, and Byzantine studies. The debates primarily revolve around the reasons for shifts in self-identification in the ancient world and the degree to which any labels (whether ancient or modern) for religious categories reflect a sense of a significant and unified social identity. There are questions about what precisely belongs to the category 'religious', especially as to whether it is adequately captured by reference to practices and beliefs. Moreover, studies of this facet of late-antique culture are starting to employ methods already used in scholarship on other forms of ancient identity politics (especially ethnic discourse concerning 'barbarians') and so are coming to explore the malleability and potential overlapping of religious identities in late antiquity, as well as their variable expressions in response to different public and private contexts.[1] Although most scholars agree that religious identities were constructed and expressed through forms of 'rhetoric', further systematic study of rhetoric's meaning and influence in this context is still required.[2] Recent scholarship has emphasized the socio-political context of late-antique rhetoric, not least the ways in which rules about appropriate discourse prescribe or seek to perpetuate various social norms. For this reason, apparently neutral or technical texts can be studied for the insights they yield about the identities of those people compiling or using them.

---

[1] On these issues, see for example: Sandwell (2007); McLynn (2009); Alan Cameron (2011); Rebillard (2012); Cribiore (2013); Johnson (2013); Boin (2014); Stenger (2014); van Nuffelen (2014); Rebillard and Rupke (2015).

[2] See especially Brown (1992); Averil Cameron (1991).

This volume therefore seeks to engage with and develop previous directions of research by exploring a wider variety of forms of construction and negotiation of religious identities (both individual and communal) in late-antique society. In particular, it emphasizes the importance of rhetoric to this question, incorporating both the rhetoric of self-presentation used by late-antique figures themselves and also the rhetoric evident in the external (and often hostile) construction and ascription of religious identity onto them by contemporary and later individuals. In addition, as well as considering the place of rhetoric in creating religious identities, it also explores late-antique discussions about rhetoric itself, particularly in the context of Christian responses to classical *paideia*. The contributors to this volume not only employ a broad conception of the notion of 'rhetoric' that includes both literary material and the artistic and architectural record, but they also seek to create a more conceptually informed and illuminating understanding of the possible interpretations of 'rhetoric' in these contexts. Recent studies of rhetoric in late antiquity have tended to reject the contention, common in early- to mid-twentieth-century scholarship, that rhetoric in late antiquity had lost its practical function (especially its grounding in argument) and had become restricted to forms of epideictic for display. This claim was sometimes linked with assumptions about the degeneration of late-antique literature (and rhetoric in particular) under the influence of the so-called Second Sophistic. More recent scholarship has developed a much more nuanced picture of rhetoric in late antiquity and has subjected the concept of the Second Sophistic to thorough critique.[3] This approach needs to be applied to the study of presentations and constructions of specifically religious identity in the period.

We also aim to move beyond claims that representations of late-antique religious identity involved (and still involve) rhetoric, in order to ask *how* that rhetoric worked, *who* used it, and in *what forms*? Expressions of religious identity provide interesting case studies of rhetoric in action, which can contribute further to our understanding of the use of rhetoric in the fourth century: in what sense are these various modes of discourse 'rhetorical'? Is rhetoric itself associated with (or disassociated from) any particular religious traditions? To what extent are the modes of discourse under discussion associated with the traditional sites of rhetoric: law, politics, and the attribution of praise or blame (each of which was a powerful site for identity-formation of several kinds)?

In sum, rhetoric and religious identity are here brought together to provide *mutual* illumination: in what way does a better understanding of rhetoric (its rules, forms, practices) enrich our understanding of the expression of

---

[3] Themistius and Penella (2000); Cribiore (2001); Whitmarsh (2001); Heath (2004); Whitmarsh (2005); Himerius and Penella (2007); Cribiore (2013); van Hoof (2014); Kim (2017); Richter and Johnson (2017); Whitmarsh (2017).

late-antique religious identity? Conversely, does an understanding of how religious identity was ascribed, constructed, and contested provide us with a new perspective on rhetoric at work in late antiquity?

In order to cover this ground, this volume employs a variety of complementary perspectives. Conceptual and methodological questions are addressed explicitly in the three chapters of Part I, as they analyse and to some degree problematize the current terms of the debate on religious identity in late antiquity: 'religion', 'Hellenism' (specifically, the Greek word '*Hellenismos*'), and 'semi-Christian'. By implication, they also deal with the concept of 'paganism'. Part II asks the question '*who* is responsible for representations of religious identity in the fourth century?' with a focus not only on famous ancient authors such as Julian and Augustine, but also on how certain debates (the relationship of magic and religious ritual) and literary forms (Manichaean dialogue literature) have been constructed by modern scholars. Part III asks *how* religious identity was expressed. A particular feature of this volume is the extension of the debate on religious identity to literary forms that have been underexplored for this purpose, including law codes and funerary art. Throughout the volume, the chronological scope is the 'long fourth century', covering the period from the Tetrarchy to the Theodosians, as this was a time of significant development and transformation of the religious life of the Roman Empire and produced a correspondingly rich variety of material for analysis. The geographical range is mostly the Roman Empire, but some of the texts discussed (notably the Manichaean literature) exceed those borders and we write with an awareness that issues of religious identity cut across political borders in interesting ways.

* * *

Part I presents a trio of discussions of the nature of religious identities and their representation in late antiquity. Each of these is centred on a particular category that has become a focus of scholarly debate, exploring the ways in which it has been interpreted and the challenges it presents for our understanding of the period. Éric Rebillard's wide-ranging piece not only problematizes the category of 'semi-Christians' but also critiques the broader scholarly method of categorizing individuals' identity by group, a practice condemned by Rogers Brubaker as 'groupism'. Instead, Rebillard suggests studying how an individual might possess several different identities, which are neither equally salient nor equally active in any given context. Some famous cases concerning religious identity—such as that of the fourth-century poet and politician Ausonius—have proven challenging to historians, not so much because religious identities are fluid, but because 'religious identities are not necessarily activated in any given context, even when available'. This question of when and why certain identities are activated (both by historical individuals and by scholars seeking to describe them) thus opens up a new avenue for exploring the rhetoric of religious identity in the past. Moreover, it simultaneously acknowledges the rhetoric implicit in modern scholarly methods, since categorization 'always does violence to individuals', even when nuanced.

Aaron Johnson's chapter, on the third-century philosopher Porphyry of Tyre and responses to him by Iamblichus and Eusebius of Caesarea, focuses on the significant and debated notion of 'religion', particularly when applied to pagans in late antiquity. This has attracted its own share of scholarly rhetoric in recent years, with most scholars now emphasizing that terms such as *eusebeia* or *religio* do not equate to the modern concept of 'religion', meaning that any sense of a collective 'pagan religious identity' is an external construct imposed by Christian authors. Whilst rejecting suggestions that Porphyry ever used 'Hellene' to denote an 'overarching identity label for a religious group that we now name pagans or paganism', as well as arguing that neither Iamblichus nor Eusebius narrowed down the concept of 'Hellenism' in such a way, Johnson nonetheless nuances approaches to 'the religious' in their writings. This chapter demonstrates that, although these three authors were 'unwilling to articulate these matters within a discrete identity category distinguished from other categories like culture, philosophy, race, or nation', their use of religious identity-labels hints at an incipient 'shift in religious conceptions, insofar as they formulate an ideal for pagan religious thought or practice'. Johnson thus points the way towards a method for studying religious categories even in late-antique authors who do not define them in the same disembedded manner that would be adopted in later generations.

Douglas Boin's contribution continues to explore the same conceptual and terminological issues as Johnson, examining how they play out in the middle of the fourth century. This chapter takes the form of a novel reinterpretation of the thorny question of the emperor Julian's employment of the term *Hellenismos*, examining it within the context of earlier Jewish and Christian uses of the word. Boin argues that its meaning and application can be traced back to Julian's Christian background and that it can therefore be regarded as an example of a 'reclaimed epithet'—that is, a previously pejorative description (of Christians who are 'acting too Greek') being adopted by an individual or group who rhetorically reinforce their identity through its use. Rather than representing 'Julian's profession of belief in a different universal religious system', which is being contrasted clearly with Christianity, his employment of *Hellenismos* is thus said to function within a specifically Christian discourse. Julian therefore emerges from this reading as a man who, rather than seeking to distinguish himself from 'Christians', may instead 'have been directly rebuking many hardline members of his own Christian community'. From such a perspective, Boin argues, this rhetoric of religious identity in late antiquity does not provide a clear window onto a Roman world divided between 'pagan' and 'Christian'; rather, it reveals a society 'being torn asunder by the fact that the Christian community could not agree on what it meant to be a "Christian"'. This chapter therefore highlights the importance of recognizing the 'in-group' nature of much polemical religious rhetoric whilst also providing a radical reappraisal of Julian's own 'apostasy'.

The methodological and theoretical discussions of Part I are complemented by the specific case studies in Parts II and III. Part II turns attention squarely to some of those figures often regarded as having been responsible for distinctive constructions of religious identity in the fourth and early fifth centuries. Besides discussions of a number of prominent individual actors and authors from the period—the emperor Julian, Augustine of Hippo, Libanius, and John Chrysostom—this part also looks at identity construction more broadly within both Christianity and Manichaeism during this period, particularly through the rhetoric of exclusion. By studying these particular conceptualizations of identity and the place of rhetoric in religious practices, this section of the volume highlights a variety of responses to the changing circumstances that came into being with the growing notion of a Christian Roman Empire during this time.

Following on from Boin's methodological consideration of Julian's self-presentation in the preceding chapter, Part II opens with Shaun Tougher's exploration of one of the emperor's lesser-studied works: the *Hymn to the Mother of the Gods*. This philosophical exploration of the worship of the Great Mother is placed in dialogue with two hostile accounts of these beliefs and practices written by the Christian authors Arnobius of Sicca and Firmicus Maternus, revealing how each of these texts employs the cult to create distinctive conceptions of religious identity. All three provide descriptions of the myths associated with the goddess, with Arnobius and Firmicus both mocking them and asserting their human origins, whilst Julian reinterprets them as a Neoplatonic allegory. Moreover, whilst the Christian works have long been characterized as apologies, Tougher argues that the same should be said of Julian's writing, which functions as a response to critiques of precisely the sort seen in Firmicus and Arnobius. The text therefore deserves to be reread as 'not just about providing a Neoplatonic interpretation of the myth and the cult; it is also apologetic—anti-Christian—in character'. In a different manner to Boin, therefore, Tougher also sees Julian's Christian background as important to understanding his writings as emperor, since he used his knowledge of criticisms of the worship of the Great Mother to defend its place in his policy of restoration and to stress 'the centrality of the cult within the identity of the Roman empire itself'.

Susanna Elm's contribution moves on to consider another figure who often appears prominently in modern explorations of late-antique religious identity —Augustine of Hippo—emphasizing how he uses the category of 'the extraordinary' to make specifically Christian claims about human identity. In particular, this chapter focuses on the reports of 'certain monstrous races of men', including a number of seemingly fantastical descriptions, which appear in chapter 16.8 of the *City of God*. As Elm demonstrates, Augustine's work was created through detailed use of, and engagement with, many other writings from the Roman world, not merely drawing on them but also seeking 'to overwrite all others, physically overpowering them and forcing them to the ground by the sheer material weight of his magnum opus, this monument for the ages that rendered all else superfluous'. In narrating extraordinary bodies, he drew on Book 7 of Pliny the Elder's *Natural History* (or Solinus' summary), the aim of which was 'the demonstration of nature's majesty through the creation of a proper *historia*'. Yet for Augustine, despite all their various and astounding appearances, all these extraordinary people were nonetheless brought together into their humanity, their shared descent from Adam and Noah, and thus testified to 'the enormous unifying power of the one God, who had created everything'.

Augustine also appears as one of the central figures in Raffaella Cribiore's chapter, which very elegantly provides a new slant on the 'Christianization as decline' thesis, arguing that there *was* a period of 'democratization of culture' (to use the terminology of Santo Mazzarino) during late antiquity, but that it neither began with Christianity nor was limited to the religion's adherents. In particular, Cribiore focuses on how this trend developed in the field of rhetorical training, drawing examples from the complaints of the fourth-century educator Libanius, who lamented the failure of many of his students to hone and maintain their speaking skills to the degree that he regarded as necessary for a member of the elite. After examining Libanius' pessimistic complaints, Cribiore then demonstrates that the Christian orator John Chrysostom shared the Antiochene rhetorician's disquiet about apparently slipping standards. This is particularly evident from his *De sacerdotio*, in which he grumbles that the audiences of sermons often do not appreciate good rhetoric and that a cleric should resist the urge to compromise his standards to win the applause of the crowd. Both men, however, stand in contrast to Augustine, who embraces the positive aspects of a more democratic literary/rhetorical culture, 'preaching the need for a more malleable approach to learning' and urging Christian orators to respond to the needs of particular audiences. As Cribiore argues, by the middle of the fifth century 'rigid education with its inflexible rules that necessitated a strong commitment for many years did not respond anymore to changing circumstances', but this shift cannot be attributed neatly to the influence of Christianity. Rhetoric about rhetoric does not divide on lines of religious identity at all.

Moving away from the Christian tradition, Nicholas Baker-Brian considers the use of one particular rhetorical form—the dialogue—in the construction of religious identity amongst late-antique Manichaeans. Building on recent treatments of dialogue literature in this period, particularly by Simon Goldhill and Averil Cameron, Baker-Brian extends consideration of this theme to Manichaean *Kephalaia* texts, arguing that these compilations of teachings were 'instrumental in augmenting core aspects of the identity of the religion'. The founder of the religion, Mani, appears as the central character in these writings, engaging in fictionalized conversations with a variety of learned interlocutors representing other systems of philosophy and belief, including those associated with Persia and India. These figures come to acknowledge Mani's superior wisdom, sometimes praising him with effusive rhetoric, and seek to be educated by him. As Baker-Brian highlights, 'in the hands of Manichaeans, dialogue became an especially potent rhetorical instrument for demarcating the religion's claim to a distinctive identity'. The use of this rhetorical form was therefore central to the construction of the religious movement's sense of itself, whose 'roots lay in the supersessionary claim of Mani that his revelation not only complemented but also completed the "wisdom and knowledge" of his prophetic predecessors'.

The final chapter in Part II, by Maijastina Kahlos, explores the use of the concept of 'magic' in the late-antique rhetoric of religious identity, demonstrating how both Christians at the time and modern scholars have constructed a narrative of 'magicless Christianity'. Taking the position that magic is 'a socially constructed object of knowledge whose content and formulations vary according to different social contexts and circumstances', this piece considers how it was used as a rhetorical category by Christians in creating a sense of their identity in opposition to pagans, heretics, and Jews. In particular, this can be observed in attempts to demarcate the miraculous achievements of 'holy men and women' from the dangerous and improper activities of 'sorcerers', despite the ostensible similarities between their spectacular interventions, such as exorcisms. Kahlos situates this rhetoric within a broader late-antique discourse in which the accusation of 'magic' was used to delegitimize opponents and was sometimes associated with the use of other devices and materials such as amulets and herbs, as opposed to simple verbal formulae. As the evidence shows, however, the use of some such practices took place amongst Christians, leading to figures such as Augustine, John Chrysostom, and Gregory of Tours wrestling with the question of how to define the limits of 'acceptable' behaviour: for example, could phylacteries containing scriptural verses or saints' relics be employed by Christians or were they not sufficiently distinct from amulets? As Kahlos concludes, authority was always a central issue in the use of this rhetoric: Christian writers emphasized the importance of the authority of any 'ritual expert' in determining the legitimacy of a practice; Christian notables employed accusations of magic as 'an effective tool against political and ecclesiastical rivals'; and Christian leaders claimed the right to determine the boundaries between 'religion' and 'magic' and thus to make this a vital facet of their own particular conceptions of religious identity.

Part III moves on to focus on the question of how religious identity was expressed, shifting attention to particular modes of expression that sought to create communal religious identities. It proceeds via a series of case studies of different literary and visual forms—law codes, chronicles, heresiologies, funerary art, ascetic texts—each of which possesses its own distinctive rhetorical conventions. Whilst constructions of religious identities are more easily recognized in some other types of writing, such as theological discourses, apologetic literature, and homilies, the studies collected in this part of the volume demonstrate the presence of this phenomenon in some lesser-studied examples from the period, including artistic material. By examining the nature and function of their individual 'rhetorics', these chapters present a richer and more complex account of the ways in which religious identity could be constructed within the educated culture of late antiquity.

In the first contribution to this final section, Mark Humphries focuses his attention on the *Theodosian Code*, compiled and promulgated in the early fifth century by the regime of Theodosius II. This is a work which has often been mined for information by historians, who have argued over the degree to which its individual laws on religion, frequently featuring ferocious and bombastic language, can be regarded as evidence of attempts to establish orthodox Christianity as the dominant religion of empire. In contrast, Humphries moves attention away from the individual texts within the *Code* and instead examines the rhetoric of the compilation as a whole, illuminating 'the extent to which the laws selected for inclusion produced a specifically Theodosian vision of a Christian Empire'. By beginning only with the reign of Constantine in the early fourth century, this collection creates 'a dramatically foreshortened vision of legal history' for the Roman Empire, with very little reference to the preceding centuries and rulers. This is particularly visible in the treatment of the concepts of *superstitio* and *insania*, which are isolated from their earlier employment as 'polemical condemnations of non-normative religious activity opposed to traditional paganism', instead featuring only as part of a new Christian rhetoric for condemning pagans. Moreover, as Humphries demonstrates through a detailed analysis of Book 16, whilst Constantine and his immediate successors do appear as authors of relevant legislation, Theodosian laws predominate, with that particular dynasty being presented as the one that ultimately established a successful definition of orthodoxy after decades of confusion. The Roman religious identity constructed by the *Code*, therefore, 'however much it reflects changes in the empire that began with Constantine, is essentially a Theodosian Christianity'.

Peter Van Nuffelen then considers the role of narrative in constructing identities in Greek chronicles of the fourth century. The ecclesiastical histories of the period, especially those written by Eusebius in the fourth century and his continuators, Socrates and Sozomen, in the fifth, have tended to receive more scholarly attention, but this chapter instead argues for the centrality of the chronicle form to Christian historical writing in the century after Eusebius' own *Chronica* was compiled. After detailing the evidence for the composition of such texts during this period and the range of different models they followed, Van Nuffelen then presents a series of case studies of their varying constructions of identity. The first of these explores early continuations of Eusebius' work, the so-called *Continuatio Eusebii antiochiensis* and *Continuatio continuationis*, neither of which conforms to the Nicene orthodoxy that would ultimately become dominant. Whilst these theological concerns are present, however, they are not necessarily paramount to the idea of Christianity constructed here, since both works 'assume a doctrinal stance without explicitly defending it'. Their focus in narrating Christian history is more outward-facing, so that 'victory over paganism and, to a lesser degree, Judaism is what counts'. The chronicle of Andreas, with its concern for establishing and affirming the date of Easter, defends the position adopted at Nicaea in 325 against other Christians who are presented as being too close to Jewish practice. Moreover, by using arguments from both the rhythm of the solar year and the biblical account of Creation to justify his arguments, Andreas seeks to make 'Christianity appear as representing the natural order: the liturgical calendar does not merely represent the history of salvation but also the cosmological order'. In the final case study, the Alexandrian Annianus is shown to display an even greater concern with 'the mapping of sacred history onto the cosmic year', as well as in correcting and extending Eusebius' chronology to help refute claims by pagans and heretics. As Van Nuffelen demonstrates, however, the local character of this chronicle is also significant, with the celebration and prominence of the bishop Theophilus helping to establish a specifically Alexandrian sense of identity.

Richard Flower's chapter considers another relatively neglected and maligned form of late-antique literature: the heresiologies that flourished from the fourth century onwards. These listings of different non-orthodox sects, usually incorporating a significant quantity of polemical and even fictional material, establish the boundaries of orthodoxy through a process of negative definition, categorizing a range of beliefs and groups as incompatible with a Christian identity. Flower explores the rhetoric employed by three heresiologists of the late fourth and early fifth centuries—Epiphanius of Salamis, Filastrius of Brescia, and Augustine of Hippo—in the prefatory material of their works. The claims they made helped to establish the authority and prestige of both themselves and their texts by employing literary techniques frequently seen in technical writing from the classical world. By examining the prefaces and paratextual material of Epiphanius' *Panarion*, with its rhetoric of responding to requests received from correspondents and also the wider needs of society, this chapter demonstrates how the bishop of Salamis uses claims to *utilitas* that also appear in earlier authors such as Pliny the Elder, Galen, and Nicander of Colophon. Epiphanius thus countered possible accusations of distortion and personal animosity by 'adopting the persona of the dispassionate scholar, who wrote what he wrote because others recognized his great learning and sought his advice', even when he did not wish to provide it. A similar 'rhetoric of compulsion' is also evident in Filastrius' preface, but this author explicitly aligns his project with Scripture, reworking Epiphanius' chronology to reflect that of Genesis and also presenting his own work as a fulfilment of prophecy, 'making it not merely exclusively Christian, but resolutely biblical'. Augustine then built on the rhetoric of necessity and modesty visible in both these earlier heresiologies and classical technical literature, but also adapted it to present himself and his project as the product of divine assistance and will.

The artistic culture of early Christianity takes centre stage in Robin Jensen's chapter, which expands the concept of 'rhetoric' beyond verbal examples to examine the funerary iconography of Christian monuments and its relationship to existing motifs in use more widely in the Roman world. The chapter opens with a consideration of methodological issues involved in interpreting both the form and content of these images, including the role of patrons in choosing decorative schemes and the problems of extracting a clear sense of 'identity' from such works. After considering developments in the pictorial decoration of Roman sarcophagi during the imperial period, including a gradual move away from mythological imagery, Jensen then explores the presence of biblical material on explicitly Christian examples from the late third century onwards. Going against the prevailing trend, the appearance of such images, which also incorporate elements from traditional non-Christian sarcophagus decoration, 'represents a significant return to narrative iconography on Roman sarcophagi after its near disappearance on pagan monuments'. The biblical episodes chosen for inclusion, however, seem to defy any single explanatory rationale, despite the various hypotheses that have been advanced by scholars. Whilst very deliberate arrangements of characters can sometimes be identified, many examples present instead an 'assembly of abbreviated figures that frequently appear to march randomly (and even awkwardly) across a sarcophagus' front panel', in contrast to the neater decorative schemes seen on earlier pagan mythological examples. Rather than being dismissed as being due to a lack of concern or skills, however, Jensen interprets this formal arrangement as 'another new kind of visual rhetoric' alongside stories from a new Christian *paideia*, with these collections representing something akin to 'the catechism at a glance'. This was a religious rhetoric that marked itself out from others not only through its vocabulary but also through its grammar and syntax.

The final case study, by Hajnalka Tamas, considers a detailed, but relatively obscure, presentation of the ideal ascetic life: the *Liber ad Renatum monachum*, written by the bishop Asterius Ansedunensis, probably in the early fifth century. This text draws heavily on the views and writings of Jerome concerning asceticism, particularly as articulated in response to Jovinian, and develops them into an even more extreme position. Asterius' ideal is primarily concerned with isolation, emphasizing *anachoresis* and 'progressive detachment from everything that might distract the mind from the contemplation of the divine', whilst criticizing those who sought public fame and recognition. As Tamas emphasizes, in this scheme the 'most important step to spiritual freedom is to renounce fellow human beings', taking this idea to such an extreme that to remain engaged with society in any way was defined as an impossibility for the true ascetic. Renunciation is therefore at the centre of this idiosyncratic conception of ascetic identity, with Asterius placing little emphasis on other activities normally associated with monks, including 'fasting, prayer, or psalmody', or vigils and biblical study. This was justified through exegesis of Scripture, most notably the story of Creation, in which Adam is to be understood not merely as the first man but also as the first ascetic, living a solitary and self-sufficient life in Paradise. Eve disrupted this situation, with her desire for companionship, and so original sin was to be found specifically in a 'voluntary dedication to human relationships'. The ideal expression of Christian identity was therefore to be found in divesting oneself of all such connections and embracing solitude, 'the natural state of the human being'.

The volume concludes with Morwenna Ludlow's exploration of 'rhetoric about literary style' amongst late-antique Christian authors, examining how they used ways of speaking about style as a method for constructing both their own individual identities and that of Christianity as a whole. As has long been recognized, some Christians, drawing on a rhetorical trope also employed by classical philosophers, claimed that they avoided artful rhetoric to speak the unvarnished truth, in contrast to their sophistic opponents. Ludlow explores this issue in much greater depth, surveying both ancient discussions of 'style' and their modern treatments in order to identify three literary 'moods' or 'sensibilities' recognized in the classical world: the 'slender', 'pleasant', and 'majestic' or 'sublime', used for different contexts and purposes and also characterized by, amongst other things, 'an intensification of emotional force' as one moved from the first to the last. A combination of these might be used by a single author, or even within a single text, when the subject demanded it, since the key determining criterion was always a sense of 'appropriateness'. This chapter illuminates how these concepts were employed by the trio of fourth-century bishops known as 'the Cappadocians'—Basil of Caesarea, Gregory of Nyssa, and Gregory of Nazianzus—who followed classical precedent in using this register of assessment, including identifying the presence of the different 'styles' within the many books of Scripture. Like other commentators on literature, they also employed the rhetoric of 'appropriate' and 'inappropriate' style in their discussions of works and authors, judging them not only in isolation, but also in comparison to each other. This is particularly evident in their attacks on the literary pretensions of the heretic Eunomius, whose prose was contrasted with both the plain-speaking biblical text and the 'sublime' compositions of Basil himself. Such characterizations are, therefore, neither absolutes nor an idiosyncratic feature of Christian authors. Rather, the 'plain–elaborate opposition is itself part of a broader rhetoric about style in classical and late antiquity', which was a major literary manoeuvre for establishing and reinforcing identity in relation to the author's own perception of the truth.

Part I

The Nature of Religious Identities and Their Representation

2

Approaching 'Religious Identity' in Late Antiquity

Éric Rebillard

INTRODUCTION

Scholars have long written about the blurring of the boundaries between Christians and pagans. Indeed, in 1923, Charles Guignebert forged the label 'semi-Christians' to describe such individuals. Though the category has often been criticized, it seems, nevertheless, to endure in contemporary discourse as a means to designate Christians who did not fully embrace Christianity.[1] A review of the use of this category, of its critics, and of some of its most recent avatars will provide us with a good introduction to current approaches to religious identity in late antiquity. Most of these approaches suffer from what Amartya Sen has called 'the presumption of the unique relevance of a singular classification'.[2] I will therefore suggest a paradigm shift: instead of classifying individuals according to one category membership, their 'religious identity', I will introduce two concepts: identity salience and arrangement of category membership sets. I will then provide a brief sketch of how religious identity can be redescribed and I will offer the case of Ausonius as a good example of how such a redescription can help us move forward in our understanding of religious identity in late antiquity.

---

[1] See Markus (1990) 8, 33 n.13.   [2] Sen (2006) 11.

ENOUGH WITH THE SEMI-CHRISTIANS

From Guignebert (1923) to Bonner (1984)

Charles Guignebert (1867–1939) was the first to use the category. An important, albeit almost forgotten, French historian, who occupied the first Chair of History of Ancient Christianity at the Sorbonne between 1919 and 1937,[3] Guignebert introduced the label in an effort to bridge the gap between the old and the new religion—a gap that historians, encouraged by ecclesiastical discourse, too often accepted as an absolute separation. In his work of 1923, he points out the historical existence of numerous people who in fact seem to have had a 'double religious life' and proposes that we call them 'demi-chrétiens'. He seeks to distinguish the semi-Christians both from those Christians who adapted pagan practices to their new faith and from those who were bad Christians and could not live up to the standards of their new obligations. Thus the semi-Christians considered themselves to be good Christians, and if they continued some old cultic practices, it was not just a matter of bad habits, nor was it simply a form of syncretism. Guignebert also insists that these people were not entirely ignorant and therefore unable to understand the difference. However, he does not attempt a more precise definition, and after these rather general remarks he undertakes a review of examples.[4]

Amongst the pre-Constantinian examples discussed by Guignebert there is the case of Martialis, a Spanish bishop.[5] A letter of Cyprian of Carthage mentions that he was deposed after he had obtained a certificate of sacrifice during the enforcement of Decius' edict in 250.[6] The letter also mentions that he was a member of a *collegium*, an association: 'And as for Martialis, not only has he been a habitué of the banquets of some pagan social club, participating in their shameful and obscure entertainments; his own sons he had buried in the manner of pagans as members of that same sodality, interred in the company of strangers among heathen graves.'[7] The important point for Guignebert is that Martialis had no intention of quitting the Church and that he fought against his deposition.

For the post-Constantinian period, Guignebert finds in the denunciations of the bishops many examples of Christians who took part in pagan festivals or continued to visit temples.[8] He also emphasizes the importance of astral cults, the solar cult in particular, and its syncretic strength in the fourth and fifth centuries.[9] Amongst several other examples, he mentions sermons of John

---

[3] See Laplanche (1999) on Guignebert's historical method and principles.
[4] Guignebert (1923) 65–74.   [5] Guignebert (1923) 77.
[6] On Martialis and Cyprian's letter, see Clarke (1984–1989) vol. 4, 139–42.
[7] Cypr. *ep.* 67.6.23. Translation Clarke (1984–1989) vol. 4, 25.
[8] Guignebert (1923) 86–9.   [9] Guignebert (1923) 89–93.

Chrysostom and of Augustine in which the preachers present, as would-be martyrs, women who would not use magic remedies when one of their children was dangerously ill.[10] He suggests, finally, that the question of the religion of Ausonius is a good case in point.[11] Ausonius has been depicted both as a pagan and as a Christian. Guignebert seems to dismiss any attempt to define him as one or the other on the basis of any particular passage of his writings and he concludes: 'Truth is, it seems to me, that Ausonius is sometimes Christian, sometimes pagan, that he is both, probably more pagan than Christian, that in sum he is a semi-Christian.'[12]

These examples are interesting, if difficult, cases.[13] They provide us with a good idea of what is at stake for Guignebert. He does not adopt the language of the Christian leadership, but he takes seriously the proposition, however implicit, that these semi-Christians consider themselves fully Christian and that they, at the same time, maintain beliefs and/or practices that belong to paganism. As we will see, this perspective was somewhat lost in the way some later scholars used the term semi-Christians.

Guignebert's category of 'semi-Christian' was resurrected by Gerald Bonner in 1984 in a paper on the extinction of paganism.[14] Bonner was looking for a 'deeper psychological factor', beyond state coercion and the influence of powerful patrons, in order to explain mass conversion.[15] According to Bonner's analysis, the semi-Christians constituted the reservoir from which the Church drew many of its converts after the Constantinian revolution.[16] Though he concedes that there were semi-Christians before the Peace of the Church, he notes that their number increased considerably afterwards: 'The negative effect on the Church of the passing away of paganism was the dilution of the quality of Christian living brought about by an influx of converts with a semi-Christian outlook.'[17] Like Guignebert, Bonner attempts to distinguish between the 'semi-Christians' and the 'paganized Christians'.[18] Paganized Christians are described as converts who retained some of their old habits of thought and practice. However, by attributing sincerity to the paganized Christians, Bonner seems to refuse it to the semi-Christians, and thus departs from Guignebert's position. Bonner clearly promotes a very different conception of the semi-Christians when he characterizes them by their refusal of baptism or martyrdom.[19] He goes further and states: 'The paganized Christians were within the circle of the Church; the semi-Christians were on the

---

[10] Guignebert (1923) 96.   [11] Guignebert (1923) 98–9.
[12] Guignebert (1923) 99 ('La vérité me paraît être qu'Ausone est tantôt chrétien, tantôt païen, qu'il est les deux, et, sans doute, plus le second que le premier, mais qu'au total c'est un demi-chrétien').
[13] See below on Ausonius.   [14] Bonner (1984).   [15] Bonner (1984) 348.
[16] Bonner (1984) 350–5.   [17] Bonner (1984) 355.
[18] Bonner (1984) 348; see Guignebert (1923) 66.   [19] Bonner (1984) 348–9.

fringe.'[20] We can surmise that in Bonner's view the Spanish bishop Martialis would not be a semi-Christian.

Though he acknowledges that there were some, Bonner does not give any example of semi-Christians from before the Peace of the Church. For the post-Constantinian period, he presents Marius Victorinus as 'the archetype of the semi-Christian', though acknowledging that he was later baptized.[21] Bonner refers to what Augustine reports about the Roman professor of rhetoric in the *Confessions*.[22] Augustine himself got the story from Simplicianus, a presbyter of the Church of Milan. Victorinus used to tell Simplicianus that he was already a Christian and Simplicianus would always reply to him that he would count him amongst the faithful the day he would see him in Church. Though Victorinus was reading the Scriptures and other Christian texts, he would not seek baptism because, in the words of Augustine, 'he was sorely afraid of upsetting the proud demon-worshipers who were his friends'.[23] The anecdote, which should in any case be read in the context of Augustine's own conversion narrative,[24] takes us far from Guignebert's semi-Christians. Indeed, Victorinus is not even mentioned by Guignebert. Contrary to what Bonner suggests, nothing in Augustine's account suggests that Victorinus was still a worshipper of idols when he declared himself to be a Christian to Simplicianus.[25] Thus the archetype of the semi-Christian appears to be a rather exceptional case of Christian self-ascription by a highly educated member of the Roman senatorial aristocracy.

Another example, one that Bonner shares with Guignebert, is that of Ausonius: 'Much which can be urged as evidence for Ausonius being a pagan—his use of classical mythology, his occasional gross obscenity, the lack of any hope of a future life in his elegies—accords very well with the concept of semi-Christianity... and it is precisely for that reason that the break with Paulinus of Nola caused him such distress, for Paulinus had determined to follow Christ whatever the cost.' It is not clear whether Bonner considers Ausonius to have been baptized, but he obviously reckons that he was not ready to 'follow Christ' at all costs and as such remained on the fringe of Christianity.

Finally, Bonner presents Constantine as 'the greatest of the semi-Christians, and certainly the most influential'.[26] In sum, Bonner's category of semi-Christian is quite different from the category introduced by Guignebert. His

---

[20] Bonner (1984) 350.   [21] Bonner (1984) 350.
[22] Aug. *Conf.* 8.2.3–5; see Courcelle (1968) 383–91; O'Donnell (1992) 2.13–15.
[23] Aug. *Conf.* 8.2.4, tr. Boulding (1997) 188.
[24] Hadot (1971) 235 mentions three possible biases that could have distorted the account; see Vessey (2005).
[25] Bonner (1984) 350 quotes the earlier description of Victorinus (8.2.3: *usque ad illam aetatem venerator idolorum sacrorumque sacrilegorum particeps*), but this refers to his career until the time he started to read the Scriptures.
[26] Bonner (1984) 351.

semi-Christians are, to a large extent, sympathizers who held back from a formal conversion, whilst for Guignebert semi-Christians were converts who had a double religious life, Christian and pagan.

Semi-Christians, Judeo-Christians, or Judaizers?

A common critique of the semi-Christian category is that it is seldom attested in the vocabulary of the Greek and Latin ecclesiastical writers.[27] Such a critique may not seem particularly relevant, as both Guignebert and Bonner make clear that it is a category they have devised for their own purpose. However, it is interesting to investigate whether and how the category was used in late antiquity, especially in the light of Emmanuel Soler's recent suggestion that it described an altogether different group of Christians.[28]

The expression '*Christianoi ex emiseias*' only appears once in Greek Patristic literature. John Chrysostom uses it in his first homily against the Jews, preached in Antioch towards the end of 386, when he was still a presbyter.[29] He interrupts a series of sermons against the Anomoeans in order to address a more urgent matter, as the festivals of the Jewish year, Rosh Hashanah, Sukkot, and Yom Kippur, are drawing near. John wants to eradicate a bad habit shared by some members of his audience: they join in these festivals and, though they are professed Christians, they more generally frequent the synagogues.[30] At one point in his sermon, he apostrophizes these Judaizing Christians: 'Do you fast with the Jews? Then take off your shoes with the Jews, and walk barefoot in the marketplace, and share with them in their indecency and laughter. But you would not choose to do this because you are ashamed and apt to blush. Are you ashamed to share with them in outward appearance but unashamed to share in their impiety? What excuse will you have, you who are only half a Christian?'[31]

The coining of the phrase '*christianoi ex emiseias*' by John Chrysostom is in keeping with the invective register that is so well exploited in his homilies *Against the Jews*.[32] We must also note that Chrysostom only uses the phrase once. Despite this, Laurence Brottier titled her dissertation on Chrysostom's preaching 'The call of the semi-Christians to the angelic life'.[33] She justifies such a general use of the expression by arguing that in other texts Chrysostom condemns Christians who go to Jewish festivals along with Christians who go to pagan festivals.[34]

---

[27] See Markus (1990) 8 n.13.   [28] See Soler (2010).
[29] Dating in Mayer and Allen (2000) 148.
[30] A classic treatment is that of Wilken (1983); see also Soler (2006) 113–35.
[31] Chrys. *Adv. Jud.* 1.4.7, tr. Harkins (1979) 16.   [32] See Wilken (1983) 112–15.
[33] Brottier (2005).   [34] Brottier (2004) 439.

Emmanuel Soler rejects the generalization and insists that the phrase be reserved for the very specific category of Christians that Chrysostom thus labelled. Soler identifies these Christians who observed the Jewish Law as belonging to the relatively amorphous group of the so-called Jewish Christians.[35] Thus, says Soler, the semi-Christians were not half pagans, as Guignebert had it, but half Jewish.[36] In the context of Antioch, these Christians would be former Arians whose subordinationism would have pushed them to frequent the synagogues.[37]

Soler finds support for his interpretation in Jerome's and Augustine's use of the Latin word *semichristianus*.[38] Jerome uses *semichristianus* twice, each time in a similar context: the discussion of Greek translations of the Hebrew Scriptures. In his commentary on Galatians, Jerome seems to attribute such a translation to Ebion and qualifies him as '*semichristianus et semiiudaeus*'.[39] In his commentary on Habakkuk, Theodotion and Symmachus, both of whom he considers Ebionites, are also qualified as *semichristiani*.[40] The use of such a label contrasts with Jerome's positive assessment of their translations in other contexts and may be explained as an attempt to distance himself from these authors because he is under attack for his own use of the Hebrew text.[41] In any case, though Jerome depends on Origen and Eusebius for his knowledge of these translators, the Latin word *semichristianus* finds no equivalent in the Greek sources about them and, therefore, seems to have no relation to Chrysostom's phrase.

The word *semichristianus* appears only three times in Augustine's works and all three occurrences are in the *Contra Faustum*. It seems to have been used by the Manichaean bishop to deride the Catholics. The first occurrence is included in the first quote of Faustus that Augustine refutes:

> FAUSTUS SAID: Since their errors have already been more than sufficiently brought into the light and since the lies of the Jewish superstition and of the semi-Christians have been amply exposed, namely by the most learned Adimantus, who alone after our blessed father Mani should be studied, it seemed, my dearest brothers, not inapropos also to write these brief and concise replies on account of the clever and cunning statements of those debating with us.

---

[35] Soler (2010) 288–9. Soler adopts Marcel Simon's definition of Jewish Christians (Simon (1964)) and ignores the many problems associated with the label; see Broadhead (2010) 6–27 for a recent overview.

[36] Soler (2010) 290.   [37] Soler (2010) 289; see Soler (2006) 124.

[38] Soler (2010) 290.

[39] Hier. *in Gal.* 3.13–14 (PL 26, 387); see Klijn and Reinink (1973) 40 and 204–5 (text and translation).

[40] Hier. *in Habacuc* 3.10–13 (CCL 76A, 641); see Klijn and Reinink (1973) 40, 53, and 208–9 (text and translation).

[41] See Jay (1985) 105–10.

Approaching 'Religious Identity' in Late Antiquity

> AUGUSTINE SAID: You think that people ought to avoid semi-Christians because you say that that is what we are. But we avoid pseudo-Christians, because we show that that is what you are. For something that is 'semi' is imperfect in some respect, but still not false in any respect.[42]

The reference to the lies of the Jews and to the treatise of Adimantus makes clear that Faustus calls the Catholics *semichristiani* because they accept the books of the Old Testament. In his reply Augustine only accepts the label semi-Christian in order to call the Manicheans 'pseudo-Christians'. If the use of *semichristianus* in this passage points to a context not very dissimilar to that of Jerome's usage, this is not the case with the third occurrence of the word:[43]

> The little ones whom you call semi-Christians are certainly opposed to you if they hear the voice of love, their mother, speaking to them from the lips of the apostle: 'If anyone preaches to you another gospel apart from what we have preached to you, let him be anathema.' (Gal 1:8–9)[44]

Augustine does not say in which context Faustus calls *semichristiani* the *paruuli*, who are the newly baptized. Nothing, however, points to their acceptance of the Old Testament, as the discussion is about the birth of Christ.

Thus the similarities between the three sets of texts in which semi-Christian is used are weaker than Soler would like. It seems better to consider the different occurrences as independent of each other and each as coined in a polemical context without a very specific target. The absence of an ancient equivalent for the categories of Christians that Guignebert and Bonner sought to isolate is interesting in itself and does not constitute a legitimate critique of their endeavour. There have, however, been other critiques addressed to the notion of semi-Christian, and I turn to these now.[45]

The Kahlos Scheme

In a series of publications, Maijastina Kahlos presents what she herself calls the 'Kahlos scheme' as a radical departure from the category of semi-Christians.[46] First, she denounces some serious flaws inherent in the term itself: it privileges a Christian perspective (these people could just as well be called 'semi-pagans'), and it is derogatory. As she writes, 'the "semi"-terminology bisects

---

[42] Aug. *C. Faust.* 1.2–3, tr. Teske (2007) 70.
[43] Soler (2010) does not mention this occurrence.
[44] Aug. *C. Faust.* 2.2, tr. Teske (2007) 72.
[45] Not discussed here is O'Donnell (1979), an important attempt to break the pagan–Christian dichotomy.
[46] Kahlos (2006b) 217 for the phrase; the scheme is first presented in Kahlos (2004); see also Kahlos (2005), (2006b), (2007a), and (2007b).

and underrates these unclassifiable individuals'.[47] Second, she emphasizes that adding an in-between category does not go far enough in the blurring of the rigid pagan–Christian dichotomy. As she states, in Guignebert's system or in Bonner's system, 'the pagan–Christian dichotomy is still there'.[48]

Developing her position out of the postmodern deconstruction of binary oppositions, she thus suggests: 'The key for exceeding the horizon of dichotomous structures might be realizing that the parts of a binary opposition need each other. In fact, they are one. The one side needs and includes its opposite side because the self cannot be conceptually defined without the other.'[49] In order to abandon the old lurking dichotomy, Kahlos invents a new concept, *incerti*: 'I have decided to call these betwixt-and-between people, who elude the binary opposition pagans–Christians, *incerti*. The new concept *incerti* is a double entendre: first, it describes the feeling or state of uncertainty on the mental level of individuals in late antiquity. Second, on the scholarly level, it calls into question categorizing and defining and also draws attention to the violence done to individuals by the rigidity of the classifications.'[50]

Kahlos finds many examples of *incerti* in Christian literature. Amongst others, she mentions Marius Victorinus and Ausonius, whom she qualifies as of an 'ambivalent and unclassifiable character'.[51] To these she joins many anonymous *incerti* denounced by bishops as living a 'double life'.[52] This expression recalls Guignebert, who described his semi-Christians as living a double religious life.[53] In the end, the Kahlos scheme seems to be more of an up-to-date (and fancier) version of the Guignebert scheme than a real breakthrough. More troubling, it assumes that all the in-between individuals were in a state of uncertainty, though there is little evidence that this was actually the case. Marius Victorinus, for example, displayed no uncertainty whatsoever as far as we can tell from Augustine's report.[54]

The concept of *incerti*, however, should serve as a good reminder for scholars that categorization always does violence to individuals and that a multiplication of overlapping categories does not avoid this fact. Thus, when Alan Cameron posits 'five overlapping categories',[55] he merely introduces more nuances to a scheme that is based on a dichotomy between pagans and Christians. Cameron's categories are, at the extremes: committed pagans (Symmachus) and committed Christians (Augustine); on the sides: centre-pagans (Servius) and centre-Christians (Ausonius); in between: 'the (for a time) perhaps rather large group of those who for one reason or another

---

[47] Kahlos (2007a) 28.   [48] Kahlos (2007a) 28.
[49] Kahlos (2006b) 218; see also Kahlos (2007a) 30.   [50] Kahlos (2006b) 218.
[51] Kahlos (2007a) 41–2.
[52] Kahlos (2007a) 38; see Kahlos (2005) on bishops' denunciations of spectacles, Kahlos (2007b) about banqueting.
[53] Guignebert (1923) 65.   [54] See above.   [55] Cameron (2011) 176.

resisted straightforward classification'.[56] What is common to all these classifications is the focus on religion as a principle of classification. However, as Amartya Sen has suggested, 'a person's religion need not be his or her all-encompassing and exclusive identity'.[57] This is the possibility that we need to explore as we formulate a new approach to religious identity in late antiquity.

A NEW APPROACH TO RELIGIOUS IDENTITY IN LATE ANTIQUITY

The Danger of 'Groupism'

It is a common postmodern cliché to understand the boundaries between religious identities as contingent and fluctuating. However, this too often results in a discourse that talks about the fluidity of identities whilst it simultaneously reifies identities by attributing them to groups together with agency, interests, and will. This is what Rogers Brubaker denounces under the name of 'groupism'.[58]

Brubaker defines groupism as 'the tendency to take discrete, sharply differentiated, internally homogeneous and externally bounded groups as basic constituents of social life, chief protagonists of social conflicts, and fundamental units of social analysis'.[59] He invites us to avoid starting our analysis with groups, and to focus instead on 'the processes through which categories are used by individuals to make sense of the social world'.[60] Brubaker also suggests that we consider the concept 'groupness': an event that can succeed but also fail, and is, even in case of success, typically just a passing moment.[61]

Following these principles, Brubaker defines as 'everyday ethnicity' the workings of ethnicity and nationhood in the Transylvanian Romanian town of Cluj between 1995 and 2001.[62] His goal is to balance the impression of the centrality of ethnicity presented by political discourse with the experiential centrality (or not) of ethnicity in everyday life. Brubaker and his students are interested in what they call 'the intermittency of ethnicity', seeking how and when ethnicity is relevant, looking for 'sites where ethnicity might—but need not—be at work'.[63] As they warn, 'in order to understand *how* ethnicity

---

[56] Cameron (2011) 177. [57] Sen (2006) 14.
[58] Brubaker (2004) 7–27 = (2002); see also Brubaker et al. (2006) 8 on 'the unhappy marriage of clichéd constructivism and engrained groupism'.
[59] Brubaker (2004) 8 = (2002) 164. [60] Brubaker (2004) 13 = (2002) 170.
[61] Brubaker (2004) 12 = (2002) 168.
[62] Brubaker et al. (2006); see Fox and Miller-Idriss (2008).
[63] Brubaker et al. (2006) 168.

matters...it is important to bear in mind *how little* it matters to much of everyday experience'.[64]

However, they are very careful to emphasize that the fundamental intermittency and the episodic character of ethnicity must not be analysed as a measure of its importance or even of its significance.[65] What it points to is that individuals have many identities and that we need to seek an understanding of their workings in relation to each other.

Individuals and Their Many Identities

Since at least William James, it is a common idea that individuals have multiple identities, 'selves' in James' words, but the relationships between and amongst identities have seldom been theorized.[66] The study of this relationship is central to the programme of identity theory.[67]

Identity theory distinguishes three bases of identities: role, group, and person.[68] A role is 'a set of expectations tied to a social position'.[69] A person's identification with a social group is the basis of his or her social identity.[70] Finally, the 'person identity' is 'the set of meanings that define the person as a unique individual'.[71] Though different theories focus on one or the other bases of identities, according to Burke and Stets, they 'all operate in the same way': 'Identities from each basis have identity standards that serve as the reference and guide behavior in situations. Whether it is a role, social, or person identity, individuals act to control perceptions of who they are in a situation to match the feedback they receive in the situation.'[72] Though the approach may seem mechanistic and emphasis on quantitative analysis is ill-suited for historical inquiries, identity theory provides us with a vocabulary that ultimately allows a better understanding of how multiple identities are handled by the individuals. The salience of an identity is its probability of being activated in a situation.[73] Activation refers to the condition in which an identity is actively engaged as opposed to being latent and inactive.[74]

Category or group memberships such as ethnicity, religion, or occupation define social identities. Each category membership can be described as a family or a set of contrastive categories in a given culture. In the religious set for late antiquity, there are, amongst others: pagan, Jewish, and Christian. Two types of arrangement of category membership sets, lateral and hierarchical, are distinguished by the anthropologist Handelman: 'Given a lateral arrangement,

---

[64] Brubaker et al. (2006) 206. [65] Brubaker et al. (2006) 362–3.
[66] Burke (2003) 195. [67] Burke (2003); Burke and Stets (2009) 130–54.
[68] Burke and Stets (2009) 112–29. [69] Burke and Stets (2009) 113.
[70] Burke and Stets (2009) 117. [71] Burke and Stets (2009) 124.
[72] Burke and Stets (2009) 112. [73] Burke and Stets (2009) 134.
[74] Burke and Stets (2009) 77.

the assumption is that various category sets (i.e., ethnic, occupational, religious, educational, etc.) are interchangeable to a certain extent in an occasion of interaction; and therefore, that the same person can be categorized according to different criteria of relevance in different situations. But if the arrangement of membership sets tends more to the hierarchical, then all categorizations about a person may be allocated according to, and interpreted in terms of, membership in a given category set.'[75] In a hierarchical arrangement, if religious membership is given salience, the entirety of an individual's behaviour should be determined and interpreted in terms of his or her religious affiliation. In a lateral arrangement, situational selection is key, and different category membership sets can be activated according to the context of the interaction.

CONCLUSION

These theoretical considerations provide us with a solid framework within which we can approach religious identity in late antiquity. Not only are religious identities fluid, that is, the boundaries between the different religious groups are permeable, but religious identities are not necessarily activated in any given context, even when available. Religious identities can enter into conflict with other identity sets and room must be made for lateral arrangements of identity as well as hierarchical arrangements.

This last point is particularly relevant for approaching religious identity in late antiquity, as most scholars have tried to determine which identity set was dominant and commonly opposed hierarchical arrangements to each other. Thus, when Jim O'Donnell challenges the received opinion that Nectarius, the correspondent of Augustine, is a pagan, he writes that he is instead 'a perfectly ordinary Christian whose main allegiances are not religious but social'.[76] I think this is too simple a representation. Once we move beyond the discourse of the bishops and its focus on religious identity, it seems that a lateral arrangement is a better representation of the workings of social identities in late antiquity.

In other words, it is not necessary to assume a hierarchy between Nectarius' multiple identities and allegiances. In their letter-exchange, Augustine vainly tries to frame their discussion within the pagan–Christian dichotomy.[77] Nectarius, however, writes to Augustine as a leading citizen of Calama, and also as an old acquaintance and a man who shares Augustine's culture. We should not infer from this that Nectarius considers a display of religious allegiance to

---

[75] Handelman (1977) 192–3.
[76] O'Donnell (2005) 185; on Nectarius's religion, see Rebillard (2012) 82–4.
[77] O'Donnell (2005) 188.

be misplaced in the public sphere.[78] He might simply think that his religious identity, whether shared with Augustine or not, is irrelevant to the present exchange.

Though it cannot be excluded that some individuals actually had a double religious life, as suggested by Guignebert,[79] the examples presented by scholars can be better understood within the framework promoted here. I will briefly consider the case of Ausonius, which has been discussed by Guignebert, Bonner, and Kahlos.

Since the publication of Labriolle's study in 1913, the consensus has been that Ausonius was a Christian.[80] Even if the arguments based on his political career in the service of a Christian emperor and the Christianity of his family are rejected,[81] two of his works (a third is considered by some as spurious) are deemed to attest to his Christianity.[82] Despite this unanimity, the question of Ausonius' religion has been raised again and again.[83] What puzzles scholars is that excepting the two pieces of Ausonius' writing that display a thorough knowledge of Christianity, all his other works are silent on the topic, and that his verses, when not straightforwardly frivolous, are full of gods and rich with references to classical mythology. When scholars are not prompted to a negative appraisal of his personal Christianity—calling him a lukewarm Christian or a semi-Christian[84]—they explain these features of his writing as characteristic of the Christianity of his time, when his former pupil Paulinus of Nola was the exception and not the rule.[85] Pierre Langlois is an exception in this respect. He writes very perceptively that 'Christianity is not the whole life of Ausonius',[86] and that if in his poetry he is the heir to the classical literary

---

[78] Isabella Sandwell introduces the dichotomy public/private for distinguishing the arrangements promoted by Chrysostom (a hierarchical arrangement giving salience to religious identity in all social interactions) and by Libanius (religious identity is confined to the private sphere whilst in the public sphere salience is given to civic or political identity); see Sandwell (2007) 125–80. The dichotomy public–private suggests that Libanius promotes two different hierarchical arrangements depending on the sphere of his interactions. The notion of a lateral arrangement in which situational selection is the key gives us a greater flexibility, which seems to fit better the evidence, and avoids the distraction of having to define public and private.

[79] Guignebert (1923) 65.

[80] See Labriolle (1910) with Bruggisser (1996). On Ausonius and his works, see an overview in Herzog and Nauroy (1993) 306–52.

[81] See Bruggisser (1996) 122–3.

[82] These pieces are the *Oratio matutina* (*Ephemeris* 3) and the *Versus Paschales*; Green (1991) 667–9 considers the *Oratio consulis Ausonii versibus rhopalicis* to be spurious.

[83] See Amherdt (2006) for a recent treatment and a bibliography of previous scholarship.

[84] Riggi (1968) 691–2 (semi-Christian); Piganiol and Chastagnol (1972) 227 and Charlet (1984) 286 ('chrétien tiède'); Herzog and Nauroy (1993) 348 ('chrétien de nom'), etc. See Amherdt (2006) 385–6.

[85] Bowersock (1986) 1 ('a man of his age'); Amherdt (2006) 388 ('un homme de son temps'). A variant consists in presenting Ausonius as a moderate Christian in contrast to his friend Paulinus of Nola; see Green (1993) 47–8. On the relationship between Ausonius and Paulinus, see the recent treatment of Amherdt (2004).

[86] Langlois (1969) 57.

tradition it is not because he is a pagan, but because he appreciates the beauty of this literature.[87]

I would re-describe Ausonius' religion in the following terms: Christianity was undoubtedly his religious identity, but only one of his many identities; he did not think of himself as a 'Christian writer', though he could occasionally compose pieces that used Christian material and topics. There is no reason to expect a full congruence between his literary work and his religious identity. Thus the question of Ausonius' religion should be considered closed.

---

[87] Langlois (1969) 58. See also Cameron (2011) 404 for 'the well-documented phenomenon, of which Ausonius is no more than the most conspicuous example, of enthusiasm for classical culture among Christians, especially Gallic Christians'.

3

The Rhetoric of Pagan Religious Identities

Porphyry and his First Readers

Aaron P. Johnson

The modern study of paganism in late antiquity has, with a welcome growth of interest and sensitivity over the last several decades, become keenly aware of, and increasingly troubled by, the fact that late-antique pagans failed to articulate a common identity for themselves in terms of their religion.[1] In no small part this is due to the fact that they lacked a singular and discretely identifiable *religion*. Indeed, scholars of Greek and Roman religion have with solemn regularity observed that there is no word for religion (in the modern sense of that term) in antiquity and often remark on the differing semantic ranges and uses of *eusebeia* or *thrēskeia*, *pietas* or *religio* (and other relevant words). The *pagani* described in invariably unflattering terms in the pages of Latin Christian authors embodied a collective identity demarcated by an exclusively religious position only in the pages of those authors (and possibly not even there).[2]

The hesitation in applying the term 'pagans' to those who would identify themselves as neither Christians nor Jews in the eastern Mediterranean is certainly justifiable, given the fact that the label draws on a Latin Christian usage of doubtful, but certainly polemical, origins. Whilst some have opted for 'polytheists'[3]—another label deriving only from Christian rhetoric and, in any case, standing as a rather uncomfortable designation for those individuals whose religious practice and thought prioritized a single 'God over all'—an alternative label deemed satisfying for many students of late-antique paganism

---

[1] I remain grateful for the hospitality shown by Morwenna Ludlow and Richard Flower during the colloquium to which this chapter contributed, as well as Gillian Clark for engaging conversation during my time at Exeter. The chapter has been sharpened considerably in its different drafts by the perceptive comments of Jason Ward and especially Christine Hecht (whose meticulous work on the *Philosophy from Oracles* has been of great importance).
[2] See Cameron (2011) 14–32; Jürgasch (2015).   [3] Fowden (2005) 521–37.

Aaron P. Johnson, *The Rhetoric of Pagan Religious Identities: Porphyry and his First Readers* In: *Rhetoric and Religious Identity in Late Antiquity*. Edited by: Richard Flower and Morwenna Ludlow, Oxford University Press (2020).
© Oxford University Press. DOI: 10.1093/oso/9780198813194.003.0003

has been found in the terms *Hellenes* and *Hellenism*. Both terms seem more appropriate at the outset since they are both Greek words that occur in religious contexts within late-antique literature. And so, a staple of modern treatments of paganism in the later eastern Roman Empire is the confident assertion that *Hellenes*, a once ethnic then cultural label, came to mean *pagans* in the Greek sources of the period.[4]

There is good reason, however, to be less optimistic about the usefulness and accuracy of this assertion. The discovery of occurrences within pagan texts where Hellenes is used as a collective label for a group whose identity was primarily or exclusively religious is rather difficult to establish, and thus the distinctively religious application of the label appears to be a Christian polemical construction rather than a self-ascription.[5] Furthermore, even in Christian authors the label continues to elicit a range of identity markers that go beyond the religious sphere.[6]

The following discussion seeks to investigate a central figure in treatments of late-antique paganism, as well as two of his first readers—one pagan, the other Christian—for what light they shed on the problem of finding a notion of pagan identity (real or imagined) in late antiquity. Porphyry of Tyre, the third-century Platonic philosopher well-known for his fascinating explorations into religious matters (even if these engagements now survive almost entirely in fragments), had to wait at least a half-century before finding a favourable reception. Instead, Iamblichus of Calchis, an associate of Porphyry known for his religiously and spiritually powerful form of Platonic philosophy, and Eusebius of Caesarea, a Christian polymath who remains simultaneously one of our best and most problematic sources for the study of Porphyry's fragmentary works, are the earliest readers of Porphyry (as far as the surviving evidence allows us to conclude with any certainty) and both represent a critical response to his religious thought.

Other figures have been put forth as early readers and respondents to Porphyry: Arnobius, Lactantius, and Athanasius.[7] Although the temptation may be strong to fill out the paucity of our evidence for Porphyry's now lost writings or to piece together tantalizing hints in the fragments of those lost works with what seem to be clues left in the writings of these Christians of the

---

[4] See Bowersock (1990) 9–11; Van Liefferinge (2001).

[5] This remains true even for those pagan authors who directly engage Christianity, such as Porphyry (on which see below), the Alexandrian poet Palladas (on whom, see Johnson forthcoming), or the emperor Julian (on whom, see Johnson (2012b) 445–51).

[6] See Johnson (2012b); *pace* Chapter 4, Boin's contribution to the present volume, as well as Boin (2014).

[7] See, for example, Courcelle (1953); Beatrice (1990), (1993); Simmons (1995); DePalma Digeser (1998). The author of the *Cohortatio ad Graecos* (attributed to Justin by the manuscript tradition) can only be considered a reader of Porphyry if we presume that the oracles cited in the latter's *Phil.Orac.* did not circulate independently of that work.

early fourth century, we must eschew the impulse to construct conjectural lines of connection between Porphyry and these Christians who nowhere name Porphyry.[8] The precise relationship between Porphyry's thought and these Christians requires sustained inquiry that lies beyond the scope of the present discussion. The following study will thus limit itself to those works of authors writing in Greek[9] who explicitly mark themselves as Porphyry's earliest interlocutors, namely Iamblichus and Eusebius.

At stake in the investigation of religious labels in Porphyry, Iamblichus, and Eusebius is not merely philological accuracy or terminological pedantry. A larger narrative of Christianity as a *religion* sui generis, or as the ideal type for the modern construct of the conceptual category of *religion*,[10] has drawn much of its power from a particular understanding of Eusebius.[11] Furthermore, if Porphyry can be taken as the first to use *Hellene* as a religious label, then this would not only lend itself to our understanding of the alleged shift of Hellenism to become the Greek equivalent of paganism, but it would stand as a self-ascribed religious label in the first place, used to signify a religious identity by a pagan himself (at least as I continue to use the term 'pagan' as shorthand to refer to someone who was identified as neither a Christian nor a Jew in late antiquity). If this were the case—although I will argue that it is not—Porphyry's role within the historical development of the conceptual category of *religion* would be revolutionary. Whilst I would argue that neither Porphyry nor his first readers foment a 'revolution' in religious conceptions or language, we shall see in what follows that they each articulate religious identity labels indicating (or, at least groping towards) a shift in religious conceptions, insofar as they formulate an ideal for pagan religious thought or practice.

ETHNICITY AND RELIGION

At the outset, I should clarify somewhat my use of the term 'religious' in this inquiry. Because of my sympathies for the various projects either seeking to deconstruct the modern academic category of *religion* as a product of particular forces distinctive to modern European and then American contexts, or aiming to provide careful and contextualized studies of ancient and late-antique phenomena (whether of literary or material culture), I prefer the

---

[8] See Goulet (2004) 102–4; Riedweg (2005); Freund (2017).
[9] The earliest Latin author to cite Porphyry by name is Firmicus Maternus, who is omitted from the present study for reasons of space rather than interest.
[10] See, for example, Dubuisson (2003).
[11] For my own interpretation, see below and Johnson (2014b) 44–6.

more malleable adjective *religious* over the noun *religion*.[12] At the same time, there are ancient phenomena—albeit within different assemblages of thinking, speaking, and practice and with different social entanglements and valences— that share significant enough resonances with modern phenomena so that the assertion that there was no religion in antiquity seems overly simplistic and might occlude as much as it illumines.[13]

I use the terms 'religion' and 'religious' to designate in a polythetic manner the range of words, acts, postures, and so on that are deemed to participate in, open up, or be reflective of, a marked relation to numina, gods, daemons, or souls—namely those practices in response to or directed towards those beings who are not (or, are no longer) simply human or animal.[14] Furthermore, although both the array of traditional religious institutions, practices, and ideas in the classical and post-classical periods and the various expressions of Christianity in late antiquity were developed within relations of power, techniques of the self, and constellations of ancient knowledge that are rather different from those of the early modern Protestant and European imperialist contexts in which the category of 'religion' was crafted,[15] I nevertheless remain cautiously comfortable seeing those activities or concerns that we today might call religious as being variously 'embedded' within the foreign frameworks of antiquity.[16] In fact, I would argue that religious elements were integral parts (but only parts) of a broader identity that was being imagined or assumed in a range of discursive contexts by the use of the label Hellene (as well as Egyptian, Chaldean, and so on). The distinction is important, since if they did not have an overarching term serving as a label for a category of 'religion' then it seems absurd to look for religious identity labels that covered the conceptual terrain that we label paganism at all. At the same time, if religious phenomena formed a part of other complex identities then we might expect to find a partial label that designated only some pagans (or only some of their paganism).

This understanding raises one more point by way of prolegomena before turning to Porphyry and his first readers, and it seeks to render explicit the relationship between my approach and that of Éric Rebillard (as presented in

---

[12] For example, Asad (1993); Dubuisson (2003); Nongbri (2013).
[13] See Frankfurter (2015).
[14] I would be hesitant to follow Bruce Lincoln (2012) 75–6 in defining religion as 'a polythetic *entity*' (emphasis mine) necessarily involving four domains (of discourse, practice, community, and institution). At the same time, I have found much to recommend the practice-centred approach to the ontology of religion formulated by Stowers (2008) (whilst I would suggest that discourses cannot so easily be filtered out of such an approach, since ways of speaking and thinking may prompt or restrict practices, even as practices certainly prompt speaking and thinking).
[15] I am becoming increasingly suspicious of vague gestures to the 'Protestant' formulation of religion as if the Protestant tradition were a monolithic and univocal discourse.
[16] For an important critique of notions of 'embedded religion' in antiquity, see Nongbri (2008).

this volume as well as in his important book, *Christians and Their Many Identities in Late Antiquity*). We both, as far as I can tell, share an assumption that identities are the results of processual social and discursive engagements that individuals articulate, manipulate, resist, or ignore at various moments and within differing contexts. An individual may choose (or have forced upon them) one or more of several identities; no single identity or category of identity is exclusive of others in practice, though rhetorically it might be declared as such. Thus, any of the otherwise non-exclusive multiple identities may be invoked and ascribed (whether to self or others) along a spectrum from minimal to maximal interpretations of its reach or its priority over a person's social stance or actions, as well as its perceived relation to other identities. The adoption by some Latin Christian authors of a category of 'semi-Christians' marks a rhetorical display of a maximal view of Christian identity in its condemnation of those with more minimal conceptions of Christianity (i.e., those who allowed commitments labelled as Christian to have a less pervasive reach over all areas of their lives).[17] Or, alternatively, the category of semi-Christians was meant rhetorically to dismiss a different configuration of the components of practice or belief than that of the author and the normative value given to his own configuration of religious elements (i.e., it rejects a non-exclusive form of a Christian identity in favour of a more exclusivist one).[18] In all this, however, it could be that these Latin authors might be working with something closer to a discrete conceptual category of *religion* as denoting a separable conceptual domain from political, civic, familial, ethnic, or other cultural domains. I have found the situation less clear amongst those writing in Greek, as will become clear from consideration of the usage of the label Hellene in Porphyry and his first readers, to whom I now turn. I should make clear that my concern is not with whether there was 'religion' or the 'religious' in antiquity in ways identifiable to a modern historian (whether embedded or disembedded, whether named or unnamed); rather my concern is with the question of whether late-antique intellectuals

---

[17] I do not address the issue of Christians or semi-Christians as identity labels in my discussion below, since my focus is upon whether there exists an identity label for pagans in the pages of a small group of Greek-speaking authors. I suppose the equivalent type of an identity label in Porphyry would need to be something like a semi-philosopher (or a sophist) who did not practise the pursuit of the divine in a philosophically serious or accurate way (see, e.g., *Abst.* 4.18.4).

[18] Of course, it is rather difficult to accept that an author is a Christian defending an admittedly non-normative construal of Christian identity under a spurned label (*Hellēnismos*) if the author nowhere self-identified as a Christian. See Chapter 4, Boin's contribution to the present volume, for such an argument (which fails, in spite of claims to the contrary, to offer a philological analysis of Julian's use of the labels Hellenes, Hellenists, or Hellenism, for which, see instead Bouffartigue (1991) or Johnson (2012b); it likewise fails to offer a compelling rebuttal of the argument offered by Van Nuffelen (2002a), which can, in fact, be further substantiated by careful philological analysis in spite of Bouffartigue's rejoinder in 2005).

articulated the category (and attendant apparatus of labels) as such, as representing a discrete sphere of human experience.

Only two passages in the corpus of Porphyry can even bear the possibility of adopting the label *Hellēn* to designate a religious position standing as an equivalent to 'pagan'.[19] In the first, Porphyry writes to his wife Marcella stating that he has had to go on a journey because of a certain 'need of the Greeks, with the gods joining in'.[20] A popular interpretation sees the Greeks of this statement as unproblematically designating pagans and thus has supposed it refers to a visit to Diocletian's court in Nicomedia to lend intellectual justification to the Great Persecution.[21] Yet, aside from there being no evidence that Porphyry had any connection to Diocletian or to the Great Persecution,[22] there is little basis for taking the Greeks here as a label for a religious identity at all. Even though the gods are mentioned as 'joining in' it seems that Marcella took the invitation as directed to her as well; furthermore, based on the evidence within the letter itself the gods are not likely to be those of popular cult.[23] Similar language, after all, occurs in other writers to refer to teachers of Greek *paideia* and their students. An understanding of the 'need of the Greeks' along these more social and even academic-scholastic lines seems reasonable, especially given the fact that the letter exhibits a rather studied detachment from contemporary pagan religion in favour of a philosophical approach to the divine.[24]

The second relevant passage is *Against the Christians*, frag. 39 Harnack (= fr. 6 Becker), which presents a fascinating critique of Origen.[25] Here Porphyry claims that Origen was raised a Greek, but committed some act of 'barbarian daring', and that he 'Hellenized' with respect to his ideas about reality and the divine whilst nonetheless living 'Christianly and lawlessly (*paranomōs*)'. Origen is also criticized for inserting Greek ideas into his interpretations of the Jewish Scriptures. The verb *Hellēnizein* cannot easily be restricted to religious activity, since it refers to his views of both 'reality and the divine' as well as his applying the ideas of many Greek philosophers (Porphyry names nine of them) in his reading of the Bible. 'Hellenizing' here indicates an intellectual philosophical process that Porphyry deemed

---

[19] A third passage, which has received much attention, is that given as No. 1 in Adolf von Harnack's collection of 'fragments and references' of the *contra Christianos* (Harnack (1916)); see earlier, Wilamowitz-Moellendorf (1900). This passage is, however, arguably not Porphyrian but a construct of Eusebius himself for what 'some Greek' might say against the Christians. It has rightly been omitted in the recent critical collection of Muscolino (2008–2009), or placed in the category of *dubia* in Becker (2016); see also, Johnson (2010), (2017); Morlet (2010) 41–8.
[20] *Ep. Marc.* 4.58–9 O'Brien Wicker.   [21] Chadwick (1955) 142–3; Beatrice (1993).
[22] See Alt (1996); Riedweg (2005); Hartmann (2017).
[23] See Alt (1996) 208; Johnson (2011) 167, (2013) 20–1, 250–1.
[24] The worship *kata ta patria* most probably refers to ancient religious practice philosophically understood; see Alt (1996); Clark (2007b) 140, and in the following paragraphs.
[25] For judicious commentary, see Becker (2016) 136–67.

inappropriate and inconsistent with Origen's lifestyle.[26] The fragment's assertion that Origen was raised a Greek does not readily entail that Origen was raised a pagan, as is sometimes thought, since Porphyry specifies that he was 'trained in Greek literature'.[27] The reference to Greeks in this fragment, as in the *Epistle to Marcella*, most naturally indicates an educational and cultural identity rather than a primarily or exclusively religious one.[28]

The label *Hellēnes* occurs as an ethnonym in numerous other occurrences throughout Porphyry's corpus of writings and even more unambiguously designates the historical people as an ethnicity or a group marked by educational or philosophical achievement. Most often it is adopted to refer to the nation (*ethnos*) of Greeks and, as such, it joins the host of other nations (from Jews to Egyptians to Troglodytes) invoked variously in Porphyry's arguments.[29] Whilst Porphyry's Greeks are, aside from Origen, certainly all pagans (that is, neither Christians nor Jews), their religious practices and ways of thinking about the divine were circumscribed within the broader contours of ethnic identity. Porphyry possessed in the *Hellēnes* no overarching identity label for a religious group that we now name pagans or paganism.

If Porphyry did not convert the ethnonym *Hellēnes* into a distinctively religious label, then possibly his first readers could have. Porphyry's *Epistle to Anebo*, which had asked many critical questions about Egyptian religious practice to an otherwise unknown (and possibly fictitious[30]) Egyptian priest, elicited a lengthy response from his former student Iamblichus. The response (given the title *On the Mysteries of Egypt* since the Renaissance) inadvertently gained Iamblichus a lasting reputation as the spokesman for the purported impulses towards magic, superstition, and the irrational that later readers saw as festering in late antiquity.[31] These impulses have too readily and too often been pinned on 'Oriental' influences upon Western rationalism.[32] Thus, Iamblichus is rarely assigned a key role in modern accounts of paganism as Hellenism in late antiquity and has only awkwardly been labelled a Hellene at all (although an unfortunately unidentified student would name him 'the common good of the Greeks' and the saviour or 'light of the Greek world' in an elite educational-cultural context).[33]

In fact, in his *On the Mysteries*, the Greeks are the one ethnicity to be named as introducing error into the religious and philosophical spheres. In this, his ethnic and cultural stance seems to be roughly similar to that of Porphyry, whose *Philosophy from Oracles* claimed that the Greeks and 'those in power'

---

[26] Becker (2016) 159.   [27] Becker (2016) 156–67.   [28] See Johnson (2012a).
[29] See Johnson (2013) 258–91.   [30] Oréal (2012); Saffrey and Segonds (2012) xxx–xxxii.
[31] Dodds (1951).   [32] For corrective, see Shaw (1995) 7–8, 29–30, 94–5.
[33] Ps.-Julian, *Ep.* 181.449B; 184.419A, B Bidez-Cumont; with more of a philosophical valence, Iamblichus is said to have mingled literature with philosophy, 'to the height of which the entire Greek [tradition] is remembered to have attained', *Ep.* 187.405D Bidez-Cumont; on the author, see Barnes (1978).

were plagued by error in contrast to various eastern peoples who had pursued the path to the gods.[34] In a discussion on sacred names,[35] Iamblichus warns that the ancient prayers must be preserved 'like inviolable sanctuaries' exactly as they were originally formulated.

> For this is the reason why all these things in place at the present time have lost their power, both the names and the prayers: because they are endlessly altered according to the inventiveness and illegality (*paranomian*) of the Hellenes. For the Hellenes are experimental by nature, and eagerly propelled in all directions, having no proper ballast in them; and they preserve nothing which they have received from anyone else, but even this they promptly abandon and change it all according to their unreliable linguistic innovation. But the barbarians, being constant in their customs, remain faithful to the same words.[36]

This disparaging description of the Greeks not only avoids treating this group and their identifying ethnonym as an exclusively religious position, but also fits well with a pervasive attempt throughout the work to delineate an authorial stance as Egyptian (or Assyrian-Chaldean).[37] If it were not for a chance remark of Michael Psellos, citing an earlier statement of Proclus, we would not even know that the author of the *On the Mysteries* was Iamblichus, since it is identified at the outset as being a response to Porphyry by a certain Abamon, a prophet and priest of Egypt,[38] on behalf of Anebo. The primary authorial stance is thus Egyptian, though we should only cautiously accept his representation as accurately reflecting what a self-identified 'native' Egyptian might have thought about religious matters.[39]

Iamblichus was a Hellenized Syrian philosopher, and in any case, explicitly declares in the prologue to *On the Mysteries* that some of his responses to Porphyry would need to be drawn from the Chaldean sages and others from the prophets of the Egyptians;[40] but then he promises that he will truthfully present 'the ancestral doctrines of the Assyrians' in his work, drawing in part from what the ancients collected in a 'limited volume' from the limitless writings of antiquity.[41] In this passage Iamblichus reveals that the treatise presents his own Chaldean/Assyrian interpretation of Egyptian religious

---

[34] See Johnson (2011) 171-3.   [35] On which, see Schott (2009).

[36] *Myst.* 7.5.[259].4-12; tr. Clarke et al. (2003).

[37] This is not to deny that Iamblichus is Hellenized in his educational background or that Greek rituals do not frequently fall within his purview; but the work is not simply defending the Greek tradition as such, as asserted by Van Liefferinge (1999) 36. The Assyrians had been identified as Chaldeans at least since Philo of Alexandria, *De Abrahamo*; see Tanaseanu-Döbler (2010).

[38] Prophet: *Myst.* 1.1.[3].8; 1.1.[4].11; priest: *Myst.* 1.1.[1].1-[2].3; 1.8.[28].8. On the pseudonym, see Saffrey (1971); Clarke et al. (2003) xxvi-xxxvii.

[39] On which, see Fowden (1983) 134-41; Clarke et al. (2003) xxxviii-xlviii.

[40] *Myst.* 1.1.[4].10-12.6.7.[249].3-6.

[41] *Myst.* 1.2.[5].7-11; Clarke et al. (2003) ad loc, suppose the 'limited volume' to be the Corpus Hermeticum.

phenomena. He thus wears his Egyptian persona lightly.[42] Later, he will report what the Chaldean prophets, as authorities on the matter, teach about pure and impure forms of divination.[43] Here, in fact, the Chaldeans seem to hold a higher position of piety in comparison with Egyptians since their invocations of the gods avoid threats altogether, whereas the Egyptians sometimes use threats.[44] Yet, later, the Egyptians take pride of place since they 'were the first to be granted participation with the gods'.[45]

Both peoples receive the epithet of 'sacred nations' (*hiera ethnē*).[46] Yet, in spite of their special status, the ethnonyms for neither nation receive any sort of special force to refer to a generic form of religion that could convey the sort of semantic weight that 'paganism' might. Whatever the precise ethnic label Iamblichus/Abamon adopted for his authorial persona, there is clearly no single label or even a single position that demarcates a primarily or exclusively religious identity equivalent to paganism. Greeks, Egyptians, and Assyrians have distinctive ways of doing ritual or thinking about religion within Iamblichus' work. These ethnonyms designate peoples with ancient ancestors, distinct languages, and geographical homelands, representative national character, and distinctive ways of living and thinking. Because the concerns of the treatise are religious it is mostly religious features of their ways of thought and life that receive attention. But, we should not therefore presume that Iamblichus considered these labels to refer to religious positions disembedded from ethnic particularity.

As a Christian who composed a masterful two-part apologetic work against the Greeks and the Jews as the two rivals of Christianity, Eusebius, it might first be thought, would be a likely candidate for framing the Greeks in a starkly religious sense.[47] If Christianity was seen as a religion, as distinct from some other type of group identity (a culture, a race, and so on), then its rivals must have been conceived as religions as well. Eusebius' Greeks would thus be roughly equivalent to 'pagans'. This approach would seem to gain even more confirmation from the prefatory statements of the second part of his great apologetic effort, namely the *Demonstratio Evangelica*, which followed the *Praeparatio Evangelica*. Mirroring the criticisms that he had specified in the programmatic opening of the former work, where he claimed that he would respond to hostile criticisms that the Christians had departed from both

---

[42] Cf., however, *Myst.* 9.4.[278].7, where 'Abamon' refers to 'the Chaldeans and us [the Egyptians]'.
[43] *Myst.* 3.31.[176].1–2; for background of classical portrayals of Chaldeans, see Tanaseanu-Döbler (2010).
[44] *Myst.* 6.7.[249].3–6.   [45] *Myst.* 7.5.[258].3–4, tr. Clarke et al. (2003).
[46] *Myst.* 7.4.[256].4–5; 7.5.[257].7.
[47] My discussion here follows that of Johnson (2014b) 44–6.

the Greeks and the Jews in an act of double apostasy, he wrote in the preface to the *Demonstratio*:

> It was said already before in the *Preparation* how Christianity is neither some Hellenism (*Hellēnismos*) nor Judaism (*Ioudaismos*), but bears a certain appropriate impress of piety towards God, and this is not a new or outlandish thing, but quite ancient... Hellenism, in a nutshell, is the improper fear (*deisidaimonian*) of many gods according to the ancestral ways of all nations...[48] Christianity (*Christianismos*) would be neither some Hellenism nor Judaism, but something between these, the most ancient pattern of the life of piety, and a certain most ancient philosophy, yet only recently legislated for all humans in the whole world.[49]

These lines have led some to suppose that Eusebius here articulates the first expression of the modern notion of 'religion' as a discrete category separated from its traditional ethnic contexts.[50] Yet, the fundamental lines of the two-part apologetic magnum opus carry out a sustained form of what I have elsewhere called 'ethnic argumentation', which requires for its persuasiveness the construal of markers of ethnic difference including the shared history of a kin group, emphasis upon central founding fathers, regional affiliation, language, dietary and sexual customs, and religious practices and ways of life.[51] In the *Praeparatio* the embeddedness of Greek religious components within a broader ethnicity is essential for his argument: the Greeks were historical latecomers to the history of great nations and stole all their best and worst ideas, stories, and practices from other more ancient peoples.

Whilst the addition of the *-ismos* endings to *Hellēnismos*, *Ioudaismos*, and *Christianismos* in the preface of the *Demonstratio* seems to indicate systems of thinking and acting—especially in the case of Hellenism, which is described as the superstition exhibited in the ancestral cult forms of many nations—these systems are integrally connected to ethnic underpinnings.[52] Indeed, even though the label of Hellenism is defined as applying to all those nations that worship many gods, it seems to have been chosen specifically (over the Egyptians, Phoenicians, or others) for its ethnic particularities of a people rooted in a specific time and place.[53]

On the other hand, the notion of polytheism enjoys a certain popularity in the pages of Eusebius' apologetic tome. One can imagine that it could have been made to carry the sort of conceptual weight needed for a circumscribed religious identity. And yet, it occurs only in adjectival form, not as a noun: as

---

[48] *DE* 1.2.1–2, 12a.   [49] *DE* 1.2.10, 14a.   [50] Boyarin (2008).
[51] Johnson (2006); see also, Johnson (2014a).
[52] This is true even of *Christianismos*, which might seem to be a clearly and discretely religious label since today Christianity is unproblematically deemed by most to be a religion; for Eusebius, however, Christians were an *ethnos*; see Johnson (2006) 220–32.
[53] Johnson (2014b) 44–6.

'polytheistic superstition' (*polutheon deisidaimonian*) or 'polytheistic error' (*polutheon planēn*).[54] The notion as well as the adjectival application remains always expressed within particular ethnic contexts (e.g., 'the polytheistic error of the Greeks', and so on) and is not employed in our two programmatic passages instead of the term Hellenism. Indebted as they are to earlier ways of framing religious difference within and between peoples, the -*ismos* labels are used as a rhetorically effective means of signifying the inadequacies of the two rivals of Christianity, at least as long as Eusebius' construction of those ethnic identities remains in play in the reader's historiographical, national, and religious imagination.[55]

Together with Porphyry and Iamblichus, Eusebius highlights the religious differences or similarities of various peoples but avoids adopting a particular term to designate an exclusively religious identity for pagans in contrast to other categories of identity (cultural, racial, legal, and so on). In none of these three thinkers is the label of Hellenes adopted as a simply religious designation for pagans or even polytheists. No doubt each of these intellectuals would have identified Hellenes as polytheists (at least most of the time, though some Hellenes might also be identified as atheists), but this was not the sum of the contents or connotations for the identity of Hellenes as discursively constructed in their writings.

RELIGIOUS IDENTITIES

There are no 'pagans' performing sacrifices, saying prayers, or displaying lives of piety in the pages of Porphyry, Eusebius, or Iamblichus, only Egyptians, Persians, Syrians, Greeks, Romans, and others. Within these larger group identities, though, there were smaller groups marked out by religious identity. These are the priests, who can on occasion be classified in kinship terms, as belonging to a priestly *genos* (a race or family) within the broader *ethnos*—a

---

[54] For example, PE 1.4.5; 1.6.4; 1.8.19; 1.9.19; 2.5.3; 3.14.1; 4.1.1; 4.15.6; 5.1.7; 5.2.3. For the related 'superstitious error' (*deisidaimona planēn*), see for example, PE 1.5.1; 2.5.2; 2.6.11; 6.6.65; cf. 2.1.52.

[55] *Pace* Boin (2014), whose argument is vitiated partly by an overly schematic understanding of *Hellēnismos* and its cognates in Jewish and Christian literature (esp. Eusebius) and partly by an uncritical privileging of the notion that the label *pagani* expressed a metaphor designating 'civilians' or those deemed to be insufficiently combative in their faith (Tertullian is over-interpreted whilst the dominant usage, as far as I have been able to determine, is glossed over or ignored; for example, Philastrius, *De div. haeres.* 11, PL 12.1233); for criticism of the military metaphor, see Cameron (2011) 15–16, 19.

point made more than once in Porphyry's *On Abstinence*.[56] There, priests are clearly defined as those who 'are able in nations and cities to sacrifice on behalf of all and by their piety bring the divine to care for them'.[57] Importantly for his vegetarian argument, all priests abstain from various types of meat regardless of whether they maintain the 'Greek or barbarian custom'.[58] His description of the Egyptian priests is lengthy and laudatory, since they are declared to embody the virtues and live austere lives of contemplation away from the crowds.[59] They were engaged in daily studies in various fields of inquiry and 'stayed awake for love of scholarship (*philologia*)'.[60] The priests were true philosophers,[61] but they remained firmly ensconced within an Egyptian ethnic context, living in their temples, conducting festivals and public rituals (4.6.2, 6), following Egyptian-centred laws (for instance, not eating food imported from outside Egypt, 4.7.1), stayed within the boundaries of Egypt (leaving was considered an act of impiety, 4.8.4); the animals they considered divine were sacred to particular regions within Egypt (4.6.4); their hymns used their ancestral language (4.9.5), as did their burial rites (4.10.4).

Less clearly located in either civic or ethnic contexts were identities marking extremes on a religious spectrum: the sorcerers (*goētes*) were located on the lawless and superstitious side and theosophists, 'those wise about the gods' (*theosophoi*), were placed on the other.[62] In fact, those who might be stereotyped as experts in sorcery, namely the Magi who were differentiated into three classes (*genē*) of people who were 'wise about the divine' (*sophoi peri to theion*) within the Persian ethnicity,[63] were explicitly not to be equated with *goēteia*.[64] If Porphyry ever used the term 'theurgy' (though it can be found in

---

[56] *Abst.* 2.30.5; 4.7.5; 4.16.1; 4.17.1, 3; for distinctions between *genos* and *ethnos*, see Johnson (2013) 191–201. On classical priesthoods bound to a *genos*, see briefly Price (2004) 303; Chaniotis (2008) 21–2.

[57] *Abst.* 4.5.4; tr. Clark (2000), modified; for broader context, see Marx-Wolf (2016) 100–25. For the imprecision and dangers of imputing modern Christian notions of priests to the various terms for priestly personnel in antiquity see Henrichs (2008); Chaniotis (2008).

[58] *Abst.* 4.5.5; significantly, Greek priests receive no sustained attention in *Abst.* 4, possibly as a result of the traditional notion of Greek priesthood as comprising a limited role without expectations of ritual expertise or pervasive lifestyle commitments; see Chaniotis (2008); Tanaseanu-Döbler (2013) 89–90.

[59] *Abst.* 4.6.1–7, citing Chaeremon. For the integration of Egyptian priests in Roman society (and for the possibility that many Egyptian priests were not in fact from Egypt), see Swetnam-Burland (2011).

[60] *Abst.* 4.8.2–3.   [61] *Abst.* 4.6.1.

[62] In his history of sacrifice in *Abst.* 2 (drawing on Theophrastus), Porphyry presents different poles of a religious spectrum: on the one side were the earliest pure and simple (non-animate) sacrifices; the other side split into two opposing problematic forms of atheism amongst the *atheoi* (who were 'non-sacrificers', *athutoi*), or of human sacrifice (by 'bad sacrificers', *kakothutoi*, marking an extreme of 'lawlessness', *paranomia*, and savage superstition); *Abst.* 2.7. Interestingly, these extremes are represented by particular ethnic examples (the Egyptians at *Abst.* 2.5.1; the Thoans at 2.8.1–2; the Bassarians and Taurians at 2.8.3).

[63] *Abst.* 4.16.1–2.   [64] *Abst.* 4.16.8.

no solidly established verbatim fragment and its rare occurrence in the polemical paraphrases of his opponents leads one to suspect its being their addition rather than his own word choice[65]) it, too, seems bound to ethnicity (in this case, Chaldean).[66] The *goētes* were thus ethnically unbounded within Porphyry's portrayal. Stirring up daemons 'to gratify their lusts', the sorcerers were identified as individuals who least exemplified holiness and assimilation to the divine, and who pursued lawlessness towards the universe (*eis ta hola paranomias*) and even necromancy.[67] They stood in direct contrast to the theosophists: 'Purity (*hagneia*) does not belong to the sorcerers but to divine men who are wise about the gods (*theosophoi*)'.[68] This latter category deserves special interest.

Porphyry seems to have been the first to coin the word *theosophia* and *theosophoi* as an identity label for these 'orders' (*tagmata*) within different nations who practised varying levels of ascetic lifestyle.[69] He may have been prompted to adopt the neologism by Chaeremon's claim that the priests of the Egyptians were philosophers,[70] although the term occurs earlier in the work,[71] and may have been a natural extension of similar locutions that occur in other works: 'those wise with respect to the divine' (*tois ta theia sophois*),[72] or the phrase, 'a theological wisdom' (*sophias theologou*).[73] In any case, the exact label is applied in the *On Abstinence* only to Egyptians and Indians, though it seems Porphyry would have had no qualms in assigning it to other ascetic groups, which he highlights in the fourth book of his treatise on vegetarianism.

---

[65] The first occurrence of *theurgia* in the fragments of the *De Regressu animae* is only ascribed to a sweeping and anonymous 'they' (fr. 286 Smith), which in a subsequent line by our single source for the fragments of this work (Augustine) narrows to include 'Porphyry, too' as admitting some limited efficacy to theurgy (fr. 288 Smith); but, these 'fragments' can scarcely be deemed faithful paraphrases rather than sweeping gestures meant to put whatever original discussion Porphyry had offered into a particular light amenable to Augustine's polemic (and in any case, we have no way to determine whether Augustine came across this treatise, if in fact it was an independent treatise, in whole or in part, in Greek or in Latin translation). Porphyry's wording may only have contained *ta hiera* or *teletai* whereas Augustine could have chosen to attack it under the label of *theurgia*, which was currently fashionable amongst his own contemporary Platonists a century after Porphyry's death.

[66] See *Regr.anim.* frs. 287, 294 Smith.   [67] *Abst.* 2.45.1–3; 2.47.2 (on necromancy).

[68] *Abst.* 2.45.2; cf. Iamb. *Myst.* 2.11, cited below.

[69] *Abst.* 4.9.9 (the Egyptian priests); 4.17.1 (the Brachmans and Samanaeans); as far as I can tell, *theosophia* only occurs before Porphyry in an odd passage of Clement of Alexandria where it is given in adverbial form (*Strom.* 1.1, PG 8, 708A); it is unclear, therefore, who (if anyone) had used the term in the little over half-century up to Porphyry and how they might have used it; see Siémons (1988) 4, 11, 17–19 for some possibilities.

[70] *Abst.* 4.6.1 (= fr. 10 van der Horst); for useful discussion of this passage, see the notes of van der Horst (1984), as well as (1982).

[71] *Abst.* 2.35.1; 2.45.2 and 4. The label also occurred in his *On the Styx* fr. 378.50 Smith and probably in his *Philosophy from Oracles*, since Eusebius invokes it sarcastically when introducing quotations of that work (see *Phil.Orac.* frs. 303.9; 323.7 Smith). On fr. 340a Smith (= Philoponus), see below. In general, see Toulouse (2005).

[72] *Phil.Orac.* fr. 326.15 Smith.   [73] *Simulac.* 351.15 Smith.

The Rhetoric of Pagan Religious Identities 41

These include the different orders of Magi amongst the Persians (since they were 'wise about the divine', *sophoi peri to theion*)[74] and the Essenes amongst the Jews (who are designated a type of philosophy and are 'distinctively pious towards the divine').[75]

Whilst these instances of *theosophoi* (and its circumlocutions) are all applied to people within a broader ethnic context, an arresting occurrence of *theosophia* arises in a context without reference to any specific ethnic identities. In a discussion of the prescriptions for purity by 'theologians',[76] Porphyry declares, as we noted above, that holiness does not belong to sorcerers (*goētes*) but 'divine and theosophic men (*theiōn kai theosophōn andrōn*)' who are pursuing likeness to God.[77] He writes:

> Purity (*hagneia*), both internal and external, belongs to a divine man (*theios anēr*) who strives to fast from the passions of the soul just as he fasts from those foods which arouse passions, who feeds on wisdom about the god (*theosophia*) and becomes like [the god] by right thinking (*orthais dianoiais*) about the divine; a man sanctified by intellectual sacrifice (*noera thusia*).[78]

Whilst we remain without a general identity label for 'pagans', what we find in this description is an identity label for the true philosopher's (pagan) religion. It designated not those for whom religious elements were an integral part of their lives and multiple identities, but those for whom all of life was subordinated to the pursuit of the divine and practices of likening oneself to God. This was a maximal view of the religious in the life of the philosopher since all of life was defined as an approach to the God over all. Throughout the second book of the *On Abstinence* Porphyry had sought to redefine holiness in terms of simplicity and virtue.[79] Crucially, he had presented a hierarchy of sacrifices that became ever more immaterial and intellectual as it ascended to higher theological levels of divine beings, so that one worshipped the intelligible gods only with words, and the 'God over all' only with pure silence and pure thoughts.[80] This is the 'intellectual sacrifice' referred to in his description of the theosophists. Such an understanding of sacrifice was not merely a cognitive grasp of religious truths, or doctrine, but a way of life.[81]

Such a religion would have little in common with the traditional forms of paganism within their local civic or ethnic contexts. Indeed, at key points in the *On Abstinence*, Porphyry had voiced a critical (sometimes even caustic)

---

[74] *Abst.* 4.16.1.   [75] *Abst.* 4.11.1; 4.12.1; 4.13.1.
[76] Theologians: *Abst.* 2.36.3; 2.43.4; 2.44.2; 2.47.1; 2.55.1 (which names Seleukos the theologian); 2.58.1; 4.44.2 and 4.47.1. It is unclear who the theologians of these passages were (Orphic or Pythagorean writers are likely candidates); see Clark (2000) 154 n.297. In any case, because Porphyry usually uses the term to refer to ancient authors and sages, I have omitted analysis of the *theologoi* from the current investigation into religious identities.
[77] *Abst.* 2.45.2; see Plato, *Theaet.* 176b.   [78] *Abst.* 2.45.4, tr. Clark (2000), modified.
[79] See his programmatic remarks at *Abst.* 1.57.   [80] *Abst.* 4.34.2–4; cf. *Abst.* 4.37.
[81] See *Abst.* 1.29; 2.61.1.

distance from the ways of living and thinking of 'the many'.[82] It would likewise have little in common with Christianity, as Porphyry represented it, which attended too closely in his mind to the recently embodied soul of a pious man and which unduly focused on the physical plane.[83] A single piece of evidence that might seem to indicate a link between the theosophist and the physical plane occurs, however, in a testimony to Porphyry's *Philosophy from Oracles* by the sixth-century Christian John Philoponus. The apologist claims that, for Porphyry, 'the practical theosophy—as he calls magic—is difficult in the undertaking for humans', because precise knowledge of the stars is impossible, causing the oracles relying on them to be untrue.[84] There is reason to suspect Philoponus' testimony here (as he generally appears not to have been precise in his citations of Porphyry), but if the phrase 'practical theosophy' and not just the term 'theosophy' was Porphyry's it would seem to apply to a wisdom about the gods[85] in relation to the stars, the sub-astral realm of the fates, and the giving of oracles. It is inappropriate to suppose that the term's covering for magic is anything more than Philoponus' own rhetorical smear (one that we find in Augustine as well).[86] If it is Porphyry's, the phrase 'practical theosophy' probably refers to the philosophically astute understanding of oracular phenomena and not the invocations, bindings, and other divinatory procedures to which the other related fragments from the *Philosophy from Oracles* refer.

Aside from the intriguing testimony of Philoponus, *theosophia* signified the true philosophical approach to the divine and thus what we might be tempted to label a truly philosophic religion. This association entailed a significant identification between the identity label of the philosopher and the priest. In the manner of a manifesto, Porphyry wrote:

> The philosopher, priest of the God who rules all,[87] reasonably abstains from all animate food, working to approach the god, alone to the alone, by his own effort... And just as a priest of one of the particular gods is expert in setting up cult-statues of this god, and in his rites and initiations and purifications and the

---

[82] 'If the many (*hoi polloi*) [do not accept abstinence from meat], it need not concern us, for among the many there is nothing reliable and consistent even in friendship and goodwill. They have no capacity for such things, or for wisdom, or even for bits of wisdom which have some worth; the common person (*ho polus*) does not understand what is advantageous... Besides, there is much licentious and unrestrained behavior among the many' (*Abst.* 1.52.4); cf. *Abst.* 4.9.10. For Porphyry's elitism, see Toulouse (2005); Johnson (2013) 179–80, 292–6. Many philosophers served as priests in spite of their philosophical scruples, in other words separated theory from social practice; see Haake (2008).

[83] See Johnson (2012a).   [84] *Phil.Orac.* fr. 340a Smith.

[85] I take the gods to be the object of the wisdom; alternatively, Van Liefferinge (1999) 184, supposes *theosophia* here to designate 'wisdom coming from the gods'.

[86] Augustine, *Civ.Dei* 10.9.1–12.

[87] Later, this philosopher will be named 'the priest of the Father'; *Abst.* 2.50.1; see Marx-Wolf (2016) 107–9.

like, so the priest of the God who rules all is expert (*empeiros*) in the making of his cult-statue and in purifications and the other rites by which he is linked to the god.[88]

That such a priestly identification for the philosopher was not merely a passing rhetorical flourish, but a more substantial identity claim, is made clear from the fact that he repeats it in his later *Epistle to Marcella*. There, he claims that 'the wise man alone is a priest; he alone is God-beloved; he alone knows how to pray'.[89] Knowledge was essential to this priestly philosopher and ignorance was impiety: 'The impious man is...the one united to the opinions of the masses regarding God'.[90]

With its focus on the intellect, the articulation of this religious identity of the philosopher-priest or theosophist presumed that knowledge was crucial to true religious expression: doctrine did matter. Correct knowledge, in the sense of theological understanding of a Platonic ontology and psychology, knowing the soul's true nature and place in relation to the three hypostases of Plotinus' formulation of Platonism, was essential to salvation of the soul.[91]

In contrast to Porphyry, Iamblichus seems entirely to avoid the labels of theosophy (aside from a single odd reference to the 'theosophic Muse').[92] Whether intentional or not, this avoidance coheres with the sustained emphasis upon ritual performance and work in *On the Mysteries*. Whilst there are scattered references to various religious identities, such as priest, diviner, prophet, the Korybantes, or the devotees of Sabazios or Magna Mater throughout the treatise, certainly the most significant and esteemed label for a person demarcating their religious position is that of the theurgist (*theourgos*). If the 'divine divination' elaborated in the third book of *On the Mysteries* can safely be equated with theurgy or at least be taken as forming a part of theurgy for Iamblichus (an equation that I think can be made based upon the high number of circumlocutions for divine divination as arising from the 'works of the gods' or 'divine works',[93] as well as passages that explicitly invoke theurgy within the context of the soul's limited role in divine divination[94]), then those 'possessed' (or 'retained', *katechomenoi*)[95] by the gods in divinatory rituals and who have 'subjected their entire life as a vehicle (*ochēma*) or instrument to the gods who

---

[88] *Abst.* 2.49.1, 3, tr. Clark (2000). [89] *Ep.Marc.* 16.280-1, tr. O'Brien Wicker (1987).
[90] *Ep.Marc.* 17. 291-2, tr. O'Brien Wicker (1987). Van Liefferinge (1999) 203 has noted the importance of 'acts' (*erga*) in Porphyry's theosophy and supposes them to be cultic rituals; I see no clear evidence to imagine these as other than acts of asceticism or intellectual training.
[91] See *De nosce te ipsum*, frs. 274-5 Smith. [92] *Myst.* 7.1.[249].9.
[93] *Myst.* 3.5.[111].7-9; 3.7.[115].5-7; 3.10.[121].3; 3.17.[140].6; 3.17.[142].6; 3.18.[144].1; 3.18.[144].7-8, 9, [145].2; 3.19.[147].9; 3.20.[149].10, 11 (in a sentence explicitly using the term 'theurgic activity'), [150].2; 3.25.[160].2; 3.27.[165].7.
[94] *Myst.* 3.20.[149].9-12; 3.22.[152].9-10; *pace* Charles-Saget (1993) 108-9.
[95] This seems to be Iamblichus' reference to the *katochoi*, a distinctively Egyptian category of religious personnel; for the earlier debate on this category, see Geffcken (1978) 6, with 18 n.68.

inspire them' are theurgists.[96] These individuals 'either exchange their human life for the divine, or they direct their own life towards the god'.[97]

Likewise, the divinatory 'expert' (*epistēmōn*) is identifiable with the 'theurgic expert' (*tou epistēmonos theourgou*)[98] and may be seen as one who ascends to superior beings and joins with them 'through assimilation and appropriation'.[99] Knowledge is thus included as a distinguishing mark of the theurgist's identity as it is construed by Iamblichus. Even in the well-known passage where he averred that symbols maintained their efficacy even when the theurgist was not doing intellectual work,[100] Iamblichus had added that 'effective union never takes place without knowledge (*gnōnai*) but nevertheless is not identical (*tautotēta*) with it'.[101] This distinguishing of knowledge as a necessary but not sufficient basis for theurgic union[102] provides an important degree of conceptual distance between Iamblichus' *theourgia* and Porphyry's *theosophia*. As Iamblichus continues: 'Thus, divine purity (*hagneia*) does not come about through right knowledge, in the way that bodily purity does through chastity, but divine union and purification actually go beyond knowledge. Nothing, then, of any such qualities in us, such as are human contributes in any way towards the accomplishment of divine transactions'.[103]

The precise role and nature of the knowledge necessary (at least partially) to the theurgist's successful ascent to the 'intelligible fire'[104] is left ambiguous. What becomes clear is that Iamblichus' theurgist can hardly be seen as a champion of the irrational.[105] Such a caricature has arisen partly from Iamblichus' own efforts to draw firm lines of distinction between his own and Porphyry's conception of the ideal communication and communion with the divine. For Iamblichus, the role of the gods was both primary and essential, whereas for Porphyry the gods assisted a soul who possessed within itself the keys to its own salvation.

Like Porphyry, the identity of the religious ideal (whether it was labelled *theosophia* or *theourgia*) was represented as one end of a spectrum that held at its other religious extreme the sorcerers (as well as 'atheists', though these individuals receive only the briefest passing mention[106]). These individuals were contrasted emphatically with the theurgist at key points in Iamblichus' argument.[107] Significantly, they are most marked by their use of artifice

---

[96] *Myst.* 3.4.[109].10–11.
[97] *Myst.* 3.4.[109].11–13; for Iamblichus' categorization of such individuals as a class of only a very few humans, see Shaw (1995) 146–52.
[98] *Myst.* 3.18.[145].13; on the theurgist as ritual expert, see Tanaseanu-Döbler (2013) 106–8.
[99] *Myst.* 3.18.[145].10–12.   [100] Shaw (1995).
[101] *Myst.*2.11.[98].6–7; tr. Clarke et al. (2003).
[102] Shaw (1995) 85, 97; Van Liefferinge (1999) 28.
[103] *Myst.*2.11.[98].7–11; tr. Clarke et al. (2003).   [104] *Myst.* 3.31.[179].7.
[105] See the important study of Smith (1993); also Van Liefferinge (1999) 29–35.
[106] *Myst.* 3.31.[179].9; the label probably designates the Christians (see note at Clarke et al. (2003) ad loc.).
[107] See Cremer (1969) 34–6.

in ritual: their apparitions were 'produced artificially (*technikōs*)' and bore no clarity or truth (in contrast to the true visions of the gods).[108] The rites of the Egyptians are in no way to be confused with the *technasmata* of the sorcerers.[109] Sorcery (*goēteia*) finds no particular attachment to a single ethnic group and it seems that Iamblichus is more concerned to combat general stereotypes of Egyptians or Chaldeans as practitioners of sorcery (probably expressed in Porphyry's *Epistle to Anebo*) and has no particular individuals or groups of individuals in mind. Whether in the identity label of the sorcerer or the theurgist, however, Iamblichus has articulated a person identified primarily for their religious activity and ideas, which, whilst possessed of more or less significant threads to broader ethnic identities (however these might be envisioned at any particular point in his argument), were separable from those identities. Yet, it was precisely as ideal types for the positive or negative poles of religious identity that they failed to convey an identity of pagan religion *tout court*.

Eusebius seems to have had no knowledge of Iamblichus or his response to Porphyry's *Letter to Anebo*, but it is highly unlikely that he would have allowed for Iamblichus' attempted separation of theurgy (a term not registered by Eusebius) from sorcery. In fact, his many harsh words against *goēteia* were aimed at the sort of polytheistic or daemonic activity represented by Iamblichus' theurgists, Egyptian priests, or sorcerers with all distinctions cast aside in a brusque rhetorical sweep. At the heart of the rise of civic religious practices, for Eusebius, were the daemons or, more sarcastically, the 'noble gods' who fostered *goēteia* and taught the 'evil contrivances' (*kakotechnai*) to those serving them.[110] Sorcery was 'a perversion of true piety'.[111] Unlike Porphyry, who sought to differentiate sorcery from the Magi and their practices, Eusebius equates sorcery and magic (*mageia*),[112] and even identifies the Apollo whose utterances were quoted in Porphyry's *Philosophy from Oracles* as a promoter of magic.[113]

Whilst given some respect by Eusebius for being one of the foremost philosophers of his time, Porphyry receives the denunciation of making sophistries and inventing clever interpretations that only concealed the impiety and unsoundness of pagan religious activity.[114] Eusebius derided Porphyry sarcastically for his *theosophia* after quoting the *On Abstinence* on the Egyptian deification of animals and again before and after quoting his *Philosophy from Oracles*.[115] It is striking, therefore, that Eusebius elsewhere applied the

---

[108] *Myst.* 3.25.[160].11–[161].2; on the varied use of *technē*, see Shaw (1995) 38–9; Van Liefferinge (1999) 40–1; Tanaseanu-Döbler (2013) 108–10.
[109] *Myst.* 7.5.[258].5.   [110] *PE* 5.2.5; 5.10.12.   [111] *PE* 6.11.82.
[112] *PE* 5.14.3; cf. 5.15.4–5.   [113] *PE* 6.4.3.
[114] For example, Porphyry's *On Images* is an example of the 'sophistries (*sophismata*) of young (or recent) men' at *PE* 3.7.5; see also 3.10.3; 3.13.9; 3.15.1; 3.16.4.
[115] Eus. *PE* 3.5.4 (referring to the occurrence of the term in the just quoted passage from the *Abst.* at 3.4.14); 4.6.4; 4.9.7; 9.10.2 (unless this latter is actually part of the quotation of Porphyry's

term in a positive manner to Christianity or its Hebrew forebears. Though rare, its positive use is well placed. For instance, in an attempt to show that Plato had borrowed the tripartite categorization of philosophy from the ancient Hebrews, Eusebius writes that for the latter the dialectical branch of philosophy was based on reality, 'which with souls illumined by divine light their *theosophoi* discovered, and were by it enlightened'.[116] More pointedly, in the prologue of the work Eusebius states that he will address the issue of 'what Christianity should properly be called, since it is neither Hellenism nor Judaism, but a new and true kind of *theosophia*'.[117] Whilst there is no good reason to suppose Porphyry was the single target lurking behind the bulk of the *Praeparatio*,[118] the fact that Eusebius seems to adopt the terms of theosophy (*theosophia, theosophos*) only in this work does reveal a certain rhetorical punch to these passages.

Theosophia, though a (now Christian) philosopher's 'religion', remained contextualized in Eusebius within the nation of ancient Hebrews or of later Christians; in other words it remained an ethnically rooted way of life and did not become a separable transcendent 'religion' according to the oft-invoked Protestant heuristic. For Christianity itself was a nation of those who were 'friends of God' and practitioners of intellectual sacrifice. Whilst Eusebius' formulations do not show a notion of religion disembedded from ethnic constructs, his privileging of intellectual religious acts for those 'wise about God' points to a religious ideal in which knowledge played a key role. Like Porphyry, Eusebius marks an identification of religion and/as philosophy in such a way that doctrine becomes essential. In so doing, his conception of religious activity would contribute to, and be representative of, a shift in Christianity towards a concern with proper doctrine. This concern would play a well-known role in fourth-century ecclesiastical politics. But it was not a distinctively Christian concern, since, as we have seen, both Porphyry and Iamblichus (in different ways) also valued philosophical knowledge, 'right thinking', as fundamental to the religious task of connecting humans to the divine.

CONCLUSION

In none of the three thinkers under consideration here was a label employed or an identity constructed that could stand as a notion of 'pagan religion' disentangled from other identities as discretely religious in conception. In

---

text). Cf. *PE* 4.2.10 (where the oracular activity of the pagan priest Theotecnus is designated *theosophia*).

[116] *PE* 11.5.1, tr. Gifford (1903), modified. [117] *PE* 1.5.12; tr. Gifford (1903), modified.
[118] See Morlet (2011).

spite of the fact that each of these intellectuals elaborated arguments clearly dedicated to matters that fall within the purview of our modern category of religion, they seem unwilling to articulate these matters within a discrete identity category distinguished from other categories like culture, philosophy, race, or nation. Whilst their various formulations of theosophists, theurgists, or sorcerers may come tantalizingly close to a disembedded conceptual category of religion, as though they were strictly religious identities, they are bound to particular embodiments within particular nations and cities. Only the rhetorically barbed label of *goēteia*, which referred to those practising artifice and sophistry, remained unmarked in terms of broader identities. But each of these thinkers would hardly have allowed sorcerers the privileged status of possessing a 'religion' rather than a delusion driven by human or daemonic technique.

Insofar as Porphyry and his first readers are representative, the conceptual revolution that carved out a notion of disembedded religion, distinguishable from the 'secular' or public sphere, seems not to have occurred in the late third or early fourth centuries and would have to await later developments. Before, however, we see them as too entirely foreign from modern Western phenomena we must appreciate the vast diversity in modern conceptions of the human relationship with the supra-human. There remain many for whom the content of one's diet is a deeply religious matter; or for whom a line between the spiritual and bodily, the heavenly and the earthly, the private and the public is to be eschewed; for whom the involvement of the divine in human affairs is to be engaged in a maximalist fashion; for whom praxis is to be privileged over doctrinal belief; for whom a separation of religion from politics is unthinkable for its driving of the divine from a purportedly neutral or secular sphere. Academic definitions of 'religion' drawing upon a narrow characterization of Protestant Christian thought may remain as unhelpful for investigating the present world as much as the ancient. More supple and polythetic approaches to both ancient and modern religious practices or ways of thinking and speaking about the divine may after all find some familiarity in the otherwise ever foreign worlds of intellectual culture in late antiquity.

4

The Maccabees, 'Apostasy', and Julian's Appropriation of *Hellenismos* as a Reclaimed Epithet in Christian Conversations of the Fourth Century CE

Douglas Boin

INTRODUCTION: THE REASONS FOR METHODOLOGICAL RIGOUR

The opening chapters in this volume by Johnson, Rebillard, and the present author have been grouped together because they offer insights on historical method.[1] This chapter, in particular, is a focused study of the Emperor Julian. I will introduce the emperor in a moment, but before beginning, I would like to offer a reflection on what my methodological conversation partners and I have in common and where we differ. As will become clear from this chapter, my interest in Julian—his language, policies, and worldview—stem from a lack of satisfaction with the way Rome's fourth-century cultural changes have been characterized in secondary historical writing. What once was seen as a time of Christian ascendancy and pagan reaction has, in many ways, remained a time of Christian ascendancy and pagan reaction. My repetition here is meant to be both intentional and surprising; even as many scholars would do their best to rub out any trace of conflict from the fourth-century story, many others see

---

[1] I would like to thank the organizers of the conference in Exeter for their invitation, their generous support, and, above all, for their encouragement and feedback as this chapter came together. I have not intended to be exhaustive in my references to the secondary literature on this topic since a re-write of Julian's reign would take a book; but I do hope that my selections will point readers towards key debates on the specific issues raised here and to the scholars who have done much to forge a path in the area of Julian's biography, fourth-century social and cultural history, and the history of religion.

Douglas Boin, *The Maccabees, 'Apostasy', and Julian's Appropriation of* Hellenismos *as a Reclaimed Epithet in Christian Conversations of the Fourth Century CE* In: *Rhetoric and Religious Identity in Late Antiquity*. Edited by: Richard Flower and Morwenna Ludlow, Oxford University Press (2020). © Oxford University Press. DOI: 10.1093/oso/9780198813194.003.0004

The Maccabees, 'Apostasy', and Julian's Appropriation of Hellenismos 49

little option but to continue to describe fourth-century actors, like Julian, in terms that are comfortably recognizable to us. The title of a 2017 book from Oxford University Press captures the entrenched obstinacy; to a certain segment of researchers, Julian will forever be 'the last pagan' who waged 'war against Christians'.[2]

What the authors in this opening section share, I believe, is a commitment to a greater precision and conceptual clarity in historical writing; and if that means scholars have to give up their usual way of doing things, then so be it. This restlessness with the status quo, to my mind, is surely the right instinct because it lies at the root of what it means for a scholar to describe, honestly and fairly, the nature of an individual's historical experience. Johnson himself frames his argument, about what the word 'Hellene' may have meant to someone like Porphyry, within the need to account for the 'sensitivity' of ancient words and their social contexts; and Rebillard, too, uses sociological theory to urge scholars to think more clearly—avoiding, for example, the gross characterizations of 'groupism' when writing about faith because of the inherent difficulty of assuming homogeneous identities across religious communities. Readers who take their history with a bit less jargon may have found other ways of solving this problem (don't refer to 'the Christians'); but at its core, these two explorations of how we write about the past have a lot of common sense. This chapter shares those same commitments.

I also think it's important, before beginning, to highlight areas of difference, not to say that I 'differ' with my colleagues' methodological choices but that I myself have different social-historical aims. Whilst Rebillard's suggestions for new ways of categorizing identity are certainly novel, I wonder how they forward the conversation amongst those with a social history approach; one of the aims in trying to tackle the complexity of fourth-century politics, as I see it in my own contribution, for example, is not necessarily the need for another system of abstract categorization to replace earlier systems of abstract categorization. Rather, the crucial matter in writing about someone like the Emperor Julian is finding the actual specificity in our words to describe both what the sources are saying *as well as* how they can be put together to form a narrative of change over time—the historian's task. Johnson, to my mind, hones in on this facet of the problem more explicitly, articulating the urgency of our methodological choices when he explains 'at stake in the investigation of religious labels in Porphyry, Iamblichus, and Eusebius is not merely philological accuracy or terminological pedantry', because it relates to 'a larger narrative of Christianity'.[3] Yet whereas Johnson is largely concerned with intellectual and ethnic histories, however, I am interested in social

---

[2] Teitler (2017) from the title, *The Last Pagan Emperor: Julian the Apostate and the War against Christianity*.

[3] See Johnson, in this volume, p. 30.

practice—Christian social practice before and after Constantine—not because I am concerned to document Christians' many identities over time but because I'm concerned to write about the *social and political impact of those Christians' choices* over time.

The life of the Emperor Julian, last representative of the house of Constantine, is an excellent case study in this regard because of his prolific written output and, more importantly, because of his language choices. As I will show here, a more rigorous look at Julian's vocabulary might even suggest new possibilities for describing the divisive politics of the fourth century. At the core of this contribution, then, is not a desire to blur the details of social and cultural life in cities of the fourth-century Roman Empire but to sharpen it.[4] In it, I advocate that Christianity's tangled relationship with Judaism—and with the legacy of the Maccabean revolt and with literary accounts like 2 Maccabees —take a more prominent place in discussions about Christian political behaviour in the Roman Empire. Christian social differences, as I will suggest, lay at the centre of Rome's 'fourth-century crisis';[5] and it is these social fissures—not the usual theological ones or even the tired assumption of a clash between traditionalists and Christians—that played an overlooked role in changing the Roman world.[6]

JULIAN AS A CASE STUDY IN HOW TO APPLY HISTORICAL METHOD

According to the bishop Gregory of Nazianzus, the identity of the terrible dragon, or serpent, of the apocalyptic text known as the Book of Revelation was none other than the Roman emperor Julian. Raised in a Christian family, and emperor for three years (r. 361–363 CE), Julian was pilloried by Gregory for being 'an apostate' from the Christian faith.[7] That label has done lasting damage to the emperor's reputation as a Christian. From Christian church historians of the fifth century CE to the politically charged anticlerical writings of Voltaire in the eighteenth century to one contemporary German scholar calling the Roman Emperor a 'Christian hater' (*Christenhasser*),[8] Julian's choices have warped many narratives of the fourth century and

---

[4] For a blurred approach to the root of Julian's complexity, which argues that the emperor's beliefs were drawn from a mix of traditional and Christian values and practices, see Nesselrath (2013) 186–7.

[5] Boin (2018).

[6] For Julian as leading up to a battle between traditionalists and Christians at the Frigidus River, see, for example, Scrofani (2010) 157.

[7] Greg. Naz. *Or.* 4.1 ('dragon and apostate'). For a discussion, see now Elm (2012) 336.

[8] Sozomen 5.2.14; Rosen (2006); a good survey of the reception of Julian's legacy as 'apostate' is Andrei (2015) 252–83, with discussion of Voltaire at 252–3.

obscured the process by which traditional religion was outlawed and Nicene Christianity established as the empire's official *religio*.[9] I would like to revisit these widely accepted interpretations of Julian, not by re-evaluating the entirety of the emperor's three-year rule (more appropriate to a larger book-length project), nor even by reviewing specific aspects of Julian's legislative programme (a much more complicated topic). Instead, I would like to focus on a narrow philological question and show how, when treated with precision, this one seemingly straightforward episode in the life of Julian can change how we write and think about much broader topics, like the nature of religious tolerance and pluralism in the later Roman Empire.[10]

Overview of the Problem: Julian's *Hellenismos*

In 362 CE, on his way to Antioch, Emperor Julian wrote to a priest in Asia Minor, Arsacius, to lay out his grand vision for Roman civic life. Romans who neglected the traditional gods should be stigmatized as practitioners of 'atheism'.[11] And if these 'atheists' did not want to participate in their local festivals and sacrifices, ceremonies overseen by a city's priests, these men and women were to be publicly shamed. If they were government officials, the punishment was worse; Julian recommended they should be removed from office.[12] The closest the emperor ever came to naming these 'atheists', in this letter, was to call them 'impious Galileans'.[13]

Julian's use of this geographical term, which historians have traditionally taken as a blanket slur referring to all 'Christians', has influenced the interpretation of the entire letter.[14] In the opening lines, Julian explained the motivations for his policy this way:

> Ὁ Ἑλληνισμὸς οὔπω πράττει κατὰ λόγον ἡμῶν ἕνεκα τῶν μετιόντων αὐτόν· τὰ γὰρ τῶν θεῶν λαμπρὰ καὶ μεγάλα, κρείττονα πάσης μὲν εὐχῆς, πάσης δὲ ἐλπίδος.
>
> *Hellenismos* is not yet the success I wish it to be, and it is the fault of those who profess it. For the matter of the gods is on a splendid and magnificent scale, surpassing every prayer and every hope.[15]

---

[9] For example, Murdoch (2003) 143; Errington (2006).
[10] Scholars of political theory will likely see parallels here to Michel de Montaigne's 1562 attempted rehabilitation of the emperor as a proponent of creating a neutral public sphere—a topic I regret not having the space to explore more fully; see Posner (2015) 71–82; see also Andrei (2015) 253.
[11] Julian *Ep.* 22, τὴν ἀθεότητα (429C, ed. Wright (1923)) (= no. 84, ed. Bidez (2004)). For a recent synthesis of Julian's reign, see Watts (2015) 109–26, who downplays any conflict in the fourth century for a picture of the time as an 'exciting, enchanting...age of gold' (220). Other studies are discussed below.
[12] Julian *Ep.* 22, 430A–B.   [13] Julian *Ep.* 22, δυσσεβεῖς Γαλιλαῖοι (430D).
[14] To cite but one example, Kaldellis defines 'Galileans' as 'what the Apostate called Christians to belittle them'; see Kaldellis (2008) 144.
[15] Julian *Ep.* 22, 429C, tr. Wright (1923), slightly modified.

The *opinio communis* is that, because Julian had expressed frustration with the lack of willingness of 'the Christians' to participate in civic sacrifices, his use of the word *Hellenismos* in this context must refer to a separate and recognizably distinct 'religion', a worldview and belief system that was opposed to 'Christianity'.[16] Wright himself, the editor of the letter in the Loeb edition, translated this word as 'the Hellenic religion'.[17] Abundant literature has been produced on the idea of Julian's support for 'Hellenism', frequently understood as a synonym for non-Christian belief, or 'paganism'.[18]

This chapter proposes an alternative way of interpreting the letter by looking more closely at the long history of the word *Hellenismos*. Moreover, instead of starting from the assumption that the emperor 'converted' and 'apostatized' from his Christian upbringing, I would like to start by interrogating what it actually meant for a fourth-century Greek Christian to embrace this term; and by extension, what it meant for a Greek Christian writer, like Gregory of Nazianzus, to hurl the derogatory language of 'apostasy' ($\dot{\alpha}\pi o \sigma \tau \alpha \sigma i \alpha$) at a man raised in a Christian family.[19] The study of the intra-group rhetoric of betrayal, often associated with tendentious charges of 'apostasy', is only beginning to be explored in scholarship.[20] I would like to contribute to this new direction by exploring the possibility that Julian used the word *Hellenismos* as a 'reclaimed epithet'. That is, rather than seeing it as Julian's profession of belief in a different universal religious system—one distinct from 'Christianity'—I suggest that Julian appropriated a term which had negative, in-group connotations in order to give it a positive, in-group spin.[21]

This act of appropriation would naturally tell us very little about 'pagan–Christian' interactions and much more about the contested nature of identifying as a 'Christian', even after the Edict of Milan, a time when Christian diversity is still largely described by scholars in theological—not social—terms. And whilst I don't deny that there is a need to use ancient sources to document the emperor's life, the testimony for his 'apostasy' is simply not as clear as scholars imply. Ammianus Marcellinus says Julian 'revealed the secrets of his

[16] A methodological point: I do not believe there is any ancient word that captures the modern idea of 'religion', so I tend to avoid references to 'religion' in my research; see Nongbri (2013). For this reason, I also part ways with scholars who approach Julian's policies with the intent to distinguish his 'religious' ideas from 'cultural' ones.

[17] Bouffartigue reviews the translation history of this word in his defence of the letter's authenticity; see Bouffartigue (2005) 233–4. I will discuss the letter's authenticity below.

[18] 'Quel que soit le degré de prudence des traductions proposées, il est néanmoins clair que pour chacun de leurs auteurs les deux noms grecs réfèrent à la religion païenne opposée au christianisme', Bouffartigue (2005) 234.

[19] On Julian's family, see Tougher (2007) 12–21.

[20] For example, see Flower (2013a) 61–78, 79–126 and Shaw (2011) 107–45.

[21] *Pace* Elm (2012) 487: 'Gregory's comprehensive vision, formulated in intense negotiation *with competing universal claims* endured because it was broader in its reach [than Julian's vision]...' (emphasis added).

heart and...ordered the temples to be opened'; Libanius, in his funeral oration, said that the emperor underwent a change and began to be 'different regarding certain things but kept the same appearance as before'.[22] And yet neither source prevents us from deducing that the emperor may have been building a broad coalition to ensure toleration for all of Rome's worship practices—or that such a noble effort may have been the very thing that earned him the label 'apostate' from other, more uncompromising Christians.

HELLENISTIC JUDAISM, INTRA-GROUP USES OF *HELLENISMOS*, AND JULIAN

In recent publications, I have argued that the meaning of *Hellenismos* in the fourth century CE is best captured by translating it as a subjectively deployed verbal noun, 'acting Greek', not as an objective, self-contained 'religion'.[23] Being accused of 'acting too Greek' was a major concern for Christians in the eastern Mediterranean in the age before and after Constantine. For that reason, Julian's decision to embrace this negative term—valorizing it, even— marks an important turning point in fourth-century political debates. At issue was the thorny, unresolved question of whether Christians should or would change the empire's laws to prohibit non-Christians from worshipping as they previously had.[24] This legislative question is related to a much more important social-historical issue about whether Christians in the Roman Empire were actually capable of embracing, adopting, or endorsing a platform of toleration; or whether Christianity as a monotheistic faith was an inherently intolerant belief system.[25] In the latter approach, Christian toleration is seen to be an invention of the modern age, not an ancient phenomenon. In my recent work, I have argued for the former position. In what follows, I would like to demonstrate how a greater attention to the meaning of *Hellenismos* as an intra-group word can help substantiate this approach.

The usual reconstruction of Julian's reign as a time of 'pagan revival' is built upon two assumptions: (1) that because the emperor himself writes about changing from one 'road of life' to another;[26] and (2) that because Gregory of

---

[22] Ammianus Marcellinus 22.5.2, tr. Rolfe (1940); Libanius, 18.19, tr. Norman (1969), slightly modified; see also Braun (1978) 159–88.

[23] Boin (2015) 117–20.

[24] Kaldellis' observations are insightful here: 'Christians inherited the distinct religious ambivalence toward Hellenism that was created through all this turmoil. They too struggled to define just what part of "Hellenism" (sic) was incompatible with their faith', Kaldellis (2008) 29.

[25] This chapter thus engages with previous work on the nature of Christian intolerance; see, for example, Stroumsa (1993); Drake (1996), (2011).

[26] Julian *Ep.* 47 (434D), with further discussion below.

54   *Rhetoric and Religious Identity in Late Antiquity*

Nazianzus referred to the Christian emperor as an 'apostate', Julian must have abandoned his Christian faith.[27] This section sets forth my philological reasons for questioning these assumptions. The next section draws upon theoretical contributions from linguistics to substantiate it.

Julian's Letter to Arsacius, 362 CE

Julian's sole reference to *Hellenismos* comes from his letter to Arsacius. Although missing from medieval manuscripts of the emperor's letters, this important Greek text is known because it was included in the *Church History* of the fifth-century CE writer Sozomen.[28] Perhaps not surprisingly, some scholars have considered it a forgery because of its sketchy transmission history.[29]

Julian's vocabulary choices also did not seem to fit a fourth-century context. Peter Van Nuffelen has suggested, for example, that *Ep.* 22 is a forgery, in part, because no *non-Christian* is known to have used the word *Hellenismos* to mean 'non-Christian religion' before the fifth century CE.[30] One does not need to accept Van Nuffelen's analysis, however, to appreciate that Julian has long been seen as a passionate advocate for the maintenance of non-Christian worship. In his survey of the emperor's life based on Ammianus Marcellinus, John Matthews argued that it was Julian's *superstitio*—a sense of zeal that fell outside the boundary of socially acceptable *religio*—which proved the defining characteristic of the emperor's reign.[31]

Although formulated in different contexts, both Van Nuffelen's and Matthews' conclusions hit a common note: Julian's identity, articulated in his

---

[27] The only smoking gun for Julian's 'conversion', however, is a letter to a community at Alexandria. In it, the emperor, discussing the importance of honouring the sun god Helios, warns his audience that they should 'not stray from the right road if you heed one who till his twentieth year [c.351 CE] walked in that road of yours but for twelve years now has walked in this road I speak of, by the grace of the gods', *Ep.* 47 434D (ed. and tr. Wright (1923)). Libanius (*Or.* 18.19) refers vaguely to this moment as Julian's 'change in beliefs' (tr. Norman (1969)); he uses the even more opaque Greek phrase ἦν μὲν περὶ ταῦτα ἕτερος. Nothing in Libanius, however, gives us enough specificity to map modern categories onto the ancient analysis (i.e., did Julian convert from 'paganism' to 'Christianity' or from an intolerant Christianity to a more tolerant one?). Given the prevalence of Helios figures in Jewish synagogue mosaics dated to the fourth to sixth century CE, it is also clear that non-Christian communities could embrace the visual language of Helios whilst not necessarily forfeiting their own monotheistic beliefs.

[28] Sozomen, *HE* 5.16.

[29] Rosen (2006) 301, with further references and discussion below.

[30] 'Cette lettre est le seul exemple d'un païen qui désigne sa religion avec un terme utilisé habituellement par les chrétiens...Le contenu pour sa part révèle aussi un anachronisme', Van Nuffelen (2002a) 138–9.

[31] Amm. Marc. 22.12.6, 25.4.17. For discussion, see Matthews (1989) 81–114.

language choices and in his political choices, must have been motivated by something other than his Christianity.[32]

From the Maccabees to Julian: *Hellenismos* as a Negative In-Group Word

There are reasons to question these starting points. One challenge comes from philological analysis. In recent years, Steve Mason and others interrogated more closely the precise meaning of *-ismos* words, such as *Medismos*, *Ioudaismos*, and *Hellenismos*. Mason's work has been instrumental in documenting how these ideas have a negative connotation, used by writers inside a group to deride fellow members, not as catch-all terms easily understood by outsiders. In Mason's view, for example, *Medismos* was used by Greeks in the archaic and classical age against *other* Greeks who had embraced too many Persian traits.[33] Before Mason, this way of understanding *-ismos* words had been noted by Seth Schwartz who, in his work on the Maccabees, had argued that *Ioudaismos* in 2 Maccabees carried a similar slur; there, it helped one group of uncompromising Jews stigmatize a group of more accommodating Jews for not being 'Jewish enough'.[34] I drew upon both Schwartz's and Mason's works to advance my philological argument about the meaning of *Hellenismos* in Eusebius ('acting too Greek') and other fourth-century Christian writers working in Greek.[35]

The mid-fourth century was an age when identifying as 'Christian' was legal but not mandatory and the religious world of Roman cities remained firmly rooted around its traditional urban centres of practice, such as temples, altars, statues, and sanctuaries. Following a faith history constructed largely by Eusebius, however—the Christian bishop who stressed rapid conversion and cultural upheaval in the wake of Constantine's rise to power—social and cultural historians have traditionally written about the mid-fourth century with one eye on Christianity's political successes and another on the eventual, if not inevitable, collapse of traditional religion.[36] Seen in this 'triumphalist' perspective, Julian's support for traditional cults, articulated forcefully in his letters and laws, has earned pages of commentary. Because 'true', or 'real',

---

[32] The literature illustrating this point is substantial. See, for example, R. Smith (1995) 182; Tougher (2007) 22–30, 54–62 (including a section on Julian's purportedly 'coming out' as a non-Christian, at 54–5); Kaldellis (2008) 143–54.

[33] Mason (2007) 463.   [34] Schwartz (2001) 32–5.   [35] Boin (2014).

[36] I subscribe to the view that traditional religious practices remained an important feature of late-antique urban life throughout the fourth century CE and have documented this work at Boin (2010), (2013a). For a recent bibliography on the same question, see Salzman et al. (2015). For the longevity of traditional cults, see Trombley (2012). For a more focused look at the effects of the Emperor Constantine, see Lenski (2016) 168–72, 235–40.

Christians were forbidden from adapting in any way to non-Christian customs, the emperor's policies became the sign of a mid-fourth-century 'pagan revival'.[37] Or so the story goes.

Understanding the complicated intra-group history of the word *Hellenismos* does not deny that many communities in the eastern Roman Mediterranean had watched the very same word acquire a positive meaning during the second and third century CE—that is, during the so-called Greek renaissance of the Roman Empire's 'Second Sophistic'. Yet, for Greek-speaking Christians of the fourth century CE, the dominant frame of reference for conceptualizing this term may have remained sectarian Jewish history, not mainstream literary discourse.[38] Thus, just as *Hellenismos* had been a negative concept in earlier periods of Jewish history, so it would remain a word with negative connotations in Christian conversations with their own Christian peers during the fourth century CE.[39]

For the historian, putting this intra-Jewish or intra-Christian shouting match into historical perspective demands that we see the perspective from inside the group and outside the group at the same time, articulating—in the most neutral language possible—what our sources are describing as they argue amongst themselves. This approach allows us to see how such highly charged rhetoric in arguments about what it meant to be a Christian eventually became, in both east and west, both before and after Julian, highly emotional affairs with much at stake.

RECLAIMED EPITHETS AND INTERNAL IDENTITY DISPUTES AS SUBJECTS OF SOCIAL HISTORY

To summarize the argument so far, I have suggested that Julian's knowledge of *Hellenismos* should be understood as a product of his own Christian upbringing, when *Hellenismos* became a frightening spectre for many hard-line Christians, especially for those who embraced the radical political stance of the Hellenistic Maccabean movement as part of their own group identity.[40]

---

[37] To be selective: Bowersock (1978) describes Julian's age as one of revival, in which the emperor tried to replace Christianity, called 'the religion of Constantine', with his version of 'paganism', 80; R. Smith (1995) 179 characterizes Julian's life as 'the best-known instance from antiquity of a [loosely defined] conversion...away from Christianity'; 'defection' at 179.

[38] For argument with a more complete bibliography, see Boin (2014); see also the discussion of the word's ethnic resonance in Johnson (2013) 1–15.

[39] Boin (2014) 183–8.

[40] Documented, for example, in the following reception studies: Pizzolato and Somenzi (2005) 79–170; Rouwhorst (2005); Ziadé (2007); Joslyn-Siemiatkoski (2009); Rutgers (2009) 19–48.

I have made the argument about Julian, specifically, by suggesting that, despite the emperor's passionate argument for a broad civic pluralism, there is no *philological* reason to question the legitimacy of *Ep. 22.* Thus, whereas Van Nuffelen has concluded that the letter must be a forgery because the emperor's use of *Hellenismos* was, inexplicably, 'the only example of a non-Christian who designated his belief system with a term regularly used by Christians [to designate it]',[41] I have suggested that we understand this word choice as a powerful reclamation of an in-group slur.

I would now like to pivot to the issue of why any Christian—let alone the Roman emperor, raised in a Christian family—might have desired to 'reclaim' this epithet in the mid-fourth century. To do so, I would first like to turn to theoretical studies of language, slurs, and other hurtful epithets, and I would propose we see Julian as the most vocal proponent of a social phenomenon that may have been more widespread than our sources have described.

Theories of Linguistic Reclamation

A historian's job is not to take sides in internal identity disputes like the ones just described in the Maccabean period or the social landscape of fourth-century Rome. In the remainder of this chapter, I would like to demonstrate how a greater sensitivity to linguistic phenomena, like slurs, can offer a more nuanced social-historical understanding of ancient cultures.[42]

Many scholars, across disciplines, have made important contributions to this literature, with many of the case studies emerging from modern contexts and involving themes that only partially overlap with the study of antiquity. Race, gender, ethnic, and queer studies have seen a proliferation of interest in this area, with some scholars narrating how specific words have changed over time and others investigating the linguistic underpinnings or the theoretical frameworks that both sustain and undermine these usages in society. Common themes do cut across these works, as echoed, for example, in the findings of political scientist Farah Godrej, who in her research has explored how 'linguistic reclamation' functions as 'a tool for disarming the power of a dominant group to control one's own and others' views of oneself, to categorize oneself or one's group in a totalizing way'.[43]

Yet a rigorous attention to specific social and cultural contexts has been a welcome feature of these conversations and one that offers a helpful reminder to the ancient historian not to make comparisons too lightly, even when borrowing theoretical approaches. Jabari Asim's and Arthur Spears' writing

---

[41] Van Nuffelen (2002a) 138–9 (author's translation).
[42] This section expands upon my work on 'social stigma' in Boin (2013b) 41–3.
[43] That is, 'consciousness-raising': Godrej (2011); the quotation is at 112.

on race and American culture, for example, or Jacquelyn Rahman's studies on the social history of words in African-American communities as in-group and out-group expressions, situate the linguistic phenomena of slurs in US contexts and explore the wide cultural reach of hurtful words, investigating how economic issues can impact group identity formation; how creative expression, like music or film making, can help give voice to resistance; and how transatlantic slavery, civil war, reconstruction, and civil rights became crucibles for social expression.[44] The matrix of these and other forces—history, economics, gender, and power, dating back to the arrival of the first colonizers of America—gave rise to the world, as Asim writes, in which African-Americans 'refused to see themselves as whites wished them to be'.[45] Spears' work, which describes how African-Americans 'defanged' the once hurtful word which was often used to humiliate them, makes a similar contribution.[46]

This cultural specificity is important to appreciate since much of what we would like to know about overlapping and intersecting matrices in the ancient Mediterranean world is missing from the historical record. There are findings and shared approaches in the modern literature that can resonate with ancient evidence, however, as emerges from the fields of political science and philosophy of language, on the nature of 'reclamation'. In Godrej's assessment, for instance, reclamation plays a forceful role in changing public conversations about a stereotyped group because it promotes 'consciousness-raising' on the part of listeners—a process which lies at the root of individual identity formation. 'We are, in different complex ways, always subject to others' stories about us', she explains, 'so that our ownership of our identity is partial at best'.[47] This process is similar to what Adam Croom has described in his work, noting how slurs 'are frequently picked up and appropriated by the very in-group members that the slur was originally intended to target, which might be done, for instance, as a means for like speakers to strengthen in-group solidarity'.[48] The tenor of these and earlier studies, like those by Ervin Goffman and John Austin, which explored the social effect of language choices on the construction of identity, have an obvious relevance to the study of ancient words, whether '*Hellenismos*' or 'Christian'.[49]

Scholars of antiquity may never be able to explain with the sophistication of their modern colleagues where, why, and how the damaging words of antiquity originated in any one specific context, and the amount of ancient evidence that does survive renders it almost impossible to construct the sorts of fully realized case studies that we see in the modern literature. There is little hope of a Roman historian's matching Croom, who uses English

---

[44] Rahman (2015) 72–4; Asim (2007). [45] Asim (2007) 14. [46] Spears (1998) 241.
[47] That is, 'consciousness-raising': Godrej (2011) 111; the lengthier quotation is at 112.
[48] Croom (2013) 177.
[49] Two key studies of the subject are Austin (1962) and Goffman (1967).

examples from comedy albums and popular culture to articulate a more nuanced, threefold taxonomy for slurs, dividing them into 'paradigmatic', 'non-paradigmatic', and 'non-derogatory in-group use', the latter of which dovetails with the concept of 'reclamation'.[50] And there are still other contemporary scholars, like Rahman, who have been successful in pointing out that 'self-labelling' is not the only strategy for managing adverse social situations; expressions of assimilation or even, what Rahman calls, 'no obvious reaction at all'—an understandable 'sense of powerlessness and total lack of agency'—can be documented in modern contexts as responses to oppression, slavery, and adverse economic conditions.[51]

But even if the depth and complexity of this modern work cannot be replicated with ancient evidence, the theoretical advances put forward by it do offer an occasion for reconsidering pieces of ancient writing that might have been overlooked or under-scrutinized by earlier scholars, who have often laboured under different interests. These modern tools are especially important, I suggest, for understanding Julian's reign because at the core of any act of reclamation is a desire to 'change the story', which it is clear the fourth-century emperor was trying to do. Godrej herself noted that 'ownership over one's life narrative is only meaningful if the world responds positively to this self-reconstruction, instead of denying or ignoring the stories one chooses to tell'.[52] I would like to conclude by exploring how Julian's reclamation may have been his attempt to change the story of Christianity's rise.

SITUATING MINORITY IDENTITY DISPUTES IN A NON-MINORITY CULTURAL FRAMEWORK ('THE RISE OF CHRISTIANITY')

In the model proposed, a fourth-century Christian's use of *Hellenismos* ('acting too Greek') is an example of taking a 'paradigmatic derogatory' word and transforming it into a 'non-derogatory in-group' term. This act of reclamation may have been unique to Roman political conversations of the fourth century CE, but as a linguistic phenomenon, it is certainly not unique to the history of Rome or early Christianity. Many scholars would agree that the term *Christianos* itself began its life as a 'paradigmatic derogatory' word which, by the late first century CE, was reclaimed by some of Jesus' followers to become an essential part of their own identity.[53] I would now like to put Julian's own reclamation into the larger history of this group.

---

[50] Croom (2013) 177; for the discussion of this threefold classification of slurs, see 188–94.
[51] Rahman (2015) 71.   [52] Godrej (2011) 118–19.
[53] Trebilco (2012) 3–4, 272–97.

At the core of many interpretations of Julian's reign is the broader issue of how Christians themselves came to 'triumph' over classical Rome, moving from a minority culture to a majority one and from an outcast worship practice to an officially sanctioned one. Traditional explanations for how, when, and why Christians won these triumphs have often relied upon presumed notions of Christians' rhetorical supremacy or their faith-based exceptionalism, whether implicitly or explicitly stated.[54] This story begins earlier in the history of the empire. Unable to adjust to life in Rome, followers of Jesus were—for three centuries—persecuted and martyred. Whether downplayed as sporadic or played-up as systematic, the details of this 'martyrdom and persecution' narrative do not matter, for the outcome is still the same. Because Christians were incapable of adjusting their identity to that of the Romans, social separation and a growing tension with their Roman neighbours was inevitable. Only with the rise to power of individuals *within the group* (as evidenced by Galerius' alleged death-bed conversion in 311 CE or the conversion of Constantine, variously dated) did this situation change. Christianity's greater visibility and eventual demographic growth thus came about from having one of their own in the seat of power, a political victory which set in motion an almost unstoppable process by which Christianity itself became the majority faith of the empire.[55] Because Julian's policies challenge the presumed inevitability of this process, his time has, not surprisingly, been characterized as an old-school, traditionalist 'revival'.

What other research has made clear, however, as an important corrective to this supersessionist approach, is that there is no social or cultural reason to believe that traditional beliefs or civic practices died with the rise of Christian social visibility. In fact, abundant archaeological, epigraphic and textual evidence—including the longevity of imperial cult practices—can be used to tell a much different narrative.[56] Combined with a greater attention to the dynamics of conversion and challenges to the 'marketplace metaphor' of ancient religions, this evidence suggests that the relationship of traditional

---

[54] For elements of the following narrative, see, for example, Chadwick (1993) and Stark (1997) 147–9.

[55] The assumption of a demographically expanding Christian community lays at the heart of many post-Constantinian studies; see, for example, Brown (2012), who argues that 'the entry of new wealth and talent into the churches' in the fourth century—a time when Christians teetered on becoming a demographic majority—led Jesus' followers 'to envision the possibility of a totally Christian society' (528).

[56] See n.26, above. For evidence of imperial cult during Julian's reign, such as the continued use of the formula '*pro salute Augusti*' in epigraphy or the evidence for a local *flamen perpetuus*, see Conti (2004) 111–12, 150–1, 157–8 (nos. 76c, 132, 141, and 143a). The longevity of the imperial cult in late antiquity is the subject of my larger study in progress.

religion, mystery cults, and Christianity was not a zero-sum game in which one faith group 'lost' as another 'won'.[57]

In addition, by looking at evidence over the *longue durée*—from the first-century CE letters of Paul, a time when there is no evidence for anyone self-identifying as a 'Christian', through to the early fourth century CE, when being 'Christian' was no longer a legal risk—there is a significant history of Christian social and cultural compromise which can challenge standard narratives of Christianity's rise. From the communities of Jesus' followers at Corinth, who attended civic sacrifices; to the Christian soldiers of Tertullian's day who honoured the imperial house at civic ceremonies; to the home renovators of Dura Europos, Syria, who built their Christian worship space by adapting—not tearing down—existing structures, the history of Christianity in the Roman Empire is much more complicated than the stories of the martyrs can lead us to believe. Yet newer paradigms, like the 'myth of persecution', which is also intended to challenge older narratives of Romans and Christians caught in existential opposition, might push the revisionism too far; many Christians no doubt encountered a significant level of social resistance to their presence in everyday interactions, a fear perhaps based on little more than conservative Roman mores and a generalized anxiety about the place of outsiders in Roman society—nothing that would classify as 'persecution' but nothing to be dismissed, either.[58] In any case, the documented legacy of Christian accommodation to Roman culture is an important phenomenon that needs to be seen as existing in tension with the traditional analyses of the early Christian community. For it belies many basic historical assumptions, such as the notion that all of Jesus' followers were zealous to convert their family, friends, and neighbours; or that they were fundamentally unable to exist in the Roman world without changing it to fit their own unique worldview.

That is what makes Julian's reclamation of *Hellenismos* ('acting too Greek') so powerful when understood in the context of the mid-fourth century CE. The emperor was boldly asserting that Christians should, just as they had for three centuries, continue to find creative ways to coexist with their Roman friends and family. In this way, he may have been directly rebuking many hard-line members of his own Christian community—people who, embracing the rhetoric of the Maccabees and others, had been arguing that social separation and radical political change were necessary if one wanted to

---

[57] For new approaches to the topic, see now Papaconstantinou and Schwartz (2015). On the nature of the ancient 'religious marketplace' metaphor, which has often led scholars to assume a model of zero-sum social relations, see the important critique by Engels and Van Nuffelen (2014).

[58] Boin (2015) 15–56.

call oneself a 'Christian' in fourth-century Rome.[59] The fact that Julian himself chose the adjective 'Galilean' to smear certain members within the 'Jesus group' would not, then, be a straightforward illustration of 'what the Apostate called Christians to belittle them'.[60] Instead, it might be an indication that confirms Julian's disillusionment with *fellow Christians*, especially those who did not recognize the value of political compromise.

In short, the Christian emperor who had grown up being taught to see the danger of 'acting too Greek' may have been—in one rhetorical move—turning the tables on members of his own Christian community who were using a selective understanding of their group history to write a radical political programme for the fourth-century empire. If these interlocutors, like Eusebius before him or Gregory of Nazianzus of his own day, could not stomach a self-identified 'Christian' to compromise with the majority Roman culture, Julian was prepared to challenge their version of Christianity as well. This reconstruction is certainly plausible because the conversation about what constituted a 'true' Christian was one of the most pressing issues for the fourth-century empire. As I have argued elsewhere, the nature of this thorny, unresolved social debate about what it meant to be a 'Christian' can explain the emergence of the Latin-based slur 'civilianism' (*paganismus*) in the western empire, where it was used as a term of disparagement by Christians who mocked their own Christian peers for not adopting a militant understanding of their faith. This intra-Christian debate between 'civilians and soldiers' (or, as we clumsily translate it, between 'pagans and Christians') would have a lasting, polarizing effect on fourth-century politics.

CONCLUSION

In the previous half-century, many scholars who have studied 'pagan–Christian' interactions have tried to steer the conversation away from examples of outright hostility and conflict between these two religious groups to search for the commonalities and grey areas that existed between them. Although a noble ecumenical endeavour, the emphasis on grey areas is also historically misleading, for it creates a false equivalency between the two groups. Christians may have remained the minority culture for much of the fourth century, and whatever grey area did exist between the Christian and

---

[59] *Pace* Kaldellis (2008), who interprets Julian's legislation against teachers as an example of Julian 'siding with the Christian hard-liners who wanted nothing to do with Hellenism...' (149); see also Tougher (2007) 56.

[60] Kaldellis (2008) 144.

non-Christian demographics was probably quite small indeed, proportionate to the larger Roman culture.

What I have suggested here, focusing on Julian's language choices, nudges this conversation into an even more nuanced direction. In this interpretation, the Roman world was *not* engaged in an empire-wide ecumenical dialogue about the universal appeal of different theological views or religious systems. It was being torn asunder by the fact that the Christian community could not agree on what it meant to be a 'Christian'.[61]

So it was for Christians like Julian who believed that political and cultural compromise was an essential part of identifying as a 'Christian'. And so it was for Gregory of Nazianzus, who believed that the performance of Roman politics was akin to waging spiritual warfare against apocalyptic demons. Indeed, the fact that both would later be buried in the Church of the Holy Apostles in Constantinople suggests that many Romans of the fourth century probably still considered both men to be legitimate members of the Christian community long after their war of words had ended.[62]

We need look no further than our own headlines to consider another example of this model. In the summer of 2005, King Abdullah II of Jordan convened an international conference in Amman to tackle the delicate Islamic issue of *takfir*. The Arabic word, which means 'unbeliever', was being hurled by radical Muslims against their own Muslim peers, charging them with 'apostasy'.[63] Some of these were dubious charges. According to one radical cleric, Abu Hamza al-Masri, Muslims who believed in democracy, voted, or even tried to participate in the political process were guilty of the label. As al-Masri had argued in his book, *Beware of Takfir*, 'It does not matter how much worship [these Muslims] do or how many times they go on Hajj [the pilgrimage to Mecca], they cannot come an inch closer to Islam because of this action'.[64] For the future historian, writing an account of the twenty-first century, this rhetoric may prove difficult to interpret. For al-Masri is adamant that being a 'Muslim' can be understood only in a way that is militantly opposed to one's surrounding culture; and that, by extension, any person whose worldview had been purged of dualistic thinking did not really belong to the group.

In January of 2015 in New York, al-Masri was sentenced to life in prison for aiding terrorists,[65] but the significance of the 2005 Amman meeting in Jordan

---

[61] Boin (2015) 110–28. [62] Constantine VII, *Book of Ceremonies* 2.42.

[63] 'Jordanian king urges Muslims to settle differences, agree basics at OIC summit [A text of a report in English by the Jordanian news agency Petra-JNA]' *BBC News* (8 December 2005). The result of the conference can be read online at: ammanmessage.com (accessed 23 July 2016).

[64] For discussion of this episode, see Aslan (2010) 101–28, with the quotation from al-Masri at 107.

[65] 'Life Sentence for British Cleric Who Helped Plan 1998 Kidnappings in Yemen', by B. Weiser, *The New York Times* (9 January 2015).

is more relevant than ever. The complicated task of sorting out who is a 'real' Muslim from who is not is raging more openly and more fiercely than ever before—only now, positions are reversed, tying even non-Muslims hopelessly in knots. That same year, an Islamic group in Britain began a hashtag campaign, 'Not in My Name', to oppose acts of Islamic extremism. The year before, the then US President Obama famously declared ISIS, or ISIL, 'not Islamic'.[66]

These contemporary examples reveal that research into late-antique rhetoric and religious identity might benefit if we shift the scholarly method away from studies of generic blurred boundaries and bring intra-group conflict back into much sharper, social focus. That is not going to be easy, of course. Whether we are writing about people who lived in 2007 or fifteen hundred years ago, there are serious and challenging methodological issues that researchers must wrestle with when they write about individuals and the communities to which they belong, how they act, how they see themselves, and how they are seen by others. As historians, we may not be able to extricate ourselves from these internal, rhetorical debates. But we do need to find a way, or perhaps even create a language, to describe the complexity of what we are seeing in our sources.

---

[66] 'Obama Says the Islamic State "Is Not Islamic". Americans Disagree', by A. Blake, *Washington Post* (11 September 2014).

Part II

Agents of the Representation of Religious Identity

5

Julian the Apologist

Christians and Pagans on the Mother of the Gods

Shaun Tougher

INTRODUCTION

The cult of the Great Mother must be one of the most written about aspects of Roman religion, by both ancient and modern authors.[1] Her importation into Rome in 204 BC in the context of Rome's ongoing conflict with Carthage is described in Livy's history, relating how the stone representing the goddess was brought from Pessinus in Phrygia with the agreement of the king of Pergamum, Attalus.[2] The annual festival created for the Great Mother in Rome—the Megalensian festival, held in April—is discussed in Ovid's *Fasti*.[3] Many aspects of the cult are still debated, such as why the Galli—the supposedly self-castrating devotees of the goddess—feature in it, whether they were actually self-castrates, and what exactly their role in it was.[4] What is clear is how much the reconstruction of the cult and its festivals (it was also celebrated in March) is based on meagre evidence, but also on evidence that is late. A significant amount of the 'evidence' for the cult comes from late Roman sources, especially Christian ones. Christians in their assessments of paganism gave a particular place to the cult of the Great Mother and the place of Attis (her human consort who castrated himself) and the Galli within it, usually in derisory and shocking terms. This chapter focuses on two examples from the fourth century—Arnobius of Sicca and Firmicus Maternus— examining how they present and comment on the cult. The main purpose of

---

[1] See, for instance, Vermaseren (1977); Beard (1994); Turcan (1996b) 28–74 and 344–9; and Roller (1999), esp. 263–325. The Great Mother is also known as the Mother of the Gods and as Cybele.
[2] Livy 29.10.4–11.8 and 29.14.5–14.   [3] Ovid, *Fasti* 4.179–372.
[4] For example, it has been common to describe the Galli as eunuch priests, but it has been argued that they were just devotees and hangers-on: Bowden (2010) 96–8.

68   *Rhetoric and Religious Identity in Late Antiquity*

the chapter, however, is to bring these Christian texts into dialogue with a pagan treatment of the cult, the discourse on the Mother of the Gods, written by the famous last pagan Roman emperor, Julian; this text is often given the title *Hymn to the Mother of the Gods*. By examining these rhetorical texts concerning religious identity, the chapter seeks to place Julian in context and in dialogue with his contemporaries, especially Christians. As Jacqueline Long has observed, it is important to 'flesh out Julian's image as a person much more integrally connected with others than historical study of his frustrated reign has always done, or even literary studies of his individual works'.[5] This approach has also been advocated and embraced by Susanna Elm, in her monumental *Sons of Hellenism, Fathers of the Church: Emperor Julian, Gregory of Nazianzus, and the Vision of Rome* (2012).[6] I will argue that Julian's discourse on the Mother of the Gods needs to be read not just as an expression of his rarefied Neoplatonic beliefs but also as a response to, and engagement with, Christian assaults on paganism, which, having been brought up a Christian, Julian would have been very familiar with: Julian was not just 'the Apostate' but also 'the Apologist'. Further, the chapter emphasizes the centrality of the cult of the Mother of the Gods in rhetorical constructions of religious identities and in the identity of the Roman Empire itself. This, in turn, heightens and elucidates Julian's particular interest in this cult.

LATE EVIDENCE, CHRISTIAN EVIDENCE

As noted, much evidence for the cult comes from the later Roman period. For instance, there is the Codex-Calendar of Philocalus of 354, which records the March festivals for Attis, and the April festival for the Great Mother;[7] there are the altar inscriptions from the Phrygianum on the Vatican Hill in Rome, commemorating taurobolia, most of which date to the fourth century AD;[8] and, from the sixth century, there is John Lydus' *On the Months*, which mentions the March festival and the role of the emperor Claudius (AD 41-54) in developing it.[9] In addition, there are numerous Christian texts which discuss the cult, including works by Tertullian and Augustine.[10] Such Christian attention to the cult has been commented on by scholars. Maijastina Kahlos, in her *Debate and Dialogue. Christian and Pagan Cultures, c.360—430*

---

[5] Long (2012) 336.
[6] And see also recent work by David N. Greenwood, for example, Greenwood (2017), which returns to the question of Julian's 'Pagan Church' and considers the role of Constantinian influence.
[7] See Salzman (1990) 86-91, 164-9.   [8] See, for instance, Cameron (2011) 144-8.
[9] *De Mensibus* 4.59.
[10] For example, Tertullian, *To the Nations* 2.7.16, and Augustine, *The City of God* 7.24-6.

(2007), examining 'how Christian argumentation against pagans was intertwined with self-perception and self-affirmation', notes that 'the cult of Magna Mater and Attis with castrated *galli* priests was a recurrent theme in Christian assaults';[11] Mathew Kuefler, in his *The Manly Eunuch. Masculinity, Gender Ambiguity, and Christian Ideology in Late Antiquity* (2001), asserts that 'Christian writers denounced the castration of men as typical of all that was immoral and effeminate in pagan culture';[12] and in a chapter entitled 'Cybele and Christ' (1996), A.T. Fear explores if 'Attis and Cybele [were] a favourite target for the invective of Christian writers' because the cult was an easy target, or because they felt threatened by a cult which had similarities with Christianity or was even deliberately copying Christianity, and he favours the view that the cult was important for them to address because it was on the front line of the religious war of the period.[13]

The specific authors and texts that are the focus of this chapter are Arnobius of Sicca and his *Against the Pagans* (*Adversus Nationes*); Firmicus Maternus and his *On the Error of the Pagan Religions* (*De Errore Profanarum Religionum*); and the emperor Julian and his *To the Mother of the Gods*. Arnobius was from Sicca in North Africa.[14] He was a teacher of rhetoric, and one of his pupils was Lactantius, famous for his *On the Deaths of the Persecutors* and teaching Crispus the son of the first Christian emperor Constantine the Great (306–337).[15] Arnobius was a pagan who converted to Christianity; it seems that his *Against the Pagans* was written as a testament of his new faith.[16] It consists of seven books, and has been dated to either 302–305 or the 320s.[17] An aspect of the text is its refutation of anti-Christian works of pagans, such as Porphyry's *Against the Christians*.[18] Firmicus Maternus was originally

---

[11] Kahlos (2007b) 1, 114.   [12] Kuefler (2001) 245.
[13] Fear (1996). On Christian (as well as pagan) responses to the cult, see also Rauhala (2011).
[14] For Arnobius see Simmons (1995); Edwards (1999); and now Champeaux (2018). For an English translation with introduction and notes, see McCracken (1949); all translations of Arnobius are taken from this unless otherwise stated. For an edition, see Marchesi (1953). The Les Belles Lettres edition is not yet complete, as Books 4 and 5 are yet to appear: Book 1 (Le Bonniec (1982)); Book 2 (Armisen-Marchetti (2018)); Book 3 (Champeaux (2007)); and Books 6–7 (Fragu (2010)).
[15] Lactantius comments on the Mother of the Gods in his *Divine Institutes* 1.17.7, when discussing that gods were humans: 'The mother of the gods loved a beautiful youth, but, having discovered him with a mistress, she emasculated him and rendered him a half-man; for this reason her sacred rites now are celebrated by Gallic priests,' tr. McDonald (1964) 69. On Lactantius' *Divine Institutes* see Schott (2008) 79–109. Attis and Cybele also surface in Eusebius' *Preparation of the Gospel*, which refers to statements of Porphyry explaining the myth, with Attis related to earth as the symbol of the spring blossom (3.11), and to the view that Cybele and Attis were humans (2.2, citing Diodorus). Sadly, Eusebius' *Against Porphyry* no longer survives. On Eusebius as apologist see Kofsky (2002); Schott (2008) 136–65.
[16] See, for instance, Masterson (2014) 387.
[17] On the date see for example Simmons (1995); Edwards (1999).
[18] On Porphyry see, for instance, Kofsky (2002) 17–36; Schott (2008) 52–78.

from Sicily.[19] He trained in rhetoric, and became an advocate. He was a pagan who converted to Christianity. He wrote the *Mathesis*, 'The largest surviving Latin treatise on astrology',[20] which was dedicated to the senator Lollianus Mavortius (consul in 355) and has been dated to 334–337. His *On the Error of the Pagan Religions* was written subsequently. It was dedicated to the sibling Christian emperors Constantius II (337–361) and Constans (337–350) (20.7: *sacratissimi imperatores*), and has been dated to 346.[21] Julian is, of course, the most famous of the three men, as the last pagan Roman emperor.[22] He was born in Constantinople in 331 or 332, and was a member of the imperial family: his father was Julius Constantius, the half-brother of Constantine the Great: they had the same father, the emperor Constantius I (Caesar 293–305, Augustus 305–306). Born into a Christian family, Julian was brought up a Christian but converted to paganism when he was about twenty years of age. He was well educated, culminating in some time spent at the university in Athens in the summer of 355. Appointed Caesar by Constantius II in the same year, Julian became sole Augustus on the death of his cousin in November 361. His discourse to the Mother of the Gods was written in 362 during the festival in March, in a single night, according to his own claim (178D).[23]

Before considering these authors and their texts individually and in more detail, some initial comparisons between the three can be made. All three authors were writing close in time to one another, especially Firmicus and Julian. All three men were also converts: Arnobius and Firmicus from paganism to Christianity, and Julian in the opposite direction; this means that they wrote with experience of the religious group that they no longer identified with, and probably had insights into both sides of the religious divide. Regarding the language of the texts, both Arnobius and Firmicus wrote in Latin, whilst Julian wrote in Greek, though they all had facility in the other language. Perhaps Julian's Latin was not as assured as the Greek of Arnobius and Firmicus, although this may be an impression he himself deliberately fostered. A key issue for this chapter is the categorization of the texts in question. The texts of both Arnobius and Firmicus have been described as apologies, and whilst their polemical nature has also been commented upon, it is acknowledged that apologies were both defensive and offensive anyway.[24]

---

[19] For Firmicus Maternus see Forbes (1970; English translation with introduction), and Turcan (1982; edition and French translation with introduction and commentary). All translations of Firmicus are taken from Forbes (1970).

[20] Forbes (1970) 5. It is usual to suppose that Firmicus was a pagan when he wrote the *Mathesis*, but Edwards (2015) 72–6 and 112 suggests he was already a Christian when he wrote it.

[21] Forbes (1970) 9. AD 350, the year of the death of Constans, is the *terminus ante quem*, and, as there is a reference to Constans' expedition to Britain, AD 343 is the *terminus post quem*.

[22] See, for instance, Tougher (2007).

[23] Rochefort (2003) 102. All translations of Julian's discourse are taken from Wright (1913).

[24] Simmons (1995) 126 asserts that apology is not the right word for Arnobius, but Edwards (1999) 202 counters this. Forbes (1970) 18 states that Firmicus 'assails the pagan religions in the

Julian the Apologist 71

Julian's text appears very different in character; as mentioned, the discourse has been described as a hymn, and Wolfgang Liebeschuetz has likened it to a sermon or homily, comparing it to Constantine the Great's *Oration to the Saints*.[25] Gabriel Rochefort concentrated on the Neoplatonic character of the text, emphasizing dogma and exegesis.[26] There is, however, an apologetic quality to the discourse, also noted by Liebeschuetz, who writes that both Julian's 'hymns' (the other is the discourse on King Helios) 'arguably represent a systematic intellectual apology for the paganism that Julian was seeking to revive'.[27] Yet there is no sustained scholarly discussion of the apologetic nature of Julian's text, and this chapter aims to foreground it. In the construction of religious identity, apologetic had an important role; as Jeremy Schott observes, 'these conflicts between pagan and Christian intellectuals proved instrumental in the production of Christian identity',[28] and one can add pagan identity too, both the construction of it by Christians and the self-construction of it by pagans. I turn now to the authors and their texts individually, and examine how they present and comment on the cult of the Great Mother.

ARNOBIUS

As noted above, Arnobius' *Against the Pagans* is divided into seven books. George McCracken defines the subject of each chapter as follows: 1. Refutation of Pagan Criticism; 2. Attack on Philosophy; 3. The Anthropomorphic Gods; 4. Criticisms of Various Pagan Gods; 5. Jupiter Elictus, Attis, Mysteries; 6. Temples and Images; and 7. Sacrifices and Ceremonials.[29] Arnobius discusses the Mother of the Gods at various points across the seven books (1.41, 4.29, 5.5–17, 5.42, and 7.49–51), addressing in particular the myth and rites of the cult. The most extensive discussion is in Book 5, in which he states that he uses Timotheus' account of the origin of the Mother of the Gods and of her sacrifices. This Timotheus is otherwise unknown, but is thought possibly to be a Ptolemaic writer, an Eleusinian Eumolpid.[30] In Book 1, in response to

---

same aggressive and trenchant way as Arnobius before him,' whilst Edwards (1999) 197 n.1 opines that his text 'is clearly more polemical than apologetic'. On apologetic in general see, for example, Kofsky (2002) 5–12; Schott (2008) 2–3.

[25] Liebeschuetz (2012) 214. On the hymn as homily, see also Long (2012) 331. For Constantine's oration see Edwards (2003) xvii–xxix and 1–62. For comment on it see also Schott (2008) 111–22, who notes its apologetic nature.

[26] Rochefort (2003) 99.

[27] Liebeschuetz (2012) 214. Fear (1996) 46 also touches on the apologetic aspect of the text.

[28] Schott (2008) 5.   [29] McCracken (1949).

[30] See Lancellotti (2002) 2 and 121; Borgeaud (2004) 44 and 46. The account is similar to the one found in Pausanias 7.17.10–12, but more extended. Even so, not everything is clear or fully explained; one has the sense that an even more extensive version has been condensed.

pagans mocking Christians for worshipping a god who died crucified, he retorts 'Do you not bear witness, with the approval of the Galli, to the fact that that Phrygian Attis, mutilated and deprived of his manhood, is a gracious god, a holy god, in the shrines of the Great Mother?' (*nonne illum Attin Phrygem abscisum et spoliatum viro Magnae Matris in adytis deum propitium, deum sanctum Gallorum conclamatione testamini?*) (1.41.4). In Book 4, arguing that the pagans treat their own gods shamefully, he mentions the marriage of the human Attis with the Great Mother and her desire for him (4.29).

Then, in Book 5, there is the extensive discussion of the myth and the cult.[31] Arnobius presents the story of the myth of Attis (5.5–7), criticizes it (5.8–15), then discusses the rites (5.16–17). The story runs as follows:[32] in Phrygia, there was a rock named Agdus, and the Great Mother derived from it. Jupiter (her son) tried to have sex with her whilst she was asleep on the rock, but was not able to, and ejaculated on the rock.[33] This resulted in the birth of Acdestis (Agdistis), who was twin-sexed, and of a lustful and destructive nature. The gods discussed what to do about the problem of Acdestis, and the god of wine, Liber, made Acdestis fall asleep by adding wine to a spring, and then tied his genitals to his feet. As a result, when Acdestis woke and stood up, he was castrated. His blood gave birth to a pomegranate tree. Nana (the daughter of Sangarius—either a king or a river) put fruit from it in her bosom, and thus fell pregnant. Her father confined her, but the Mother of the Gods kept her alive by feeding her. Nana had a child whom the father ordered to be exposed, but it was found and brought up, and given the name of Attis. He became the beloved of both the Mother of the Gods (his grandmother) and Acdestis (his father) (admitting to the latter relationship when he was inebriated). Midas, the king of Pessinus, arranged the marriage of Attis with his daughter, to save the boy. He closed the gates of the town, but the Mother of the Gods raised up the walls with her head. Acdestis filled the guests with frenzied madness. A daughter of the mistress of Gallus cut off her breasts, whilst Attis cut off his genitalia under a pine tree. From his blood a violet sprang. The bride (named Ia by Valerius the pontifex, notes Arnobius) covered the breast of Attis with wool and killed herself. From her blood sprang purple violets. The Mother of the Gods wept and from her tears an almond tree grew. She then took the pine tree away to her cave, and she beat and wounded her breast, lamenting with Acdestis. Acdestis begged Jupiter to restore Attis to life, which he did not consent to, but allowed 'that his body should not decay, that his hair should ever grow, that the very smallest of his fingers should live and alone

---

[31] Arnobius 5.5–17, ed. Marchesi (1953) 253–71, tr. McCracken (1949) 414–26.
[32] See also the summary in Lancellotti (2002) 3–5; Borgeaud (2004) 44–6.
[33] For discussion of the obscene character of the account of this episode see Masterson (2014) 388–9.

react by continued motion'. Acdestis consecrated the body in Pessinus and honoured it with annual rites and a priesthood.

In the course of relating the story, Arnobius also provides asides explaining elements of it, perhaps following Timotheus too.[34] He states that the name of Attis derived either from the fact that he was fed on he-goat's milk (Phrygians call goats *attagi*)[35] or from the fact that it is Lydian for 'handsome'; since Attis admitted his unseemly relationship with Acdestis when he was drunk, drunks are not allowed in his sanctuary; the Mother of the Gods is depicted with a turreted crown as she raised up the walls of Pessinus; Attis' sacred pine is decorated with violets as they derived from his blood; the almond tree signifies the bitterness of mourning.

Then Arnobius begins to comment on the myth, mocking the tale and its details (5.8–15). He observes that this is a shocking way for pagans to honour their gods. It is shameful that Jupiter wants to have sex with his own mother. The love of the Mother of the Gods for Attis is not appropriate, as they see in theatres that it was 'infamous and scandalous' (*infamis et flagitiosa*) (5.13). He notes absurdities in the story; chronologically, the Mother of Gods cannot be the mother of the gods, and must be human not divine. How is the birth of Acdestis possible, he asks. He observes that the castration plan makes no sense as it does not lead to calm: '[a]s if, indeed, those who have been subjected to such mutilation of body become less brazen, and as if we do not daily see them becoming more wanton and laying aside every restraint of shame and modesty breaking forth into filthy vileness, making open admission of their abominable conduct' (5.11). He exclaims, '[w]hen these things are brought forward, are you not ashamed and confounded to say things so indecent? We wish to hear or learn from you something befitting the gods; but you, on the contrary, bring forward to us the cutting off of breasts, the lopping off of men's members, ragings, blood, frenzies, the self-destruction of maidens (*mammarum expromitis exsectiones, amputationes virilium veretrorum, iras, sanguinem, furias, interitus virginum voluntarios*), and flowers and trees begotten from the blood of the dead' (5.14).[36]

He then turns to the rites (5.16–17). He contrasts the pagan rejection of the literal truth of the myth with the fact that they nevertheless continue to commemorate it in annual rites. He asks, 'for all that, how can you assert that representation not to be true when the very rites you continue to practice

---

[34] See the comments of Turcan (1996a) 387–90.

[35] On the identification of the goat as male see Borgeaud (2004) 108, understanding this in relation to the complete hostility to male roles in Arnobius' account of the myth: 'Even the animal that nourishes and cares for the abandoned Attis loses its virility; it is a billy goat that gives milk'; and see also 169–70 n.76, which cites a reported case of a billy-goat giving milk in Palestine in 1995. On the he-goat in the myth see also Lancellotti (2002) 4 n.14.

[36] Tr. Bryce and Campbell (1886) 495. This is a better translation than that of McCracken for this section; perhaps McCracken did not want to offend by being explicit.

at each returning anniversary are evidence that you believe it to be true and consider that it has been verified and found worthy of credence?' (5.16). He points specifically to the pine tree brought into the sanctuary of the Mother of the Gods, the fleeces of wool which bind and surround the tree trunk, the branches of the tree decorated with violets, 'the Galli with hair dishevelled, beating their breasts with their hands', and the abstinence from eating bread on certain feast days. He asks if these are not commemorating the details of the myth, what then do they signify: 'if what we say is not so, speak out, tell us yourselves: those eunuchs and effeminates (*evirati isti mollesque*) we see in your midst in the services of the divinity—what is their business there, what their concern, their charge? And why do they like mourners beat their arms and breasts and represent the misfortune of those who experience a woeful lot?' (5.17). Ultimately, Arnobius considers that the rites just mark sad human events rather than divine matters, but if not, and there is some secret reason for them, they are still about some shameful deed. He declares, 'who is there that would believe that there is anything noble in what those worthless Galli put their hands to, what effeminate debauchees perform?' (*Quis est enim qui credat, honestatis aliquid in ea re esse quam initiant viles Galli, effeminati conficiant exoleti?*). Thus, Arnobius focuses his attack on the degeneracy and absurdity of the myth and the rites associated with it, emphasizing in particular the role of the Galli within these.

Later in Book 5, Arnobius imagines that pagans will make the defence that the narratives are allegorical, that Attis signifies the sun (*sol*). He responds,

> if Attis is the sun, as you refer to him and call him, who is that Attis supposed to be whom your literature records and declares was born in Phrygia, who suffered certain things, likewise did certain things; whom all the theaters know in their stage plays; whom every year we see receiving special and individual veneration in the calendar of sacred cults? Was the transference of his name made from the sun to a man or from a man to the sun? But if that name was derived in the beginning from the sun, what in the world, I ask you, has the golden sun done to merit from you that you make him share his name with a half-man (*semiviro*)? But if the name is derived from a goat and from Phrygia, of what has the father of Phaethon, the father of this light and brightness, been guilty, that he should appear to deserve to be named for a castrated (*absciso*) man and should become more august when marked with the appellation of a mutilated person (*evirati corporis*)? (5.42)

Again Arnobius attacks the absurdity and sordidness of the myth and cult, again he emphasizes the place of castration within it.

Finally, in Book 7, at the very end of his apology, Arnobius comes to the question of the special relationship between the Mother of the Gods and the Roman Empire (7.49–51). Addressing how she was summoned to Rome he imagines or responds to a pagan account of the importance of this, that the goddess was summoned to save and protect Rome from Hannibal, and this led to the general expansion of Roman power. Again Arnobius mocks the absurdities of the story. He asks, how could a stone save Rome? How can a stone be the Mother of the Gods? Why did she not save Rome earlier? To the pagan defences that she had not yet been asked for help and that she was not in Italy yet, he responds that she should not have needed to be asked, and 'to a god—if god he be—to whom the earth is a mere point and to whose nod all things are subject, nothing at all is far away'. He further argues that her inequitable behaviour also demonstrates that she is not a real god.

FIRMICUS MATERNUS

Firmicus Maternus' *On the Error of the Pagan Religions* (*De Errore Profanarum Religionum*) consists of 29 chapters, organized in 3 sections. Clarence Forbes provides a useful summary of the structure of the text: 1: 'account of Oriental and Greco-Roman cults, with naturalistic and euhemeristic explanations' (1–17); 2: symbols, mythology (18–27); 3: urging 'the triumph of Christianity' (28–9).[37] Unfortunately, the beginning of the text is lost. It picks up with a description and denouncement of the worship of the divinized elements: water, earth, air, and fire. The element of earth brings him to the Phrygian worship of Magna Mater and Attis (chapter 3).[38] He writes: 'the Phrygians who dwell in Pessinus by the banks of the Gallus River assign the primacy over the other elements to the earth, and maintain that she is the mother of all things' (*omnium esse matrem*). 'Then, desirous that they too should get themselves a set of annual rites, they proceeded to consecrate with annual lamentations the love affair of a rich woman, their queen, who chose to avenge in tyrannical fashion the haughty snub that she suffered from her young beloved' (*adulescentis amati*). To please her, they claimed that the beloved had been resurrected after burial, and they built temples to him. 'Thereafter what the angry woman had done to avenge the insult to her slighted beauty, this they insist that the priests whom they ordain should suffer (*hoc ordinatos a se pati volunt sacerdotes*).[39] Thus in annual rites honoring the earth there is drawn up in array the cortege of the youth's funeral, so that people are really venerating an unhappy death and funeral when they are convinced that they are worshipping the earth.'

---

[37] Forbes (1970) 221 n.514.
[38] Tr. Forbes (1970) 47–9. See the comments of Forbes (1970) 132–3; Turcan (1982) 188–97. On the earth aspect of Attis see also Eusebius' *Preparation of the Gospel*, which refers to statements of Porphyry explaining the myth, with Attis related to earth as the symbol of the spring blossom.
[39] That is, castration.

76   *Rhetoric and Religious Identity in Late Antiquity*

Continuing with his focus on the rites of the cult, he asserts that they seek to hide this error by declaring that the rites are organized according to a naturalistic explanation. 'The earth, they maintain, loves the crops, Attis is the very thing that grows from the crops, and the punishment which he suffered is what a harvester with his sickle does to the ripened crops. His death they interpret as the storing away of the collected seeds, his resurrection as the sprouting of the scattered seeds in the annual turn of the seasons.' He says he wants to ask them questions about their behaviour: 'Why did they combine this simple matter of seeds and crops with a funeral, with death, with a haughty snub, with a punishment, with a love affair?', and 'Do you howl as a mark of thanksgiving for the new growth of the crops, do you mourn to show your joy? And when you do see the true explanation, do you still not regret your past behaviour, but persist in busying yourself with annual lamentations, always running away from life and seeking death?' Essentially, he wants to ask them why they bother with all these rites, what is the point of them. He asserts that a farmer knows what he is doing anyway, following the 'laws of the seasons', so they have to admit that 'these rites were organized not in honor of the crops but in honor of an irrelevant death'. In comparison with Arnobius then, Firmicus presents a much more allusive, even coy, explanation for the existence of the cult and its rites; as Forbes comments, 'Firmicus habitually speaks of delicate matters in delicate terms'.[40] He is distinctive for his emphasis on the earth aspect of the cult, as well as for suggesting that Cybele was a queen of Pessinus, and that Attis was resurrected.[41] What he has in common with Arnobius is his assertion that there was nothing divine here, just a story of a sad human affair. They can both pose as hard-headed practical and rational interpreters of affairs.

In addition to considering the origins of the cult and nature of the rites, Firmicus also turns to other questions. He finishes chapter 3 by considering 'the claim that earth is the mother of all the gods'. His response is essentially 'Whatever!'; he observes that 'she is the mother of *their* gods...they are forever making their gods out of stone or wood gathered from the earth'. Here he alludes to the Mother of the Gods as stone and Attis as a pine tree.[42] He also remarks that the earth is constricted by other elements anyway. He concludes that the gods daily confess their weakness to humans.

In chapter 8, Firmicus returns to the subject of mourning for the dead Attis. In this chapter, the Sun (Sol) is speaking to the assembly of humankind, denouncing Heliolatry. It reckons Attis amongst several others that they mourn for—Liber, Prosperina, Osiris—but asks that they 'do so without heaping indignity upon me'. Attis is also meant when the Sun comments 'others cut out my manhood and mourn the loss' (*alii amputatis viribus*

---

[40] Forbes (1970) 148 n.49. On Arnobius' contrasting use of obscenity see Masterson (2014).
[41] See the comments of Forbes (1970) 148 nn.46 and 47.   [42] Forbes (1970) 149 n.60.

plangunt).[43] Here Firmicus is referring to the conflation of Attis with Sol, as indicated by Arnobius too.

In his last two references to the cult, Firmicus explicitly contrasts it with Christianity. Chapter 18 compares the rites for Attis with the Eucharist, focusing on the signs and symbols used.[44] He records the ritual words that have to be spoken by a devotee in the temple, supplying the Greek also: '"I have eaten from the tambourine (*tympanum*), I have drunk from the cymbal, and I have mastered the secrets of religion"'.[45] The contrast is between the damning food and drink of the pagan ritual and the saving bread and wine of the Eucharist, between death and immortality. Finally, in chapter 27, Firmicus compares the pine tree with the Christian cross, the former being one of several counterfeits of the wood (*ex ligni imitatione*) in pagan cult. He records that 'In the Phrygian cult of her whom they call the Mother of the Gods, a pine tree is cut every year, and an image of a youth (*simulacrum iuvenis*) is fastened on the middle of the tree'. Again, he supplies unique information regarding the attachment of the image of Attis to the tree.[46] Although not explicitly spelled out, there is an implied contrast between the spring festival for Attis with the key symbol of the pine tree, and Christian Easter with the key symbol of the cross.

JULIAN

Having reviewed how Arnobius and Firmicus have presented and discussed the myth and the cult of the Mother of the Gods, I turn now to Julian. Often remarked upon for his Neoplatonic navel-gazing—or more accurately Neoplatonic star-gazing—Julian, in his discourse on the Mother of the Gods, presents a Neoplatonic interpretation of the meaning of the myth, particularly the role and symbolism of Attis within it.[47] His text has a clear structure: he describes how the Mother of the Gods came to Rome, then establishes the Neoplatonic worldview and the philosophical framework, and finally returns to the myth and the rites and interprets them in that light.[48] She came from the Phrygians to the Greeks, specifically the Athenians, he emphasizes. There follows the familiar story of how she was transferred to Rome, in the context

---

[43] See Turcan (1982) 244.   [44] Forbes (1970) 80–4.

[45] Note that the Latin does not translate the Greek literally; it should say 'I have become an initiate of Attis' (*religionis secreta perdidici*; γέγονα μύστης Ἄττεως). See the comments of Forbes (1970) 195 n.338; Turcan (1982) 289.

[46] Forbes (1970) 217 n.490; Turcan (1982) 335.

[47] For Julian on the Great Mother see, for instance, Turcan (1996a), (1996b) 71–3; Lancellotti (2002) 125–35.

[48] For discussion of the text see Smith (1995) 159–62; Rochefort (2003) 94–102; Liebeschuetz (2012).

of the war with Carthage, involving the role of the oracle at Delphi and the request that the statue be brought to Rome. Julian dwells on the episode of the transport ship stopping once it reached the Tiber, which demonstrates the power of the goddess. The supposedly tainted priestess, Claudia, was blamed for the halting of the ship, but Claudia proves her chastity by being able to pull the ship with her belt. Julian says 'the goddess showed the Romans' 'two things' (160D): 'first that the freight...was priceless, and that this was no work of men's hands but truly divine, not lifeless clay but a thing possessed of life and divine powers', and second, 'that no one of the citizens could be good or bad and she not know thereof' (161A). With the installation of the goddess, the war with Carthage went Rome's way.

The emperor then provides his own philosophic interpretation of the myth. He understands Gallus/Attis (he uses both names) in Neoplatonic terms, as 'the substance of generative and creative Mind (Nous) which engenders all things down to the lowest plane of matter, and comprehends in itself all the concepts and causes of the forms that are embodied in matter', and states 'we believe that Attis or Gallus is a god of generative powers' (165B). Focusing on the details of the myth, he says Attis was exposed at birth near the river Gallus, but grew up, tall and beautiful. He was beloved by the Mother of the Gods, who entrusted all things to him and put a starry cap on his head. This cap is understood as the visible sky, the river Gallus as the Milky Way, and Attis himself resembles the sun's rays. However, Attis then passes to the lowest region, symbolized in the myth by his descent to the cave to marry the nymph; she thus represents the dampness of matter. Gallus constitutes the connecting link between forms embodied in matter beneath the region of the moon. The Mother of the Gods is the source of the intellectual and creative gods, who in their turn guide the visible gods. She is both mother and spouse of Zeus. Her love for Attis is passionless, chaste ($\dot{a}\pi a\theta\acute{\eta}s$). She does not want Attis to be 'allured into generation' (166C). Julian declares: 'This is what the myth aims to teach us when it says that the Mother of the Gods exhorted Attis not to leave her or to love another' (167A). Nevertheless, Attis descended to the lowest limits of matter, which was terminated by the intervention of Helios through his persuasion of the Lion, who contends with the nymph. Julian continues: 'Then [the myth] says that by detecting and revealing the truth, [the Lion] caused the youth's castration. What is the meaning of this castration? It is the checking of the unlimited'. After his castration, Attis is led upwards again to the Mother of the Gods.

Having provided a Neoplatonic interpretation of the myth, Julian then connects this with the season of the rites. The sacred tree is cut at the spring equinox (23 March), and trumpets are sounded. Then, 'on the third day the sacred and unspeakable member of the god Gallus is severed' (24 March). There follows the Hilaria (25 March, the day of the resurrection of Attis) and the festival. The castration denotes 'the halting of [Attis'] unlimited course'; when he touches the equinox, he is stopped. Regarding the rituals of the cult,

Julian observes that some are secret, but some not. He observes that 'the cutting of the tree belongs to the story of Gallus and not to the Mysteries at all, but it has been taken over by them, I think because the gods wished to teach us, in symbolic fashion, that we must pluck the fairest fruits from the earth, namely, virtue and piety (ἀρετὴν μετὰ εὐσεβείας), and offer them to the goddess to be the symbol of our well-ordered constitution here on earth'. Like the tree, he says, they need to 'strive upwards to the goddess...who is the principle of all life' (169B-C). As for the trumpet, it 'sounds the recall for Attis and for all of us' who have fallen to earth but belong to heaven. Hilaria—Joy—follows of course, as souls return to the gods.

Julian then summarizes aspects of the myth and the cult and their interpretation and significance. For instance, he asserts 'the association of Attis with matter is the descent into the cave', and 'forever is Attis the servant and charioteer of the Mother; forever he yearns passionately towards generation; and forever he cuts short his unlimited course through the cause whose limits are fixed, even the cause of the forms'. He notes that of the two equinoxes the spring equinox is more honoured as it signifies the sun coming close, with its uplifting rays (171D-172A). He notes the significance of the equinox in the rites of the Eleusinian Mysteries too. He comments also on the aspect of chastity, present in both cults. In that of the Great Mother, 'the instrument of generation is severed' (173C-D); the importance of chastity is that it signifies union with 'the One, stainless and pure' (so avoiding generation).[49] Finally, he turns to the sacred rite, and the purification (173D), discussing the food restrictions within the cult and explaining them. These relate to Attis as 'the direct creator of the material world'.

Julian then concludes his discourse, asking 'And now what is left for me to say?' (178D). He reflects on the circumstances of the composition of the text and on the nature of Attis again, as the Logos, then offers a hymn (ὕμνος) to the Mother of the Gods.

JULIAN THE APOLOGIST

Within his Neoplatonic interpretation of the myth and the cult, evidently in discourse with other pagans,[50] Julian is also clearly pursuing an apologetic

---

[49] It is notable that Julian does not address the issue of real castration; perhaps it was too sensitive a subject for him. One wonders if he might have justified it on the grounds of the importance of chastity, a virtue valued by Christians too of course, and some Christians did embrace self-castration on the grounds of Matthew 19.12: see, for instance, Caner (1997).

[50] Note, for instance, Julian's emphasis on his own theory about why they cannot eat the fruit of the date-palm, as the tree is perennial and sacred to the sun: 176B. It seems that Julian, like Arnobius and Firmicus, was addressing both pagan and Christian intellectuals.

80 *Rhetoric and Religious Identity in Late Antiquity*

agenda, responding to criticisms of the myth and the cult of the kind we have already witnessed from Arnobius and Firmicus. Having run through the story of how the goddess came to Rome, Julian discusses reaction to it. He remarks that 'some will think it incredible and wholly unworthy of a philosopher or a theologian', but declares that this is what had been recorded by historians, and also in statues in Rome. He continues: 'yet I am well aware that some over-wise persons (τινες τῶν λίαν σοφῶν) will call it an old wives' tale (ὔθλους εἶναι γραδίων), not to be credited', but he defends it, saying 'I would rather trust the traditions of cities than those too clever people (τοῖς κομψοῖς), whose puny souls are keen-sighted enough, but never do they see aught that is sound' (161B). Julian then says he has been told that Porphyry has written a treatise on the same subject as him, but asserts that he has not read it and then goes on to provide his own philosophic interpretation of the myth.[51] Whether Julian had read this text of Porphyry or not, his reference to the famous opponent of Christianity is telling.

Subsequent to explaining the meaning of the rites, Julian proceeds to defend the gods: he declares 'let no one suppose my meaning to be that this was ever done or happened in a way that implies that the gods themselves are ignorant of what they intend to do, or that they have to correct their own errors. But our ancestors in every case tried to trace the original meanings of things... then when they had discovered those meanings they clothed them in paradoxical myths. This was in order that, by means of the paradox and the incongruity, the fiction might be detected and we might be induced to search out the truth' (169D–170B). Julian was certainly a proponent of the value of myths, as can be seen for instance in the myth of his own life he supplied in his oration against the Cynic Heraclius and in his myth of the dinner party of the gods to decide who was the best emperor, the *Caesars*.[52]

When summarizing aspects of the myth and the cult, and their interpretation and significance, Julian also seems sensitive to criticism. He insists that Attis' descent into the cave did not occur 'against the will of the gods and the Mother of the gods, though the myth says that it was against their will' (171B), and that the Mother of the Gods was not hostile to Attis in the myth after his castration. His discussion of the food restrictions is especially interesting, as he prefaces this by referring to criticism of them: 'everyone thinks that the following is ridiculous. The sacred ordinance allows men to eat meat, but it forbids them to eat grains and fruit' (174A). He then continues: 'but the following ordinance is ridiculed by the most impious (οἱ δυσσεβέστατοι) of

---

[51] See Smith (1995) 161, who wonders if Julian is referring to Porphyry's *On the Cave of the Nymphs*. See also Wright (1913) 481 n.1; Rochefort (2003) 106 n.3. On Julian and Porphyry, and Julian's originality, see also the comments of Turcan (1996a) 396. On Porphyry and Julian against the Christians see Meredith (1980).

[52] See also Tougher (2018) 89.

Julian the Apologist 81

mankind also' (174B), meaning the Christians.[53] This ordinance is about vegetables that grow upwards being allowed to be eaten, whilst roots that grow downwards are not, and that figs are allowed to be eaten but not pomegranates or apples. Julian continues: 'I have often heard many men saying this in whispers, and I too in former days have said the same, but now it seems that I alone of all men am bound to be deeply grateful to the ruling gods, to all of them, surely, but above all the rest to the Mother of the Gods. For all things am I grateful to her, and for this amongst the rest, that she did not disregard me when I wandered as it were in darkness' (174B–C). This discourse clearly had great personal meaning to Julian, and situates him as a convert to paganism, rejecting his former Christian views. The sense of the personal is reinforced when Julian recalls that he himself was questioned by someone (presumably, in this case, a pagan) about his assertion that they should not eat fish as they do not sacrifice them (176C–177A).

Finally, the anti-Christian agenda of Julian is revealed in his terminal hymn to the Mother of the Gods, when he requests the goddess to 'grant to all men happiness, and that highest happiness of all, the knowledge of the gods; and grant to the Roman people in general that they may cleanse themselves of the stain of impiety (τῆς ἀθεότητος τὴν κηλῖδα)'.

Thus, Julian's discourse is not just about providing a Neoplatonic interpretation of the myth and the cult; it is also apologetic—anti-Christian—in character. Interestingly, soon after Julian wrote his discourse, his friend and ally and fellow-pagan, Salutius, the Praetorian Prefect of the East, wrote his *On the Gods and the Universe*, often seen as a kind of 'Guide for Dummies' to Julian's religion. In it he also deals with the Mother of the Gods and Attis,[54] and follows the same plan as Julian; as Arthur Darby Nock observes, 'the general sequence is the same in the two: myth, theological explanation, description of ritual, significance of time of rites, significance of the sacred season at Eleusis'.[55] Notably, Nock asserts that Salutius' 'statement of faith is so made as to parry the usual onslaughts of Christian polemic',[56] but it is clear that Julian is also doing this.

In his discussion of Julian's discourse, Liebeschuetz emphasizes the 'cosmological and soteriological meaning' that the emperor gave the myth and ritual, eschewing the straightforwardly earth interpretation seen reflected, for instance, in Firmicus. Liebeschuetz comments that 'the ancient, and very earthy, fertility festival has been transformed into a celebration of the hope of personal immortality'—and is thus comparable, he says, to 'the Christian Easter'.[57] For Liebeschuetz, this reflects the influence of Christianity on Julian's religious

---

[53] Rochefort (2003) 123 n.2.   [54] 4.7–11, ed. Rochefort (1960) 7–8, tr. Nock (1926) 7–11.
[55] Nock (1926) li, though he notes there are differences too. See also the comments of Turcan (1996a) 401.
[56] Nock (1926) cii.   [57] Liebeschuetz (2012) 221.

project. In his reading, Attis is a Christ figure, the Mother of the Gods the Virgin Mary. But clearly Julian was not alone in seeing these connections and associations; as seen, Firmicus, writing before Julian, presents the resurrection of Attis as a parody of the Easter mystery.[58] Thus, one has the sense that Julian is responding to Christian attacks, and drawing on his own experiences and understanding as a Christian; as David Hunt has shown, Julian utilizes his knowledge of contemporary Christian debates about the nature of Christ in his *Against the Galileans*.[59] Arnaldo Marcone situates Julian within the 'pagan' response to Christian attacks, viewing Julian's discourse as a 'nice example' of 'the attempt to allegorize disreputable forms of traditional mythology in order to neutralize criticism of the myths'.[60] Further, as Jacqueline Long has said, in discussing Julian's writings in general, it is 'worth considering whether... the *Hymn*... reflect[s] not impervious hostility but an engaged intellectual confrontation. The extent to which Julian's texts stage conflict in order to highlight ideas before a broader audience or to appeal for sympathy is... worth examining.'[61]

CONCLUSION

Julian's discourse on the Mother of the Gods is important not just for the emperor's Neoplatonic interpretation of the myth and rites of the Great Mother and Attis. The text also speaks to Julian's larger concern with the Christianization of the Empire, and should be understood as a response to Christian apologetics as well as an engaged pagan exchange. This conclusion supports the need for Julian to be seen firmly within the context of his own times and in relation to contemporary Christian culture. Further, however, this chapter emphasizes the centrality of the cult within the identity of the Roman Empire itself. Pagans and Christians alike were aware that the importation of the cult into Rome was associated with, and understood to be vital for, the earthly success of the Roman Empire. Thus, Christians were keen to attack this pagan touchstone of empire, to replace the Great Mother with Christ, whilst for the pagan convert Julian she was a central part of his programme of religious restoration and restoration of the Empire. This is laid bare towards the end of Julian's hymn to the Mother of the Gods, when he beseeches that she helps the Roman people 'to guide their Empire for many thousands of years' (180B). In rhetorical constructions of religious identity, for both Christians and pagans, the Mother of the Gods had a critical role.

---

[58] Perhaps Julian was inverting this point and suggesting that Christian beliefs were a parody of pagan ones; I thank the editors for this suggestion.
[59] Hunt (2012).   [60] Marcone (2012) 247.   [61] Long (2012) 331.

6

Bodies, Books, Histories

Augustine of Hippo and the Extraordinary (*civ. Dei* 16.8 and Pliny, *HN* 7)

Susanna Elm

The histories of the nations tell of certain monstrous races of men. If these tales are to be believed, it may be asked whether such monsters are descended from the sons of Noah, or rather from that one man [Adam] from whom the sons of Noah themselves have come. Some of these are said to have only one eye, in the middle of their forehead. Others have feet that point backwards, behind their legs. Others combine in themselves the nature of both sexes, having the right breast of a man and the left of a woman, and, when they mate, they take it in turns to beget and conceive... Elsewhere we come across females who conceive at the age of five and do not live to be more than eight years old... There are some men without necks... and... other man-like creatures are depicted in mosaic on the marine parade at Carthage, taken from books as examples of the, as it were, too curious history (*curiosioris historiae*)... It is not, of course, necessary to believe in all the kinds of men which are said to exist. But anyone who is born anywhere as a man (that is, as a rational and mortal animal), no matter how unusual he may be to our bodily senses in shape, color, motion, sound... derives from the original and first-created man; and no believer will doubt this. It is, however, clear what constitutes the natural norm in the majority of case and what, in itself, is a marvelous rarity (*raritate mirabile*).[1]

---

[1] Aug. civ. Dei 16.8: *Quaeritur etiam, utrum ex filiis Noe uel potius ex illo uno homine, unde etiam ipsi extiterunt, propagata esse credendum sit quaedam monstrosa hominum genera, quae gentium narrat historia, sicut perhibentur quidam unum habere oculum in fronte media, quibusdam plantas uersas esse post crura, quibusdam utriusque sexus esse naturam et dextram mammam uirilem, sinistram muliebrem, uicibusque inter se coeundo et gignere et parere; aliis ora non esse eosque per nares tantummodo halitu uiuere, alios statura esse cubitales, quos Pygmaeos a*

Being Christian whilst being Roman was by no means straightforward. Nor was it evident what being Christian meant for those one might want to consider 'ordinary' Romans.[2] For us, as scholars, the vast majority of Romans, Christian and otherwise, become tangible only if they belonged to the elites, however broadly defined, and yet even here, it is hard to see how 'ordinary' members of the Roman elites defined and enacted their being Christian. Many texts showcase how extraordinary Roman Christian men prescribed codes of conduct for other Christian men and women, but these texts often sought to instruct their audience how to be an extraordinary rather than an ordinary Christian and even they convey the difficulties their authors faced in crafting a Christian Roman identity: who should these new Romans, these Christian Romans be? How should they behave, what should they look like?

I have been trying to locate these 'new' Romans through slightly oblique angles of approach, here through the relation between particular bodies, books, and histories.[3] These are the topics addressed in the brief passage from Book 16.8 of Augustine of Hippo's *City of God* quoted above and they will guide what follows.

When reading Augustine's *'magnum opus et arduum'* (*civ. Dei Praef.*), I have always wondered why he sprinkled so many references to extraordinary bodies throughout his work. What might these bodies signify in the context of the *City of God*? Augustine was, of course, acutely aware of 'all those manifold signing systems without which human society either cannot function at all or at least function much less conveniently'.[4] Thus, it is safe to assume that his references to extraordinary bodies are not accidental, that Augustine wrote about them because he found them interesting, but also because he wished to explore their potential for the *innumerabilia genera significationum* to the fullest for the society he envisioned. What, then, might these bodies signify, what knowledge did Augustine want them to impart?

cubito Graeci uocant, alibi quinquennes concipere feminas et octauum uitae annum non excedere. Item ferunt esse gentem, ubi singula crura in pedibus habent nec poplitem flectunt, et sunt mirabilis celeritatis; quos Sciopodas uocant, quod per aestum in terra iacentes resupini umbra se pedum protegant; quosdam sine ceruice oculos habentes in umeris, et cetera hominum uel quasi hominum genera, quae in maritima platea Carthaginis musiuo picta sunt, ex libris deprompta uelut curiosioris historiae. Quid dicam de Cynocephalis, quorum canina capita atque ipse latratus magis bestias quam homines confitetur? Sed omnia genera hominum, quae dicuntur esse, credere non est necesse. Verum quisquis uspiam nascitur homo, id est animal rationale mortale, quamlibet nostris inusitatam sensibus gerat corporis formam seu colorem siue motum siue sonum siue qualibet ui, qualibet parte, qualibet qualitate naturam: ex illo uno protoplasto originem ducere nullus fidelium dubitauerit. Apparet tamen quid in pluribus natura obtinuerit et quid sit ipsa raritate mirabile; translations in the following, with modifications, by Dyson (1998).

[2] Rebillard (2012). [3] Elm (2013), (2015), (2017a), (2017b), (2018).

[4] Aug. *doctr. christ.* 2.25: *commodo vero et necessaria hominum cum hominibus instituta sunt, quaecumque in habitu et cultu corporis ad sexus vel honores discernendos differentia placuit, et innumerabilia genera significationum, sine quibus humana societas aut non omnino aut minus commode geritur*...; Conte (1994); Doody (2010) 11–39.

On first reading Book 16.8, one might think that Augustine's primary concern are these extraordinary bodies per se, simply because they are such *rara mirabilia* and *curiosa*. Some have a firm place in the literary imagination, such as the men with one eye in their forehead, or those that are 'only a cubit high, and these are called pygmies by the Greeks, after their word for a cubit, *pygme*'. Others are rarer, more of a *curiositas*, such as 'those with no mouth, who live only by breathing through their nostrils', or 'those whose feet are attached to a single leg which does not bend at the knee'. However, as Augustine points out, his source for at least some of these extraordinary bodies are the *historiae gentium*, chief amongst them the elder Pliny's *Natural History*, and that fact should alert us that curious bodies are not the sole issue at stake here.[5]

For Augustine and his Latin contemporaries and precursors, *curiositas* denoted a suspect form of inquisitiveness, a desire for knowledge with a tinge of the transgressive, especially when directed towards *mirabilia*.[6] Curiosity in the context of *historia* was, however, different.[7] When writing history, *curiositas* meant careful, diligent, comprehensive study. Granted, even here an erudite man might be tempted into excess and carry his studiousness too far, might become a little too curious, especially when investigating *mirabilia*, so even here discernment was required. Yet, a *curiosa historia* was a priori a good thing.[8] Thus, on second glance, Augustine's description of these extraordinary bodies gestures at correct and incorrect ways to be a proper historian and, moreover, at the correct themes and subjects of history done properly. What, then, might Augustine be saying here through extraordinary bodies and the books describing them about history?

HISTORY AND BOOKS

Augustine's *City of God* is in many ways a history.[9] Hence, it is not surprising that he began his opus at the beginning, not of the world but *ab origine* of the *civitas Romana* (*civ. Dei* 2.2), the most important earthly city, to narrate its

---

[5] Plin. *Nat. Hist.* 7.2.10–30; cf. Aug. *civ. Dei* 16.11. Beagon (1992), (1994) esp. 72–5; Gevaert and Laes (2013); Murphy (2004).

[6] Sen. *De brev. vit.* 13; Tert. *praescr.* 7.7, 7.12; Aug. *mor.* 1.38; Plutarch, *On Curiosity, Mor.* 517–21; Labhardt (1960) esp. 211–13; (1996–2002); on Augustine and *curiositas* see also Wild (2011).

[7] Aug. *doctr. chris.* 2.17.27: *Varro, quod nescio utrum apud eos quisquam talium rerum doctior vel curiosior esse possit*; Aug. *en. Ps.* 34.2.3; Cic. *Tusc.* 1.108; Plin. *Ep.* 9.28.5; Sogno (2012); Beagon (1994).

[8] Plin. *Ep.* 3.5, about the elder Pliny's extra-ordinary studiousness; Sen. *Brev. vitae* 13.3; Naas (2011).

[9] Müller (1993) 156–69; and especially Studer (1996); Markus (1970) 1–21.

'origin, progress, and appointed end' (*civ. Dei* 18.1). However, this does not mean that linear history was Augustine's primary concern. Rather, in Mark Vessey's words, 'Augustine had a way of beginning at the beginning, and then beginning again', and again.[10] Thus, he introduced the beginning of the other crucial city on earth, Babylon, in Book 16, the one of the extraordinary bodies of the *historia gentium*, whilst the beginning of the heavenly city had to wait until Book 10 (*civ. Dei* 10.32). The focus of the *City of God* is 'the origin, progress, and appointed end' of the *civitas terrena* and of the heavenly city, but as this multiplicity of beginnings already indicates, the history of these cities cannot be properly narrated and comprehended in linear fashion.

Thus, the *City of God* is to a significant degree also a meditation on history as cognitive endeavour, on the correct way to perform historical inquiry, *historialis cognitio*.[11] As Augustine makes clear, appropriate *historialis cognitio* relies on linear history, but it uses linear histories in the plural. *Historialis cognitio* properly done requires many different histories, because its aim is to be comprehensive: it turns to the past to foretell the future, the properly appointed end. Therefore, *historialis cognitio* wishes to uncover the hidden mechanisms and driving forces that govern origins, progress, and end. Historical inquiry thus becomes analogous to divination and prophecy, in particular if it uncovers a singular authority driving the whole and hence becomes universal history. To be universal, history must be comprehensive, which demands the inclusion of *curiosa* and *mirabilia*, albeit in correct measure.[12] As a consequence, true *historialis cognitio* relies on other *corpora*, bodies of knowledge, because only a multiplicity of divergent voices can bring to the fore a unifying authoritative one.[13]

Augustine's *historialis cognitio* thus relied on other *corpora*, other foundational bodies of knowledge, the more extraordinary and diverse the better. Here, Porphyry's monumental work *On the Return of the Soul* was central. As Augustine informs us in Book 10.32, Porphyry had thoroughly investigated the histories of many peoples to discern one authoritative voice, a singular 'universal way of the soul's deliverance'.[14] Porphyry concluded that *his historialis cognitio* did not result in a singular way to the One, but instead revealed as

---

[10] Vessey (2012) 14. The following is deeply influenced by Vessey's work on Augustine and the book.

[11] Aug. *civ. Dei* 10.32; *c. Faust.* 12.22, 13.2; Studer (1996).

[12] Studer (1996) 57–60; Beagon (2007) 20–2.

[13] On books and writings as *corpus* see, for example, Aug. *Ep.* 149; *Retr.* 2.13: *liber cuius est titulus adnotationes in iob utrum meus habendus sit, an potius eorum qui eas sicut potuerunt vel voluerunt redegerunt in unum corpus descriptas de frontibus codicis, non facile dixerim*; see also *Retr.* 2. 45; *Sermo* 313C: *et quid plura dicam? Multi usquequauqe habent magnum corpus librorum eius.*

[14] Vessey (2012) 16; Studer (1996) 54–6.

many diverse ways as the recorded voices of different peoples. Alas, countered Augustine, Porphyry's inquiry had been incomplete.

> And when toward the end of his first book on the soul's deliverance, Porphyry says that no system of thought which contains the universal way of the soul's deliverance... has yet come to his knowledge from his historical inquiry (*historialis cognitio*), he acknowledges beyond doubt that there is such a way, but that he does not yet know what it is... But what more illustrious history can be found than that which has taken possession of the whole world (*universum... orbem... obtinuit*) because its authority is so eminent? Or what history could be more faithful than that which narrates past events and foretells future ones, so many of the predictions of which have been fulfilled that we are able to believe without doubt that the rest will be fulfilled also?[15]

Porphyry had been searching in vain, because he had overlooked the one illustrious history based on true authority. His mistake could, however, be forgiven, since he had not been able to read the *City of God*. Based on the same fundamental methodological assumptions regarding correct *historialis cognitio*, Augustine refuted Porphyry with his one history of two particular peoples in direct succession to demonstrate beyond doubt that *this historialis cognitio* was the only relevant one for *omnes gentes*; a 'narrative and cognitive unit rendered through writing'.[16] In this unit, past, present, and future, though distinct, merged into one and functioned as a synchronic whole.[17]

To collapse past, present, and future into one Augustine provided a continuous stream of evidence demonstrating that *his* particular history not only predicted the present and the future, but *was* past, present, and future, and hence truly universal. To accomplish this Augustine relied, just like Porphyry, on the written record of other inhabitants of the *civitas terrena*, the Roman Empire above all, canonical and authoritative 'bodies of knowledge' produced by Vergil, Sallust, Cicero, Pliny, Terence, and in particular Varro.[18] Indeed, he did not so much rely on these works, but dissected and devoured, ingested and digested them—like another one-eyed Polyphemus—to create an immense new body of knowledge. Augustine's own *historialis cognitio* sought to overwrite all others, physically overpowering them and forcing them to the ground

---

[15] Aug. civ. Dei 10.32.3: *Quid hac historia vel inlustrius inveniri potest, quae universum orbem tanto apice auctoritatis obtinuit, vel fidelius, in qua ita narrantur praeterita, ut futura etiam praedicantur, quorum multa videmus impleta, ex quibus ea quae restant sine dubio speremus implenda?*

[16] Vessey (2012) 16–20, quoting 16.

[17] Feeney (2007) 229 n.110 on Augustine's synchronicity.

[18] Studer (1996) 56, 60–3; O'Daly (1999) 236–8; Vessey (2014) 253–77; McRae (2016) 129–40.

by the sheer material weight of his *magnum opus*, this monument for the ages that rendered all else superfluous.[19]

Augustine had to prove irrefutably that 'the City of God, of which we speak', as he phrased it at yet another beginning, that of Book 11, 'is one attested by that writing (*scriptura*), which, in its divine authority, excels all the literary resources (*litteras*) of all the nations'.[20] These *litterae*, much like those Porphyry had perused for his historical inquiry, represent what Jan Assmann has called the archival and canonical resources of cultural memory, foundational for the formation of a *civitas* and hence for the identity of 'peoples'.[21] For Porphyry, the sheer diversity of these resources, *litterae*, their variations, and oddities, in short, their curiosities and *rara mirabilia*, illustrated the diverse ways towards the one divine.

Augustine argued the opposite: such divergences and oddities, these very *mirabilia*, point instead powerfully towards the unifying force of a single God. *Scriptura*, singular, is his evidence, because, as he is at pains to show, it contains the necessary and sufficient written resources of the entire world (*toto orbe*) and embodies the principal narrative and cognitive unity, from Genesis to Revelation.[22]

> There is but one single discourse of God *(unus sermo Dei)* amplified through all the scriptures *(scripturae)*, dearly beloved. Through the mouths of many holy persons a single word makes itself heard *(sonet)*. That Word, being God-with-God in the beginning, has no syllables, because it is not confined by time. Yet we should not find it surprising that to meet our weakness he descended to the discrete sounds we use, for he also descended to take to himself the weakness of our human body.[23]

One voice through many mouths: a voice that is at once extraordinary, requiring no syllables, and embodied in ordinary speech. This is the process Augustine's *City of God* explicates and performs through the past for the present and the future: the unity of *Scriptura* and history, attested by the very diversity and multiplicity of many voices, including the *rara mirabilia* of the extraordinary.[24]

---

[19] Plin. *Ep.* 7 to Tacitus: *Auguror nec me fallit augurium, historias tuas immortales futuras*; Vessey (2012) 20–5.
[20] Vessey's translation (2012) 15.   [21] Assmann (2008).
[22] Aug. *civ. Dei* 18.37; 18.40–1.
[23] Aug. *En. Ps.* 103.4.1: *Meminit Caritas Vestra, cum sit unus sermo Dei in Scripturis omnibus dilatatus, et per multa ora sanctorum unum Verbum sonet, quod cum sit in principio Deus apud Deum, ibi non habet syllabas, quia non habet tempora; nec mirandum nobis sit, quia propter infirmitatem nostram descendit ad particulas sonorum nostrorum, cum descenderit ad suscipiendam infirmitatem corporis nostri*; Augustine, *Exposition of the Psalms*, tr. Boulding (2004); Cameron (2012).
[24] Vessey (2012) 15.

HISTORY AS BODY

To this performance of history as cognitive unit, bodies were central.[25] So far, I have focused on *corpora* in the form of books, but for Augustine *human* bodies were equally significant. Because time and history begin with the human body, as Augustine made clear in the brief passage from the *Enarratio in Psalmos* cited above, without human bodies there would be no history. Conversely, physical human bodies make tangible the synchronicity of history as both linear and three-dimensional, in space and time. At this juncture Augustine's extra-ordinary bodies gain their heuristic value as more than *mirabilia* or curiosities. Because these bodies are extraordinary, they stand outside 'all those manifold signing systems without which human society either cannot function at all or at least function much less conveniently'.[26] However, the bodies described in Book 16.8 are those of human beings and as such inextricably linked to the ordinary: simultaneously extra- and ordinary.[27]

What are we to make, then, of these extraordinary bodies in the context of Augustine's Book 16.8? First, it is important to situate Book 16 within the overall structure of the *City of God*. As Gillian Clark has pointed out, 'Augustine was particularly aware of *City of God* as a book, as a physical object used by readers'.[28] He consciously configured the *City of God* as a *corpus*, a physical, material, three-dimensional body of knowledge.[29] The format of this object was the spine-hinged book or codex rather than the scroll, and we know that in composing the *City of God* Augustine paid careful attention to its shape so that the physical form of the codex reinforced his arguments about history.[30] From the outset, Augustine had designed the *City of God* to fit into two codices (*Ep.* 1A*.1). The first ten books narrating the linear progress of the *civitas terrena* ought to form one codex, whilst Books 11–22, narrating the progress of the *civitas Dei* and the appointed end of both cities, should comprise the second. Should this division prove too unwieldy, the first codex might be divided into two after Book 5, whilst the second part might be subdivided into three smaller codices of four books each, the second of which should comprise the historical development of the two cities in Books 15–18.[31]

Augustine wrote the *City of God* such that its material shape furthered his cognitive intent: thanks to the codex format, readers would be able to follow

---

[25] Aug. *Gen. litt.* 9.14.24; *civ. Dei* 10.29; 22.26; *Retr.* 1.4; Paulsen (1990) 105–16; Hunter (2012) esp. 357; Miles (2012) esp. 77.
[26] Aug. *doctr. christ.* 2.25.
[27] For an analysis of Augustine's extra-ordinary bodies and their fate in *civ. Dei* 21-2 in the context of disability studies see Upson-Saia (2011).
[28] Clark (2007a) 120.   [29] See, for example, Aug. *Retr.* 2.13.
[30] Spiegel (1990); Jager (2000) 33–8, 43; Hurtado (2006) 43–93; Vessey (2012) 27–32.
[31] Aug. *Epp.* 1A*.1 and 2*.2–3 to Firmus.

the histories of the two cities synoptically from beginning to end, just as it unfolded. Indeed, this history looks like a double-helix, one strand following the *civitas Dei*, the other the *civitas terrena*, which consists in fact of *two* cities, Rome and Babylon, but all three cities and their histories are always interwoven and intertwined. To ascertain further the proper reading of his writings, Augustine recapitulated, 'Varro-like in his care to apportion his subject matter into its respective containers', the actual history of the two cities in Book 18, so massive that it could form its own codex.[32] Book 18 provides an epitome of the intertwined history of the two cities Augustine had delineated in Books 15–17 'for the overall view of the readers' (*consideratione legentium*; *civ. Dei* 18.1). Varro's pre-Roman chronology in his *De gente populi Romani* and Jerome's Latin translation and continuation of Eusebius' *Chronicle*, both read on the fundament of *Scriptura*, provide the sources of Book 18.[33] These sources confirmed that the history of the *terrena civitas* was that of two powers dominating all others in succession, Assyria/Babylon and Rome.[34] Babylon and Rome had won the race amongst all the different human peoples, but not coincidentally they were 'neatly ordered and well spaced from one another in terms of both time and place. For the former arose earlier, and the latter later; the one in the East, and the other in the West. Again, the beginning of the one came immediately after the other's end' (*civ. Dei* 18.2). Thus, the consecutive history of Assyria/Babylon and Rome formed one linear strand, the axis around which Augustine narrated the history of the *civitas terrena* in its relation to the *civitas Dei*: 'Babylon, as the first Rome, runs its course next to the city of God... and Rome itself is like a second Babylon'.[35]

However, prior to the rise of Assyria/Babylon and subsequently Rome, Augustine had no other resources at his disposal than *Scriptura*. Books 16 and 17 had to be written *in meo stilo*, since Scripture was the only book available for the history of the *civitas terrena* for 'a period of over a thousand years': from the time after Noah and the flood to Abraham, a period that witnessed the actual foundation of the city of Babylon (*civ. Dei* 16.2). Further, not even Scripture was forthcoming in telling details about this period, so that Augustine had to take recourse to other bodies of knowledge when narrating the history of that time: enter the extraordinary bodies.

---

[32] Quote Vessey (2012) 24; McRae (2016) 138–9.
[33] For Eusebius' *Chronicle* see O'Daly (1999) 236–8; Burgess (2002); Grafton and Williams (2006); Vessey (2010).
[34] The foundational study for Augustine's concepts of Rome, Babylon, and Jerusalem remains van Oort (1991) esp. 93–163.
[35] Aug. *civ. Dei* 18.2: *Babylonia, quasi prima Roma, cum peregrina in hoc mundo Dei civitate procurrat... et ista Roma quasi secunda Babylonia est*; cf. Aug. *civ. Dei* 16.7; 18.22.

EXTRAORDINARY BODIES—PLINY AND HIS APE

Book 16 had to address two problems raised by the paucity of information provided by the principal repositories of cultural memory: first, 'whether the holy city ran a continuous course after the flood, or was so interrupted by recurrent periods of irreligion that not a single man worshipped God', since from Noah and his sons to Abraham not a single man is mentioned 'whose devotion to God is clearly attested' (*civ. Dei* 16.1). Second, given the comprehensive nature of Noah's flood, where did subsequent generations come from? Even more pressing, from whom did certain monstrous types of men (*monstrosa hominum genera*) described in the history of the nations (*quae gentium narrat historia*) descend? From the sons of Noah or from Adam?

Where *Scriptura* is silent, extraordinary bodies speak. But what do they say? The *historia gentium* to which Augustine here refers is yet another form of *historialis cognitio*: Pliny the Elder's *naturalis historia*, more specifically the collection of human animals in all their variety assembled in Book 7 of the *Natural History*.[36] Augustine might well have owned a copy of the sizeable Book 7 that Pliny had structured 'as a self-contained unit'.[37] As Pliny had stated in the preface of the entire work, his topic was 'nature, that is, life' (*rerum natura, hoc est vita, narratur*; *HN Praef.* 13), and to represent 'life' he chose a method that was not dissimilar to that of Porphyry, but in some ways the opposite of Varro's (whose *Divine Antiquities* he seems to have used): instead of subdividing knowledge into compartments, he assembled a comprehensive overview of life in all its variety and diversity, *varietas naturae*, including the many diverse human bodies.[38] Preserving knowledge assembled in the past and everything he could acquire at present, Pliny wished to demonstrate through the sheer diversity of nature, her *rara mirabilia* encountered in regions remote and central, the equally enormous, multidimensional power of the *pax Romana*, which had brought all this variety into one.[39]

Rara mirabilia could be found in Africa as well as in Italy, in the past as well as the present, and hence also in the future.

However, as he had stated at the outset, Pliny's project encompassed even more than to showcase Rome's unifying control of the *orbis terrarum*. After all, his topic was *nature* herself.

> For instance, who believed in Ethiopians until they had seen some? What isn't amazing when first discovered? How many things are judged impossible before

---

[36] Naas (2002) 293–325; Doody (2010) 11–14, 25–30.
[37] Hagendahl (1967) 670–3; Beagon (1992) 34, 40–3.
[38] For Pliny's likely use of Varro's lost *Antiquitates Rerum Humanarum et Divinarum* or the equally lost *Admiranda* in Book 7 see Beagon (1992) 31; Naas (2002) 294–6.
[39] Plin. *HN* 27.3; 37.201; Beagon (1992) 23–6, (2007) 22–5, 29–40; Murphy (2004) 197–201; Naas (2011) 61–70; but see Doody (2010) 20–1.

they occur? As it is, in every instance the power and majesty of the nature of things is unbelievable if your mind grasps only parts of it, and not the whole thing.'[40]

For Pliny, every single individual aspect, the more extraordinary the better, served to illustrate the overwhelming power of nature as a whole, at least for those capable of grasping how the numerous detailed observations coalesced. This was Pliny's project: the demonstration of nature's majesty through the creation of a proper *historia*, the proper cognitive unit of nature's many individual, extraordinary parts composed to illuminate the whole.

Even if Augustine did not have direct access to Pliny, we know for certain that he used another work that did use Book 7: Solinus's *Collectanea rerum memorabilium*.[41] Rather than being merely 'Plinie's ape', as which he had been belittled in the sixteenth century, Solinus had compiled his *memorabilia* in a systematic geographic fashion along a map that began in Rome and spiralled outward in a counter-clockwise direction to delineate the circumference of the *orbis Romanus* in the mid-fourth century.[42] Like Pliny, Solinus informed his readers that he too had been driven by the *fermentum cognitionis* to be comprehensive and hence had included *mirabilia* and curiosities, especially those attested by 'the most accepted writers'.[43]

Thus, Solinus's version of Pliny's *Natural History's* Book 7 also emphasized the all-encompassing, unifying force of the Roman Empire. Even more so, here too one could observe the power of nature to speak through the many curious forms of human bodies, all those *mirabilia* that had provided the blueprint for the mosaics depicting extraordinary bodies on the marine parade at Carthage. And yet, for Augustine these *historiae gentium* were *curiosiora*, a little bit too curious. Evidently, their authors had included *rara mirabilia* that revealed a certain lack of discernment so that they, like Porphyry, had failed by a slight yet crucial margin to achieve perfect *historialis cognitio*.

The human and quasi-human bodies depicted on the mosaics in Carthage, in Pliny, Solinus, and in Augustine's Book 16.8 include persons with faces that had only one eye in the middle of the forehead; faces without a mouth; persons with the soles of their feet turned behind their legs; feet so large they provide shade in the summer; persons only a cubit high; men without a neck and eyes in their shoulders. Some of these persons were *utriusque sexus*, inter-sexual, the right breast male, the left breast female, so that they conceive and beget with themselves. Of course, Augustine concedes, one does not have to believe that all these varied types of man, 'taken from books as examples of the curious

---

[40] Plin. *HN* 7.6–7; 8.42; Doody (2010) 25.
[41] Paniagua (2014) esp. 131–40; Schlapbach (2014).
[42] Arthur Golding in his introduction to the 1578 English translation; Aug. *civ. Dei* 21.4–5 and 8; Belanger (2014); Romer (2014); von Martels (2014).
[43] Solin. *Coll. Praef.* 1.3–5.

things to be found in natural history' actually exist. Indeed, Pliny and Solinus, driven by vanity, went too far when they sought to add apes and sphinxes to the list of such extraordinary bodies, even though we know 'that monkeys and apes and sphinxes are not men but beasts' (*civ. Dei* 16.8). All the other extraordinary bodies are, however, decidedly human. 'But anyone who is born anywhere as a man (that is, as a rational and mortal animal), no matter how unusual he may be to our bodily senses in shape, color, motion, sound... derives from the original and first-created man; and no believer will doubt this' (*civ. Dei* 16.8). This is Augustine's point: such bodies are human and therefore their many mouths, however diverse, sing in one voice.

At a time when other *corpora* of knowledge were not forthcoming, extraordinary human bodies with their manifold signing systems proved beyond doubt to the true believer (which Pliny, after all, had not been, so that he had missed the one true God who had created the nature he so assiduously praised) that the enormous unifying power of the one God, who had created everything, was fully and continually operative. 'For God is the creator of all things: He himself knows where and when anything should be, or should have been, created; and he knows how to weave the beauty of the whole out of the similarity and diversity of its parts' (*civ. Dei* 16.8). Furthermore, God does so in extraordinary ways that do not always conform to the ordinary signing systems of human society. 'The man who cannot view the whole is offended by what he takes to be the deformity of the part; but this is because he does not know how it is adapted or related to the whole' (*civ. Dei* 16.8). Men of greater discernment, such as Pliny and Augustine, recognize in the extraordinary, the curious, the monstrous even, proof of a cognitive and narrative unit, of a history rich in evidence of the unifying power—not simply of nature, as Pliny had mistakenly thought—but of the one God and of the world's progress towards its appointed end.

Because Augustine had to rely on his own resources for a long period of history where neither Scripture nor any other history could tell him 'whether the holy city ran a continuous course', had been interrupted, or could even count a single man 'whose devotion to God is clearly attested' (*civ. Dei* 16.1), he turned to natural history and the extraordinary bodies it had confirmed through *cognitio*—human bodies and thus neither the product of myths, miracles, or any other supernatural force—, to supply the answers to the questions he posed at the outset of Book 16. Such human bodies were tangible, three-dimensional testimony to God's continuous unifying power, especially, as Augustine was at pains to show, since such bodies were not merely the product of archives and mosaics but continued to exist in the present and hence in the appointed future. 'There is at Hippo Zaritus a man who has crescent-shaped feet with only two toes on each; and his hands are similar. If there were any with this feature, it would be added to the curious and the marvelous (*curiosae atque mirabili*) of history'—but this is a contemporary

94 *Rhetoric and Religious Identity in Late Antiquity*

person. Likewise, 'though they are rare, it is difficult to find times when there have been no *androgyni*, also called hermaphrodites: persons who embody the characteristics of both sexes so completely that it is uncertain whether they should be called male or female. However, the prevailing habit of speech has named them according to the superior sex, that is, the male; for no one has ever used the term androgyness or hermaphroditess' (*civ. Dei* 16.8).[44]

Such bodies, then, though extraordinary—neither male nor female but both—are neither mythical nor miraculous. They are assigned the male gender to make them fit the 'signing systems without which human society either cannot function at all or at least function much less conveniently' and such attempts to make even the extraordinary align with our ordinary *genera significationum* highlight Augustine's point: though no doubt extraordinary, these bodies are human and real.[45] They belong into the realm of *historia*, not of *mythos*. Thus, 'some years ago, but certainly within my memory, a man was born in the East with a double set of upper members, but a single set of lower ones. He had two heads, two chests and four arms, but only one belly and two feet...and he lived long enough for his fame (*fama*) to draw many people to come and see him'.

That such extraordinary human beings are attested as fact in the past and present indicates that they will continue into the future, and the same is true for the extraordinary message they conveyed when *Scriptura* was silent.[46] More precisely, even when the written resources of *Scriptura* were silent, God's voice, which does not require the syllables of ordinary human speech, nevertheless pronounced his unifying force through extraordinary bodies: all men, especially those enshrined in natural history as *curiosae*, derive from one man, Adam, and the holy city continued its run uninterrupted.

For those who know how to listen, who know better than most what conforms to God's hidden plans and how to classify it, that is, Augustine and his audience, such signs of divine utterance are discernible everywhere. Hence, when trying to untangle the utterly puzzling report of Scripture that angels had intercourse with human beings, Augustine concedes that this would have required gigantic women.[47] Such women exist, however, without any recourse to the miraculous, and hence Scripture as actual history is once again confirmed.

> Even in our own times...men have been born whose bodies far exceed our ordinary stature. A few years ago, in Rome, as the destruction of the city by the Goths was drawing near, was there not a woman living with her father and

---

[44] Kelley (2007) and Trentin (2011) discuss the complex attitudes towards anomalous bodies.
[45] Aug. *doctr. christ.* 2.25.
[46] For the intensification of the description of such bodies as Augustine approaches the appointed end see Burrus (2009) 250–6; Miles (2012).
[47] Muehlberger (2013) 79–88.

mother who stood so much taller in body than all other inhabitants as to be in fact gigantic? A wondrous (*mirabilis*) crowd rushed to see her wherever she went; and what amazed them most of all (*maxime admiratione*) was the fact that neither of her parents was even as tall as the tallest men that we normally see.[48]

Right before the sack of Rome, the event that prompted the writing of the *City of God*, a historical woman's real body, both ordinary and extraordinary, spoke in circumstances where God's will was hard to discern—until Augustine explicated it.[49]

BODIES OF EXTRAORDINARY KNOWLEDGE

It is to this last aspect, the simultaneous knowability and unknowability of God's will, of his system of classification, that Augustine's extraordinary bodies also speak. Augustine made it clear that persons 'who can do things with their bodies which are for others utterly impossible and well-nigh incredible when they are reported', can easily be seen as an affront, perhaps even, for those foolish enough, as divine error.[50] However, such reactions are merely the result of ignorance: 'the man who cannot view the whole is offended by what he takes to be the deformity of the part; but this is because he does not know how it is adapted or related to the whole' (*civ. Dei* 16.8). God's plans for the whole, his signing systems, are always at the same time clear and hidden. On the one hand it is evident that all the various extraordinary human bodies, even those of children utterly unlike their parents, 'derive their origin from that one man, Adam'. Yet, on the other, even as a factual part of *historia* they are so curious and *mirabilis* that they cannot be easily comprehended or fully understood.

True, God gave to the world his Word, and to be understood the Word assumed a human body. 'That Word, being God-with-God in the beginning, has no syllables...Yet...he descended to the discrete sounds we use, for he also descended to take to himself the weakness of our human body'.[51] Human

---

[48] Aug. *civ. Dei* 15.23; cf. 15.9: *Quasi vero corpora hominum modum nostrum longe excedentia, quod etiam supra commemoravi, non etiam nostris temporibus nata sunt. Nonne ante paucos annos, cum Romanae urbis quod a Gothis factum est appropinquaret excidium, Romae fuit femina cum suo patre et sua matre, quae corpore quodammodo giganteo longe ceteris praemineret? Ad quam visendam mirabilis fiebat usquequaque concursus. Et hoc erat maxime admirationi, quod ambo parentes eius nec saltem tam longi homines erant, quam longissimos videre consuevimus.* Pliny also grappled with the question whether or not extraordinary bodies resulted from inheritance, for example, 7.33–7; Naas (2002) 306–10.

[49] For further bibliographical references to reactions to the sack of Rome in 410 see Elm (2017a) 53–8.

[50] Aug. *civ. Dei* 14.24.   [51] Aug. *En. Ps.* 103.4.1.

bodies therefore speak of the divine, but as the extraordinary bodies demonstrate, what they say cannot easily be deciphered. For example, the fact that God revealed himself through the Word incarnate, through Christ's body, does not mean we know God better the closer we make our own body approximate what we think Christ's human body looked like. Those who think that they can achieve greater comprehension of the divine by disciplining their bodies to resemble that of Christ are utterly mistaken. Extraordinary bodies are better embodiments of the unknowability of God and hence of the operation of his grace than ascetic bodies *wrongly* acquired, because God created them thus: they are *mirabilia* by divine design and not as the result of human will.[52]

Their marks of difference or apparent defect are not the result or consequence of individual volition or of a person's life or actions, either good or bad. Though persons with extraordinary bodies share the defects of mankind, born from Adam and hence inheritors of his guilt *per originem*, their external marks of difference unlike wounds or scars do not, according to Augustine and in contrast to much ancient thinking, point to any particular interior moral failure or social inferiority.[53] Nor are they marks of particular virtue, since they do not result from extraordinary transformative endeavours on the part of human beings.[54]

Instead, they are the living embodiment of divine design, and hence—through their uninterrupted presence—also portents of the appointed end. To flesh out this impression further I would like to return briefly to the beginning of Book 16 (rather than to Book 22, where Augustine tries to visualize bodies at the proper end, in the heavenly city).[55] Just prior to his detailed engagement with the extraordinary bodies of the *historia gentium*, Augustine discussed the foundation of Babylon by one of Noah's descendants, Nimrod. Nimrod, who happened to have been a giant (*gigante*), had founded Babylon at a time when all men were united by speaking only one language. Such unity gave strength, but that strength gave rise to arrogance and excess. 'For they proposed to build [Babylon] to a height so great that it would, as they said, 'reach onto heaven'; although we do not know whether this referred to a single tower...or to all the towers' (*civ. Dei* 16.4).

When God noticed that the inhabitants of Babylon were building a tower intended to reach his own realm, he punished them for this affront by

---

[52] Anon. Rom. *On Wealth* 9.3; Pel. *Ad Dem.* 1; Jacobs (2000) esp. 724–35. Though some, like the persons described in *civ. Dei* 14.24, are able to induce their extraordinary states at will, they have been given their faculties at birth, not because they strove to achieve them.

[53] Hence, these bodies do not signal disability in the modern sense; Garland (1995); Kelley (2007); Claes and Dupont (2017). For additional bibliography on the social significance of scarred bodies, see Lössl (1999); Salazar (2000) 127–58; Elm (2017a) 68–72, (2017c).

[54] Pel. *Ad Dem.* 2; Goff (1991).

[55] For discussions of the bodies in Book 22 see Burrus (2009) 250–6 and Hunter (2012).

confounding the languages, creating confusion, and scattering Babylon's inhabitants over the earth: 'the name Babylon indeed means Confusion'. Excess, arrogance, and the resulting desire to create an extraordinary city caused Babylon's 'deformity'. The city 'whose wonderous construction (*mirabilem constructionem*) is mentioned by historians of all nations (*gentium... historia*)... [and] that took precedence over all others, where the king had his dwellings as in a capital city (*metropolis*)... was not brought to the perfection, which, in their proud ungodliness, its builders had expected' (*civ. Dei* 16.4).

Augustine's evocation of Babylon's gigantic expanse echoes, I think, Pliny's description of Rome, where he imagined that if all its buildings were 'piled up together and placed in one huge heap (*universitate... acervata et in quondam unum cumulum coiecta*), such grandeur would tower above us to suggest another world concentrated in one place was being described' (Pliny, *HN* 36.101). Both, Babylon and Rome had been and still were gigantic cities that defied (or tried to defy) time and space. These extraordinary cities represented extraordinary empires, in strength, size, height, and the expanse of time they endured. However, Babylon's (and hence Rome's) extraordinary characteristics led to *superbia* and a lack of humility and thus to the flawed conclusion that the city's extraordinary characteristics merited for its founder and inhabitants an approach to divine immortality through their own strength and volition.

God's rebuke was swift and to the point. 'Because the power of a ruler resides in his tongue, it was there that Nimrod's pride was condemned' (*civ. Dei* 16.4). Nimrod's tongue was split, one language divided into many, the city destroyed, its inhabitants dispersed in confusion across the earth, mankind irretrievably divided into multiple nations to clarify that God accomplished things 'in ways that are hidden from us, and which we cannot understand' (*civ. Dei* 16.4).

Augustine inserts his extraordinary bodies into this state of mankind, irretrievably differentiated and unable to comprehend each other's language. Nimrod, too, had an extraordinary body; like the city he founded, he too had been a giant. Being a giant per se did not lead to his mutilation, his divided tongue. Only once he abused his extraordinary strength to expand his and his city's powers excessively, beyond the human realm towards the divine, did his gigantic proportions mutate into something illicit, only then was his body disabled and the instrument of his power, his tongue, muted.

When Scripture too became silent, other extraordinary bodies spoke. Whilst their characteristics located them at the outer edge of human imagination, made them into *rara mirabilia* and *curiosa*, these bodies were created such by divine design, not human will. Through them, God demonstrated that 'Babylon... runs its course next to the city of God' (*civ. Dei* 16.1). 'He is always present everywhere, but he is said 'to come down' when he is performing an action on earth that is miraculous (*mirabiliter*) because beyond the ordinary course of nature... by so doing... he reveals his nature' (*civ. Dei* 16.5). Even in the depth of Babylonian confusion, God's unifying power is active, bringing together the most extraordinarily diverse human beings, then as now and hence in the future: the city of God and the *civitas terrena* both include extraordinary bodies as symbols of the divine will to create in ways that are both beautiful and manifold.

7

Classical Decadence or Christian Aesthetics?

Libanius, John Chrysostom, and Augustine on Rhetoric

Raffaella Cribiore

In appropriating part of the title of an essay of Carol Harrison on Augustine's *De doctrina Christiana*,[1] I am aware that both elements need to be considered in evaluating how Christian rhetoric veered off from pagan classical rhetoric. And yet, are these elements sufficient to explain the new modes of communication? In this chapter, I would like to investigate to what extent what Santo Mazzarino[2] called 'the democratization of culture' impacted both pagan and Christian rhetoric. Years ago this historian used the expression 'democratization of culture' with regard to late antiquity, opposing past concepts of decadence of the Roman Empire. He devoted only a few pages to this idea and did so in connection with the spreading of Christianity, but scholars nowadays recognize that the concept could be adapted to a global experience of culture and strive to identify its application.[3] Mazzarino mainly discussed the situation of city versus country with a focus on fourth-century Rome but the concept of 'democratization of culture' is useful to interpret many phenomena.[4] In what follows I would like to apply it to education and especially to rhetoric. I am arguing that though it is obvious that Christianity addressed larger and more mixed audiences, and that this factor made a conspicuous impact on cultural communications, this phenomenon started earlier and not only in Christian milieus.

The new eloquence, which was more spontaneous and emotional and required less respect for the rules, does not appear to have been strictly

---

[1] Harrison (2002).
[2] Mazzarino (1988) 433–647 and on the cultural characteristics of the period, 743–8; see also Mazzarino (1989) 63–4. Mazzarino concluded that Christianity had democratized culture. This must have been only one factor amongst others.
[3] See Giardina (2001).   [4] Brown (1997) 13.

associated with religious identity but was the result of a trend to acquire education with a minimum amount of effort that was visible already in the writings of pagan rhetors such as Libanius.[5] The desires of families to have their sons enter promptly in society called for a rhetorical practice that was less laborious and more conducive to immediate success, for example as advocates or in the retinue of an official. A fourth-century sophist could not do much to retain students and 'forcing' a supposedly dull youth to learn the theory was counterproductive.[6] In confronting the unexpected success of one of these students, Severus, who left during the second year, Libanius reported the opinion of some who attributed it to the hiring of a magician observing the boy's lack of elegance and style.[7] Severus was at the beginning of his training but was able to surpass everyone in court. This was a lesson that Libanius found hard to digest.

Like Libanius, both John Chrysostom and Augustine had a profound knowledge of rhetoric and were sophisticated and formidable speakers, yet they became aware that the categories of cultural catalysts had changed and that the observance of the principles of eloquence had to be less rigorous. In works such as Chrysostom's *De sacerdotio* and Augustine's *De doctrina Christiana*, one perceives the authors' discomfort at contemplating the lower standards of learning but also feels their recognition that change was affecting the aristocratic nature of classical culture. Both Christian writers 'lived in an age oppressed by reverence for the expert', as Peter Brown said,[8] but had to acknowledge the new criteria for success. Culture was a product of society, with the result that inflexible standards could not exist at that time.[9]

In discussing pagan and Christian eloquence, it is fundamental to exercise some caution. I have tried to show in my last book on Libanius, *Libanius the Sophist: Rhetoric, Reality, and Religion in the Fourth Century*, that there are many more details to the seemingly black and white picture of pagan and Christian relations and that this sophist was not deaf to the discourses of traditions apparently different from his own.[10] These two groups were not written in stone, were not bounded and enduring, but were in continuous evolution.[11] Christian and pagan allegiances were defined not only by practices and convictions but also by social relations. Distinctions could be perceived even in the oeuvre of a single author by keeping in view the dictates of different

---

[5] In this chapter I will be using the term 'pagan' throughout. It is a historical construct but is still the most convenient term; see Jones (2014).

[6] Cf. *Or.* 38.2–3: the student Silvanus leaves the school and practises as an advocate.

[7] See *Or.* 57.3–5; Casella (2010) 93.   [8] Brown (1967) 264.

[9] *DDC* 2.4.5. I am aware that it is impossible to talk about a single Christian discourse because there was a series of them, complementing each other and overlapping as Averil Cameron (1991) 5 remarked. Here I will focus on homiletic eloquence.

[10] Cribiore (2013).

[11] On moderate pagans emerging from Libanius' letters, cf. Cribiore (2013) 168–81.

genres. The letters of Libanius give a more nuanced view of this period and of his close interactions with certain Christians, whilst a sharper dichotomy between pagans and Christians emerges from the speeches where the sophist presented himself rhetorically as the spokesman of pagan beliefs.

Pagan and Christian youths frequented the same schools and no distinctions were perceivable amongst them in terms of attendance and curriculum, at least not in the higher grades. The school exercises from Graeco-Roman Egypt provide some help in further illuminating the situation. They show that Christian students with minimal literacy (perhaps in monasteries) wrote crosses or chrisms (the Christ monogram similar to a cross) at the beginning of their elementary exercises, but these Christian signs disappeared at higher levels of instruction so that nothing distinguished Christian literary exercises from those of pagan classmates.[12] Before Julian's Edict of June 362, pagans did not grudge Christians *paideia* and Christians taught Greek literature and philosophy at every level and were accepted by their pagan colleagues. Several students of Libanius became powerful Christian figures. Amongst them were John Chrysostom and Amphilochius 4.[13] The latter wrote a didactic epistle, *Iambi ad Seleucum*, which recalls the work of another student of the sophist, Basil of Caesarea, who supposedly followed the classes of Libanius in Constantinople or at Nicomedia. In his last years, Basil left a testimony of his appreciation of classical *paideia*, *Ad adulescentes, On the Value of Greek Literature*.[14] Another Christian student of Libanius is less known, Optimus 1. In his letter 1544 the sophist complimented him for his excellent Greek.[15] On his return home, Optimus continued to make and deliver speeches, but at a certain point was elected bishop of Agdamia in Phrygia and later of Antioch in Pisidia.[16] After Julian, some Christians were confident that they were going to be able to absorb entirely traditional pagan culture delivering fully rhetorical speeches but had to wrestle with the limitations of the times.

In his book *Changes in the Roman Empire*, Ramsey MacMullen entitled a chapter 'Distrust of the mind in the fourth century'.[17] Since the aim of that chapter was to throw into relief the period's firm hostility to intellectualism, its tone was unabashedly negative and was seemingly tied to theories of 'decline'. How different were the words of Averil Cameron: 'It was a period of

---

[12] Cribiore (1996) 87–8. Nathan Carlig has recently made a list of Christian exercises. The list of the papyri can be found at: 'Papyrus scolaires grecs et latins chrétiens' (2012), http://web.philo.ulg.ac.be/cedopal/judaica-et-christiana/. Cf. Carlig (2013).

[13] On Chrysostom see below. Cf. *Ep.* 634 sent to Amphilochius 4 PLRE 1; Cribiore (2007) 240 (appendix I, text no. 16).

[14] Wilson (1975). Basil addressed his nephews. Basil's text is further examined later in this chapter.

[15] Cribiore (2007) letter no. 155.

[16] Cf. Socrates 7.36, 20, who includes Optimus in a list of bishops transferred from one see to another.

[17] MacMullen (1990) 117–29.

unprecedented literary energy and the rhetorical education thus revived was to continue long afterwards'.[18] It cannot be denied, however, that notable cultural changes had taken place. A gradual development of specialization was visible, for example in the legal training that complemented literary rhetoric. Libanius responded bitterly to the change.[19] Manuals that summarized knowledge started to circulate accompanied by commentaries and paraphrases of literary texts that had to take the place of the originals.[20] Texts in question-and-answer format, which belonged to school practice and to the culture of conversations, debate, and disputation, provided intellectual games of persuasion. This format was employed in medical and mathematical texts and in a wide range of technical literature, such as grammatical and rhetorical treatises.[21] Technical literature flourished and practical value dictated the transmission of a text.[22] As Guglielmo Cavallo has shown, a 'consumption literature' attracted new classes of readers with, for instance, epic texts in paraphrase, biographies, or, in the Christian milieu, apocryphal Gospels and Acts of the martyrs.[23] Learning was subdivided in manageable portions and consisted of more easily digestible pills. In a period of social and cultural changes, a fast absorption of notions, easily obtainable results, and tangible success mattered more than before.

From the early fourth century onwards, 'the cream of the provincial aristocracy were making their careers in state service'.[24] An important question is how much rhetorical education affected social success. Was a strong rhetorical background a sine qua non for a gubernatorial office? Libanius had a very uneven relationship with governors, as is evident especially from the second part of his *Autobiography*.[25] Their rapport usually depended on their appreciation of his rhetorical ability. He considered hostile those who did not attend the delivery of his speeches and did not follow the persistent (and unwelcome) advice he constantly gave them. He dismissed wholeheartedly those who possessed only Latin literacy (like Festus in Or. 1.156) and presented them as complete ignoramuses. A good education had to be the chief quality for a governor because the manner in which an official governed was a direct reflection of his upbringing. When Libanius launched personal and bitter attacks against some officials whom he considered incompetent or brutal towards the common people, he attacked first their lack of a classical

---

[18] Cameron (1998).   [19] Cribiore (2007) 205–13.
[20] On earlier technical texts, see Fögen (2009); on authors of technical works, Horster and Reitz (2003); see Moreschini (1995).
[21] Volgers and Zamagni (2004); Leith (2009).   [22] See McCabe (2007).
[23] Cavallo (2001). Much of this 'letteratura di consumo' was found in Egypt. Cf. Pecere and Stramaglia (1996).
[24] Mitchell (2014) 193–201, at 193.
[25] He composed the first part from section 1 to 155 in 374 and the second that runs from there to the end between 374 and 393 when he presumably died.

education.[26] He showed once that he was startled by the unexpected success of a certain Heliodorus who had become governor without possessing a classical education in rhetoric. This man had become familiar with the laws by frequenting the law courts and then became rich and famous by practising oratory.[27] The explanation Libanius gave of this story of success that was unjustifiable in his eyes is telling. He clarified that people believed that Heliodorus had *really* gone through the mill of an education in rhetoric and thus they had rewarded his supposed upbringing. Even in moments of disappointed hope, the sophist tried to convince himself that rhetoric was the key to success, but bitter disappointment jumps up from many of his pages.

In encomiastic orations, *paideia* and the respect of justice appear as the chief virtues of governors. Libanius celebrated the incorruptibility, disregard for wealth, and just behaviour of governors whose conduct he approved of.[28] Likewise Himerius extolled the justice of magistrates as an alliance of their love of the Muses. Thus Cervonius in *Or.* 38 was 'the eye of Justice and the Law and the prophet of the Muses and Hermes'.[29] In praising another governor, Hermogenes, Himerius also hailed his cultivation of justice and his education, saying that a god had brought him to Greece as proconsul of Achaea so that rhetoric would be youthful.[30] Yet, turning to another form of evidence, the verse epigrams on stone that celebrated the attainments of governors are surprising to a degree.[31] These inscriptions were engraved on buildings, fountains, and statues, and date from the third to the fifth centuries. They almost never allude directly to governors' attainments in *paideia* but insist only on their building activities and administration of justice. Though justice is an omnipresent theme, it represented an ideal and should be considered the counterpart of the literary and legislative sources that attacked governors' misdeeds. The epigraphical evidence is incomplete but from there one might evince that a high level of education was not a strict requirement for advancement. It is interesting that Gregory of Nazianzus in a letter to Olympius also omitted *paideia* amongst the attainments of governors whilst praising their justice and honesty.[32]

Libanius could do little to slow down this process. An examination of the length of attendance of his students[33] reveals that by far most remained in Antioch only a few years and took what I have called 'the short path to rhetoric'.[34] The sophist never said precisely how long a complete education

---

[26] Cf. the governor Tisamenus (*PLRE* 1: 916–17) in *Or.* 33 who was accused of withdrawing from rhetoric even though he was of a good lineage and his father had been a rhetor.
[27] *Or.* 62.46–8. Heliodorus (*PLRE* 1: 411).   [28] See, for example, *Or.* 50.19.
[29] He was the proconsul of Achaea, *Or.* 38.9.
[30] Himerius *Or.* 48. Hermogenes *PLRE* 1: 424–5.
[31] Robert (1948). See Cribiore (2009).   [32] *Ep.* 140; Olympius 10, *PLRE* 1.
[33] See Cribiore (2007) 323–7, appendix I.
[34] Cribiore (2007) 174–83. The image of a shorter path going up to the hill of rhetoric is taken from Lucian's *The Professor of Rhetoric*.

should take and used vague expressions such as 'the whole or what is necessary' but it is clear that he would have liked to lock his students in the process of *paideia* forever.[35] His ideals of creating academic alter egos clashed with reality and with the plans of parents. Reacting strongly to the personal *insult* he felt he received from those who favoured other disciplines at the expense of rhetoric, he said: 'You dishonoured my teaching chair, adding to the injuries of this critical time, and bringing the Greek language, which was already bespattered with mire, into greater dishonour. You caused me to toil amidst a small group of students, all but proclaiming in a clear voice: "Fathers, most foolish of all men, avoid these rocks on which you waste your seed. Send your sons instead to rich Rome, where one can reap the fruits that bring success"'.[36]

His lamentations, however, were not completely unrealistic. Notwithstanding the duration of their attendance, his former students were not willing to continue cultivating the art. The whole of *Oration* 35 concerns the disappointment of Libanius because of their passive behaviour and silence in the council. He compared them unfavourably with other young men who were active in the council, insisting that rhetoric needed to be cultivated regularly otherwise it vanished.[37]

> Your natural intelligence was able to receive the art and you spent in addition no little work, but the time afterwards was not the same because those students held on to what they had acquired but it slipped away from you. The cause is that they are in touch with texts but you would rather touch snakes than books; they did not prefer horse races, which are life's profit for you; you neglect everything else and only pay attention to how one driver will surpass another.

Rules had to be continually refreshed and contacts with the ancient authors had to be frequent and renewed periodically. The discipline of rhetoric was gruelling and demanded constant commitment. In *Or.* 62.21–3, Libanius insisted that those who acquired knowledge of Roman law after rhetoric were unable to retain the rules of rhetoric that inevitably faded. In *Or.* 40.6 he presented 'the plight' of one of the sons of a certain Alexander who had sent his children to Rome to learn Latin rhetoric.[38] When the youth came back to Antioch, it seems that he had completely forgotten Greek rhetoric. 'He was no better than a slave nor a phantom since he did not say anything nor did he pay attention when anyone spoke: he so shrank from using his mouth that even nodding assent was exhausting for him.' Naturally Libanius gloated.

Centuries before, Quintilian in Rome had argued that a rhetor had to practise all the time and had to study everywhere. Mastering the rules of

---

[35] Cf. *Or.* 55.12 and 32.   [36] See *Or.* 40.5.
[37] See Cribiore (2007) 153 and *Or.* 35.13. Cf. Himerius *Or.* 63: exercises should follow a progression from the easiest to the most difficult.
[38] The sophist considered Latin and shorthand as disciplines that rivalled Greek rhetoric.

rhetoric took long but keeping them fresh had to be a daily preoccupation. A rhetor who wished to maintain the excellence he had acquired had to use some strategies. He had to cultivate writing and speaking every day even when he was occupied with business and had to practise before a group of people whose judgement he trusted. Only then did a composition and superficial verbal ability acquire power.[39] We will see that John Chrysostom followed Libanius in maintaining that daily practice was indispensable but had to witness the growing nonchalance of the times.

It is uncertain for how long John Chrysostom attended Libanius' school. Since he resided in Antioch, he did not have a previous teacher of rhetoric in a different province. Judging from his rhetorical expertise and what Wendy Mayer and Pauline Allen call 'the full range of his rhetorical tricks',[40] his attendance must have been rather long.[41] The traces of his rigorous education are visible throughout his sermons. The principles that he states in *De sacerdotio* 5.1–8 betray the student of Libanius. This is one of those treatises that appeared in the second half of the fourth century to define priestly duties and the new episcopal model.[42] In spite of the fact that they were written in different periods, the image they presented was similar because of the same social, cultural, and rhetorical background of the writers. One of the appeals of *De sacerdotio* is that we seemingly catch Chrysostom almost off guard as he remembered the training he had received and the frustration he encountered whilst preaching in his first years. This work has been criticized for lack of consistency and because preaching occupies too large a space (one-third of it) but it can be very helpful in revealing Chrysostom's initial struggles and in pointing to the audience he had to confront. I suggest that the few contradictions that appear in this work are especially interesting because they are indicative of his disappointed expectations. He had left the school of Libanius a few years earlier and his passion for rhetoric is tangible as well as his awareness that many Christian preachers did not try to reach good standards because their audiences were unprepared and loved to be entertained.

In books four and five, Chrysostom mentions that a future priest and preacher must have a grasp of theological doctrine and must be able to serve the congregation with his sermons without looking for applause. He remarks that great toil is required from a preacher to make sermons and that he has to work constantly on them: 'He is not allowed to repeat his compositions too soon. For most people usually listen to a preacher for pleasure, not profit, like judges of a play or concert. The power of eloquence is more necessary in a

---

[39] Quintilian 10.7.27–8. He mentions the authority of Cicero regarding constant application in *De optimo genere oratorum* 4.
[40] Mayer and Allen (2000) 27–8.
[41] In *De sacerdotio* 1.5 (SC 272, 1980) his mother mentions the heavy expenditures she had incurred for his education.
[42] See Lizzi Testa (2009).

106   *Rhetoric and Religious Identity in Late Antiquity*

church than when sophists have to contend against each other'.[43] John had been exposed to Libanius' public contests and orations in Antioch and experienced the unrelenting competition of sophists. This remark and the whole of book five betray his uneasiness in the contacts with the congregation.[44] Unlike the preachers he despised and following Libanius' firm belief, Chrysostom seems to know only one way, incessant work, something that we will see Augustine rejected in the preparation of his ideal preacher.

Chrysostom does not believe that speaking ability comes from nature. A man can be a forceful speaker and even reach perfection in the art but he needs daily application:[45]

> Though a man may have great power as a speaker (which you will find in few people) still he is not excused continuous effort. The art of speaking comes not by nature but by learning. Even if a man reaches perfection in it, it may abandon him unless he cultivates its force by constant application and exercise. So gifted people have even harder work than the unskilled. The penalty for neglect is not the same for both but varies in proportion to their attainments. Nobody would blame the unskilled for producing nothing remarkable but gifted speakers are pursued by frequent complaint from all, unless they continually surpass the expectation that everyone has of them. The unskilful can win great praise for small successes. But as for the others, unless their successes are very startling and marvellous, they not only relinquish all praise, but have a host of disparaging critics.

If tradition is right, John was the favourite pupil of Libanius, who had expected that he would embark on an academic career. Sozomen (*Church History* 8.2.2) reported a charming anecdote, which surely was embellished by Christian sources, that the sophist had acknowledged John's excellence on his deathbed and had wished for him to become a sophist and a teacher. There are no letters of Libanius that mention John,[46] but we may think of him in reading a letter that refers to another student, Eusebius.[47] In this letter Libanius mentioned that he cared particularly for Eusebius who had attended his classes for the longest time. 'His effort, talent, and fortune made him an orator of a high standard. I have talked to him wishing to make him an educator of young men, but he listened to his mother and uncle and went the way he went'. Eusebius became a lawyer, John instead joined the Christian church but, for different reasons, they both denied their teacher's wish. Libanius had high standards

---

[43] 5.1. I am adapting slightly the translation of the *De sacerdotio* done by Neville (1977).

[44] Though I feel that the early *De sacerdotio* testifies to John's initial dismay in confronting the kind of rhetoric used by preachers, there is also no doubt that this piece has rhetorical overtones.

[45] *De sacerdotio* 5.5.

[46] Letters regarding John may have been included in the batch from the years 365–388. Only a few letters were preserved from those twenty-three years, either because of an accident in the manuscript tradition or because Libanius did not keep duplicates for that period.

[47] Eusebius 25 *PLRE* 1. See Foerster *Ep.* 884, Cribiore (2007) 266 (appendix I, text no. 78 dated to 388).

and both students must have experienced a very demanding teacher who had high expectations for them. When John says that those who had a predisposition for speaking were less forgiven their imperfections than the unskilled and had to work even harder, it is possible that he was influenced by school experience. As a student of Libanius, Chrysostom was aware that the question of the relationship between natural ability and training was a vexing one.[48] A good training could not remedy a lack of predisposition but education could bring nature's promises to fulfilment. Libanius never let a gifted student escape from taxing discipline. He was very harsh with pupils he considered slow of intellect and sometimes discouraged them from continuing. He forced and stimulated those of average nature but worked the hardest with those who could become his successors or occupy the most distinguished offices.

Book five of the *De sacerdotio* reveals the disappointments of Chrysostom, who met the congregation as a well-trained and accomplished speaker. In his view, audiences were unforgiving. If a speaker stumbled, people jeered at him, and yet trying to please them and looking for their applause had to be avoided because he would become the slave of their desires. He recognized that it is natural to delight in applause and that the lack of it might bring some dejection, but was determined not to make concessions to the crowds. He argued that the public, which did not care for excellent rhetoric, despised the preacher who shunned praise and who refused to deliver what people wanted. In his view, sermons should please only God and the standards of good oratory, but reality was different and the Christian crowd was not looking for excellence.

So far in the text Chrysostom projected the image of a speaker of great ability who was overlooked by an amateurish audience that could not appreciate his gifts. There are, however, some contradictions that resurface in the *De sacerdotio*. At times the carping critics change faces and appear even too capable to evaluate his power. From that deep resentment ensued a desire to harm him. John mentions in fact that, besides people with inferior tastes who punished good oratory, there were others who envied an accomplished speaker for his popularity. The consequence, however, was identical. Good oratory was always belittled:[49]

> They hate him without having anything against him except all his popularity and he must put up with their bitter envy with composure. Since they do not cover up and hide the tremendous hatred that they entertain without reason, they shower him with abuse and complaints and secret slander and open malice. The soul begins by feeling pain and annoyance about each of these things and then cannot avoid being desolated with grief. They do not attack him by their own efforts but set about doing so through others as well. They often choose someone who has no

---

[48] Cribiore (2007) 129–34.   [49] *De sacerdotio* 5.6.

speaking ability and cry him up with their praises and admire him quite beyond what he deserves.

John resented the lack of recognition of his oratorical power but in this passage he appears to acknowledge that he was not entirely unpopular. Nonetheless, those who envied him for his ability also attacked his reputation and favoured undeserving and inferior speakers. He was dismayed, annoyed, and then was reduced to grief.[50] He presented the situation as a conspiracy of which he was the victim. Of course we should not lose sight of the fact that in later years Chrysostom may have concluded that more colourful and less difficult sermons would please his congregation. He was a very successful preacher judging from the large numbers of the sermons preserved.[51] His speeches do not present the same difficulties as Libanius', concentrate on providing the same entertainment that he initially criticized, and offer vivid narrations to hold people's attention. But this is a different matter.[52]

The early *De sacerdotio* sheds light on Chrysostom's initial perception that rhetoric had started to make concessions to a different public for several reasons. In addition, what this work discloses about the cultural level of audiences puts again into discussion a question that was debated especially by Ramsey MacMullen and Wendy Mayer, who did not take into account this particular work. MacMullen, in an article written in 1989, argued that the congregations to which Chrysostom preached were made up of wealthy individuals, the natural leaders of the city.[53] These were the affluent members of Antiochene and Constantinopolitan society. This scholar based his conclusions on the mention of luxurious items in the sermons and on Chrysostom's frequent ranting against wealth. Wendy Mayer pointed, however, to the fact that this did not necessarily reflect a real preponderance of wealthy people in the congregation and argued for a more varied audience that at times included women, slaves, and visitors of different linguistic background. Both scholars discussed the social and economic status of people with little attention to their education. I would like to point out, however, that there are many degrees between illiteracy, literacy, and a rhetorical education, and that members of the prosperous class did not necessarily possess the last of these. Wealthy individuals might not be so cultivated as to appreciate rhetorical subtleties. Some Homer at the school of the grammarian was enough to qualify a person as *pepaideumenos* (educated).

---

[50] On eloquence rewarded by praise and renown, see Quintilian 10.7.17.
[51] See Mayer and Allen (2000) 39 who point to his success that the Church historians also disclose. Cf. Hartney (2004) 83–98.
[52] Dating his speeches is very arduous but a careful examination of early and late sermons would be enlightening.
[53] MacMullen (1989). On preaching places in Antioch's churches, see Shepardson (2014) 50–7.

In the *De sacerdotio*, in fact, Chrysostom reveals his low opinion of the education of the congregation. Those who could appreciate his rhetorical subtleties were very few. An undisciplined crowd, which was unable to hear and speak uncritically, gave unreliable judgements that were far from the truth. He says: 'The priest should treat those he rules as a father treats very young children. We are not disturbed by children's insults or blows or tears nor do we think much of their laughter or approval. So with these people we should not be much elated by their praise nor much dejected by their censure.'[54] He thus underlines the superiority of the preacher who is clashing with an unprepared congregation. 'It is impossible for it to be made up of men of distinction and it generally happens that the greater part of the Church consists of ignorant people.'[55] Even the rest who are better are not men of critical ability. Consequently the most experienced speaker receives less applause because only 'one or two present' have acquired a real capability to judge rhetoric. The ignorant and 'unlearned' (*atechnoi*) will consider a poor speech wonderful and charming. Here Chrysostom is not mentioning the social and economic status of the congregation but sharply disparages its degree of education. Classical rhetoric needed to adapt to new times.

In turning now to Augustine to try to understand his position towards classical rhetoric, it is significant that he wrote *De doctrina Christiana* in two phases, the sections on education in book two in 396 and the account in book four in 426–7. Scholars remark that it is clear that his hostility to traditional rhetoric started before and was not a product of his old age.[56] Mistrust in rhetoric and conflicts with philosophy were old and they went back to Plato, Socrates, and the sophists.[57] More recently in the time of the Second Sophistic they persisted in spite of the fact that some sophists performed with great acclaim and were worshipped by an enthusiastic public. In the second century Philostratus denounced the lingering prejudice against rhetoric. Whilst some people honoured greatly skilful men in other branches of science and the arts, 'even while they praised rhetoric, they suspected it as being wicked and mercenary'.[58]

In spite of the lapse of time, books two and four of Augustine's *DDC* are regarded as sharing an organic unity and pursuing the same line of argument. There are of course many similarities between the two accounts so that book four grew out of two, but I would like to focus on the differences. Like John Chrysostom, Augustine was a consummate rhetorician who had assimilated a large dose of classical education but in this work he seems to be a step ahead of John in denying its usefulness and preaching the need for a more malleable

---

[54] 5.4. See below on Augustine on the status of preachers.   [55] 5.6.
[56] He began this work in 396 but completed book three and wrote book four much later, reflecting on his experience as rhetor and preacher.
[57] See Plato's *Gorgias* and *Phaedrus*.   [58] Philostratus *Lives of the Sophists* 1.15.499.

approach to learning. A consideration of the audience—or, rather, of the different audiences—that emerge from Augustine's accounts is crucial in my view to attempt to understand his motivations. Augustine addressed specific audiences, responding to their anxieties and needs. Of course the *DDC* is a treatise, so I am not arguing here, as Éric Rebillard has done for some of Augustine's sermons, that an audience played a direct role and continued to give feedback to a preacher.[59] Yet a book is also a product of communication and originates from the interactive dialogue of a writer and his public. We will see that different audiences dictated Augustine's responses.

The account of education in book two is shorter and less extreme than that in book four. Augustine maintains that the rules of rhetoric are valid and are not reprehensible per se. They can sharpen the intellect of the learner provided he does not develop a sense of superiority. Yet, even though rhetorical precepts help people develop a better understanding, he wonders whether they are absolutely necessary because a clever person could pick them up spontaneously (something he will develop in book four). The rest of the book contains a curriculum of pagan and Christian studies, including the Scriptures, history, science, mathematics, and philosophy.[60]

In book two Augustine addresses *studiosi et ingeniosi adulescentes*, 'young men capable and studious, who fear God and seek a life of true happiness'.[61] Are these very different from the *neoi* for whom Basil a few decades earlier wrote his *Address to Young Men on the Right Use of Greek Literature*?[62] Whatever the audience was for Saint Basil (his nephews, the emperor Julian perhaps?),[63] Augustine referred to eager students who may have asked for such an account. Basil's book appears to be the original model for Augustine's curriculum but it covered almost exclusively pagan literature (poets, historians, rhetors, philosophers) asking young men to look for 'the silhouette of virtue in the pagan authors' (10). Augustine broadened the curriculum, adding the study of the Scriptures, but the method was basically identical. He advised young men who read or wished to read classical literature: 'Do not venture without due care in any learning disciplines that are pursued outside the church of Christ as if they were a means to attain happiness but discriminate sensibly and carefully between them.'[64] Not only could they find useful knowledge in all the branches of pagan learning 'but also studies of liberal education that are more appropriate to the service of the truth and some very useful moral instruction as well as the various truth about monotheism to be found in their writers. All these...that were used wickedly and harmfully in

---

[59] Rebillard (2013) 15–26.   [60] Grammar is not included.
[61] *DDC* 2.39.58.139. I am using the text and translations of Green (1995) which I adapt sometimes.
[62] Wilson (1975) dates the work to the middle or late seventies.
[63] Moffatt (1972) 74–86.   [64] *DDC* 2.39.58.139.

the service of demons must be removed by Christians'.[65] Classical *paideia* and the pagan authors could not be dismissed so easily. Christians could not reject the past altogether but needed to filter it extrapolating those that Catherine Chin called 'spolia'.[66] In his zeal to acquire a secular education, however, a student was not supposed to exaggerate devoting himself wholeheartedly to study. Augustine immediately quoted the Seven Sages' maxim 'nothing in excess'.[67] Quintilian or Libanius would have considered this aphorism an educational paradox.

The immediate audience of book four is made up of people who were expecting Augustine to expound the classical precepts of rhetoric that he had learned and taught. To them he says at the beginning of the book that his purpose was different and they had to learn the rules independently, especially if they were young and learned fast. This audience, however, is always in his mind throughout the book and he measures his ideas against them, polemically arguing for a less elaborate (but not less effective) eloquence. There is, however, another audience he is thinking of, people of mature or advanced years (*maturas vel etiam graves aetates*). He glosses them as 'those whom we desire to be educated for the good of the church' and it is the needs of these preachers that he is addressing.[68]

In the *DDC* the argument is not straightforward and there are contradictions but the main line of reasoning is clear. Whereas Libanius regarded studious application (*ponos*) as a partial remedy for lack of natural endowments, Augustine rejects rhetorical *ponos* categorically though he believes in the value of strenuous physical work.[69] The account of rhetoric and education in book two becomes more rigid thirty years later. It did not adequately cover the needs of the pool of Christian learners, at which Augustine now glanced realistically, making distinctions between clever individuals and those who were slower. He claimed that the labours of rhetoric could not remedy a lack of natural predispositions and since they involved gruelling work they had to be shunned altogether. Libanius' students learned that the art of persuasion followed strict principles, which were actually a formidable help in structuring their writing, in creating effective strategies of argument, and in problem solving.[70] The sophist and at least a young Chrysostom considered it

---

[65] *DDC* 2.40.60.145.
[66] Pagans did not create these treasures but dug them out so that Christians could appropriate them. See Chin (2008) 88-93.
[67] He quoted in Latin from Terence, *Andria* 61, but this was one of the Greek maxims of the Seven Sages that were carved on the temple of Apollo at Delphi. It expressed an ideal of moderation in all aspects of life including politics, aesthetics, and culture. Here Augustine quoted it in reference to education.
[68] *DDC* 4.3.4.7.   [69] See MacCormack (2001).
[70] Consider the advice of Quintilian 10.3.13-15 to the student Secundus: only structure and not sudden inspiration will allow him to write.

fundamental to practise the rules daily so that rhetoric would not slip through their fingers. Augustine claimed that clever individuals did not need them, whilst dumb people were unable to learn them. Those without practice of writing and speaking could not assimilate them and moreover, even if the precepts of rhetoric could be drummed into them, they were of no benefit.[71] Somewhat paradoxically, Augustine maintained that rather than assist the uncertain speaker, the rules actually hampered his delivery. An orator could not keep them in mind and speak at the same time because his attempt to remember them made him forget what he was saying. 'Indeed', he said 'there are hardly any who are capable of doing both, that is, speaking well and considering as they speak the rules of eloquence which promote good speaking. There is a danger of forgetting what one has to say while working out a clever way to say it.'[72] In addition, Augustine (115) regarded as the foremost duty of a preacher making himself understood. A matter might be quite difficult to grasp in its complexity but a mode of expression should not be. Meticulous observance of the precepts of classical rhetoric would hamper understanding.

In my view, another sign of the rather low opinion that Augustine had of his audience of preachers is that the student of eloquence curiously appears to regress and is brought back to his early years. He had stated already in book two (62) that it was impossible to teach someone how to walk by giving him minute details about the front and back foot and how to move joints and knees. Children walked instinctively, not by paying attention to rules but by actually making steps.[73] Thus in book four he stated: 'Infants acquire speech only by learning the words and phrases of those who speak to them. So why should the eloquent not be able to acquire their eloquence without the traditional teaching?'[74] This is what he observed around him: 'Isn't this precisely what we see in practice?' He remarked that very many speakers who did not know the rules were more eloquent than those who had learned them. The spontaneous assimilation not only of eloquence but also of grammar would take place through reading and listening to the speeches of eloquent speakers and not by learning through the methods of a Quintilian or a Libanius. Augustine claimed that if children grew up and lived amongst adults who spoke properly they would not have any need of the art of grammar and its rules because they would learn by habit.

So, returning to the initial question of this essay, classical decadence or Christian aesthetic? To properly understand the condition of rhetoric in the fourth to the fifth centuries we cannot divorce it from the state of other disciplines. If we judge by the standards of traditional rhetoric from Plato to

---

[71] DDC 4.3.4.10.
[72] DDC 4.3.4.11. Augustine here is not regarding rhetoric as a help to writing good prose.
[73] DDC 2.37.55.134–5.   [74] DDC. 4.3.5.12.

the third century, undoubtedly those were lowered. One (but not the only) cause was the changes in the composition of the audience. Such changes, however, were at work already within a general pool of privileged students who could afford the high tuition of rhetorical schools but chose a limited attendance in search of prompt and easier success. Parts of the *DDC* are devoted to the need of preachers who had to spend their time in preparation wisely and thus had to dispense with preceptive rhetoric.[75] Yet I think that it is reasonable to suppose that Augustine was also witnessing the change in the transmission of knowledge and in rhetorical modes of communication that were generally more accessible. These concerned not only students but also a general public, both pagan and Christian, that was impatient with traditional, painstaking methods. He must have been aware to a degree of the existence of epitomies, Virgilian *centones*, paraphrases, even perhaps abridgements of the speeches of his cherished Cicero.[76] In 4.10.27, Augustine called the useless key of rhetoric 'golden', perhaps with an allusion to the privileged elite who had used it in the past, and claimed that the Christian wooden key could open many doors. Fewer pagans and Christians were willing to spend an inordinate amount of time locked in education. Traditional, rigid education with its inflexible rules that necessitated a strong commitment for many years did not respond anymore to changing circumstances. In the hands of pagans and of those Christians who were interested in eloquence (two very fluid groups) the golden key had indeed lost its lustre.

[75] Fulkerson (1985).
[76] See Horster and Reitz (2010). On abridgement of Cicero, see Dyck (2010).

8

'Very great are your words'

Dialogue as Rhetoric in Manichaean Kephalaia

Nicholas Baker-Brian

INTRODUCTION

Considerable attention has been paid over recent years to the genre of dialogue and its role in ancient literature stretching from classical Athens to late antiquity.[1] In a collection of essays entitled *The End of Dialogue* from 2008, the editor, Simon Goldhill, conceded that dialogue as a genre 'is always a conflicted, self-conscious and multiple form',[2] whilst nonetheless challenging the possibility of dialogue's existence—defined as 'the generous, sincere and engaged exchange of views'[3]—in early Christian literature. The role of dialogue, and more broadly the importance of disputation, in late-antique literature has long been acknowledged. Studies by Averil Cameron and Richard Lim have proved especially influential in shaping understandings of the relationship between dialogue, rhetoric, and religious identity.[4] In a recent reply to Goldhill's introduction, Cameron proposes a more 'generous definition of dialogue'[5] than the classical philosophical model argued for by Goldhill, in order to draw attention to the ways that Christians in late antiquity and the Byzantine period transformed dialogic forms to meet their own needs. The broader definitional approach taken by Cameron undermines the established idea that Christianity closed-off dialogue—both real-world and literary instances—based on an incorrect assumption of a preoccupation with orthodoxy,[6] and in so doing Cameron promotes the important but rarely discussed

---

[1] The quotation in the chapter title comes from 2 Ke 335.388.26–9. Translation Gardner et al. (2018). All translations from 2 Ke are taken from this edition.
[2] Goldhill (2008) 4.   [3] Goldhill (2008) 7.   [4] Cameron (1991); Lim (1995).
[5] Cameron (2014) 59.   [6] So, Goldhill (2008) 5–8; cf. Cameron (2014) 7–21.

Dialogue as Rhetoric in Manichaean Kephalaia 115

feature of dialogue's rhetorical role. Cameron cites the maximalist interpretation of rhetoric proposed by Chaïm Perelman as 'the entire universe of argumentative discourse',[7] in order to illustrate the importance of the genre of dialogue as central to the rhetorical cultures of late-antique and Byzantine Christianity. For Cameron, dialogue is nearly always rhetorical, and it was thus instrumental in effecting religious change ('Christianization') and reinforcing the concomitant concern with establishing religious identity.

Despite the criticism levelled at his argument, Goldhill, in his brief overview of dialogue in the Talmud, asks a very important question, 'Is dialogue only possible for the marginal?'[8], to which he offers no real answer. One area to which we can perhaps profitably apply his question is Manichaeism, a tradition whose sect-like or heretical status—according to its portrayal in normative Christian literature—gave it the appearance of a marginal religion within the broader context of eastern-leaning dualist ('gnostic') movements that began to appear in earnest during the second century CE. Amongst the most important surviving works from Manichaeism are the two *Kephalaia* (*Chapter-Books*), both of which qualify as 'dialogic'—an emphasis employed by Cameron to convey the sense in which a text may contain features of dialogue, 'express[ing] debates and arguments and differing points of view',[9] whilst not qualifying as instances of actual philosophical dialogue in the sense deemed to be exemplified by the Socratic model (an interpretative standard which is also now beginning to unravel[10]). These *Kephalaia* comprise two codices identified by their page headings as, *The Chapters of the Teacher* (1 Ke), and *The Chapters of the Wisdom of my Lord Mani* (2 Ke), which were amongst the Coptic works recovered from near Medinet Madi at the southern end of the Fayyum in 1929.[11] Neither Goldhill's volume nor Cameron's monograph make any reference to the *Kephalaia* codices, serious oversights in light of the depth and importance—hadith-style collections of teachings attributed to the 'founder' of a universal religion—of Manichaean dialogic evident in the chapter collections, although both studies do acknowledge the role of dialogue elsewhere in late-antique Manichaeism.[12] This chapter argues that Manichaean kephalaic material was instrumental in augmenting core aspects of the identity of the religion—as a cumulative, and universal faith—by portraying Mani as a forensic figure whose explanations for the origin and workings of the universe trumped all others. In this chapter, I focus in particular on a selection of chapters from 2 Ke (327–38), isolating those instances whereby the portrayal centres on Mani establishing his authority through dialogue. Rather than close down discussion in a triumphalist

---

[7] Arnold (1982) x; Cameron (2014) 1.   [8] Goldhill (2008) 8.
[9] Cameron (2014) 20.   [10] Cameron (2014) 12–13.
[11] See the detailed discussion in Robinson (2013) *passim*.
[12] Clark (2008); Cameron (2014) 26–8.

fashion, Mani's success is presented as genuinely rhetorical: the divine nature of the wisdom (*sophia*) conveyed in his lessons (*homilia*) persuades his opponents that no additional explanation can improve on the one that he has offered. Thus, a figure called Goundesh, a sage based in the palace of Shapur I who features in a number of chapters in 2 Ke, declares at the end of one dialogue: 'For that lesson that you recounted (is) established (in truth?), (and) is a better one than mine! From today (what is proper for me?) is silence when I follow (after?) you'.[13] 1 Ke is by far the better-known text of the two chapter collections. Research on 2 Ke, in the Chester Beatty collection in Dublin, was until recently confined to a facsimile edition produced by Søren Giversen,[14] and a small number of interpretive studies including a formative article by Michel Tardieu.[15] However, the work has recently given up some of its treasures as a result of the labours of Iain Gardner, Jason BeDuhn, and Paul Dilley, who in 2015 produced a collection of essays on aspects of the contents of 2 Ke,[16] followed in 2018 by the first in a series of editions with an accompanying English translation of portions of text.[17]

The 2018 edition of 2 Ke comprises pages 343–442 of a codex that is estimated to have been around 496 pages in length.[18] Portions of the codex are relatively well-preserved, whereas other portions have suffered significant deterioration (including the dialogue between Mani and Shapur I in chapter 338, pp.407–8). Editorial work continues on this *Kephalaia*, and a summary of publication plans for the remainder of the text is provided in the latest edition. The editors argue that the two works comprised 'a formal unit', since the chapter numbers appear consecutive.[19] Whilst prior scholarship has emphasized the apparent differences between the two chapter collections,[20] both *Kephalaia* represent the Manichaean response to a wider, cultural phenomenon of the period that has been characterized as, 'the constant reconfiguration of bodies of knowledge in late antiquity'.[21] In both collections, Mani is the figure of authority who makes the case for the 'Manichaean' interpretation of religious spheres of knowledge, comprising topics relating to cosmology, anthropology, and ethics. Whilst not overstating the differences between the two works, it is apparent that both approach their roles in reconfiguring knowledge in distinct ways. Indeed, the ancient authors of the chapters and the compilers and editors of the codices appear to have conveyed the contrasts in format and purpose between the two works through the inclusion of attendant page headings. These headings serve as paratexts[22] by providing a singular identity to an occasionally disparate collection of teachings, and which in turn augment the intertitles that accompany each chapter division.

---

[13] 2 Ke 335.388.26–9. [14] Giversen (1986). [15] Tardieu (1988).
[16] Gardner et al. (2015). [17] Gardner et al. (2018). [18] Gardner et al. (2018) 3.
[19] Dilley (2015a) 16; and the comments of Gardner (2015a) 75–7.
[20] cf. Tardieu (1988). [21] Pettipiece (2013) 60. [22] See Jansen (2014) 1–18.

Whilst both *Kephalaia* are didactic without being necessarily dialectical (a feature noted for the earlier portions of 2 Ke also[23]), the *Chapters of the Teacher* is a collection characterized more by monologue than by dialogue. Mani's lessons are addressed to his disciples who have prompted him through their questions. Mindful of not imposing a framework over the text, it is reasonable to suggest that an insular quality defines 1 Ke since Mani is for the majority of the work teaching his immediate circle of disciples. This is not, however, an observation that can be applied across 1 Ke, and some chapters bear comparison with examples in 2 Ke, such as 1 Ke 76 (Mani's journeys), and 1 Ke 89 (Mani in dispute with a Nazorean). Thus, 2 Ke is characterized by considerably more dialogic exchanges with non-Manichaeans (a vassal king, other holy men, and Shapur I himself) and by Mani moving around the Sasanian Empire (Ērānšahr[24]). In contrast to 1 Ke, 2 Ke conveys the portrait of Mani and his wisdom on the move, in turn reinforcing Mani's own self-proclaimed hope for his church (*ecclesia*) from his *Šābuhrāgān*,[25] which was further articulated in 1 Ke (chapter 151, following Wolf-Peter Funk's numeration[26]), that 'it is provided for it to go out from all cities, and its good news attains every country'.[27]

1 Ke has, therefore, qualified as an example of the genre of *erōtapokrisis*, a literary format comprising questions and answers that was utilized across a broad range of religious traditions during late antiquity.[28] Texts of this type are dialogic, although the nature of the dialogue—certainly in the case of 1 Ke—is of a somewhat limited nature. Paul Dilley has correctly identified (to my mind) the genre's adoption by the Bardaisanites (i.e., *Book of the Laws of Countries*) as the most likely immediate influence on the development of the kephalaic tradition within Manichaeism.[29] With the awareness, however, that the Manichaean religion was geographically medial from the earliest days of its existence, situated nexus-like amidst the Roman 'west' and the Sasanian 'east', Dilley has sought to advance discussion of the genre of the *Kephalaia*, moving away from the tendency to evaluate it according to purely Graeco-Roman models and towards an appreciation of the ways in which cognate genres from Iranian or Indian traditions may have influenced the compilers responsible for the texts. In order to appreciate more suitably the hybridized blend of monologue, dialogue, and didacticism evident in the chapters of the recent edition of portions of 2 Ke, Dilley has proposed the influence of cognate literary forms on the authors and compilers of *The Chapters of the Wisdom of My Lord Mani*: thus, '... the genre of the *Kephalaia* was likely understood, depending on the cultural location of its authors and readers, as a modified example of Graeco-

---

[23] Dilley (2015a) 16.   [24] MacKenzie (1998).   [25] See Lieu (2006).
[26] Funk (2002).   [27] Gardner and Lieu (2004) 266.
[28] See Pettipiece (2013); Dilley (2015a) 19–24; also the comments by Cameron (2014) 20–1.
[29] Dilley (2015a) 19.

Roman *erōtapokrisis*, Iranian *frashna*, or Buddhist dialogue. This generic polymorphy reflects the production and circulation of the *Kephalaia* across the two distinctive borderlands of Syro-Mesopotamia and Gandhara'.[30] Both collections, however, likely underwent an identical process of development. This process is complex and contested. However, by way of some brief remarks, I reproduce here the hypothetical stages of textual history and transmission for the *Kephalaia* that Timothy Pettitpiece proposed in his monograph on 1 Ke: first, the oral and written traditions attributable to Mani himself emerged; these were then promoted in oral and written forms by Mani's disciples in both Syriac and Greek; some of these traditions were organized into 'proto-*Kephalaia*', likely by disciples active in western regions (i.e., the limits of Sasanian expansion in the west, and across the western frontier with the Roman Empire), which can be evidenced by the existence of *Kephalaia*-genre material separate from the Coptic volumes in, for example, Iranian Manichaean texts;[31] and finally, 'the translation, redaction, and collection of what came to be an enormous amount of *Kephalaia* material into large volumes, such as those found at Medinet Madi, exclusively in Coptic'.[32]

The chapters from 2 Ke under discussion (327–38) engage with the established idea of wisdom as a form of cultural capital, the exposition of which legitimizes the one who propounds it. Evidence for Mani's own works indicates the priority placed on the formulation of his teachings as divine wisdom,[33] and the central nature of this idea in 2 Ke again highlights the role played by these chapter collections in reinforcing, ramifying, and interpreting core aspects of the identity of the Manichaean religion.[34] Mani himself, according to the evidence for schema that posited the ten 'advantages' of his religion over prior traditions,[35] identified his teaching as wisdom and knowledge (cf. Col. 2.2–3) that was 'above and better than those of the previous religions'.[36] In the kephalaic version (1 Ke 151) of the advantage,[37] Mani claims to have added, 'the writings and the wisdom and the revelations and the parables and the psalms of all the first churches' to his own wisdom in a way that, quoting Dilley, is 'selective and supercessionist'.[38] The broader context for the disputatious treatment of wisdom in the *Kephalaia* is the long-running conversation about the value of 'alien' wisdom—its alterity defined according to its perceived difference from Greek conceptions of knowledge—which intensified with the concerns of post-Hellenistic philosophy.[39] Mani's own theological claims ('Apostles of God have constantly brought wisdom and deeds in

---

[30] Dilley (2015a) 23. [31] See Sundermann (1992). [32] Pettipiece (2009a) 12–13.
[33] Dilley (2015a) 24–32. [34] Pettipiece (2009a) 3–19. [35] Lieu (2006).
[36] Lieu (2006) 526. [37] See Gardner and Lieu (2004) 266. [38] Dilley (2015a) 27.
[39] See esp. Parker (2008) 251–307; Burns (2014) 20–8; Dilley (2015a) 24–32.

successive times'[40]) and the portrayal of his life in Manichaean biography—his journey to 'India' ('a very imprecise term'[41]), and his engagement with eastern-orientated systems of knowledge[42]—betray his familiarity with this cultural movement. The Manichaean awareness of these claims may either have been instigated or catalyzed by the efforts of the Sasanian court itself: Shapur I was clearly 'open-minded and receptive to new ideas'[43], evident for example in the practical support offered to Mani,[44] but it may also have been the case that the court pursued an ideology that promoted 'home-grown' Iranian knowledge, undergirded perhaps by a belief in the primacy of ancient Iranian wisdom: according to claims stated in a number of sources (collected by Kevin van Bladel[45]), Iranian/Persian knowledge became dispersed across Egypt, India, and China following the conquests of Alexander of Macedon, and it was Shapur I's father and founder of the dynasty, Ardašīr, who began efforts to reclaim this heritage. The portrait of Mani in 2 Ke, contending with and ultimately triumphing over sages whose identities within the narrative are either implicitly or explicitly 'eastern', should then be read against the wider concern with the Sasanian reclamation of epistemological 'patrimony'.[46] The very fact that a number of the dialogues conclude (e.g., 2 Ke 327.367.27; 2 Ke 337.406.9) with Mani's opponent declaring Mani to be Buddha (Coptic: *Bouddas*) serve to reinforce the impression of cultural appropriation on the part of the authors/compilers responsible for the chapters concerned.[47]

One of the concerns of 2 Ke was to advertise Mani's 'exceptional intimacy'[48] with the sages associated with the court of Shapur I. The historicity of such episodes—Mani engaging with figures in court settings—is traditionally moot.[49] The awareness that literary *exempla* depicting the conversion of sages, priests, and monarchs by prophets—frequently in the context of missionizing journeys, for example *The Acts of Thomas*[50] and the biography of Zoroaster[51]—were active forces in shaping Mani and his disciples' engagement with travel and patronage and their subsequent memorialization in Manichaean literature, has contributed to scepticism towards such episodes.[52] However, Mani did gain practical support from Shapur I in the form of letters that served to introduce him to regional rulers across the Sasanian Empire,[53] something akin to travel permits that made his ability to move around the

---

[40] From Mani's *Shābuhragān*, preserved in al-Bīrūnī's *Āthār*: see now Reeves (2011) 102–3.
[41] de Jong (2008) 92.   [42] Sundermann (1986).   [43] van Bladel (2009) 42.
[44] *Manichaean Homilies* 48.2–9 in Pedersen (2006).   [45] van Bladel (2009) 30–9.
[46] Dilley (2015a) 31–2.
[47] For insightful commentary on references to Buddha in 2 Ke, see Pettipiece (2009b).
[48] Whitmarsh (2007) 33, with reference to Philostratus' portrayal of his place in 'the circle' of Julia Domna.
[49] Sundermann (2009).   [50] Parker (2008) 297–301.   [51] de Jong (2014).
[52] Tardieu (2008) 31–2; cf. Sundermann (2009); Baker-Brian (2016).
[53] *Manichaean Homilies* 48.2–9 in Pedersen (2006).

totality of Sasanian territory relatively frictionless.[54] The chronology of events concerning Mani's contacts with the Sasanian court is impossible to isolate with precision,[55] yet Mani's initial introduction to Shapur appears to have occurred *c.*241–242 following his return from the Indian sub-continent.[56] The fact that this introduction is situated towards the end of the edited material in 2 Ke (chapter 338), in addition to appearing at the very beginning of 1 Ke (1.15.24–216.1), illustrates the importance of Sasanian patronage to the master biographical narrative of Mani's life.[57] The significance of the episode's appearance in 2 Ke, however, lies in the portrayal of precisely how this patronage was acquired, namely as a result of Mani's command of wisdom in disputatious settings.

Whilst Mani's primacy as an exponent of wisdom is acknowledged in chapters prior to chapter 327,[58] it is this section in 2 Ke where the exchanges between Mani and various sages begin in earnest. The principal figure in this regard is Goundesh, who is identified as being closely associated with the palace (*palation*) of Shapur (most likely Shapur I rather than Shapur, the king of Touran, whose exchange with Mani is found in an earlier chapter [323][59]). Goundesh features in twelve chapters of the codex, and his presence plays a key role in the portrayal of Mani and the dialogic presentation of his teachings. In the partially preserved opening section of chapter 327, Goundesh's credentials as a master of discourse are outlined in the following terms: '...some people of philosophy, the people of truth, came and they...He [Goundesh] debated with each one of the...and he was victorious over them in his speech and his discourse (*homilia*)'. Here and elsewhere, Goundesh's expertise as a victor over opponents 'in the wisdom of philosophy' (380.26) is emphasized, thereby intended perhaps to indicate his expertise as a dialectical-dialogic thinker. He is also identified (chapter 336) as one of the king's (Shapur's?) favourites. It is later disclosed in chapter 337 that Goundesh was a pupil of a certain Masoukeos (395.26–7) who also seems to have been a familiar figure at the Sasanian court and whom Mani also bests in debate. Goundesh's performances are witnessed by disciples of Mani, which they report to him, in particular 'the way that he debated with the people, being victorious [over them]...they told the Apostle [Mani] about him, the way that he debates with the people and catches them and binds them with the words that he...to them'.[60] How precisely Goundesh's identity functioned in these chapters remains an open question. The sage's place in Manichaean literature has long been identified: he appears in a series of fragments in Parthian (M6040

---

[54] An idea conveyed, perhaps, by Mani's warm reception at the court of Shapur, the king of Touran, 2 Ke 323.353.28–9. See the discussion in BeDuhn (2015a).
[55] Sundermann (2009). [56] Sundermann (1986). [57] Gardner (2015a) 82.
[58] For example, 2 Ke 322.350.6–7; 2 Ke 323.356.12. [59] See BeDuhn (2015a) 56–66.
[60] 2 Ke 327.365.3–6.

and M6041), in texts bearing the heading, 'The Wīfrās of the Path'—wīfrās equating to 'homily' or 'sermon'[61]—which depict Gundēsh engaging Mani in debate. Whilst the content of these fragments bears very little relation to the dialogues in 2 Ke,[62] the Iranian fragments are a witness to the circulation of *Kephalaia*-genre material independently from the great Coptic collections of the fourth century. With reference to the Parthian fragments, Werner Sundermann noted the possibility that Gundēsh may render the name of an Indian sage (Govindeṣa or Guṇādhyeṣa), but he was unable to verify the claim.[63] More recently, Jason BeDuhn has suggested that the name may bear some relationship to Gondeisos, the name of a waterway in the province of Khuzestan, thereby denoting a person or sage 'of Gund-dēz', similar to the way Bardaisan denotes, a 'son of the (river) Daisan'.[64] Thus, whilst we cannot say with certainty that Goundesh is emblematic of a non-Iranian (alien) intellectual tradition in the chapters preserved in 2 Ke, the portrayal of his standing in the Sasanian court, his role as a conduit for religious teachings that are distinct from those of Mani, and his familiarity with 'eastern' traditions—including what appears to be his willingness to share an anecdote from the life of the Buddha (327.367–68)—makes his defeat by Mani all the more potent for the cultural context of the *Kephalaia*.

Mani overcomes Goundesh very early in the cycle of stories as presented in 2 Ke. This may be a literary contrivance in order to transform the renowned Goundesh into a disciple of Mani at an early stage, or it may simply be due to the absence of narrative finesse—the 'coarse redaction'[65]—of the codex as a whole. In chapter 328, following a (fragmentary) exchange over the merits of responding with a 'yes' or 'no' to a holy or wicked command ('So look, I have told you about the "yes" which has two forms [of] good or evil. I have also told you about the "no" which [has the] two forms of good and evil'), Goundesh paid homage to the Apostle [Mani], saying 'From now on, [I will be your] disciple! Because there is no wiser man...'. There is considerable variety in the nature of the debates between the two figures, but cosmology, anthropology, and ethics are unifying features of the dialogues. Their initial exchange (chapter 327) focuses on the core components of Manichaean theology, namely the dualism of good and evil and the commandments of righteousness (fasting, prayer, alms-giving). Whilst Goundesh is familiar with both as categories of religious thought and action, it is the depth of penetration of Mani's replies that reduce Goundesh to silence (366.27). Thus, on good and evil, Mani teaches about the nature (*phusis*) of good and evil via a series of qualifying questions ('Have you known [the nature of the] good? What it is?

---

[61] Sundermann (1981) 85–8; BeDuhn (2015a) 66–72. [62] BeDuhn (2015a) 66–9.
[63] Sundermann (1981) 87 n.3; Sundermann (1992). [64] BeDuhn (2015a) 71–2.
[65] Gardner et al. (2018) 105 n.17.

122 *Rhetoric and Religious Identity in Late Antiquity*

Or who is the doer [of the good? Or] where he will go?'[66]) Although much of the lesson is unrecoverable, it is evident that Mani is portrayed as offering Goundesh an explanation that he has never previously considered. Mani's forensic ability stands therefore in contrast to Goundesh's lack of insight.

The author(s) of the Goundesh-material demonstrates this feature most keenly in the portrayal of Goundesh's style of teaching. In chapter 332, Goundesh is sat with Mani whilst the latter reads from his *Treasury of Life*. One of Mani's 'canonical' works that was deemed to have a special significance for the eastern development of Mani's teachings,[67] the chapter appears to disclose important information about the *Treasury*'s structure when Goundesh speaks about the 'fourteen words/lessons (*logoi*)' contained in the *Treasury* (377.9), and which Mani also describes as being a 'new book' (374.23).[68] Prompted by Mani, Goundesh recognizes the value of the new work: '...nothing compares to it in my regard; there is no greater and stronger than this book' (375.1–2), and so offers a parable to highlight its importance. The *Treasury* is like a precious stone owned by a king that brings him seven advantages. For instance, the stone ameliorates the difficulties faced by the king against his opponents in battle, including improving the situation of his camp when the environment is against them, for example, by sweetening bitter waters when cast into them, and overcoming famines by bringing abundance to his camp 'So, in the manner of this great, honoured [stone], this is indeed the way with this great book, the one about which you proclaimed these fourteen *logoi* to men (for they are written?) in it, just like this stone, that it gives benefit in everything'.[69] Whilst Mani applauds the comparison of the *Treasury* to the precious stone of the king, the Apostle pushes Goundesh to interpret in greater depth the constituent parts of his parable. Goundesh admits that he is unable to progress any further with his interpretation: 'Says Goundesh to him: I (have given you a parable), the one that I recited, because I had heard it. But I do not know the interpretation (*hermēneia*) of this parable, what it signifies.'[70] The format of qualifying questions is used once again to develop the dialogue: '[Then] says the Apostle to him: Listen to me. Now I will tell you what is the interpretation of this parable. Who is the king? Or what is his precious stone? Or what are these things that give benefit in that stone?'[71] According to Mani's interpretation, Mani himself is the king and the stone is 'the great wisdom of differentiation', that is, knowledge of good and evil, which has been granted to Mani by God: like the stone's role for the king in matters of combat, Mani's wisdom is also 'weaponised',[72] being the thing

---

[66] 2 Ke 327.366.11–13.
[67] Purportedly the book that Mar Ammo recited before Bagard, the spirit of the east, prior to entering the Kushan, according to an Iranian source: see Klimkeit (1993) 204.
[68] On the *Treasury*, see now Stein (2016).   [69] 2 Ke 332.377.5–10.
[70] 2 Ke 332.337.24–6.   [71] 2 Ke 332.377.27–378.1.
[72] Cf. Gardner and Lieu (2004) 111.

that determines the success of his and his community's endeavours in the face of adversity. Mani's interpretation of the parable is therefore intended to highlight Goundesh's partial apprehension of the truth, and reinforce Mani's authority. Indeed, the portrayal of Mani's interpretation of the parable of the king and the gemstone augments the portrayal of Mani in 2 Ke and elsewhere in Manichaean literature (e.g., *Homilies* 61.16–18) as supreme interpreter. The portrayal in chapter 341 of Mani's interpretation of passages from the 'law of Zarades', an early textual compilation of teachings associated with Zoroaster,[73] and sayings written 'in the law of Jesus',[74] regarding the parameters of forgiveness in relation to acts of blasphemy, offers a further example of the Apostle unravelling another thorny parable (417.12–13) following questions from Pabakos, 'a faithful catechumen'.[75]

The impression of a grand agonistic struggle is rarely conveyed in the dialogues between Goundesh and Mani. More frequent is the portrayal of Goundesh approaching Mani like a dutiful disciple and surrendering with little resistance to Mani's superior wisdom. Thus, dialectic as a core feature of 'classical' models of dialogue[76] is hardly a concern of the majority of the sage chapters of 2 Ke. There are, however, some exceptions. One example is chapter 331, where Goundesh's question to Mani about how the soul of a sparrow-foetus can come out of its egg when there is no visible 'door nor break' in its shell, prompts a lesson on the pneumatic nature of the soul. The chapter's focus is on 'solving' the conundrum posed by Goundesh, and no claim is made about the superiority of Mani's lesson. The chapter, however, stands out for this reason. More commonly, it is the rhetorical force of the claims voiced by Mani's vanquished opponent that promote the superiority of Manichaean wisdom. In chapter 332, Goundesh signals his assent to Mani's lesson at the end of the debate over the *Treasury* by comparing himself to a champion (Coptic: *čalašire*) who had fought and conquered twelve other champions but who came up against a stronger combatant—the text is illegible at this point—and appears to have been defeated by him. The meaning of the comparison is clear, but the following gloss is added:

> Until I saw you I debated with those who are wise; I was victorious over them in the wisdom of philosophy. Now, see, you have been victorious over me in wisdom and...also, those that you do [more than] me. There is no righteous person (so good?); there is no sage equal with [you]. You have been victorious over me![77]

In chapter 337, following a lesson outlining the numerical association between the apostolic foundation of Mani's church and the arrangement of the heavens, Goundesh's repentance (*metanoia*) is reported to Masoukeos, his former

---

[73] See Dilley (2015b). [74] For details, see Gardner et al. (2018) 153.
[75] For discussion, see Dilley (2015b) 116–17. [76] Cameron (2014) 12–14.
[77] 2 Ke 332.380.25–9.

teacher, who responds in turn with an angry missive. Goundesh's response (392.28) to Masoukeos highlights the superior nature of Mani's wisdom against the wisdom taught to him by Masoukeos by way of a series of analogies. For example, Goundesh explains how he 'wore' his former wisdom like a person who wears a set of dishevelled clothes: not realizing that he was wearing a collection of rags, it was only when he encounters a group of finely dressed nobles (*eugenēs*) in a great city that the person realizes how poorly attired he is. The pride felt by the person in his appearance prevented him recognizing his true state: both Goundesh (327.365.11) and later Masoukeos (337.396.10) are portrayed as proud sages who fail initially to recognize the deficient nature of the wisdom they espouse. As Jason BeDuhn has noted, chapter 337 is an awkwardly conceived *kephalaion*, appearing 'to be a piece of continuous narrative that has been rather arbitrarily fitted into the kephalaia-genre thanks to its initial question',[78] the purpose of which is to build 'a narrative climax' into the following chapter (338), in which Mani's agonistic engagements culminate with the appearance of Iodasphes, the one who is, according to the intertitle of the chapter, 'greater than Masoukeos and Goundesh'. Masoukeos' capitulation occurs after a largely illegible debate about the origin of souls and the gradual diminution of the world. In contrast to Goundesh's statements of effusive praise of Mani's wisdom, Masoukeos declares simply, 'your [wisdom] (surpasses) all the wisdom that is in this world', following which he is reduced to silence.[79]

The climax of the sage cycle occurs in chapter 338, where Mani enters into debate with Iodasphes. At the beginning of the chapter, Iodasphes is proclaimed, 'the wise man who is from the east',[80] and who is 'greater than Masoukeos...[and] superior to Goundesh'.[81] The setting is once again at the court of Shapur (I?), where Iodasphes appears and challenges the king to find a sage within his kingdom who is able to defeat Iodasphes in debate and thereby confirm Shapur's reputation:

> Then says Iodasphes to Shapur the King: You are Shapur the King, the great king: the [master?] lord of a multitude of lands. There is no other king greater than you... There is no other kingdom equal to your kingdom. (You are) rich in every thing, except this one only which you lack: You do not have a single person in your kingdom who is able to give a defence (*apologia*) to me and debate with me and be victorious [over me].[82]

Iodasphes is etymologically derived from *bodhisattva*,[83] the Sanskrit term denoting a 'Buddha-to-be',[84] the significance of which is developed at the

---

[78] BeDuhn (2015a) 70.   [79] 2 Ke 337.400.22–3.
[80] 'The land of the east' denoting, in the Manichaean *Synaxeis* codex, India; see the reconstruction in Funk (2009) 121, and the brief note by Gardner (2015a) 83 n.21.
[81] 2 Ke 338.400.30–401.1.   [82] 2 Ke 338.401.4–10.
[83] See the discussion in Gardner (2015a) 83–4.   [84] Roebuck (2010) xvi.

end of the chapter following Iodasphes' admission of Mani as Buddha.[85] The figure of Kirdīr (Coptic: Kardel) ('the son of Artaban'), a dignitary at Shapur's court (to be distinguished from Kartīr the *mobed*[86]) who is attested in the trilingual inscription of Shapur I at Naqš-e Rostam,[87] introduces Mani to the royal court as one who can win a victory over Iodasphes.[88] The dialogue between Mani and Iodasphes is based on the question of the world's eternity ('Do [you: sc. Mani] declare about this established world (that) it is eternal, having existed from its own self from eternity? Or else...was it built (and) produced by (the...of) God...?'[89]) which, as Gardner has pointed out is one of the fourteen unanswerable questions put to Gautama Buddha by his devotees, and became associated with followers of Būdāsaf (which van Bladel notes is the Iranian-Arabic rendering of *bodhisattva*[90]) according to Bīrūnī's *Chronology*.[91] As Gardner notes, the reference to this debate and the appearance of Iodasphes highlights the importance of 2 Ke as a text that anticipates 'traditions otherwise only evidenced in texts from many centuries later'.[92] The broader cultural significance of the role of these markers of the east for both Greek and Iranian imaginations, specifically wisdom from 'India' and its attendant mystification,[93] thereby appears to be emblematized in the figure of Iodasphes. Their placement in a Sasanian (courtly) setting is a further indication of the extent to which the author(s) of the chapter and the compilers of the *Kephalaia* acknowledged the veracity of the nativist claims for wisdom that had been conceived by the Iranian ruling elite.

Mani's answer[94] to Iodasphes' conundrum prompts an effusive description of Mani's place in the firmament of stars[95] (thereby offering a further indication of the role played by the *Kephalaia* in mediating early ideas about *bodhisattva* [as Būdhāsaf], in this instance as a conduit for astrological teachings in India[96]). The ultimate importance of Mani's success in overcoming Iodasphes in debate rests with Mani's emergence—following the challenge laid

---

[85] 2 Ke 338.406.9.   [86] Skjaervø (2011).
[87] Gardner (2015a) 84–8. Kartīr the *mobed* is also listed in the inscription of Shapur. See the discussion by Rubin (2002).
[88] 2 Ke 338.401.15–23.   [89] 2 Ke 338.402.21–5.   [90] van Bladel (2009) 116.
[91] See Gardner (2015a) 87–8 n.37. Also, Gardner et al. (2018) 125. On the eternity of the world as a tenet of Būdhāsaf, see the remarks of Crone (2012).
[92] Gardner (2015a) 87–8 n.37.   [93] Parker (2008) 251–4.
[94] The remains of Mani's response in chapter 338 to the 'unanswerable question' of Iodasphes are such that it is difficult to judge the precise nature of the apostle's reply. On page 402, line 25 f., Mani begins addressing Goundesh (rather than Iodasphes) with the statement, '...this constructed world is a product. It was fashioned (by the...) of God. There is a (?) beginning for the product that has come about...' The illustrative core of Mani's explanation can only be partially reconstructed (pages 403–4). The debate concludes on page 406, lines 4–8) with Mani saying (to Iodasphes?): 'If this world were eternal thing, there would be nothing new revealed in it. Rather, that which exists in it from the first day, it also is that which you will find apparent in it (now). There is nothing new would...forth in it; not also would they (?) generate in it.'
[95] 2 Ke 338.406.2–9.   [96] See van Bladel (2009) 115–18.

down by Iodasphes—as claimant of the crown of sagacious pre-eminence in the territory of Shapur I. It is Kirdīr, the son of Artaban, who conveys the news of Mani's success to Shapur, which in turn results in Mani attending Shapur's court, and engaging him in a discussion. As noted, these portions (chapter 338, pp.407-8) of the codex are illegible, but it may reasonably be surmised that it is at this point that Mani gains the favour of Shapur, which leads to the endorsement memorialized in the *Homilies* (48.1-9). As Gardner has highlighted, how the account of this incident in chapter 338 of 2 Ke squares with the other accounts (in 1 Ke, and also in al-Nadīm's *Fihrist*[97]) recounting Mani's first contact with Shapur remains an important question.[98] However, an attempt at reconciling these different narratives may be missing the point of the episode as it came to be embedded in the *Kephalaia*. The overall aim of the sage cycle from chapter 327 to chapter 338 is relatively straightforward: it is intended to demonstrate Mani's persuasive brilliance in the face of challenges brought by a series of religious authorities who, if not demonstrably, are at least tacitly representative of 'alien wisdom'. According to the *Kephalaia*'s portrayal of Mani, his success against these authorities derives from the divine nature of his wisdom.[99] As Mani explains to Iodasphes: 'Ask me everything that you want! I will explain it to you, for the wisdom (given by?) God (is) from me (?)'[100] Thus, whilst the explanations attributed to Mani in 2 Ke cannot be regarded as dialectical, they certainly qualify as 'dialogic' in the sense of a term denoting an emergent genre that blended the concerns of dialogue with the concerns of rhetoric. In the light of the dialogic strain running through the Coptic *Kephalaia*, the Manichaean contribution to the development of dialogue and rhetoric during late antiquity should no longer be overlooked. In the hands of Manichaeans, dialogue became an especially potent rhetorical instrument for demarcating the religion's claim to a distinctive identity. Distinctiveness was a familiar feature of Manichaean identity: its roots lay in the supersessionary claim of Mani that his revelation not only complemented but also completed the 'wisdom and knowledge' of his prophetic predecessors (as seen in the remains of his *Shābuhragān* and manifest in later versions including in 2 Ke[101]). However, the 2 Ke conveys a more assertive portrayal of Mani with regard to how his religious rivals were engaged and subsequently defeated in debate. Further work is required in order to comprehend the precise historical circumstances underlying the

---

[97] See Reeves (2011) 38.   [98] Gardner (2015a) 88.
[99] According to chapter 342, Mani's wisdom was acquired following a rapture when he saw both the land of light and hell with his own eyes.
[100] 2 Ke 338.402.17-19.
[101] See Reeves (2011) 102-3 and 2 Ke 342.422.28-423.12. For commentary, see BeDuhn (2015b).

representation of Mani as an icon of dialogue. Its origin, however, evidently lay in the efforts of Manichaeans to establish a closer relationship with the rulers of Sasanian Persia where the impression of Mani as a combative figure was understood to align with the competitive ethos of elite culture at court. Mani's ultimate fate, however, illustrates the sizeable gulf that existed between religious rhetoric and political reality in third-century Iran.[102]

[102] Cf. Gardner (2015b).

9

'A Christian cannot employ magic'

Rhetorical Self-fashioning of the Magicless Christianity of Late Antiquity

Maijastina Kahlos

'A CHRISTIAN CANNOT EMPLOY MAGIC'

In the *Life of Hilarion*, Jerome tells us of the circus races in Gaza. There is a citizen called Italicus, *municeps Christianus*, who keeps horses for the races and competes with an unnamed *duumvir*, thus a man from the leading elite of the city. This *duumvir* is said to be a worshipper of Marnas, an important local deity.[1] With a few words Jerome outlines a highly competitive atmosphere in the urban life between the Christian and pagan population.[2] The account is in all probability fictive but reveals the attitudes and mental universe of the time as well as the tensions in society in Gaza.

According to Jerome, Italicus' rival has commissioned a sorcerer (*maleficus*) to speed up his own horses and slow down the other horses using some demonic incantations (*daemoniacis quibusdam imprecationibus*). The Christian Italicus seeks help from the Christian holy man Hilarion, in Jerome's words, 'not so much for damaging his opponent as for protecting himself' (*non tam adversarium laedi quam se defendi*).[3] At first Hilarion is reluctant because one should not waste prayers on such trivialities. Italicus answers that

---

[1] Hier. *Hilar.* 20.

[2] Being terms formulated from outside, words such as pagans and heretics should be read with inverted commas throughout this article.

[3] Hier. *Hilar.* 20. This kind of fear was not necessarily groundless. We have plenty of evidence that competitors in horse races sometimes attempted to harm each other by magical means: curse tablets with the aim of harming the horses and charioteers of rival circus teams have been found in ancient circus areas in Carthage and Beirut: Jordan (1988) 117–34, (1994) 325–35. *CTh* 9.16.11 (in 389) was issued against magic used in the circus; Amm. 26.3.3, 28.1.27, 29.3.5 reports charioteers who were punished for having used magic. In the sixth century, Cassiodorus

this is his public duty (*functionem esse publicam*) and he is acting not for his own benefit but out of duty. Thus, Italicus also belongs to the local elite and sponsoring races is part of his communal duties.

Two members of the local elite are in competition but Italicus makes his personal concern a public cause for Christianity. He struggles 'against the enemies of God' (*contra Gazenses adversarios Dei*) who were insulting, not so much Italicus but Christ's church (*ecclesiae Christi insultantes*). Moreover, Italicus states, 'a Christian cannot employ magic (*nec posse hominem Christianum uti magicis artibus*), but rather he can seek for help from the servant of Christ'—hence the words in the title of my chapter.

Persuaded by this argument, Hilarion has his drinking cup filled with water and given to Italicus who then sprinkles the stable, horses, charioteers, carriage, and the barriers of the course with the water. Jerome paints a lively image of the excitement at the races, the adherents of both circus parties in eager anticipation. The horses of one team almost fly to the finish line, the others are slowed down. Consequently, Italicus wins the race, which raises a great clamour in the people of Gaza, and even pagans themselves cry that the god Marnas has been overcome by Christ (*Marnas victus est a Christo*).

Italicus' pagan rivals were furious at their downfall and urged that Hilarion should be executed as a Christian sorcerer (*Hilarionem maleficum Christianum ad supplicium poposcerunt*).[4] In line with the prevailing worldview, the Gazans understandably interpret Hilarion's activity as counter-magic. Jerome's narrative reveals that there always was a risk for a Christian ritual expert of being labelled a practitioner of magic. Jerome does not think so: for him, Hilarion is a holy man whereas the opponent's ritual expert is a sorcerer (*maleficus*) as Jerome clearly states. However, how could an ordinary person in late antiquity make a distinction between proper holy men and sorcerers?

CHRISTIAN SELF-FASHIONING IN RHETORIC: A MAGICLESS SELF-IMAGE

Modern scholars have the same problem. I agree with Stephen D. Ricks who states, '...where religion ends and magic begins on the religion–magic

---

(*var.* 3.51) writes about a victorious charioteer called Thomas who was blamed for using magic by his rivals. For competition curses, see Graf (2000) 54–5; Ogden (1999) 33.

[4] Hier. *Hilar.* 20. Jerome also states that Italicus' success made many people convert to Christianity. Miracles play a significant role in earlier Christian accounts of conversion; for conversion stories, see MacMullen (1981) 95–6 (who regards miracles as crucial for conversions) and Shumate (1996) 27 (who questions MacMullen's view).

continuum depends upon the stance of the person speaking or writing, since it is not possible to divide religion and magic on the basis of any objective set of criteria'.[5] Therefore, I understand the concept 'magic' as a discursive category that is dependent on the perceiver—an ancient perceiver as well as a modern one. Consequently, 'magic' is a socially constructed object of knowledge whose content and formulations vary according to different social contexts and circumstances.[6]

How did people in late antiquity understand magic? Almost no one considered their own rituals and beliefs as constituting magic. Magic was understood as, if not always illegal and illicit, something socially disapproved of and deviant. At its worst, magic was comprehended as surreptitious and harmful practices, detrimental to individuals and the whole community. Therefore, nearly every group and all ritual experts did all they could to keep away from the label of magic.[7] In their avoidance of the label of magic, Christians did not differ from other religious groups.

In this article, I discuss the use of rhetoric in building and reinforcing Christian identity in which magic had no part to play. The image of magicless Christianity was enhanced in many contexts—apologetic treatises, tractates, sermons, and especially hagiography. I show that, in situations of rivalry between ritual experts—holy men and/or magicians—it was imperative for Christians to refute accusations of magic and redirect the slander against their opponents. This applied to the pre-Constantinian period as well as to post-Constantinian circumstances. In these situations of rivalry, Christian writers were at great pains to create a distinction between proper Christian holy men and those others (pagans, Jews, heretics) who were practising either injurious magic or just harmless tricks.

Making distinctions between the proper, authorized and approved behaviour (religion) and the improper, unsanctioned, and deviant one (magic) is also an issue of authority. In analysing magic as a social discourse and discourse of alterity, we can observe the changes in power relations in late Roman society. To put it bluntly, the pattern usually follows the universal saying 'my religion, your magic', and this is how Christian writers and church

---

[5] Ricks (1995) 143.

[6] I follow the theoretical consideration of magic as a discursive formation, outlined by Stratton (2007) xi, 2–3, 14–17, 23; Stratton (2015) esp. 86 for magic as social discourse and discourse of alterity; Gordon and Marco Simón (2010) 5. According to Stratton (2007) 16, magic as a discourse provides 'an understanding of magic that bridges the gulf between those who reject the use of magic as a concept altogether and those who seek a universal heuristic definition'.

[7] This applies to most of the groups and individuals in ancient sources. However, some ritual experts in the so-called Greek magical papyri and a few Babylonian rabbis styled themselves as magicians and their practices as magic, with a positive twist. A few ritual experts are known to have adopted a self-consciously subversive stance as magicians and deliberately transgressed the religious norms of the surrounding society. Smith (1995) 18; Stratton (2007) 15, 37; Janowitz (2002) xii; Ogden (1999) 84, 86.

leaders in their rhetoric also defined the relationship between beliefs and practices they accepted and those they condemned. Ecclesiastical leaders insisted upon a Christian self-image according to which *genuine* Christians neither practise magic nor employ extravagant equipment in their rituals. The words from the *Life of Hilarion*—'a Christian cannot employ magic'—precisely represent this magicless self-image.

This magicless Christianity was already stressed in the second and third centuries, often when facing slander coming from hostile outsiders. For example, in his defence against the literary assaults of the Platonist Celsus, Origen declares that Christians exorcise demons without any strange arts of magic or incantations; instead they use only prayers and simple adjurations. Christians did not cast spells but only used 'the name of Jesus and other words from the sacred Scriptures'.[8] In the early fourth century, Eusebius of Caesarea replied to accusations that Jesus and his disciples were sorcerers and asserted that Christians did not resort to the usual magical techniques such as incantations, amulets, and magical verse even to help the sick. No disciple of Jesus had yet been proved to be a magician. No Christian had ever admitted to being a sorcerer. Christians used 'the mere name of Jesus and the purest prayers' to exorcise demons.[9] Eusebius also described Christians whose presence, glance, mere breath, and voice were enough to expel wicked spirits.[10] But no magic.

According to the magicless self-image, Christian charismatics did not need any sophisticated equipment for accomplishing their miracles. The mythicized figure of Moses, who eventually was added to the Christian assembly of holy men, was thought to show his superiority in using a wand as his *only* equipment; moreover, he resorted *only* to the power of words—verbal formulae. For instance, Origen defended Moses against suspicions of magic, stating that Moses did not do all his wonder-working with his wand (*rhabdos*) but

---

[8] Orig. *c. Cels.* 7.4; 1.6. Moreover, Origen stresses that these exorcisms are mainly performed by unlearned Christian folk. As Kofsky (2002) 200 points out, Origen himself was well-informed about those practices and beliefs that he deemed to be magic: *c. Cels.* 1.22, 1.24, 1.25, 4.33–4, 5.9, 5.46, 7.69, 8.58, 8.61. Another Christian writer, Tertullian, declared that Christians did not rely on astrology, divination, or magic. Tertullian, *apol.* 35.12: *astrologos et haruspices et augures et magos… Quas artes… ne suis quidem causis adhibent Christiani*. Tertullian's denial is connected with the idea that astrologers, diviners, and magicians try to consult the fates for emperors and makes it clear that this is a condemnable practice.

[9] Eus. *dem. ev.* 3.6. In his defence, Eusebius argues that Jesus forbade his disciples to take anything with them when sending them on their journeys. Moreover, Jesus, his disciples, and Christians in general did not want to make money from their miracles as charlatans did. In addition to money-seeking, Eusebius also mentions the thirst for glory and (sexual) pleasure as characteristics of sorcerers and charlatans. These were the basic elements in the label of magicians; see Kahlos (2015) 152–3.

[10] Dionysius of Alexandria in Eus. *eccl.* 7.10.4. See also Tertullian (*apol.* 23.15–16) on the power of the name of Christ as well as mere touch and breath, and Minucius Felix (*Oct.* 27.5) on the power of Christians' words and prayers.

also with his hands and by word (*logos*) in order to avoid the crowd accusing him of using magical tricks.[11]

This idea is connected to late-antique discussions on rituals in which a number of Greco-Roman, Jewish, and Christian writers stressed that tools and other materials were used in baser rituals, whilst in more subtle rituals there were only verbal formulae. Accordingly, the Greek writer Philostratus portrayed his hero, the miracle-worker Apollonius of Tyana, as not relying on sacrifices, prayers, or even words. The philosopher seems to have had the strictest view since he writes that only contemplation (*theoreia*) is untouched by magic.[12]

The ancient writers wanted to depict the rituals and ritual experts of their own inclination as superior in respect. Consequently, it was the rival groups that were depicted as employing all sorts of paraphernalia, incense, herbs, charms, and devices. According to Justin, the apologist and martyr, Christians used the name of God alone and this practice was better than the incantations and incense of pagan and Jewish exorcists.[13] In the early fourth century, again replying to slander against Christians, Arnobius assured his readers that Christ acted 'without the power of incantations, without liquids from herbs and plants, without any scrupulous observation of rituals, libations, and opportune moments'. Christ had no need of any *adminiculum*, auxiliary device, because he achieved all miracles in the power of his own name. Arnobius contrasted this with his opponents, who resorted to magical devices for seeing the future, curing disease, opening locked doors, silencing people, holding back the competition in races, and inciting love.[14] Later, Augustine of Hippo declared that the Manichaeans used magic arts (*per magicas artes*) 'to get unto wives of others'.[15]

Late-antique inscriptions and papyri show that, very much in line with their contemporaries, Christians also made use of amulets, charms, spells, and rituals that their bishops frequently condemned as magical. Ecclesiastical

---

[11] Orig. *Selecta in Exodum* (PG 12, 284B). Janowitz (2002) 14. Cf. a Jewish writer, Artapanus, who implied Moses' superiority to Pharaoh's magicians, depicting Moses as causing the Pharaoh to fall down mute only by a whisper in his ear: *FGrH* 726 F 3 (= Clem. *strom*. 1.154.2; Eus. *praep*. 9.27). Bremmer (2000) 221, (2002) 65.

[12] Philostr. *v. Apoll.* 7.38. Plot. *Enn.* 4.4.44. Plotinus also despised prayers: Plot. *Enn.* 2.9.14, 4.4.26. Irenaeus of Lyons (*Adv. haer.* 1.21.4) refers to an early Christian group that opposed the use of water in Christian rites. For a discussion of the equipment and verbal formulae, see Janowitz (2002) 14–16.

[13] Justin, *Tryph*. 85.3.

[14] Arn. *nat*. 1.43: Qui sine ulla vi carminum, sine herbarum et graminum sucis, sine ulla aliqua observatione sollicita sacrorum, libaminum, temporum?; 1.44: Atquin constitit Christum sine ullis adminiculis rerum, sine ullius ritus observatione vel lege, omnia illa quae fecit nominis sui possibilitate fecisse... The uses of spells that Arnobius lists are similar to those in the so-called magical papyri in Greek and Coptic.

[15] Aug. *contin*. 12.27. Graf (2002) 95. For Christian love spells, see Meyer and Smith (1999) nn.73–84.

leaders stuck to the magicless self-image according to which good, genuine Christians did not resort to magic, not even to healing devices when faced with the gravest illness of their children.[16] It was the heretics who were involved in magical practices. Therefore, it is heretical Christians who practise magic, not proper Christians, Origen writes. His manoeuvre functions in a twofold manner: first, he frees his own group of Christians from the accusations of magic and second, he undermines rival Christians by saddling them with the label of magic.[17]

THE SIGN OF CHRIST OR THE SIGN OF THE DEVIL

Augustine, Bishop of Hippo, is one of the church leaders who fashioned the magicless self-image of Christians. In the *Tractate on the Gospel of John*, he blames his parishioners who run to (as he calls them) enchanters and diviners (*ad praecantatores, ad sortilegos*) to receive remedies for their illnesses. This blame is connected with Augustine's complaints about Christians who take part in the pagan festivities of Magna Mater. Instead, he offers Christian festivals for Christians (*Ecce spectacula Christianorum*).[18] Augustine dismisses other rituals and festivities as counterfeits of Christian ones: 'For evil spirits forge certain shadows of honour to themselves so that they may deceive those who follow Christ'.[19] He rebuffs a pagan priest who claimed that the deity called the 'capped one' (*Pilleatus*) was himself a Christian, too (*et ipse Pilleatus christianus est*).[20] Whilst discussing this combination of the *Pilleatus* deity and Christ, Augustine refers to 'those who seduce, by means of amulets, by incantations, by the devices of the enemy, mingle the name of Christ with their incantations'. The reason is, Augustine states, that nowadays these people are not otherwise able to seduce Christians. He uses the metaphor of

---

[16] See Augustine's argument below.   [17] Orig. *c. Cels.* 1.57.
[18] Aug. *tract. in Ioh. ev.* 7.6–7.
[19] Aug. *tract. in Ioh. ev.* 7.6. The idea of falsification is old and already appears in second- and third-century Christian apologetics: demons try to deceive people by imitating Christian rituals, even before the birth of Christ because demons could predict the establishment of Christianity.
[20] Aug. *tract. in Ioh. ev.* 7.6. The deity referred to as *Pilleatus* is probably Attis since Augustine also discusses the festivities in honour of Magna Mater. It is not clear what the priest of *Pilleatus* implied when stating that his god was Christian. Chadwick (1993) 29 n.14 excludes the possibility that a temple of Magna Mater had been transformed into a Christian place. Sometimes pagan gods were said to be made Christian, for example, when Jerome writes about the devastation of the Serapeum in 391 (*ep.* 107.2: *Iam et Aegyptius Serapis factus est Christianus*). A plausible explanation (also given by Boin (2014) 194) is that Augustine's audience did not feel that they compromised their Christian identity by participating in the festivities of Magna Mater.

poison mixed with honey, common in ancient literature,[21] so that 'by means of the sweet, the bitter may be concealed, and be drunk to ruin'.[22] Augustine is strongly against any kind of mingling of what he regards as separate, Christian and non-Christian. At the same time, his rhetorical twist is to pile together everything he finds distasteful—festivities of Magna Mater, *Pilleatus*, amulets, incantations—into the one concoction of magic and idolatry.[23]

Augustine insists that his parishioners not seek Christ elsewhere.[24] He forbids his audience to go to the healers, in Augustine's words, 'sorcerers, diviners, and remedies of vanity' (*ad praecantatores, ad sortilegos et remedia vanitatis*) when their head is aching.[25] He complains: 'Daily do I find such things; and what shall I do?' He asks how many have died with remedies and how many have lived without remedies. 'But if one dies with such a remedy, with what confidence will the soul go forth to God?' Augustine argues that a person who has sought a cure from these healers has lost the sign of Christ (*signum Christi*) and has taken the sign of the devil (*signum diaboli*). Augustine also refers to possible objections that might arise amongst his parishioners: 'One may claim that he has not lost the sign of Christ'.[26] The voice of protest is fictive but is credible enough in this context.[27] Ordinary people from Augustine's congregation did not necessarily see their visits to healers, soothsayers, and other ritual experts as being in contradiction to their participation in Christian communal life. Nonetheless, Augustine did. He proclaims that they cannot have both signs. He exclaims: 'Woe to the double-hearted (*vae duplici corde*), to those who in their hearts give part to God and part to the devil!'[28]

As an alternative, Augustine advises his listeners to place the gospel as a phylactery on one's head rather than an amulet (*ligatura*) of those unacceptable healers.[29] What does Augustine mean here? He probably refers to little copies of gospel texts that were used as amulets. Amulets with invocations to deities, angels, demons, saints, and other mighty powers were a widespread everyday phenomenon all over the Mediterranean area. They were a kind of *koine* of prophylactic practices shared by Greco-Roman, Jewish, and Christian populations alike. Amulets were expected to provide their wearers with protection against diseases such as fever, headache, and colic as well as many other troubles. For example, John Chrysostom mentions several times the use

---

[21] Kahlos (2006a) 53–67.   [22] Aug. *tract. in Ioh. ev.* 7.6.
[23] For Augustine's views on magic and paganism, see Markus (1996) 131–9; Graf (2002) 87–103; Kahlos (2015) 158–9.
[24] Aug. *tract. in Ioh. ev.* 7.7.   [25] Aug. *tract. in Ioh. ev.* 7.7.
[26] Aug. *tract. in Ioh. ev.* 7.7.
[27] For similar fictive voices of protest in the sermons of bishops in late antiquity, see Kahlos (2016) 11–31.
[28] Aug. *tract. in Ioh. ev.* 7.7.   [29] Aug. *tract. in Ioh. ev.* 7.12.

of phylacteries in Antioch, with women and small children wearing gospel texts around their necks as 'a powerful amulet' (φυλακῆς μεγάλης εὐαγγέλια).[30]

Augustine grumbles about the use of these gospel texts for disease prevention but still regards them as a better option than the devices provided by the rival ritual experts. He says that he rejoices when he sees a person in bed, wracked with fever and pains, placing hope in nothing other than the gospel placed on the head. Augustine reminds his listeners that he is pleased, not because the gospel was used for this healing purpose, but because the gospel is in any case preferable to amulets (*quia praelatum est evangelium ligaturis*).[31] Thus, as we can see, Augustine was distressed about the use of amulets; furthermore, he was somewhat uncomfortable with the use of gospel texts as objects of ritual power. However, sacred objects used for purposes other than the ecclesiastical were far better than the options of the rivals, which he deemed magical and pagan. Placing the gospel on someone's forehead was the lesser evil—a compromise. Finally Augustine reminds his audience that the best alternative would be to use the gospel in the heart to heal the heart from sin.[32]

In his catechetical teaching, John Chrysostom also takes a negative stance towards phylacteries and incantations, especially complaining about the invocations by 'drunken and half-witted old women' whom Christians bring to their houses. Similarly to Augustine's preaching, John Chrysostom mentions the protests that his parishioners make: they defend their practices as Christian, for the female enchanter 'is a Christian and pronounces nothing except the name of God'. This is a special abomination for John Chrysostom because the name of God is used in the wrong manner. He reminds his readers that even demons uttered the name of God and they were demons nonetheless.[33] John Chrysostom stresses that good Christians should resort only to words and the sign of the cross.[34]

In a sermon commentary, John Chrysostom discusses phylacteries, with very similar expressions to those in the catechetical teaching. Wretched Christians resort to charms and old wives' fables, and 'Christ is cast out, and a drunken old woman is brought in'. People are again represented as defending themselves by arguing that their practices are Christian—saying, 'we call

---

[30] Ioh. Chrys. *hom. de statuis* 19.14; also *hom. in Matth.* 72.2. For Christian use of amulets, see Ogden (1999) 51; Janowitz (2001) 42, 56–7; Nieto (2010) 578; Gordon and Marco Simón (2010) 33, 37–8; Engemann (1975) 25, 41; Kotansky (2002) 45; Lambert (2010) 642; Magoulias (1967) 240–1.

[31] Aug. *tract. in Ioh. ev.* 7.12.

[32] Aug. *tract. in Ioh. ev.* 7.12. For the ritual power of the gospels and other sacred books, see Escribano Paño (2010) 129.

[33] Ioh. Chrys. *catech.* 2.5 (PG 49, 240). John also complains about Christians using golden coins of Alexander of Macedon as phylacteries, encircling their heads and feet with these coins. He contrasts this custom with wearing a cross that has undone the power of the devil and that is worth resorting to even for the health of the body.

[34] Ioh. Chrys. *catech.* 2.5 (PG 49, 240); *hom. Col.* 8.5 (PG 62, 357–9).

upon God, and do nothing extraordinary'. The old woman is said to be Christian and 'one of the faithful'. They claim that 'there is no idolatry, but simple incantation' (ἐνταῦθα δὲ οὐκ ἔστιν εἰδωλολατρεία, ἀλλ' ἁπλῶς ἐπῳδή, φησίν). This is, however, devil's deceit, John Chrysostom proclaims, using the same metaphor as Augustine, the deleterious drug in honey.[35]

John Chrysostom insists that good Christians would rather die and let their children die than resort to phylacteries. He parallels a mother who did not use amulets for her child with the behaviour of martyrs: 'She chose rather to see her child dead than to fall into idolatry'.[36] Augustine takes a similar stance in one of his sermons when he states that it is better for a Christian to die of a disease than resort to amulets and spells. Such rites, he explains, 'are unlawful, diabolical, to be detested and cursed'. He denounces them as the work of sorcerers and wizards (*magi*).[37]

RIVALRY BETWEEN RITUAL EXPERTS

As Jerome's narrative on Hilarion reveals, for ritual experts, including Christian ones, there was always a risk of being labelled a practitioner of magic. In competitive situations between ritual experts, it was imperative for Christians to refute accusations of magic and redirect them against their opponents. Christian writers aimed at drawing a distinction between their holy men and the magicians of their rivals by appealing to unselfish motives, thus leaning on the idea shared in Roman society that charlatans seek their own glory and financial profit whereas the genuine holy men never take rewards for their efforts. For example, the Apocryphal *Acts of the Apostles* describes the Apostles Andrew and Thomas as refusing money offered as a reward.[38]

During the post-Constantinian period, as the many different versions of Christianity were slowly expanding in the Mediterranean area, the rivalry between ritual experts continued and perhaps even intensified.[39]

---

[35] Ioh. Chrys. *hom. Col.* 8.5 (PG 62, 357–9).
[36] Ioh. Chrys. *hom. Col.* 8.5 (PG 62, 357–9).
[37] Aug. *sermo* 306E. Augustine also complains about phylacteries in Aug. *ep.* 245.2: *superstitio ligaturarum*; *enarr. in ps.* 34.1.7.
[38] *Act. Andr.* (Lat.) 7; 15–16; *Act. Thom.* 20. Other assurances: for example, Tert. *apol.* 37. Similarly, Philostratus (*v. Apollonii* 4.45) represents the Greek philosopher-miracle worker Apollonius of Tyana as refusing the money offered to him as a reward. Stratton (2007) 114; Bremmer (2002) 55.
[39] Bremmer (2002) 70 places the competition between magic and miracle in the period between the birth of Christianity and the arrival of Constantine and the Christian Empire and states that after their rise to power, Christians eliminated the contest. However, I am inclined to see the competition between magic and miracle as continuing intensively in late antiquity, as the hagiographical material indicates.

In fourth- and fifth-century sermons, theological tractates, and hagiography, magic and miracle were under vigorous discussion. Christian hagiographers in particular contrasted the two. For them, miracles were the monopoly of Christian holy men and women whilst opponents—pagans, Jews, or rival Christians—were practitioners of magic.[40] Jerome's account of Hilarion illustrates the contest between religions and the roles of magic and miracle in it. The contest goes on not only on the everyday level of the circus races, but also between the worshippers of rival deities in the Gazan community and between the Christian God and demons on the cosmic level. Similar contests on various levels abound in late-antique and early medieval hagiography.

For instance, a Christian holy man, Shenoute of Atripe, encountered resistance to his attempts to Christianize the Egyptian countryside. On his way to the village of Plewit to destroy local shrines, Shenoute is reported to have come across magical binding spells that the ritual experts amongst the villagers had buried on the way to prevent him coming into the village. Nonetheless, Shenoute finds them out and reverses the spells against his rivals.[41]

In these hagiographical accounts, the local experts are marked with the label of magician and thus distanced from the holy men whose ritual power is characterized as legitimate. Gregory of Tours contrasts the miracles of his saint, Martin of Tours, with the local healers whom he labels *sortilegi* (diviners) and *harioli* (soothsayers). Gregory contrasts their bandages and potions with the dust of Saint Martin's basilica that is more powerful than their 'witless remedies'.[42] In these accounts, the power of Christian ritual experts is depicted as coming from the Christian God, the only acceptable source, whereas that of the experts of the competing side comes from unjustified supernatural sources. The power acts are also compared in strength and effect. The miracles of Christian holy men are seen as mightier than those of rival wonder-workers. For instance, even though Augustine argues for the legitimate source and noble motivation of Christian miracles in contrast to the malicious power and selfish intentions of magicians, he also makes a comparison between the powers of the Christian God and lesser supernatural powers: magicians perform their trickeries in the name of inferior deities.[43]

---

[40] This idea was proverbially expressed by Grant (1966) 93: 'Your magic is my miracle, and vice versa', and has since been quoted in abundance, for example, Remus (1999) 270. For the relative and perspectival nature of miracle and magic, see also Stratton (2007) 8, 114; Neusner (1989b) 61.

[41] Besa, *Vita Sinuthii* 83–4. Tr. Bell (1983) 66 (CSS 73). Frankfurter (2008) 152–3, (1997) 125–6; Magoulias (1967) 235.

[42] Greg. Tur. *mirac. Mart.* 26–7. According to Frankfurter (2005) 276–7 (see also Frankfurter (2002) 165), they are probably local healers whom Gregory associates with fortune tellers traditionally held with suspicion in Roman society in order 'to mask a historical rivalry between the regional shrine of the deceased saint and ritual experts of the local milieu'. Trombley (1985) 336, 340 and Frankfurter (2005) 276–7 with a number of other examples.

[43] Aug. *div. quaest.* 79.2: per sublimiorum nomina inferiores terrent.

The mythicized Moses, as mentioned above, was adopted into the gallery of Christian holy men and his figure functioned as an exemplar when the boundaries of religion and magic were discussed, especially by Augustine. Moses was used as proof of the supremacy of God's holy men in comparison to any magician. The figure of Moses was, however, problematic since he was also regarded as one of the greatest ritual experts in the Mediterranean tradition, Jewish, Greco-Roman, and Christian alike. His name was invoked in many of those incantations and spells that ecclesiastical leaders vociferously condemned.[44] How could an ordinary person make a distinction between the accepted Moses and the censured one?

APORIA AND AUTHORITY

This leads us to the question of how an ordinary individual in late antiquity could make a distinction between proper holy men and sorcerers.[45] Here I refer to the distinction between what was permitted and legal versus what was prohibited and illegal—therefore, the difference was an issue of authority: who had the authority to define the limits of permitted practices? In distinguishing between legitimate religious activities and illegitimate ones, even the Christian clergy was not always sufficiently informed to mark out border lines clearly. Or they simply were not willing to go along with the lines that the church councils and leading bishops had set. In many regions, for instance in Gaul, Hispania, Syro-Palestine, and Egypt, the boundaries between local charismatic monks and other ritual experts were blurred.[46] Bishops and ecclesiastical councils disapproved of sorcery amongst the clergy. For instance, the council of Laodicea (around 380AD) specifically prohibited priests to act as magicians, enchanters, 'mathematicians', and astrologers (*magoi, epaoidoi, mathematikoi, astrologoi*) or to make amulets (*phylacteria*).[47]

The problematic boundaries between legitimate and illegitimate use of supernatural powers were also pondered in the *erotapokriseis* (question-and-answer) literature. For example, a seventh-century writer, Anastasius of Sinai, is still dealing with the question of how to distinguish between the two ritual

---

[44] For example, in Acts 7:22, Moses is said to have been 'taught the whole wisdom of the Egyptians, and he was powerful (*dynatos*) in words and in deeds'; also Phil. *v. Moys.* 1.5. Several spells and writings were attributed to Moses. In *PGM* 5, 109 a ritualist identifies himself as Moses. Gager (1972) 140–61; Wischmeyer (1998) 96; Luck (1999) 115.

[45] Cf. Breyfogle (1995) 450 who, when discussing the miracles of Martin of Tours, remarks 'how difficult it is to distinguish between holy man and magician' in late antiquity.

[46] For the blurred boundaries, see Frankfurter (1997) 127–30, (2002) 168, 172; Brakke (2008) 94; Wischmeyer (1998) 103; Velásquez Soriano (2010) 603, 618.

[47] The Council of Laodicea, can. 36. Klingshirn (2003) 80; Flint (1999) 345.

experts in his *Questions and Answers*. It is asked (with a reference to Matthew 7:22-3) what it means that the Lord does not recognize all miracle-workers even though they have cast out demons, prophesied, and done many deeds of power (*dynameis*) in his name. In his reply, Anastasius explains that miraculous signs (*semeia*) turn out to be beneficial, even when performed by worthless persons. He gives the Biblical examples of Balaam (Num. 22-3) and the witch of En-Dor (1 Sam. 28). Anastasius stresses that the miracles achieved even by heretics and infidels (*apistoi*) happen by the will of God and hence, the orthodox faith should not be shaken because of these signs and miracles. Therefore, one should not make a great fuss when seeing some worthless person or infidel performing miracles.[48] One might wonder if this explanation was much help in distinguishing between permitted and forbidden activities. As H. J. Magoulias argued in his research on hagiography, it was only the involvement of a saint—thus, a person with appropriate authority—that determined the legitimacy of the actions.[49]

Ecclesiastical writers such as Martin of Braga stressed that Christians should utter only prayers, in contrast to the spells that rival experts chant. He wrote that Christian prayers were a form of sacred incantation (*incantatio sancta*) and they were substitutes for the incantations (*incantationes*) of magicians and sorcerers.[50] Evagrius Ponticus compiled a collection of Biblical passages for monks who could fend off demons with suitable verses—appropriate and authorized weaponry for Christians.[51] Ritual texts have been preserved in late-antique papyri in Egypt and inscriptions in Hispania and Italy. There are curative and protective texts, texts with curses and love charms, and they cover various kinds of everyday issues, childbirth, love, impotence, diseases, horse races, commerce, and so on. In these texts, the Christian God, Jesus, the Virgin Mary, and the Apostles are mentioned, as well as angels, demons, and saints.[52] The archangels Michael, Gabriel, Raphael, and Uriel are the most powerful names. Biblical figures such as Abraham, Jacob, Moses, and Solomon are often invoked. Many of these ritual texts were probably condemned by some church authorities but possibly approved by other ecclesiastical leaders if these texts had some authoritative backing.[53]

---

[48] Anastasius Sinaita, *Erotapokriseis*: Quaest. 62, eds. Richard and Munitiz (2006). Stolte (2002) 110.

[49] Magoulias (1967) 228-69.

[50] Martin. Brac. *corr*. 16. Klingshirn (2003) 81. For the difficulties of making distinctions between prayers and spells, Janowitz (2002) 95-6 and Velásquez Soriano (2010) 616. Already Irenaeus (*haer*. 2.32.5) wanted to draw a distinction between the pure, sincere prayers of genuine Christians and the spells of competitors.

[51] For Evagrius Ponticus' *Antirrheticus* as an apotropaic weapon, see Clark (2004) 559.

[52] Egypt: Meyer and Smith (1999); Hispania: Velásquez Soriano (2010) 620-5; Italy: Manganaro (1963) 57-74.

[53] The invocations of angels were regarded with mistrust by many Christian leaders (for example, already Iren. *haer*. 2.32.5; Council of Laodicea: can. 35, around 380). Nieto (2010) 575-8.

As we saw above, Augustine was troubled about the Christian use of phylacteries, even if Christian objects were more commendable than the pagan options. For his part, Ambrose of Milan did not have that austere stance with regard to amulets as he tells us about Constantine's mother Helena who had sent her son a bridle and a diadem equipped with the nails of the holy cross. These gave the emperor 'the support of divine protection (*divini muneris...auxilium*) so that he might take his place in battles unharmed and be without fear of danger'.[54] Similarly, the power of martyrs and other saints was recognized as appropriate and in most cases received the backing of local bishops. The relics of saints were the phylacteries that were used to protect fields, heal diseases, and drive away demons.[55] Gregory of Tours illustrates the rivalry between ritual experts in late antiquity. On the one hand, he approves the phylactery equipped with relics that his father used for protection from 'the attacks of bandits, the dangers of floods, the threats of violent men, and assaults from swords'. On the other hand, he stresses that a Christian must follow the codex of the Scriptures, not 'whispered incantations, cast lots, and amulets around the neck' but this implies the ritual protection from the false, unauthorized side.[56]

THE IMPORTANCE OF BEING MAGICLESS

Magic functioned as a boundary-making concept when Christian identity, orthodoxy, and orthopraxy were negotiated and redefined. The canons of church councils produced lists of forbidden practices, thus making their definitions by means of exclusion. For instance, the *Apostolic Constitutions* (from the late fourth century) listed unsanctioned ritual experts such as a magician, enchanter, astrologer, diviner, wild beast charmer, mendicant, charlatan, maker of amulets, charmer, and soothsayer (*magos, epaoidos, astrologos, mantis, thêrepôdos, lôtax, ochlagôgos, periammata poiôn, perikathairôn, oiônistês*).[57] The Council of Ancyra in 314 forbade Christians from performing divination and following the customs of pagans, as well as bringing people into their houses for sorcery or for lustrations. Here, as in many other regulations, divination, magic, and 'pagan' customs were paralleled.[58] Similar lists were repeated in the records of succeeding councils—it is debated in present scholarship whether this may be the result of a topos, the traditional manner

---

[54] Ambr. *obit. Theod.* 41.47–51, tr. Liebeschuetz (2005) 197–8.
[55] For the power of relics, see Brown (1996) 198; Magoulias (1967) 252–6.
[56] His father's medallion: Greg. Tur. *glor. mart.* 83, 108, tr. Van Dam (1988) 108; the rival medallion: Greg. Tur. *mir. Iul.* 45, tr. Van Dam (1993) 192; Brown (1996) 105–6.
[57] *Const. Apost.* 8.4.32.   [58] Council of Ancyra, can. 24 = cap. 71, in Barlow (1950) 140.

of repeating these sorts of lists, or the factual annoyance caused by continuing practices.[59] The list is repeated in the accounts of the Council of Braga in 572 which forbade people from bringing diviners (*divini*) and especially *sortilegi* into their houses in order to cast out evil (*malum*), detect witchcraft (*maleficia*), or perform pagan purifications (*lustrationes paganorum*).[60] Likewise the Council of Trullo (in 691) banned cloud-chasers, sorcerers, purveyors of amulets, and diviners who were to be cast out from the church if they persisted in 'these deadly pagan practices'.[61]

The label of magic was by no means innocuous, and it was in the interests of all religious groups to avoid it. During the early Empire, religious groups acting on the margins, outside the public civic sphere, were already always at risk of being associated with magic or even charged with practising it. To be associated with magic was a matter of serious concern—for Christian groups from the first to the early fourth century, and for other groups, pagans, and heretics later on. Christian emperors outlawed *maleficium*, harmful magic that was performed to hurt other people.[62] In late-antique legislation, harmful magic was classified as the third gravest crime after high treason and murder.[63] What the specific forbidden rituals were varied from decree to decree and from emperor to emperor. The rulers of early medieval kingdoms continued the policies of western emperors as the words of King Theoderic show: 'It is not allowed to be involved in magical arts in Christian times'.[64] In late-antique power struggles, accusations of magic or paganism or the combination of both were used as an effective tool against political and ecclesiastical rivals.[65]

CONCLUSION

The self-fashioning rhetoric of magicless Christianity has been persuasive enough to convince modern scholars. Consequently, Christians who do not

---

[59] For a discussion of lists of forbidden practices, see Hen (2015) 183–90.
[60] Council of Braga in Barlow (1950) 140. Klingshirn (2003) 68.
[61] Council of Trullo, can. 61. Stolte (2002) 114.
[62] For example, *CTh* 9.16.9 (in 371); 9.16.10 (in 371); 9.38.4 (in 368). Escribano Paño (2010) 122; Fögen (1993) 38.
[63] *CTh* 9.38.7 (in 384); also 9.38.3 (in 367); 9.38.4 (in 368). Escribano Paño (2010) 123.
[64] Cassiod. *var.* 4.22: Versari non licet magicis artibus temporibus Christianis. Dumezil (2005) 595 n.56.
[65] Denigrations sometimes led to official charges and criminal proceedings as in the case of the Neoplatonic philosopher Sopater whom Constantine had executed because he had allegedly prevented the corn supply from arriving on time in Constantinople by magical means (Eun. *v. soph.* 6.2.10, ed. Wright (1961) 384) or in the case of the Roman senator Boethius who was charged with practising magic (Boeth. *cons.* 1.4.36–7). For the political instrumentalization of magic accusations, see Escribano Paño (2010) 123–5; Graf (2000) 59; Trombley (1993) 65.

fit into the boundaries of the magicless image have caused considerable headaches for researchers.[66] Are the ritual experts who have written the so-called magical papyri to be recognized as proper Christians or not? What about those people who resorted to phylacteries? Are those people, who use amulets equipped with relics and authorized by bishops, genuine Christians? Whose authorization is valid?

I have preferred using words such as rituals and ritual experts instead of magic—except when referring to how writers in late antiquity themselves applied the term 'magic' *from their own viewpoint* in their condemnations of certain beliefs and practices.[67] By using the word 'magic', we would bring with it all the condemnatory attitudes—the discourse of ritual censure—that have been associated with it by generations of Greco-Roman elite writers, then Christian ecclesiastical elite writers, medieval elite writers, Reformation theologians, Counter-Reformation theologians, European colonial powers, and finally modern scholars.

In Greco-Roman and Christian antiquity, making boundaries and defining what constituted proper religion and what constituted magic was a matter of authority. For example, Jerome asserted that Hilarion's miracles were not magic. Defining and making boundaries is also a matter of authority in scholarly discussions: who has the authority to define by which criteria we scholars make a distinction between religion and magic? It would be fair play to do justice to each individual and group in the past and speak of rituals and beliefs only. Thus, the question of whether Christians were involved in magic or not is irrelevant. Instead, the issue of analysing rhetoric and self-image is important because it may also reveal ruptures in ancient texts and even in our modern prejudices.

---

[66] One example is the second-century writer Julius Africanus whose encyclopaedic knowledge of healing devices, incantations, and different rituals caused some modern scholars to cast doubts on his Christianity. For a reappraisal, see Wallraff (2009) 51 who parallels Julius Africanus' *Kestoi* with the *Stromateis* by Clement of Alexandria, a writer whose Christianity is not challenged.

[67] I have adopted the term 'ritual expert' from Frankfurter (2005). In recent scholarship, the distinction between magic and religion has been challenged over and over again, for example, Smith (1995) 16: 'substantive definitions of "magic" have proven empty in concrete instances and worthless when generalized to characterize entire peoples, whole systems of thought or world-views'; Gordon (1999) 168: 'Magic may be a practice, but more than anything else it is a shared construction, a child of the imagination'; also Gordon and Marco Simón (2010); Meyer and Mirecki (1995); Neusner (1989a) 4–5; Ritner (1995) 43–4; Ricks (1995) 143; Remus (1999) 258–98; Meyer and Smith (1999) 1–5; Meltzer (1999) 13–14; Frankfurter (1997) 131; Frankfurter (2002) 159; Janowitz (2002) xiv–xviii.

Part III

Modes of the Representation of Religious Identity

10

The Rhetorical Construction of a Christian Empire in the *Theodosian Code*

Mark Humphries

INTRODUCTION

The *Theodosian Code* (*Codex Theodosianus*), initiated by Theodosius II (408–50) at Constantinople in 429 and promulgated by that same emperor's first *lex novella* in 438,[1] has long provided scholars with a challenging resource for understanding how the Christian Roman Empire functioned.[2] Part of the challenge derives from the condition of the text itself: its complex transmission means that only about three-quarters of the original Code has survived.[3] But even what does survive is not always easily explained. Scholars have stressed how the Code is the product of nearly a decade of collaborative work by legal experts, and covers a great deal more than just Christianity, a consideration which ought to temper overenthusiastic efforts to see it as a compilation guided in every respect by Christianity.[4] As Tony Honoré observed: 'The Code is a cool document. Its aim is, faithfully and perspicuously, to record. It is the work of lawyers and administrators, not fanatics.'[5] In a landmark study of the evidence for religious change provided by the laws assembled in the Code, David Hunt offered a cautious verdict: '[p]apers and books about Christianising the Roman Empire ought not to be encouraged'; he contended, furthermore, that 'laws, of course, "do not a Christian make"', and concluded that 'the laws...led the regiment of Christianisers from the rear'.[6]

---

[1] On the preparation of the Code, see Matthews (2000) 55–84; for a detailed reassessment of its promulgation, see Salway (2013).
[2] A classic example, amongst numerous others, is MacMullen (1986) 324–5 (slavery), 331–7 (games and punishments).
[3] Salway (2013) para 16. In more detail, see Matthews (2000) 85–120.
[4] For an overview (particularly useful on the early modern editors and interpreters), see Germino (2012).
[5] Honoré (1986) 183.   [6] Hunt (1993) 143, 158.

Mark Humphries, *The Retorical Construction of a Christian Empire in the Theodosian Code* In: *Rhetoric and Religious Identity in Late Antiquity*. Edited by: Richard Flower and Morwenna Ludlow, Oxford University Press (2020).
© Oxford University Press. DOI: 10.1093/oso/9780198813194.003.00010

146   *Rhetoric and Religious Identity in Late Antiquity*

Even so, the temptations offered by the Code have continued to prove alluring to scholars, particularly in terms of its sixteenth book, which assembles imperial legislation on a variety of religious matters, and which has seemed to offer an opportunity to examine the extent to which Christianity informed the actions of emperors from Constantine I (306–37) down to the time of Theodosius' codification.[7] One reason for this is that the very arrangement of the Code encourages us to regard it as a narrative of sorts. Within each book, laws are gathered into titles dealing with specific areas of legislation; and within each title, the laws are arranged in chronological order. Theodosius, in his law of 429 announcing the codification project, explained the rationale for this: the Code would include not just the laws currently in force, but also, for the benefit of the legal experts who would use the Code in judicial contexts, the laws they had superseded.[8] As a result, individual titles within the Code allow us to see how legal pronouncements and practice on various issues changed over time. Thus book 16, title 10 (*de paganis, sacrificiis et templis*), famously assembles twenty-five laws condemning pagan cult practice from Constantine in 320/321 to Theodosius II and his western colleague Valentinian III (425–55) in 435.[9] From them, it would appear at first sight that we can construct a story of Christian imperial attitudes to paganism marked by mounting rhetorical intransigence and increasingly stern punishments. But any enthusiasm for such a narrative constructed from the Code should be resisted.[10] It needs to take account of the reality observable from the Code itself that the suppression of traditional cult required the constant reiteration of laws condemning it. At the same time, any analysis needs to interpret individual laws not only with an eye to the original circumstances, and places, in which they were issued, but also with an awareness that the form in which they survive (in many cases, they are brief extracts from longer pronouncements) reflects the editorial choices of the fifth-century compilers.[11]

An attempt to use the Code to trace such religious changes was offered, however, in an article published by Michele Salzman in the same year as Hunt's words of caution. She analysed the materials in book 16 of the Code for what they reveal about the processes of Christianization, arriving at altogether

---

[7] It is worth noting that this approach is perhaps encouraged by the presentation of the Code in the Sources chrétiennes series, where book 16 comprises a separate volume by itself (Rougé et al. 2005), whilst legislation from books 1–15 and other legal collections comprised a second volume (Rougé et al. 2009).

[8] *CTh.* 1.1.5: *Sed cum simplicius iustiusque sit praetermissis eis, quas posteriores infirmant, explicari solas, quas valere conveniet, hunc quidem codicem et priores diligentioribus compositos cognoscamus, quorum scholasticae intentioni tribuitur nosse etiam illa, quae mandata silentio in desuetudinem abierunt, pro sui tantum temporis negotiis valitura.*

[9] See McLynn (2009) 574–5, arguing that this grouping of 'pagans, sacrifices, and temples' encourages us to think of these concepts as naturally belonging together. Cf. Belayche (2009) for the image of late paganism that emerges from the Code.

[10] Humphries (2018) 73–4.   [11] For the editors at work, see Matthews (2000) 200–53.

more optimistic conclusions than Hunt. She certainly acknowledged the limitations of the Code as a source, 'for it reveals how people were expected to act, even if it does not tell us how people actually did act', and observed that any account of Christianization aiming at completeness would need to appeal to a much broader range of sources, both textual and material.[12] Nevertheless, she maintained that the Code had its uses, not least as a guide to imperial aspirations. The compilers working under Theodosius II had, after all, begun their compilation with Constantine and continued down to laws issued in the 430s by Theodosius and Valentinian.[13] Therefore the laws they gathered together belonged to Christian emperors, with the sole exception of the pagan Julian (361–3); but whilst some of his laws are preserved in the Code, none pertain directly to matters of religion and there are none by him in book 16.[14] Therefore, Salzman argued, the laws are representative of emperors who

> wanted the Empire to become a Christian one, and believed that it was their duty to bring that about. To that end, emperors willingly used law as a means of conversion; by and large, their laws offered positive incentives and negative punishments that would affect either one's social identity or one's material well-being in the world, keeping in mind that the two were interconnected.[15]

Later treatments, by contrast, have tended towards a more cautious approach. Thus, when John Curran used the Code as a guide to the fate of the traditional cults of the city of Rome in the fourth century, he too acknowledged the limitations of the Code, particularly bearing in mind that the stated purpose of the compilation, as set out in laws issued by Theodosius describing the project, meant that some laws were excluded from it, and that others were excerpted under different titles.[16] Therefore, Curran warned against using the Code as if it were some sort of handbook, since the evidence it provides even for the aspirations of emperors is, at best, partial.[17] As for the importance of Christianity in the Code overall, Benet Salway has argued more recently that '[d]espite the innovation of including [an] entire last book devoted to Church matters (*CTh* 16) and the undoubted piety of the imperial households at both Constantinople and Ravenna, the extent of the Code's Christian character should not be exaggerated'.[18]

It strikes me, however, that another approach to Christianity in the Code is possible, one which foregrounds the impact on it of its compilation under Theodosius II rather than treats it as a repository for a history of

---

[12] Salzman (1993) 362–3.
[13] See below p. 148. A similar formula is used in the law announcing the final stages of the editing process, *CTh* 1.1.6 (435): *omnes edictales generalesque constitutions... quas divus Constantinus posterioresque principes ac nos tulimus.*
[14] For Julian's legislation in the Code, see Germino (2009); Harries (2012).
[15] Salzman (1993) 363.   [16] *CTh* 1.1.5–6 (quoted in nn. 8 and 13 above).
[17] Curran (2000) 161–9.   [18] Salway (2013) para. 15.

148 Rhetoric and Religious Identity in Late Antiquity

Christianization. As Salway has remarked in terms of what we can deduce of the editorial process, some aspects of the Code reflect an unmistakably Constantinopolitan and Theodosian outlook: for example, the majority of laws from the period of the Code's compilation (429–437) that are included within it come from Theodosius' eastern court rather than from Valentinian III's in the west.[19] In what follows, therefore, an attempt is made to examine the Christianity of certain parts of the Code in terms of the time and place in which it was compiled, and to examine how the Code represents a specifically mid-fifth-century perspective on recent imperial history. It examines a series of interrelated themes: the chronological parameters of the compilation; the selectiveness of the compilers, and how this shapes the materials preserved in the Code; and the extent to which the laws selected for inclusion produced a specifically Theodosian vision of a Christian empire.

Christiana Res Publica: From Constantine to Theodosius II

In the law initiating the Code and those referring to its completion and promulgation, there are explicit comments that it encompasses materials from the reign of Constantine down to that of Theodosius II. The letter of Theodosius II on 26 March 429 that initiated the project referred explicitly to the tetrarchic Gregorian and Hermogenian codes, before stating that his compilers would gather laws from a period that began with Constantine and continued down to that of Theodosius himself.[20] A further law of 20 December 435, announcing the final stages of the project, makes a similar assertion.[21] Theodosius' first *novella*, which validated the Code on 15 February 438, similarly alluded to the Constantinian starting point.[22] The question of the starting point with Constantine has attracted comment, if not always firm conclusions, but William Turpin was surely right to argue that the choice was in large measure ideological.[23] In it is embedded some sense of a self-conscious historical caesura between the tetrarchic period and the Constantinian one, as if the latter represented some kind of new beginning.

---

[19] Salway (2013) para. 18.

[20] *CTh* 1.1.5, which was also read out when the *Code* was promulgated at Rome in 438 (*Gesta Senatus* 4): *Ad similitudinem Gregoriani atque Hermogeniani codicis cunctas colligi constitutiones decernimus, quas Constantinus inclitus et post eum divi principes nosque tulimus, edictorum viribus aut sacra generalitate subnixas.*

[21] *CTh* 1.1.6 pr.: *quas divus Constantinus posterioresque principes ac nos tulimus.*

[22] *Nov. Theod.* 1.3: *Quamobrem detersa nube voluminum, in quibus multorum nihil explicantium aetates adtritae sunt, conpendiosam divalium constitutionum scientiam ex divi Constantini temporibus roboramus, nulli post Kal. Ian. concessa licentia ad forum et cotidianas advocationes ius principale deferre vel litis instrumenta componere, nisi ex his videlicet libris, qui in nostri nominis vocabulum transierunt et sacris habentur in scriniis.*

[23] Turpin (1985) 344–7.

Such a view would surely have been doubly relevant from the perspective of the Theodosian court situated in Constantinople, where the city's founder cast a long shadow.[24] Theodosius' reign also saw, for instance, the production of a sequence of ecclesiastical histories by Socrates, Sozomen, Theodoret, and Philostorgius that took Constantine as their starting point. Whilst in part this reflects the urge of these writers to continue the narrative of Eusebius of Caesarea (which, in its final redaction, concluded with Constantine's victory over his last imperial rival, Licinius, in 324[25]), they do not necessarily start exactly where he left off. In particular, those of Socrates and Sozomen, which might perhaps be the most representative of mainstream Constantinopolitan elite opinion (and Sozomen's is dedicated to Theodosius), began specifically with Constantine's conversion, so that their accounts overlapped with certain parts of Eusebius' narrative.[26] This was, of course, part of a trend to idealize Constantine that had a long history, stretching back into the fourth century.[27] But there is good reason to see it as reaching a crescendo in the mid-fifth century, culminating with the acclamations of Theodosius' successor Marcian (450–457) and his empress (also Theodosius' sister) Pulcheria at the Council of Chalcedon in 451 as New Constantine and New Helena.[28] The *Theodosian Code*, by adopting a starting point in Constantine's reign, articulates a similar view.

But this starting point with Constantine achieves something else too. There are very few references to the laws of earlier emperors: two each to Hadrian, Antoninus Pius, and Diocletian.[29] Whilst we need to bear in mind here the influence of both the editorial excisions made by the compilers of the Code, and the fact that the transmitted text does not represent the whole text as originally compiled, the paucity of these back references is still striking. It means that the laws assembled in the Code present us with a dramatically

---

[24] In spite of Theodosius I's suspension of display of Constantine's image around the city at the commemoration of its dedication on 11 May: see Croke (2010) 249. As Croke also shows ((2010) 253, 259, and 263) many of Theodosius I's interventions were calculated to present him as almost a second founder of the city.

[25] Eus., *HE* 10.9.

[26] Soc., *HE* 1.2–4 begins by recapping, in summary, Constantine's conversion and his conflict with Licinius; Soz., *HE* 1.2–7 offers a more detailed account, starting with Constantine's rivalry with Maxentius and concluding with Licinius' deposition and death; dedication to Theodosius at *HE* prol. Thdt, *HE* 1.1 merely summarizes Constantine's victories. As far as it can be reconstructed from the surviving fragments, Philostorgius also provided some background information on Constantine's father, Constantius I, before detailing Constantine' conversion in the context of his conflict with Maxentius (*HE* 1.5–6). Dissatisfaction with the ending of Eusebius' final edition of his *HE* had also been expressed in the early 400s by his Latin translator and continuator, Rufinus (*HE*, prol., with discussion in Humphries (2008) 154–5).

[27] For fourth-century rewritings of Constantine: Humphries (1997); at greater length, see Flower (2013a) 89–97.

[28] Gaddis and Price (2005) 2.214, 216, 240.

[29] *CTh* 4.4.7.1 and 11.36.26 (Hadrian); 8.12.4 and 9.19.4 (Antoninus Pius); 8.4.11 and 13.10.2 (Diocletian).

foreshortened vision of legal history, something resembling a bubble from the Christian empire, in which legislation issued between Constantine and Theodosius II is to be understood largely on its own terms.

Does this mean, therefore, that attitudes to crime and punishment in the Code reflect a specifically Christian ethos? It is important to be clear about what this does *not* mean. It would be unwise to see this as reflected in attitudes to social mores—however alluring such a possibility might be.[30] The work of Judith Evans Grubbs on Constantinian marriage legislation has shown that seeking to identify a Christian influence there is a misguided task.[31] Rather, the attitudes on display are largely typical of late Roman legal culture more generally: that is why it should not be at all shocking that Constantine issued legislation that threatened those guilty of a variety of crimes with burning alive, condemnation to the beasts in the arena, being sown into sacks with beasts, and having molten lead poured down their throats.[32]

Perhaps, then, it would be a more reasonable expectation to suspect that legislation on religious matters will be more revealing of specifically Christian ideals. An example of this is the usage of the term *superstitio* in the Code, with particular emphasis on the distinction the extant laws make between *superstitio* and *religio*. In short, *superstitio* came to be used to define non-normative forms of cult, specifically paganism, in contrast and opposition to officially sanctioned Christianity. The most important factor here is that the terminology becomes more trenchant as the fourth century progresses, and as Christianity becomes more dominant.[33] That this was an ideologically driven, polemical usage seems implied by the use of the term outside the Code, for example in Ammianus' denigration of the religious proclivities of Constantius II and the excessive devotion to sacrifice of even his hero Julian.[34] But we might go further than that. Since the texts in the Code only include *superstitio* used in a Christian sense of identifying paganism as non-normative religious activity, this obscures an essential point: that the term could—and indeed had—been used polemically of Christianity itself, as had been the case in

---

[30] Julian's celebrated denigration of Constantine as a pernicious innovator (Amm. Marc. 21.10.8: *memoriam Constantini ut novatoris turbatorisque priscarum legum et moris antiquitus recepti vexavit*) needs to be read in context: this claim was made in the highly charged atmosphere of Julian's bid for power in 361.

[31] Evans Grubbs (1989) 75–6; Evans Grubbs (1995) 317–21; cf. Gustafson (1997) 85–6 on penal tattooing.

[32] *CTh* 9.16.1 and 9.24.1 (burning); 9.18.1 (condemnation *ad bestias*); 9.15.1 (sack); 9.24.1 (lead); cf. Corcoran (2000) 251.

[33] References collected and analysed in Salzman (1987) 177–83.

[34] Amm. Marc. 21.16.18 (that Constantius *Christianam religionem absolutam et simplicem anili superstitione confundens*) 25.4.16 (on Julian as *superstitiosus magis quam sacrorum legitimus observator*).

Pliny's correspondence with Trajan.[35] The term had also been used in a legal context in in the celebrated letter of Diocletian to Julianus, proconsul of Africa, concerning Manichaeans in North Africa, in either 297 or 302, and preserved in the late-fourth-century *Mosaicarum et Romanarum Legum Collatio* (*Comparison of Roman and Mosaic Laws*).[36] But such non-Christian usages of *superstitio* are obscured in the Code by the editorial decision to begin its compilation with the reign of Constantine.

One of the most celebrated uses of *superstitio* is in a famous law issued by Constans against pagan sacrifice:

> Superstition shall cease; the madness of sacrifices shall be abolished. For if any man in violation of the law of the deified Emperor, Our Father, and in violation of this command of Our Clemency, should dare to perform sacrifices, he shall suffer the infliction of a suitable punishment and the effect of an immediate sentence.[37]

The polemical import of this text cannot be doubted, even if it is clear from the very next law in the Code (issued the very next year) that its rhetorical intransigence had to be qualified by messier realities.[38] But equally striking in this law is its imputation that pagan cult was a sign of *insania*, mental disturbance or weakness. That too had previously been a feature of polemical condemnations of non-normative religious activity opposed to traditional paganism. Diocletian's condemnation of the Manichaeans decried their 'worthless depraved minds', whilst Galerius' proclamation of toleration in 311 sought to justify the initiation of the Great Persecution in 303–4 as an effort that aimed at restoring Christians 'to a sound mind'.[39] Again, however, such connotations are obscured by the omission of pre-Constantinian material from the Code.

In short, then, the laws in the Code, as the famous example of Constans in 341 demonstrates, deployed the rhetoric of *superstitio* to construct a particular

---

[35] Plin., *Ep.* 10.96.8–9; cf. Pliny's acquaintance Suetonius using similar language: *Nero* 16.2. Recent discussion, with references, in Corke-Webster (2017) esp. 386–7 and 394 (noting the absence of the concept from Trajan's reply at *Ep.* 10.97). For a discussion of the use of the word over the longer term: Gordon (2008).

[36] *Collatio* 15.3.1: *otia maxima interdum homines in communione condicionis naturae humanae modum excedere hortantur et quaedam genera inanissima ac turpissima doctrinae superstitionis inducere suadent, ut sui erroris arbitrio pertrahere et alios multos videantur, Iuliane karissime*. For the date of the anti-Manichaean law, see Corcoran (2000) 135 and n.49; commentary in Frakes (2011) 301–2.

[37] *CTh* 16.10.2 (341): *cesset superstitio, sacrificiorum aboleatur insania. Nam quicumque contra legem divi principis parentis nostri et hanc nostrae mansuetudinis iussionem ausus fuerit sacrificia celebrare, competens in eum vindicta et praesens sententia exeratur.*

[38] *CTh* 16.10.3 (342); cf. Humphries (2018) 76–7.

[39] *Collatio* 15.3.3: *unde pertinaciam pravae mentis nequissimorum hominum punire ingens nobis studium est*. Lactantius, *De Mort. Pers.* 34.1: *ad bonas mentes redirent*. Later, during his attempted pagan restoration, Julian (361–3) sought to justify his controversial prohibition on Christian teachers as a project to cure madness: *Ep.* 42 (36 Wright), 424A.

152   *Rhetoric and Religious Identity in Late Antiquity*

image of religious identity for the Roman Empire. As the examples cited above have shown, however, the use of rhetoric to such ends was nothing new, and nor had been peculiar to Christian writers. And yet, in the Code, the accusation of *superstitio* becomes a central prop of the denigration of paganism. The exclusive use of the word in these terms has been achieved by excluding earlier material from the compilation, and seeing the laws from Constantine onwards as representing some sort of new beginning, rather than seeing his actions as continuing those of his predecessors.[40] The next section of this chapter, therefore, will subject these editorial principles to closer scrutiny in order to explore how they yield a picture of Christianity in the Code that coheres with mid-fifth-century Constantinopolitan ideology.

EDITORIAL PROCESSES AND THEODOSIAN CHRISTIANITY

Selection and Omission

A major challenge in using the Code at all is that its compilers were at liberty to edit laws to make them fit their context within the compilation—as is explicitly stated in the letter of Theodosius from 20 December 435 hurrying the project towards completion.[41] These editorial principles have been elucidated by comparing laws as they are preserved in the Code with surviving examples of fuller texts, whether in the form of inscriptions, or in other compendia such as the *Collatio* or the *Sirmondian Constitutions*.[42] We can observe this process at work even for legislation very close in time to the editing of the Code thanks to the survival of *Sirmondian Constitution* 6, a law issued to Amatius, praetorian prefect of Gaul, on 9 July 425 at Aquileia as part of the restoration of order in the western provinces following the removal of the usurper John and the establishment of Valentinian III as western emperor.[43] It addresses a number of religious issues, such as clerical privileges, the negation of John's legislation as it pertained to the Church, actions against

---

[40] In other words, precisely the opposite of how most modern scholars have sought to present him: for example, Curran (2000) 114.
[41] *CTh* 1.1.6.1: *Quod ut brevitate constrictum claritate luc[e]at, adgressuris hoc opus et demendi supervacanea verba et a[di]ciendi necessaria et demutandi ambigua et emendandi incongrua tribuimus potestatem, scilicet ut his modis unaquaeque inlustrata constitutio e [mineat.]*
[42] Matthews (2000) 121–65 (*Sirmondian Constitutions*), 254–79 (epigraphic attestations and compendia such as the *Collatio* and the appendix to Optatus). See also Frakes (2011) 265–6 on *Collatio* 5.3 and *CTh* 9.7.6.
[43] Context: Humphries (2012) 164–6.

religious sectarians (oversight of which is entrusted to bishop Patroclus of Arles), and various measures to be taken against religious dissidents (Jews, pagan astrologers, and Manichaeans; the non-ownership of Christian slaves by Jewish owners). Fragments of more or less identical laws (the wording is often exactly the same) survive elsewhere in the Code, and show that in July and August of 425 similar commands were issued from Aquileia to Faustus, the prefect of Rome, George, the proconsul of Africa, and Bassus, a financial official at Rome.[44] Completely missing from the fragments transmitted in the Code, however, is anything relating to the ownership of Christian slaves by Jewish owners, perhaps because the editors of the Code were satisfied that they had sufficient rulings on this from other emperors.[45] The survival of *Sirmondian Constitution* 6 not only allows us to see that such a ruling was enacted in 425, but also how the Code's editors omitted it from their versions of Valentinian's laws.

We may apply these principles of editorial excision in a quest for another Christian dimension to the Code. Whilst the Code omits laws issued by emperors later condemned as *tyranni*,[46] it does not leave out legislation enacted by the emperor Julian, the sole legitimate Augustus who did not subscribe to the project of a Christian empire.[47] Yet as Jill Harries has argued, the Julian in the Code is a very different creature from that found in his own writings, in those of admirers like Ammianus, or even in those of vociferous detractors, even if his distinctive voice can be seen to remain.[48] This can be seen particularly where a text in the Code is paralleled by Julian's writings. Examples adduced by Harries are his edict on funerals, which seems to have been explicitly aimed at the proliferation of martyr cult, and his edict against Christian teachers of pagan classics.[49] As Harries notes, the versions of these laws preserved in the Code are relatively toothless compared with Julian's own writings on the topics. The edict on teachers had been particularly contentious, provoking objections from pagans and Christians alike about the emperor's equivalence of culture and religion. Julian's own letter on the topic fizzes with polemic, accusing Christians of dishonesty and, in essence, madness. But the Julianic law on this matter that survives in the Code is an

---

[44] Faustus: *CTh* 16.2.62 (17 July); George: *CTh* 16.2.63 and 16.5.46 (4 August or 6 July); Bassus: *CTh* 16.2.64 and 16.5.47 (6 August: the transmitted date, 8 October, must be wrong, since Valentinian was in Rome, not Aquileia, by October; I would suggest emending the transmitted 'Oct' to 'Aug'). For a reconstruction of this legislative activity, see Gaudemet (1969).

[45] *CTh* 3.1.5; 16.8.22; 16.9 *passim*.

[46] See Corcoran (2000) 274–9 on the suppression of Licinius' name in surviving laws from 313–24.

[47] For an overview of Julian's laws in the Code, and the criteria for identifying them, see Germino (2009) 167–70.

[48] Harries (2012) 124–31; see also Germino (2009).

[49] *CTh* 9.17.5 and 13.3.5, with Harries (2012) 129–31.

altogether more measured document, and makes no mention of this contentious religious background.[50]

But we may go further even than Harries, and consider another editorial contribution by the editors of the Code. In his revised instructions of 435 for the completion of the Code, Theodosius implies that the arrangement of the laws under individual titles follows a logical and chronological sequence.[51] Returning to Julian's laws in the Code, it is interesting to see how they fit with the legislation of other emperors contained under the same titles. Thus the law on funerals reaffirms concerns about pollution and the violation of tombs found in a sequence of laws from Constantine to Theodosius II found in book 9, title 17: even the likely impetus for Julian's law—concern about the cult of the martyrs—is included, but not in Julian's version: rather, the worry is expressed by Christian emperors keen to regulate against unscrupulous exploitation of the cult.[52] Meanwhile, the version of the law on teaching coheres with the wider concerns of the other laws gathered under book 13, title 3 expressing the expectation that teachers should be of good character and that they should receive legal privileges commensurate with their important duties.[53] In both cases, the laws, when seen in their context within the Code, cohere with the aims of the other laws that flank them, rather than with Julian's specifically anti-Christian agenda.

Beyond Constantine: Presenting Theodosian Christianity

Such selectiveness in the approach of the editors of the Code can be seen also in the religious laws assembled in book 16. Hunt had noted precisely this in respect of the opening title of the book which addressed definitions of Catholic faith and offered a specifically *Theodosian* version.[54] But when we look at book 16 of the Code more broadly, we see that its Theodosian flavour is even more pronounced, with all of the titles there, at least in the form in which they are handed down to us, dominated by legislation issued by the Theodosian court. The table below sets out the laws in the different titles of book 16, contrasting laws issued by Constantine with those issued by the Theodosian dynasty. For the purposes of the table, 'Theodosian' is defined as any law issued between 379 and 438, with the following qualification: until the death of Valentinian II in 392, it only counts as 'Theodosian' those laws demonstrably issued by Theodosius I himself—either from one of his eastern residences, such as

---

[50] Matthews (2000) 274–7, arguing that *CTh* 13.3.5 likely predates Julian's famous letter.
[51] *CTh* 1.1.6 pr. *Omnes edictales generalesque constitutiones vel in certis provinciis seu locis valere aut proponi iussae, quas divus Constantinus posterioresque principes ac nos tulimus, indicibus rerum titulis distinguantur, ita ut non solum consulum, dierumque supputatione, sed etiam ordine compositionis apparere possint novissimae.*
[52] *CTh* 9.17.6–7.   [53] *CTh* 13.5.4–5.   [54] Hunt (1993) 146.

Table 10.1. Constantinian and Theodosian Legislation in *CTh* 16.

Title	Total	Constantine (313–337)	Theodosian (379–438)
1 (Catholic faith)	4	0	4
2 (bishops, churches)	47	7	23
3 (monks)	2	0	2
4 (religious dispute)	6	0	6
5 (heretics)	66	2	61
6 (rebaptism)	7	0	5
7 (apostasy)	7	0	5
8 (Jews, Samaritans)	29	5	22
9 (Jews and slaves)	5	1	3
10 (Pagans)	25	1	19
11 (Religio)	3	0	3

Source: Author's own compilation.

Constantinople or Thessalonica, or from western cities during his sojourn there after the civil war against the usurper Magnus Maximus in 388.

Two factors are immediately apparent from this tabulation: the preponderance of Theodosian legislation in every title and the remarkably slight presence of Constantinian laws in comparison. Given the ideological decision, discussed earlier, to begin the Code with Constantine, the sheer paucity of Constantinian laws in this of all books is striking.

A further observation might be made about the selection of emperors whose laws are contained in book 16. There are naturally no laws on religious matters by Julian as Augustus—though his name appears (usually with the title of Caesar) in several laws of Constantius II issued before November 361.[55] Mention of Constantius II prompts another observation, given that this emperor was so clearly identified with opposition to Nicene orthodoxy. His laws are included, but only in contexts where questions of heresy or orthodoxy do not arise: thus the Code contains rulings by him on clergy and the use of churches, about Jews and their ownership of Christian slaves, and about the regulation of pagan ritual and space.[56] The same is true also for legislation, even more meagerly represented than that of Constantius, issued in the name of Valens.[57] When it comes

---

[55] *CTh* 16.2.13–16; 16.8.7; interestingly, *CTh* 16.2.16 lists Julian as Augustus on 14 February 361: presumably this is a retrospective recognition of Julian's elevation made following Constantius' death on 3 November that year.

[56] *CTh* 16.2.8–16 (clerical privileges); 16.8.6–7 (Jews and property); 16.9.2 (Jews and Christian slaves); 16.10.4–6 (pagan ritual and space).

[57] Only one law issued by Valens made it into book 16, namely *CTh* 16.2.19 (protection for decurions joining the clergy). All other laws from the period of Valens' reign were issued either jointly with his brother Valentinian I or nephews Gratian and Valentinian II: see Rougé, et al. (2005) 40–1 for a convenient tabulation.

156   *Rhetoric and Religious Identity in Late Antiquity*

to substantive matters of faith, the laws that made it into the Code are all culled from unimpeachably orthodox emperors.

The only exception to this rule comes in the final law cited in the title *de fide Catholica*.[58] This law was issued in the names of Valentinian II, Theodosius I, and Arcadius at Milan on 23 January 386. Its inclusion seems to have arisen from its statement that orthodoxy had been confirmed by a church council at Constantinople (*Constantinopolitano etiam confirmata in aeternum mansura decreta sunt*). As Neil McLynn has noted, this represents a glaring error on the part of the compilers, who seem to have mistaken this as a reference to Theodosius I's pro-Nicene council in 381.[59] But the content of the law, which refers to Constantius II's heterodox council at Rimini in 359, makes it abundantly clear that it is the council held at Constantinople in 360 that is meant.[60] In reality, this law had been issued by the heterodox court of Valentinian II during its conflict with the pro-Nicene bishop Ambrose of Milan. That seems to have completely escaped the compilers of the Code, who included the law under the mistaken assumption that it confirmed Catholic orthodoxy. In executing this mistake, they inadvertently reveal that they were aiming at a specifically Theodosian definition of orthodoxy. This is even more particularly evident in those titles where Theodosian legislation makes up the majority of the assembled laws, and where the picture of the church that emerges is one dominated by the dynasty's rulings.[61]

This prompts another observation, which coheres with Hunt's caution about using the Code as a guide to Christianization, and that is to notice how little concern there is with paganism. To be sure, title 10 addresses matters such as pagan worship, sacrifice, and the use of temples, but its concern above all is as much with regulation as it is with prohibition, and a major focus is with the conduct of public officials.[62] In other words, this is not really a collection of laws designed to coerce conversion, even if the terms of individual laws are trenchant and intransigent, and reflect a hardening of attitudes across the period from Constantine to Theodosius II. On the contrary, the religious boundaries with which the laws in book 16 are most concerned are those between Christians and Jews (titles 8 and 9, with thirty-four laws between them) and, above all, between, on the one hand, the right sorts of Christians, and, on the other hand, heretics and, to a lesser extent, schismatics (the four laws in title 1, and the sixty-six in title 5, especially; also the prohibitions on rebaptism in title 6, the laws on religious contention in

---

[58] *CTh* 16.1.4.   [59] McLynn (1994) 181 and n.84; cf. Hunt (1993) 149.

[60] *CTh* 16.1.4: *Damus copiam colligendi his, qui secundum ea sentiunt, quae temporibus divae memoriae Constanti sacerdotibus convocatis ex omni orbe Romano expositaque fide ab his ipsis, qui dissentire noscuntur, Ariminensi concilio, Constantinopolitano etiam confirmata in aeternum mansura decreta sunt.* For Constantius' councils, see Ayres (2004) 160–6.

[61] For example, *CTh* 16.2 on clergy, containing 23 Theodosian laws out of a total of 47.

[62] Hunt (1993) 157.

title 4, and the provisions against Donatism in title 11). In other words, the major concern of the laws in book 16 is not about being Christian, but about being the right sort of Christian—and those definitions cohere most strongly with Theodosian orthodoxy.[63]

To these observations, we might add one further verdict. As noted above, the laws initiating the project of codification admitted that it would include laws that had subsequently been superseded. In several of the instances noted above (even the mistaken inclusion of the law of Valentinian II of 386) the confused state of the laws, even when issued by impeccably Christian emperors like Constantine, was ultimately resolved only in the legislation enacted by the Theodosian dynasty, particularly that of Theodosius II himself. In this respect, the laws resemble another Constantinian project brought to fruition in the Theodosian age: the council of Nicaea. Its status as 'ecumenical', as well as its reputation for unimpeachable orthodoxy, had been fiercely debated throughout the fourth century: the council sponsored by Theodosius I at Constantinople in 381 had reaffirmed its foundational status for orthodoxy within the Church, whilst the Code contained a law issued a few months before the council, advertising the emperor's adherence to Nicaea as the benchmark of Catholic faith.[64] All of this serves to underscore the fundamental point, that the Christianity of the Code, however much it reflects changes in the empire that began with Constantine, is essentially a Theodosian Christianity.

CONCLUSION: ROMAN LAW FOR A CHRISTIAN EMPIRE

In sum, the laws in book 16 of the Code represent a vision of religion and society that reflects the concerns of Theodosian Constantinople. In terms of a rhetorical construct of religious identity, that is pretty much what we might expect. But it might be objected that to dwell on the contents of book 16 is to allow a reading of it to dominate our understanding of the Code. It is not, after all, all about religion, even if religious concerns should appear prominently in some apparently surprising places, such as in book 2, title 8, where a string of laws concerned with the suspension of public business in the courts addresses

---

[63] This is most striking in *CTh* 16.5 *de haereticis*: there are two laws of Constantine, two of Valentinian I and Gratian, and one of Gratian in favour of Catholic hegemony in 379; the remainder are Theodosian (Theodosius I: laws 6–24; Arcadius: laws 24–41; and Theodosius II: laws 42–66).

[64] For Constantinople 381 and its relation to Nicaea, see Ayres (2004) 253–60. The law affirming Nicene orthodoxy: *CTh* 16.5.6 (10 January 381).

mainly the matter of not conducting such affairs on a Sunday, or in book 9, title 38, where a number of laws speak of amnesties for criminals at Eastertide, albeit with the restriction that the worst sorts of malefactors—murderers, sorcerers, rapists, and the like—should not expect a reprieve.

Even so, such explicit expressions of a Christian ethos are scattered. Thus we might conclude that use of the Code to trace religious identity is a fruitless undertaking; what the Code is really about is a well-ordered society, free from legal ambiguity, as Theodosius himself makes clear in the letters commissioning and promulgating the text. But that is to take a rather minimalist view of what constitutes a Christian society. Whilst the Code might not provide a Christian charter for the empire, it nevertheless offers instruction on how to apply law in an empire that was Christian. A helpful parallel to the portrait it offers might be found in the ecclesiastical historian Socrates, one of the continuators of Eusebius of Caesarea at Theodosian Constantinople. In the preface to his fifth book, he reflected on how the convergence of Church and State that had begun with Constantine meant that he needed to weave a narrative of *secular* affairs into his ostensibly *ecclesiastical* history.[65] And that, I think, neatly describes the *Theodosian Code* too. To be sure, the vast majority of its laws did not address matters of religion or religious identity. But, like the narratives of the mid-fifth-century ecclesiastical historians, the Code charted the development of a Christian imperial project, begun under Constantine and reaching fruition under the Theodosians.

Moreover, this interweaving was something of which Theodosius II himself was acutely aware in his performance of imperial duty. Nestorius, when he was appointed bishop of Constantinople in 428, had sought to exploit precisely this connectivity of heaven and earth when he asked Theodosius to give him a world purged of heretics in return for victory over the Persians: Theodosius duly delivered, and Nestorius found himself deposed.[66] The cosmic sympathy between heaven and earth, of course, had been a concern shared by pre-Constantinian pagan emperors.[67] But the *Theodosian Code*, by excluding those emperors and taking Constantine as its starting point, made it an emphatically Christian matter. When the Code was promulgated at Rome in 438, and after the Theodosian letters commissioning the Code had been read out, the assembled senators chanted acclamations advertising their assent. They began with acclaim for Theodosius II and Valentinian III, repeating it eight times; but then they chanted twenty-seven times the formula 'God gave you for us! God save you for us!'[68] This was no empty rhetorical performance, but rather an eloquent expression of the intimate connection between heaven

---

[65] Soc., *HE* 5 pr.
[66] Soc., *HE* 7.29.5. For Theodosius' responses to heresy, see Millar (2006) 149–67.
[67] Humphries (2018) 68–9, 72.
[68] *Gesta Senatus* 5: *Deus vos nobis dedit, deus vos nobis servet. Dictum XXVII.*

and earth. These senators were in no doubt that the emperors mediated law from God on high: the *Theodosian Code* provided tangible evidence of what living in the Theodosian Empire, at once Roman *and* Christian, entailed.[69]

---

[69] I am grateful to Richard Flower and Morwenna Ludlow for their invitation to contribute to the Exeter conference and the resulting volume, their saintly patience as editors, and their acute comments on an earlier draft. The content was much improved by the probing questions of the conference audience. Above all Neil McLynn, who encouraged me to subject *CTh* 16.1.4 to deeper scrutiny.

11

What Happened after Eusebius? Chronicles and Narrative Identities in the Fourth Century

Peter Van Nuffelen

The human self is constituted by narrative, so we have been taught by H.-G. Gadamer and P. Ricoeur.[1] Numerous studies explore how individual and social identity is constituted by means of narrative.[2] For scholars of late ancient historiography, in particular those with a background in the study of the early Middle Ages and that of Eastern Christianity,[3] such theories allow us to analyse more subtly narratives that used to be read as early articulations of a national or ethnic-religious identity, such as the histories of Gregory of Tours for the Franks and those of John of Ephesus for Syriac Christians. For Greek and Latin historiography written within the Empire, scholarship focuses rather on religious identity, that is, for ecclesiastical history on confessional identities,[4] and for secular history on their authors' attitude towards paganism[5]—even if there are quite a few more identities at play.

This body of scholarship tends to focus on narrative works, that is, secular and ecclesiastical histories and large-scale narrative chronicles and chronological histories,[6] although some chronicles have received attention.[7] One may

---

[1] Ricoeur (1991); Gadamer (2006) (orig. 1960).
[2] Somers (1994); Whitebrook (2001); Weedon (2004).
[3] Morony (2005); van Ginkel (2006); Wood (2010); Pohl et al. (2012); Debié (2015). The references in this and the following notes are illustrative.
[4] Marasco (2005); Blaudeau (2006).   [5] Kaldellis (2004); Cameron (2011).
[6] For historiographical genres, I adopt the nomenclature proposed in Van Nuffelen and Van Hoof (2020). Narrative chronicles are works like the *Chronica* of Sulpicius Severus; chronological histories are works in the line of the *Chronicle* of Dexippus (e.g., that of Hesychius the Illustrious). References and basic bibliographies for the authors mentioned in this chapter can be found at P. Van Nuffelen and L. Van Hoof, *Clavis Historicorum Antiquitatis Posterioris*: http://www.late-antique-historiography.ugent.be/database/—henceforth designated as CHAP.
[7] Muhlberger (1981); Kötter and Scardino (2017).

suspect here the impact of the traditional depreciation of chronicles as texts either of low culture or with a purely factual interest. For the Greek-speaking world, with which this chapter is concerned, another factor is the low rate of survival of chronicles after Eusebius, with that of John Malalas in the sixth and the Paschal Chronicle in the early seventh as the sole (almost) fully preserved late ancient texts. Another reason is that it is commonly assumed that little happened after Eusebius published his path-breaking chronicle in 325 until its reworking by the Alexandrian monk Annianus in the early fifth century.[8] The development there tends to be attributed to scholarly arguments about the date of birth of Christ, in line with the view that chronicle writing is a technical and erudite activity.[9] Two elements counsel against such a picture. First, as we shall see, there is extensive evidence for Greek chronicle writing in the fourth century. Second, the apologetic intention of Eusebius' chronicle is obvious, seeking to establish the priority of the Hebrews and hence Christianity over Greco-Roman history.[10] Such an intention is also visible in Jerome's translation of Eusebius, intent on offering a Christian history to Latin-speaking Romans.[11] It would be strange if no other specimen of the genre would share this interest.

This chapter focuses on Greek chronicle writing in the fourth century, after Eusebius (325) and until Annianus (412). The first section argues that in the fourth century the chronicle and not ecclesiastical history was the main historiographical genre for Christians. This does not mean that chronicles were the prime locus for narrative identity, let alone identity discourse in general, amongst Christians in this period. But if we are interested in if and how religious identity plays out in historiography in the fourth century, we ought to look first and foremost at chronicles. Subsequent sections look at three different sets of works: the two anonymous Antiochene continuators of Eusebius, the chronicle by Andreas, the brother of Magnus, and Annianus. If scholars have tried to contextualize these socially, they have tended to focus on confessional identities, that is, the position taken in the so-called Arian controversy of the fourth century. This may seem logical. Doctrinal polemic hardly plays a role in Eusebius' Chronicle and his apologetic is mainly directed towards paganism. Yet, his successors wrote in an empire ruled by Christian emperors, with the exception of Julian. Confessional conflict, not persecution, dominates our accounts of fourth-century church history. We shall see, however, that doctrinal conflict rarely comes to the fore in the first two case studies, even if it is present in the background. When it does surface, at least rhetorically, in Annianus, we are in 412, decades after the moment the 'Arians' lost their ascendency.

---

[8] Inglebert (2014) 364; Debié (2015) 51–2. See also Burgess and Kulikowski (2013) 125.
[9] Adler (1992) 484.   [10] Burgess and Kulikowski (2013) 119–23.
[11] Jerome, *Chronicle* pr.; Vessey (2010); Burgess and Kulikowski (2013) 126–30.

FROM EUSEBIUS TO ANNIANUS

The Appendix in this chapter lists eighteen works that can be called chronicles and that are composed after Eusebius until Annianus, whose work is dated to c.412.[12] Our group consists of several chronica, defined by Burgess and Kulikowski as 'any historical work that meets the following criteria: it is brief, annalistic (i.e., recounts a year-by-year chronology), concerned in some way with chronology, be that annalistic (year by year) or absolute, paratactic in its narrative and extensive in its chronological coverage (i.e., usually aspiring to cover hundreds or thousands of years rather than individual years or decades)'.[13] Eusebius' *Chronica*, that is the second book of his two-book *Chronicle*, is the prime example of this and it was continued in the same mode by the *Continuatio Eusebii antiochiensis*, which was in turn continued by what I call the *Continuatio continuationis*. Jerome's translation and continuation of Eusebius is another example, as possibly is the chronicle of Ausonius. A chronography is a work that collects regnal lists and other information to calculate the years—which is the material we find in the first book of Eusebius' Chronicle. The *Liber generationis* I and II are clear examples in our catalogue, and Dexter's *Omnimoda historia* may have been one, if it was indeed a translation of the first book of Eusebius,[14] whilst Metrodorus, Andreas, Epiphanius, Panodorus, and Annianus are possible ones: the fragments suggest explicit discussion of chronological problems, which is something one would expect in a chronography and less so in a chronicle. Even so, given the Eusebian precedent of combining chronica and chronography, one may wonder how fundamental the distinction is for understanding these works. Heliconius composed in Greek a chronological history, that is, a work that covered all history but in a narrative form, whilst Severus did the same in Latin by composing a narrative chronicle.[15] Hilarianus, finally, composed a computation of years, which one could call a chronography but also a computus, that is, a theoretical treatise on time reckoning.

Beyond the variety in form, we notice different responses to Eusebius. Some works are Eusebian in nature, either by continuing him in Greek (the *Continuatio Eusebii antiochiensis* and its continuation) or by translating him into Latin (Jerome and Dexter). Yet even amongst these authors, no one tries to follow Eusebius by combining chronography and chronica in a single work. Many authors, in fact, explicitly return to pre-Eusebian approaches. The dating of the Incarnation to AM 5500, which derived from Julius Africanus, had been rejected by Eusebius, whose own date is AM 5199. If Andreas chooses the unique AM 5600, the other chronographers (at least those of

---

[12] For generic classification of chronicles, see Van Nuffelen and Van Hoof (2020), largely inspired on the recent taxonomy by Burgess and Kulikowski (2013).
[13] Burgess and Kulikowski (2013) 60.   [14] Van Hoof (2017).
[15] For these definitions, see above n.6.

whom we know the date they propose) return to AM 5500, with Panodorus proposing the fairly close date of AM 5493. Equally, whereas Eusebius had started with Abraham, all chronicles start with Adam or Creation. This, in turn, allowed for the incorporation of Old Testament apocrypha, in particular the book of Enoch (Severus; Panodorus; Annianus). Again, already Africanus had relied on the book of Enoch.[16] Further, Eusebius had not bothered to bring his chronology in line with Easter calculations and, related to this, with astronomical calculations. This had been a feature of the chronography of Hippolytus (writing c.235),[17] whose work would prove to be popular in the fourth century and later (cf. *Liber genealogus* I and II, Andreas),[18] and it is prominent in Metrodorus, Andreas, Hilarianus, and Annianus. Eusebius may have attempted to find safe ground by excluding the earliest part of mankind's history and by calculating the duration of the existence of the world so that his own times remained far removed from the possible end of the world in AM 6000.[19] In doing so, Eusebius diminished his own usefulness in the eyes of his successors. If the chronicle was a step forward because of the scope of its tables, it also marked a step backwards by excluding the possibility of providing a coherent solution for the full chronology of mankind's history. Moreover, he implicitly rejected the possibility of fully correlating sacred history to astronomical chronology, a task that shall be taken up by his successors, as we shall see. Post-Eusebian chronography is, then, not just a scholarly reaction against perceived errors, but started out from principles and concerns that Eusebius had tried to avoid. Unavoidably, this meant a return to the heritage of Africanus and Hippolytus that Eusebius had tried to supersede.

Eighteen works, many of which respond to and interact with Eusebius, is a rather high tally: chronicle writing was intensively practised in the fourth century. Ecclesiastical history was, by contrast, a less popular literary pursuit.[20] Much of the evidence of the fourth century is problematic. A late Syriac source attests to a history written from Christ to Constantine by a certain Sabinus the Arian.[21] He may be identical to Sabinus of Heracleia (second half of fourth century), a homoiousian, who composed a collection of documents on fourth-century church history,[22] but the evidence is too limited to build much of an argument on. At any rate, the later source probably took Sabinus' collection to be an ecclesiastical history rather than it actually being such a work. The same

---

[16] Adler (1992) 484 notes that the Byzantine chronicler George Syncellus returns to Africanus and thus relies on the book of Enoch. George was not unique in doing so.

[17] I accept the traditional idea that Hippolytus of Rome wrote the chronography known as *Synagoge chronon*. Burgess and Kulikowski (2013) 117, 366-71 argue against this identification. Whether the attribution is correct or not, does not matter for the argument here.

[18] Hippolytus, *Chronicle* VIII, §689-700 Bauer/Helm; Andrei (2006).

[19] Adler (1992) 471-8; Adler (2006) 156; Burgess and Kulikowski (2013) 125.

[20] For the works discussed in this paragraph, full references can be found in CHAP (n.6 above).

[21] Nau (1915-1917).   [22] Van Nuffelen (2004) appendix IV.

holds for the 'church history' of Timothy the Apollinarian, which seems to have been a collection of documents.[23] Collections of documents, like the polemical works of Athanasius, were close to ecclesiastical history, but included only brief narrative connecting passages between the documents and were not ecclesiastical histories like that of Eusebius. The so-called Anonymous Arian historiographer is not a church historian but a chronicler, or, in fact, two: it is the older name given to the *Continuatio Eusebii antiochiensis* and the *Continuatio continuationis*. On the Nicene side, evidence is not much better: Alexandria may have produced a history of its see under Theophilus (385–412), but its aspect, as we can gather from the fragments, is that of a collection of documents.[24] Gelasius of Caesarea (d.395) is said to have composed a church history at the end of the fourth century, but extant fragments indicate a use of Socrates, which turn this into a pseudonymous work.[25] The first certain evidence for an ecclesiastical history after Eusebius is that by Philo of Carpasia (c.375–400), who seemed to have focused on edifying stories about martyrs and confessors and clearly was not a continuation of Eusebius.[26] The first continuation of Eusebius is the Latin translation and continuation by Rufinus (402/403) and given the fact that he was used by all orthodox Greek church historians writing in the middle of the fifth century, and possibly by their contemporary the Eunomian Philostorgius too, his work may have played an important role in starting off ecclesiastical historiography in Greek again. This is all the evidence there is, and even if one wishes to salvage one or more of the uncertain authors just mentioned, production started later than chronicle writing and was never as intense, nor is there the same degree of engagement with the Eusebian precedent: only Gelasius of Caesarea and Rufinus are continuators of Eusebius. Chronicles, not church history, were therefore the form preferred by fourth-century Christian scholars. In the following I shall present three case studies of Greek chronicles, focusing on the narrative identities they convey.

CHRISTIAN IDENTITY IN THE SLIPSTREAM OF EUSEBIUS

For the years 325–363 the seventh-century Paschal Chronicle and the ninth-century Chronicle of Theophanes show up clear parallels that indicate the

---

[23] Lietzmann (1904) 279.   [24] Bausi and Camplani (2013), (2016).
[25] Wallraff, Stutz and Marinides (2017) defend the authenticity of the transmission, but I am not sure they do justice to its complexity: see Van Nuffelen (2002c) and (2019); as well as Blaudeau (2006) 500.
[26] Van Hoof et al. (2017).

presence of a shared source. That common source is, in fact, composed of two works.[27] First, a continuation of the chronicle of Eusebius from 325 until 350, also attested in Syriac sources (in particular the *Miscellaneous Chronicle* of the early seventh century) and reconstructed by R. Burgess as the *Continuatio Eusebii antiochiensis*.[28] He suggests it formed a single continuous text with the chronicle of Eusebius itself, although in the *Miscellaneous Chronicle*, which is the best witness to the *Continuatio*, it is attached to an originally Greek epitome of Eusebius. As a continuation, the work is anonymous and does not include any authorial statement at the beginning of the continuation, even if the selection of items implies an Antiochene or at least Syrian standpoint. The first continuation was continued by a second one, which is only attested in the *Paschal Chronicle* and Theophanes. It ran from 350 until 363, halting at the end of Julian's reign; we do not know if it included the emperor's death. Assuming a broadly Syrian perspective similar to its predecessor, the *Continuatio continuationis* is more expansive and includes substantially more narrative in its entries than the rather terse notices of the *Continuatio antiochiensis*. Again, there are no authorial statements indicating that a new text begins, but the difference in composition and in reception (the *Continuatio continuationis* is absent in the Syriac tradition) leave little doubt that we are dealing not with one but with two subsequent continuations of Eusebius.

The common source of the *Paschal Chronicle* and Theophanes is traditionally called the Anonymous Homoean historian, thus drawing attention to its doctrinal position. Both works would then represent the dominant non-Nicene position of the middle of the fourth century in the East. Once one separates the single common source into two works, one notices that things are not that clear. In addition, doctrinal stance may not be the best way to characterize the tendency of the works. In contrast to earlier scholarship, R. Burgess proposed that the *Continuatio Eusebii antiochiensis* was composed by a Nicaean layman, given that it mentions the council of Nicaea as an ecumenical council and has further little interest in expanding on ecclesiastical issues.[29] Yet, less fittingly for a Nicene text, it accepts the deposition of

---

[27] The reconstruction proposed here differs from that by J. Bidez in 1913 (cf. Bidez and Winkelmann (1972) appendix VII), namely that we are dealing with a lost narrative history running until 378. Bidez built upon Gwatkin (1882) 220-2 and Battifol (1895), who studied the parallels between the Paschal Chronicle and Theophanes for the years 325-63 and extended the end point, through reliance on mainly Syriac sources, to 378. Even though it is widely accepted (e.g., Brennecke (1988); Ferguson (2005)), this reconstruction cannot be correct. In fact, Burgess and Witakowski (1999) show that the material for the years 325-50 must derive from a chronicle. Van Nuffelen (forthcoming) shows that there are no reasons to accept Bidez's argument that the work continued until 378 and that the material for the years 350-63 must also derive from a chronicle, a separate creation from the first one.
[28] Burgess and Witakowski (1999).
[29] Burgess and Witakowski (1999) 122-8. Cf. *Continuatio Eusebii Antiochiensis* a. 327 (Burgess and Witakowski (1999) 167).

Athanasius in 339 and his replacement by the 'Arian' Gregory.[30] Moreover, the author accepts the succession of non-Nicene bishops of Antioch after the deposition of the Nicene Eustathius in 330, and even attaches the laudatory epithet *hagnos* to Leontius.[31] This has led J. Reidy to reaffirm the Homoean nature of the *Continuatio Eusebii antiochiensis*,[32] but even if one rejects this idea, the acceptance of the Council of Nicaea as an ecumenical council—and indeed the only council mentioned in the work—contrasts with the usual response to Nicaea by its opponents in the first decades, namely silence.

A decade or so later, the tone of the *Continuatio continuationis* is markedly different. The chronicle, in fact, is construed around a contrast between Constantius II and Julian. The former receives divine help in battle against the Persians during the siege of Nisibis,[33] whilst Julian persecutes Christians. We do not know if the chronicle included the death of Julian on Persian soil, but if it did, the contrast would be rhetorically enhanced. A divinely favoured Constantius is succeeded by Julian who immediately reveals his anti-Christian intentions.[34] This opposition reminds one of the invectives of Gregory of Nazianzus, where a similar contrast is construed between Constantius II and Julian[35]—even though Gregory is a Nicene and Constantius II favoured the Homoeans. In Theophanes and the *Paschal Chronicle* an extensive account of martyrs under Julian appears for the years 362–363, but in its present state it

---

[30] *Continuatio Eusebii Antiochiensis* a. 339 (Burgess and Witakowski (1999) 171).

[31] *Continuatio Eusebii Antiochiensis* a. 344 (Burgess and Witakowski (1999) 171). Cf. Reidy (2015) 477–778, correcting Burgess and Witakowski (1999) 126.

[32] Reidy (2015) also proposes Eusebius of Emesa as the author of the continuation, the one-time bishop of Emesa of Homoean tendency who was known for avoiding implication in polemics. The argument cannot be accepted. There is, first, a methodological objection: one should avoid sticking names onto anonymous texts unless there is explicit evidence for identification, which there is not in this case. Our transmission is highly lacunose and there are many authors whose names we simply do not know. Second, Reidy's starting point is that Jerome's 'testimony reveals that Eusebius composed works of an historical nature that were popular reading among some' ((2015) 481), with reference to Jerome, *De viris illustribus* 91: *Eusebius Emisenus, elegantis et rhetorici ingenii innumerabiles et qui ad plausum populi pertineant confecit libros, magisque historiam secutus ab his qui declamare volunt, studiosissime legitur.* Jerome does not say that Eusebius composed works of an historical nature. Rather, his rhetorical works, to which the first clause refers, are 'diligently read by those willing to exercise their oratory' because Eusebius 'rather follows the historical [or literal] meaning [of Scripture]'. In the next sentence, omitted by Reidy, Jerome cites works against the Jews, Gentiles, and Novatians, and homilies on the Gospels—but no historical works. Third, this list of works reveals that if Eusebius of Emesa was reputed to have steered clear from anti-Nicene polemic, he did attack other traditional groups. The generally factual nature of the *Continuatio Eusebii antiochiensis* does not reveal that kind of polemic. Fourth, as my next section shows, it is not correct to say that Nicenes were 'too beleaguered' in the 350s to think of writing history (Reidy (2015) 479, with reference to Brennecke (1988) 95). With Andreas we have a Nicene contemporary.

[33] *Paschal Chronicle* a. 350 = Anonymous Homoean Historian F 24 (Bidez and Winkelmann (1972) 216–18).

[34] *Paschal Chronicle* a. 361 = Anonymous Homoean Historian F 32 (Bidez and Winkelmann (1972) 227).

[35] Gregory of Nazianzus, *Orations* 4–5, for which see now Elm (2012).

may well be interpolated with material from the fifth-century church historians.[36] Even so, the chronicle did mention how under Julian the bones of 'saint' Patrophilus were dug up and how 'blessed' Eustathius of Epiphaneia died before having to witness the desecration of his church by pagans.[37] In the account of events under Julian, these are the only two individuals who get an epithet of praise. Both were Homoean and this therefore is likely to be the doctrinal position of the author, as is also indicated by his registering the Homoean council of Constantinople of 360. Even so, that confessional identity is assumed and not polemically defended, incidentally explaining why a non-Nicene account could be incorporated without much problem in the clearly orthodox *Paschal Chronicle* and Theophanes.[38] Indeed, by including one anti-Jewish story early in the continuation,[39] and thus highlighting the difference with the other traditional Christian opponent, the author suggests a greater concern with a Christian identity rather than a particular doctrinal position within Christianity.

This may be explicable in the light of the time of writing. The fact that we do not know when the work ended, before or after the death of Julian, makes it hard to weigh exactly its intentions. It may be that the *Continuatio continuationis* was an Antiochean response to Julian's presence in the city during his preparation for his Persian campaign, strengthening local Christians in the face of what they experienced as persecution. Alternatively, if composed after Julian's death in Persia, it may be an immediate reaffirmation of the church's endurance in the face of opposition and an attempt to construe Julian's reign as the brief interlude that it has actually become. In both cases, the anti-Jewish anecdote may reflect the Jewish attempt to rebuild the Temple under Julian. Another, more traditional possibility is that the text sought to affirm Homoean identity at the moment when the doctrinal stance of the new emperor Jovian was unclear, but this seems less likely, for the text assumes the validity of the Homoean position more than it defends it.

The discovery of non-Nicene histories has intrigued scholars, hoping to get a glimpse of non-orthodox and maybe unorthodox representations of church history. The focus on doctrinal identity may seem logical, as it is an important

---

[36] Cf. Van Nuffelen (forthcoming).

[37] *Paschal Chronicle* a. 361 = Anonymous Homoean Historian F 33 (Bidez and Winkelmann (1972) 228, 230).

[38] Not differentiating between the two chronicles, Ferguson (2005) 74–8 argues that the Homoean character of the anonymous historian has been overestimated. The emphasis on Constantius II and the signs he receives need not be more than statements that God supports the Christian empire, and are not necessarily an indication of support for the doctrinal position of that emperor. Moreover, the author may simply be recording stories that circulated. Finally, ecclesiastical policy of Constantius II has been depicted as strongly anti-Nicene in later Nicene historiography, but was in reality much more conciliatory. These are valid points, but the explicit praise for clearly Homoean individuals would be remarkable if the author were a Nicene.

[39] *Paschal chronicle* a. 350 = Anonymous Homoean Historian F 24 (Bidez and Winkelmann (1972) 215).

feature in shaping the fifth-century ecclesiastical historians: the representation of fourth-century ecclesiastical history in the Eunomian Philostorgius is markedly different from that of Socrates of Constantinople and Sozomen. Such a focus on doctrinal position may not be very helpful, for the two chronicles studied here assume a doctrinal stance without explicitly defending it. Their concerns lay elsewhere: if the *Continuatio Eusebii antiochiensis* complies with the conciseness typical for chronicles, the *Continuatio continuationis* breaks that mould to construct a grander narrative of Christian-pagan opposition. Modern attempts at pigeon-holing their authors are, in fact, stronger at revealing scholarly presuppositions than reaching clear results. Why should a terse chronicle be written by a layman and why would a bishop be unable to do so? Eusebius' own Chronicle is there to illustrate the point. That doctrinal stance would be the key to the interpretation of the work, assumes that doctrinal differences were the key social identifiers for Christians in the middle of the fourth century. Yet we have evidence for bishops shifting sides (like Meletius of Antioch) or steering clear of doctrinal debate (Cyril of Jerusalem). It also assumes that individuals were able to identify doctrinal parties and groups, which were at the time shifting coalitions that only in retrospect gain genealogy and demarcation.[40] Finally, the focus on doctrinal position also reveals the assumption that a literary work gains its identity from contemporary circumstances. Yet, the two works we are discussing were continuations of Eusebius and attached to (a version of) his text. The dating by so many years after the peace of the church that we find in the *Continuatio continuationis*[41] reflects Eusebius' assessment of the importance of Constantine's conversion. The lack of polemics in the *Continuatio Eusebii antiochiensis* may well reflect an appropriation of that view: after the end of the Great Persecution the church has entered a period of peace and the quarrel about Arius should not detract from that—a view that is also implicit in Eusebius' own *Ecclesiastical History* and *Life of Constantine* and for which he was criticized by the later historian Socrates.[42] Regarding the *Continuatio continuationis*, the focus on pagan-Christian opposition, but also the polemical story about the Jews, picks up two themes that are central to Eusebius' conception of early Christian history.[43] In doing so, it emphasizes continuity with Eusebius but also acknowledges the limits of the hope that underpinned Eusebius' Chronicle and the *Continuatio Eusebii antiochiensis*: the challenges for the Church are not over yet. In that way, the two continuations fail to attribute importance to doctrinal conflict because it is not what matters in

---

[40] Cf. Gwynn (2007).
[41] *Paschal Chronicle* a. 361–362 = Anonymous Homoean Historian F 32–33 (Bidez and Winkelmann (1972) 226).
[42] Socrates of Constantinople, *Ecclesiastical history* pr.
[43] Note that the *Continuatio Eusebii Antiochiensis* (a. 349; Burgess and Witakowski (1999) 173) has a story about pagan conversion (which was not completely sincere) towards its end.

church history when one inserts oneself into the long view that writing a continuation of Eusebius implies: victory over paganism and, to a lesser degree, Judaism is what counts. As a consequence, they claim a Christian identity, even if they do not hide their doctrinal stance.

INSTITUTIONAL AND NATURAL IDENTITY

The two *Continuationes* inscribe themselves into the Eusebian project whilst offering an original contribution in the realm of contemporary history. Yet, the principles of Eusebius, including the reliance on the chronology of the Hebrew Bible, the exclusion of Pre-Abrahamic history, and hence his calculation of the age of the world, were soon challenged. The earliest correction to Eusebius was proposed by Andreas, often styled as 'the brother of bishop Magnus'. Writing in Greek, he is known as the author of a paschal cycle that was remembered in the Armenian tradition, but further Armenian and Syriac evidence shows that he also wrote a chronicle, a treatise on Easter and a geographical treatise.[44] As his Easter cycle began in 353, he must be dated to the middle of the fourth century. His reliance on reworking of the paschal cycle of Anatolius by Athanasius of Alexandria, produced for the council of Serdica (343) implies that he was a Nicene.[45] We shall see that his work defended the Nicene calculation of the Easter date. It is unclear what the relation is between the chronicle, the Easter treatise and the paschal cycle of 200 years. They are cited as separate treatises, but there is evidence that the chronicle contained also astronomical explanations, suggesting a discussion of the paschal cycle too. The cycle itself also contained explanatory canons,[46] and references to it expand also on his AM dating.[47] Whatever the precise make-up of the various works and their interrelation, we are entitled to assume that the views expressed in the various works and fragments were related to one another.

Andreas' work was clearly different from that of Eusebius, which the witnesses suppose that he knew. The Incarnation is dated to AM 5600 instead of AM 5199 and Andreas started with Creation. He reaffirms the Septuagint chronology over

---

[44] Full references at CHAP (see above n.6).   [45] Mosshammer (2008) 252.
[46] Elias of Nisibis, Chronicle Vol. 2, ed. Brooks (1910), p.52.12–16 T, p.73.32–36 V: 'The computation of Andreas' Chronicon declares that the spring equinox fell on 21 March and (there are) more than 300 years from the time of the appearance of our Lord until the time when Andreas composed the Chronicon. During them, the equinox descended of three days.' Anonymous, *Dialogue on the birthday of Christ* (Conybeare (1904) 328; Strobel (1977) 156 n.3) refers to the third canon of the Paschal Cycle.
Fragment numbers refer to the edition of fragmentary Greek chronicles that L. Van Hoof and I are preparing. Translations from the Syriac by M. Mazzola, from the Armenian by A. Hilkens.
[47] Anonymous, *On Easter* (Dulaurier (1859) 58–9; Strobel (1984) 141; Mosshammer (2008) 248–9).

that of the Hebrew Bible and includes Qainan, the son of Arphaxsad, whom Eusebius famously had left out.[48] F1 may imply that he copied material from Hippolytus, Eusebius' predecessor.[49] As said, he linked paschal calculation and chronicle writing, a link that had been present in Hippolytus but was absent in Eusebius. As such, Andreas is the first chronicler in which we see features appearing that would mark the general fourth-century response to Eusebius.

A series of extracts, from the *Treatise on the feast of unleavened bread*, explain why it was important to celebrate Easter on the right day by arguing that the Jews have forgotten the right way to celebrate Easter:

> From the Treatise on the feast of the unleavened bread of Andreas, the brother of the bishop Magnus. In order that the convention and the model (*typos*) that (the feast) occurs in the first month would be established, it is not lawful for the Church of God to celebrate this feast in the twelfth month. Again he says: because of this, it is necessary that carefully, year by year, the feast of the unleavened bread is celebrated in the first month. But the Jews, as [they are] blind in everything, even in this they are an exception. Again he says: many generations ago, before the Messiah suffered, the Jews were led away captive from their country to Babel, and the Babylonians who went up in their place and settled in Palestine, their land, and are called Samaritans, received from those Jews the tradition of when and in which time or not to observe the feast of Easter. Following the tradition that they received from them, the Samaritans still celebrate the Easter after the equinox until this day. Thus, the Samaritans observe what has been given them by the Jews and the Jews do not continue what they taught themselves. Again he says: the equinox is the beginning of the year and of the first month. Indeed, the first month begins thence. Again he says: also the Jews, although they make intercalary months, many times celebrate Easter feast two times in one year.[50]

[48] See the fragment in the previous note.

[49] Anonymous Chronicle (P'ilon Tirakac'i) (Abrahamyan (1944) 357–9). Note that the edition of the same text by Sargisean (1904) 1 l.5–3 l.17 does not have the reference to Andreas. Neither edition is a critical one, so at present we cannot know what the best reading is.

[50] Elias of Nisibis, Chronicle, ed. Brooks (1910) vol. 2 109–10 T, 119 V: ܕܐܢܕܪܐܘܣ ܐܚܘܗܝ ܕܡܓܢܘܣ ܐܦܝܣܩܘܦܐ: ܡܢ ܡܐܡܪܐ ܕܥܠ ܦܛܝܪ̈ܐ܀ ܡܛܠ ܗܘܒܠ ܕܛܘܦܣܐ ܘܫܘܪܐ ܦܩܕ ܕܒܝܪܚܐ ܩܕܡܝܐ ܢܗܘܐ܆ ܠܐ ܫܠܝܛ ܠܗ̇ ܠܥܕܬܗ ܕܐܠܗܐ: ܕܒܝܪܚܐ ܕܬܪܥܣܪ ܬܥܒܕܝܘܗܝ ܠܗܢܐ ܥܐܕܐ.. ܘܬܘܒ ܐܡܪ: ܡܛܠ ܗܕܐ ܐܠܨܐ ܕܒܚܦܝܛܘܬ ܫܢܐ ܒܫܢܐ. ܒܝܪܚܐ ܩܕܡܝܐ ܢܬܥܒܕ ܥܐܕܐ ܕܦܛܝܪ̈ܐ. ܐܠܐ ܝܗܘܕ̈ܝܐ ܐܟܘܝܐ ܕܒܟܠܡܕܡ ܒܗܢܐ܆ ܗܪܟܐ ܐܦ ܒܗܕܐ ܐܬܬܠܠܘ.. ܘܬܘܒ ܐܡܪ. ܡܢ ܩܕܡ ܕܪ̈ܐ ܣܓܝ̈ܐܐ܆ ܩܕܡ ܕܢܚܫ ܡܫܝܚܐ: ܝܗܘܕ̈ܝܐ ܗܘܘ ܕܐܫܬܒܝܘ ܡܢ ܐܬܪܗܘܢ ܠܒܒܠ ܘܒܒܠܝ̈ܐ ܗܠܝܢ ܕܣܠܩܘ ܚܠܦܝܗܘܢ ܘܐܬܬܘܬܒܘ ܒܗ̇ ܒܦܠܣܛܝܢܐ ܐܪܥܗܘܢ ܘܐܬܩܪܝܘ ܫܡܪ̈ܝܐ: ܘܩܒܠܘ ܗܢܘܢ ܡܢܗܘܢ ܕܝܗܘܕ̈ܝܐ ܡܫܠܡܢܘܬܐ: ܕܐܡܬܝ ܘܒܐܝܢܐ ܙܒܢܐ ܘܠܐ ܠܡܛܪ ܠܥܐܕܐ ܕܦܨܚܐ ܗܢܐ܆ ܐܝܟ ܕܗܟܢܐ ܩܕܡܝܐ ܕܩܒܠܘ ܡܢܗܘܢ ܢܛܪܝܢ ܗܢܘܢ ܫܡܪ̈ܝܐ ܒܬܪ ܫܘܝܐ ܠܗܫܐ ܠܡܥܒܕܗ ܠܦܨܚܐ. ܡܢ ܟܠܗ̇ ܕܫܘܬܐ ܐܫܬܘܝܐ ܘܠܠܝܐ. ܫܡܪ̈ܝܐ ܗܟܝܠ ܡܕܡ ܕܐܫܬܠܡ ܠܗܘܢ ܡܢ ܝܗܘܕ̈ܝܐ ܢܛܪܝܢ. ܘܝܗܘܕ̈ܝܐ ܒܗ̇ܘ ܡܐ ܕܐܠܦܘ ܠܐ ܩܘܘ.. ܘܬܘܒ ܐܡܪ. ܫܘܘܝܘܬܐ ܗܝ ܕܐܝܡܡܐ ܘܕܠܠܝܐ ܪܫܐ ܐܝܬܝܗ̇ ܕܫܢܬܐ ܘܕܝܪܚܐ ܩܕܡܝܐ. ܝܪܚܐ ܗܝ ܩܕܡܝܐ. ܡܢ ܬܡܢ ܫܪܐ ܠܡܣܪܚܘ.. ܘܬܘܒ ܐܡܪ. ܐܚܢܐ ܕܐܦ ܗܢܘܢ ܝܗܘܕ̈ܝܐ: ܟܕ ܡܟܒܣܝܢ ܝܪ̈ܚܐ ܒܙܒ̈ܢܐ ܣܓܝ̈ܐܐ: ܬܪܬܝܢ ܙܒ̈ܢܝܢ ܒܫܢܬܐ ܚܕܐ ܥܒܕܝܢ ܠܗ ܠܥܐܕܐ ܕܦܨܚܐ܀

The passage makes the traditional case against following Jewish custom in determining the Easter date, yet in a somewhat uncommon way. In the series of excerpts, Andreas first starts out from the fact that biblical Passover should be celebrated in the first month of Nisan and not in Adar, the twelfth month. Then he argues that the Jews fail to do this: they sometimes celebrate Passover before the equinox, whereas the Samaritans preserve the original Jewish custom of doing so after the equinox. Then he specifies what this presupposes: that the Jewish calendar should be articulated on the solar year. The reference to Samaritan practice as a justification for an Easter date after the equinox is rare in Easter discussions. It occurs in the fifth-century Church historians Socrates and Sozomen, within a context of refutation of Christians following Jewish practice, that is, Quartodecimans, Christians who celebrated Easter on the day of Jewish Passover, or Protopaschites, Christians who celebrate Easter on the Sunday after Passover thus following the Jewish calendar and not the Julian one.[51] Andreas probably has the same target. It is a variant of the Christian argument playing contemporary Jewish practice against the more ancient one as found in older Jewish literature, such as Philo of Alexandria.[52] Andreas' target, then, was Christians following Jewish customs, which in turn makes it likely that he was defending the common date of Easter established at the council of Nicaea, which was depicted as targeted against Jewish practice.[53] That turns this anti-Jewish argument into basically an intra-Christian one.[54] The existence of a treatise by Eusebius of Caesarea, aimed at convincing opponents of the Nicene decisions on Easter and dated in or just before 335, implies that the Nicene decision was not swiftly accepted. Moreover, the treatise by Eusebius picks up some of the anti-Jewish arguments hinted at in the excerpts of Andreas, suggesting there was a shared stock of arguments.[55] It is possible to think that Andreas' renewed interest in the Septuagint chronology was related to this tendency to differentiate Christian from Jewish practice. What we see, then, is an institutionalization of Christian identity:

---

[51] Socrates of Constantinople, *Ecclesiastical history* 5.22.72; Sozomen, *Ecclesiastical history* 7.18.9. See Pummer (2002) 214–18. The argument also occurs in the seventh-century Armenian scholar Ananias of Shirak (Strobel (1984) 141), who may have known Andreas.

[52] For example, Eusebius, *Ecclesiastical history* 7.32.15–16; Peter of Alexandria, in *Chronicon Paschale* pr. = PG 18.512b–520b. Stern (2001) 66–88 has further references.

[53] See the letter of the Nicene Fathers in Socrates of Constantinople, *Ecclesiastical history* 1.9.12; the letter of Constantine in Eusebius, *Life of Constantine* 3.18; Eusebius, *On the feast of Pascha* PG 24.693–706 (DelCogliano (2011)).

[54] Cf. for an earlier period Huttner (2011).

[55] Eusebius, *On the feast of Pascha* 1–11 discusses the typological nature of Jewish Passover. But there are also differences. Eusebius (*On the feast of Pascha* 20–1) argues that the Jews were wrong at the time of Jesus and celebrated Easter on the 15th of Nisan whilst Jesus did so correctly on the 14th, but Andreas' argument is even more fundamental: the Jews had completely forgotten the right practice. The argument that the Jews sometimes celebrated Easter twice in a Julian year is also found in the letter of Constantine cited by Eusebius, *Life of Constantine* 3.18.4 and Epiphanius, *Panarion* 70.11.5–6. On the treatise of Eusebius, see DelCogliano (2011).

after the first ecumenical council, conformity to agreed rules has become important, even if, both in Eusebius and Andreas, the argument is not about conformity to institution but correctness of the practice.[56]

Differentiation from Jewish practice was important in early Christian calendar discussions, but the excerpts from Andreas imply another concern: to celebrate Easter at the moment when it was fit in the solar year, that is, when the new solar year had started. Such concerns with the position of Easter in the solar year were obviously not new. In his treatise *On the Feast of Pascha*, Eusebius defended springtime as the best season to celebrate Easter, because that season teems with God's gifts.[57] Yet Eusebius did not pursue that argument very far and argued basically that Jewish Passover was established by God to take place at 15 Nisan because He had planned that his Son's resurrection was to happen at that moment.[58] Andreas, by contrast, emphasizes that the equinox is the beginning of the astronomical year. Easter thus happens at the beginning of the new year. Regularity was important in calendar discussions and Andreas produced another argument in his Paschal cycle:

> Andreas states literally this, when saying the following in the third canon of the cycle of 200 years: every year, the 17th of the month of March, the 7th of April, and the 6th of January, when Epiphany of our Lord Jesus Christ takes place, fall on one and the same day.[59]

The argument was used in a dialogue situated in the early seventh century about the question of why the Armenians celebrate Easter on 6 January and not, as all other Christians, on 25 December. Andreas presumed a birthday of Christ on 6 January, and one justification he produced was that 17 March, 7 April, and 6 January all fall on the same weekday. If 6 January is the birthday, 7 April is the moment of conception, exactly nine months earlier, and 17 March must be the day of the Creation. According to F3,[60] Andreas put the vernal equinox on 21 March. Five days earlier is 17 March and the sun and moon were created on day 4: on day 5 the sun rose for the first time in the position of the vernal equinox. The date of 25 December does not obey this regularity and hence cannot be the day of birth of Christ for Andreas. We may

---

[56] DelCogliano (2011) argues that Eusebius promotes a specifically Constantinian agenda. This should be nuanced given the shared stock of arguments, nor need it be the case that imperial loyalty was the main motive for supporting the decisions agreed on at the ecumenical council of Nicaea. For further emphasis on political motives, see Stern (2001).

[57] Eusebius, *On the feast of Pascha* 4.   [58] Eusebius, *On the feast of Pascha* 11.

[59] Anonymous, Dialogue on the birthday of Christ (Conybeare (1904) 328): Andreas ex ipsis verbis constat, qui hoc modo in tertio canone ait CC annorum cycli, singulis annis diem xvii Martii mensis, diem vii Aprilis, sextamque Ianuarii, ubi epiphaniam esse domini nostri Iesu Christi, in una eademque die concurrere. The text is unedited and I therefore rely on Conybeare's Latin translation.

[60] See above, n.46.

presume that he was aware of the celebration of Christmas on 25 December in Rome and thus that he consciously defended an Eastern position.[61]

Passover, then, was not simply meant as a prefiguration of Christ's resurrection but coincided broadly with the beginning of the solar year. By linking major Christian celebrations to regularities in the calendar, Andreas operates a naturalization of the Christian year. This allows him to refute wrong moments of celebration, like the 25 December by other Christians, or the Jewish date for Passover, which was not strictly articulated on the solar year. More broadly it makes Christianity appear as representing the natural order: the liturgical calendar does not merely represent the history of salvation but also the cosmological order.

Andreas, then, clearly defends an Eastern, Nicene position, but no more than in the two *Continuationes* does this come to the forefront. Even when adopting the cycle of Athanasius, he does not borrow that bishop's famous anti-Arian polemic. The fragmentary nature of his works may conceal such polemic, but the Easter date was, probably, the least controversial decision of Nicaea and Andreas' defence of it need not betray any particular strong doctrinal stance. Equally absent as a motivation is millennialism: putting the Incarnation in AM 5600 and calculating a cycle of 200 years until 552, well into the seventh millennium, concerns about the end of times can hardly have played a role. The defence of the Easter date of Nicaea (and other feasts) through reference to the natural order bears witness to the changed self-perception of Christians: they are no longer the exception but the rule, that is, they represent the natural order of things, from which Jews and pagans deviate. Such a view generates, in turn, the need to integrate Jewish and pagan knowledge, be it by showing where it went wrong, as Andreas did regarding the original Jewish practice kept by the Samaritans. As we shall see presently, this also is visible in our last chronicler, Annianus.

THE CENTRE REGIONALIZED: ANNIANUS

Long perceived as the first real innovator after Eusebius, the Alexandrian monk Annianus provided, in fact, an original synthesis and development of tendencies one can already observe in Andreas and in Panodorus, his immediate Alexandrian predecessor, the author of a chronicle that Annianus apparently used. Just as Andreas seems to have sought to create a correct chronology of the period before Abraham by using and correcting the tables

---

[61] This would make Andreas a very early witness to the debate about the date of Christmas: the date of 25 December is first attested in the *Depositio Martyrum* integrated in the so-called *Chronograph of 354* (cf. CHAP s.v. Valentinus).

174 *Rhetoric and Religious Identity in Late Antiquity*

drawn up by Eusebius in his chronography, Panodorus wished to harmonize the king list of the Chaldeans, provided by Eusebius and drawn from Alexander Polyhistor, with biblical chronology. Panodorus also incorporated the data of the book of Enoch, as Julius Africanus had already done, besides returning to an Incarnation date close to AM 5500 (that is, 5493). Panodorus developed a narrative of progress in astronomical knowledge: at some point, mankind started to count with solar years after having used different lengths for the year,[62] thus allowing him to integrate the deviating Chaldean lists, which were said to have used a different calculation of the year.

Annianus clearly wrote what he himself presented as an improved version of Eusebius, for the main chronological end point was the same: the twentieth year of Constantine.[63] As was usual by his time, he started with Adam. He did calculate the years until 412, but does not seem to have added chronographic content to the years after Constantine. Much of what he did can be found in his predecessors: in Panodorus and earlier chronicle writers the criticism of Eusebius, in Panodorus the calculation of Pre-Abrahamite chronology and the use of the book of Enoch, and in Andreas the combination of paschal cycle and chronography; with AM 5501 Annianus returns to a date of the Incarnation close to that of Julius Africanus.

The mapping of sacred history onto the cosmic year that we have seen in Andreas, was taken to new lengths by Annianus. Creation, Incarnation, and Resurrection took place on 25 March, which was for him the beginning of the year (T1). Moreover, Annianus produced a perpetual paschal table of 532 years, which generated in AM 5534 (= AD 42) the lunar date that Hippolytus had determined as that of the year of the Passion. Cosmic regularity linked to accuracy in the Paschal table led to Jesus' ministry being moved about a decade in time in comparison to earlier datings,[64] demonstrating the force astronomical arguments had. The system implies a Christmas date of 25 December (nine months after the conception on 25 March), a date that also had the authority of Hippolytus,[65] but deviated from earlier Alexandrian practice. Annianus is, in fact, the earliest Alexandrian source to date Christmas on 25 December and not on 6 January.[66]

The evidence we have suggests that Annianus provided a corrected version of Eusebius' chronology, but, as noted above, it is unlikely that he produced new, historical entries, even not for the period from 325 until 412. He was interested in establishing a correct chronology of world history rather than in

---

[62] Georgius Syncellus, *Chronographia* p.89.2–5 ed. Mosshammer (1984).
[63] Michael the Syrian, *Preface*, ed. Sawalaneanc (1870) 3 l. 3–5; F1 = Georgius Syncellus, *Chronographia* p.32.29–34.2 ed. Mosshammer (1984).
[64] Mosshammer (2008) 359–65.   [65] Schmidt (2015).
[66] It has gone, it seems, unnoticed: it is, for example, absent in Förster (2007).

offering an account of events. This squares with the single attestation we have for Annianus' aim:

> Moreover, on the basis of the men whose genealogies have been traced in divine Scriptures, from Adam up to Theophilus, destroyer of idols, the praiseworthy twenty-second archbishop of Alexandria, Egypt, and the two Libyas, I shall compute the chronology, and set forth the total number of years as 5904—this, so that both the heresiarchs and pagans, wise in their self-conceit, may find no basis of support in our divine Scriptures. For the pagans, wise in their self-conceit, believed that the universe was many thousands of years old, whereas the heresiarchs, by contrast, confess that Christ the creator of time was subject to time, saying, 'there was a time when he was not'. But let all of them withdraw from before the catholic Church when they hear, 'Beloved one, how do you come in, not wearing the garb of marriage?' (Mt 22.12)[67]

The aim of the work is, then, to trace a chronology of the world on the basis of the genealogies of biblical figures. This is set off against pagans, who believe in a much longer duration of the world—an allusion to the Chaldean chronology. Annianus also contrasts his undertaking with the Arians, by citing the catch-phrase doctrine the Nicenes ascribed to them. The suggestion probably is that an Arian would need to find a moment in his chronology when Christ was created—although Arian theologians never asserted that Christ was created in time.[68]

The hint at Arianism is, however, significant in that it points to an alignment with official ecclesiastical discourse. Annianus wrote his work when Theophilus was bishop of Alexandria (385-412). Theophilus himself had dedicated a list of Easter dates for a hundred years since 380 to the emperor Theodosius I, at a date between 385 and 395.[69] It was conceived as a celebration of Nicaea and its Easter date, noting how after 95 years the paschal moon returned to the same day of the month and of the week.[70] Regularity was, again, an important argument, but it was now also tied into a defence of Nicene orthodoxy. Theophilus is also styled by Annianus 'destroyer of idols'

---

[67] Georgius Syncellus, *Chronographia* p.32.29-34.2 ed. Mosshammer (1984); tr. Adler and Tuffin (2002) 42-4.

[68] Note that Annianus' double target may have been habitual by the end of the fourth century: Hilarianus, *De cursu temporum* 1: *Igitur ex lege fratribus coram, sapienta duce, tractatus foret opponeturque ab eisdem mundi initium finemque eius penitus nobis sciri non posse—quoad alii adfirmant plus XX annos habere iam mundum, alii initium et finem ei dare nolentes, alii initium concedentes, aeternum fore voluerunt—at haec ego aio adstruere qui per artem philosophicam mundi et inanem deceptionem verborum pompam opinionesque magis quam veritatem amavere et sunt amatores.* Yet, Hilarianus has philosophers defend the eternity of the world instead of Arians. Cf. Conduché et al. (2013).

[69] Mosshammer (2008) 191-3, (2017).

[70] Gennadius of Marseille, *De viris illustribus* 34. Mosshammer (2017) does not seem to mention this witness in his reconstruction of the text. On the mechanism, see Mosshammer (2008) 55.

176   *Rhetoric and Religious Identity in Late Antiquity*

and the reader is thereby invited to link Annianus' taming of the Chaldean numbers to the destruction of idolatry. More broadly, under Theophilus' episcopacy a (quasi-)historiographical work was produced, the so-called History of the Alexandrian Episcopate. It focused on the see of Alexandria, with a particular interest in Athanasius and his enemies, the Melitians and the Arians (which were linked in that work).[71] Annianus, then, inserts himself into the self-presentation that the see of Alexandria projects of itself as a bulwark against heresy and idolatry.[72] Indeed, by taking Theophilus as the end point of the chronology, and not a particular year of the ruling emperors, as was common in historiography, he admits to writing an Alexandrian work that takes its bishop as the culmination of its chronology.

In Annianus the institutionalization and naturalization that we noticed in Andreas are much more pronounced. Yet, the emphasis on Alexandria and Theophilus marks the return of an explicitly regional standpoint, yet one that is supposed to represent universal truth. The *Continuationes* and Andreas betrayed regional perspectives (Antiochene, and more broadly Eastern) but they were not advertised as such. In Annianus, by contrast, we see a geo-ecclesiological perspective that will be more prominent in later historiography, in which one major see tends to be represented as the true standard of orthodoxy.[73]

CONCLUSIONS

The ecclesiastical histories of the fifth century tend to focus on the Arian controversy, tracing the victory of the Nicene faith. It is often assumed that such a doctrinal identity is the main story told in fourth-century chronicles too and that it is the key to unlock the meaning of those works. This chapter has argued that doctrinal identities are assumed in the three case studies, but are not central to them. Rather, they convey a more general Christian identity, one that is naturalized by locking world history into the solar year. Post-Eusebian chronicle writing abandons the intellectual modesty of Eusebius and affirms that we can calculate an exact chronology from Creation until our own day, one that incorporates or explains the different calculations of pagan sources, is aligned with astronomical data, and is fully consistent with the Bible. As such,

---

[71] Bausi and Camplani (2013), (2016). Van Nuffelen (2002b) argues it was rather a collection of documents with narrative sections: see above p.164.

[72] Cf. Camplani (2015), who does not discuss Annianus. The clustering of evidence under Theophilus and his personal involvement suggest a conscious strategy to project a strongly Nicene image through historiography.

[73] For the concept, see Blaudeau (2006).

chronicle writing becomes an affirmation of Christian intellectual superiority and of the trustworthiness of the Bible.[74] 'Biblicization' goes hand in hand with 'naturalization', the tendency to see biblical chronology as harmonious with, and rooted in, the regularities of the solar year. Being a Christian thus becomes a very natural thing to be. The wide scope of chronicles, which included pre-Christian history and pre-Nicene church history, favoured such a downplaying of doctrinal identities, whilst distinction from paganism and, to a lesser degree, Judaism was more important.

Doctrinal identity is explicitly articulated only towards the end of the period surveyed. The *Continuationes* and Andreas have confessional identities but do not foreground them. Andreas' adoption of the Nicene date of Easter betrays the impact of the council of Nicaea, but its principle for establishing the Easter date was shared by Nicenes and 'Arians' alike, even if opposing councils may have produced their own calculations. It is only with Annianus that a doctrinal identity, closely tied to a geo-ecclesiological one, is rendered explicit. One may be inclined to attribute this to his alignment with the self-representation of Theophilus, but there may be other factors at play too. By the time Annianus was writing, Arianism had largely disappeared from the public scene: both successors of Theodosius I had remained Nicene. As such, Arianism was safely on the wrong side of history, as much as Judaism was. In this respect, it may be good to remind ourselves that, with the possible exception of Philo of Carpasia and maybe Gelasius of Caesarea, ecclesiastical historiography knew a new flourishing in the first half of the fifth century, when the victory of Nicaea had become obvious. Histories are often read as creators of identities, but in this case they rather reflect battle lines that were already drawn. Labels like Arianism had the advantage of allowing a historian to trace clear distinctions in the past and situate oneself on the right side of the fence. The late appearance of doctrinal identity in chronicles may reflect the same dynamic.

---

[74] Such emphasis on biblical precision may have caused the return of millennialism. As we have seen, calculating the end of the world was not a concern for Eusebius and there is no trace it was so for Andreas or Annianus. Meier (2002) 155 notes that the chronology of Annianus implies that AM 6000 would fall in 508, less than a century from the moment of writing. There is little sign that Annianus cared. At the end of the fourth century, the Latin author Hilarianus does calculate the end of the world, even though he does not make much of it. A Greek pseudepigraphical work attributed to James of Nisibis, but probably dating from the fifth century, argues strongly against millennialism, even though it is said to build its chronology entirely on the Bible (Gennadius of Marseille, *De viris illustribus* 1). Hence, I would suggest that millennialism was a consequence of the intellectual ambition of chronicle writing in the fourth century rather than a cause of it.

APPENDIX[75]

Eusebius of Caesarea (Greek; 1st ed.: 311; 2nd ed.: 324)
Chronicle (Χρονικαὶ κανόνες καὶ ἐπιτομὴ παντοδαπῆς ἱστορίας Ἑλλήνων καὶ βαρβάρων)

Metrodorus (Greek; early fourth or sixth centuries?)
Chronicle; a 532-year Easter table from Diocletian onwards

Liber generationis II (Latin; 334)
Translation of adapted version of chronicle of Hippolytus (*Synagoge chronon*)

Continuatio Eusebii antiochiensis (Greek; 350)
Continuation of Eusebius for the years 325–50

Andreas, brother of Magnus (Greek; c.353)
Chronikon; *Liber de azymis* (Easter treatise); Paschal cycle; Geographical treatise (?)

Valentinus, Chronograph of 354 (Latin; 354)
a compilation of various chronographic material

Liber generationis I (Latin; 359/365)
Translation of adapted version of chronicle of Hippolytus (*Synagoge chronon*)

Continuatio continuationis (Greek; 363)
Continuation of *Continuatio Eusebii antiochiensis* for the years 350–63

Jerome (Latin; 379–81)
Chronicon/temporum liber; translation and adaptation of Eusebius (*canones* only)

Diodorus of Tarsus (Greek; before 390)
Chronikon

Nummius Aemilianus Dexter (Latin; before 392/3)
Omnimoda historia (a translation of Eusebius' chronography?)

Heliconius (Greek; after 395)
Chronike epitome

---

[75] References to editions and studies can be found in CHAP (above n.6). The list does not include possibly fourth-century texts mentioned in John Malalas, of which the existence and date are debated (Anthios; Domninus; Irenaeus; Theophilus). Burgess and Witakowski (1999) 114 n.7 suggests the existence of a continuation of Eusebius until 333 because the *Chronicle of Zuqnin* p.119.30-3 and 127.33–128.7 (ed. Chabot (1927)) has supputationes at that point. This may be the case, but the material attributed to that continuation has material from Socrates, the fifth-century church historian. So at the very least we are dealing with an interpolated text. Odorico (2014) has identified the *Commentary on the Hexaemeron* by Pseudo-Eustathius (PG 18: 707-94) as a chronicle. He argues for a date between the early fifth and ninth centuries, with a preference for a later date. Zöpfl (1927) 53–4 preferred a date before the sixth century.

Quintus Julius Hilarianus (Latin; 397)
De cursu temporum; Expositum de ratione paschae et mensis

Ausonius (Latin; before 398)
Cronica ab initio mundi usque ad tempus suum

John Chrysostom (Greek; before 403)
Letter to Acacius (chronology from Adam to Constantine; possibly pseudepigraph)

Epiphanius of Salamis (Greek; before 403)
Chronicle (possibly pseudepigraph)

Sulpicius Severus (Latin; 403)
Chronica

Panodorus (Greek; before 408)
Chronicle

Annianus (Greek; c.412)
Chronography

12

The Rhetoric of Heresiological Prefaces

Richard Flower

In the twelfth year of the reign of the emperors Valentinian and Valens, and the eighth of Gratian's, two presbyters named Acacius and Paul wrote to Epiphanius, the bishop of Salamis in Cyprus.[1] In their letter, they apologized for not visiting him, but proclaimed that both they and others had come to regard him as 'a new apostle and herald' and 'a new John', who would provide them with guidance.[2] In particular, having heard that he had given names to various heretical sects, they asked him to 'explicitly clarify the heresy of each of these superstitions'.[3] This request survives as a preamble to Epiphanius' *Panarion*, or *Medicine Chest*, a massive compendium that describes the characteristics of eighty different heretical sects, arranged chronologically across the work's eighty chapters. From the wording of their request, it is not clear whether Acacius and Paul expected the bishop to respond with quite so extensive a treatise, although the title that has been transmitted with their letter presents them as having this aim, stating that they asked Epiphanius to write about 'all heresies' and that 'not only they but also many others persuaded and, you might almost say, forced him to do this'.[4]

This letter has frequently been employed by scholars not only to explain why the *Panarion* was written, but also to demonstrate that Epiphanius was revered and popular in his own day, even if his modern reputation is less positive.[5] We must, however, be careful about how we use this document, and be alive to how it rhetorically frames the *Panarion* in our interpretation, both through the

---

[1] *Letter of Acacius and Paul* Title. All references to the works of Epiphanius use the three-volume GCS edition of Holl, revised variously by Dummer, Bergermann, and Collatz (1980–2013). The dating formula is somewhat confusing, but appears to refer to the year 375. Epiphanius using similar dating formulae in *Ancoratus* 60.5, 119.1, where he refers to the fact that he is writing in the ninetieth year of the era of Diocletian, the tenth of Valentinian and Valens and the sixth of Gratian.

[2] *Letter of Acacius and Paul* 1.6. All translations are my own unless stated otherwise.

[3] *Letter of Acacius and Paul* 1.9.   [4] *Letter of Acacius and Paul* Title.

[5] See, for example, Pourkier (1992) 47–51; Williams (2009) xv; Berzon (2016b) 130.

statements it makes and by its very paratextual presence. Epiphanius' reply to the presbyters' letter follows this, forming the first of the *Panarion*'s two prefaces, although it does not specifically refer to Acacius and Paul's request.[6] Instead, it outlines in more general terms Epiphanius' methodology for the work and his hopes for how it will be read, before providing a table of contents for the whole work, listing and numbering the eighty chapters, and outlining their division into seven sections split across three books. Epiphanius' second preface does, however, contain a direct address to Acacius and Paul, claiming that they and others had 'put pressure on and, you might almost say, forced' him to write this catalogue, using language that is reminiscent of the title appended to their prefatory letter.[7] Oddly, however, the second preface also states that it is written in the eleventh year of Valentinian and Valens and the seventh of Gratian, one year before Acacius and Paul had supposedly asked Epiphanius to compose the work.[8] Scholars have struggled with this paradox: Karl Holl, editor of the standard critical edition about a century ago, concluded that the transmitted date for the letter must be incorrect.[9] Aline Pourkier proposed that Epiphanius had received such a letter from the two presbyters, but had failed to keep the original. He had decided to rewrite it the next year so that he could attach it to his work, and in doing so 'il a alors daté tout naturellement cette écriture nouvelle de l'année en cours'.[10] It could also be that Epiphanius invented the letter entirely, although there is no particular reason to jump to that conclusion. Another possibility is that Acacius and Paul really did write to Epiphanius to ask him to explain heresies to them, but that in the meantime he had independently decided to begin work on the *Panarion*. When their letter arrived, a year after he embarked on this enterprise, he may then have attached it to the front of the completed work and inserted their names into his second preface, thereby presenting the whole text as a response to their request, as well as those of other people who urged him to write such a treatise.[11] This theory is given some support by the fact that Epiphanius was clearly already interested in the subject before 375, as demonstrated by the presence of the almost identical list of heresies in his *Ancoratus*, composed the year before he started work on the *Panarion*.[12]

Whatever the truth of this matter, it is clear that, by placing this letter at the beginning of his great compendium of heresy, Epiphanius presented his work to the audience as a grudging response to vehement requests, as the labour of a

---

[6] *Panarion* Proem I. The transmitted title calls this preface 'the reply of Epiphanius to the presbyters Acacius and Paul in response to their letter to him concerning him writing against heresies'.
[7] *Panarion* Proem II 2.5.   [8] *Panarion* Proem II 2.3.   [9] Holl (1915) 153.
[10] Pourkier (1992) 50-1, quoting 50.
[11] On the position of the *Letter of Acacius and Paul* at the start of manuscripts of the *Panarion*, see Holl et al. (2013) 724, 743.
[12] *Ancoratus* 12.7-13.8.

diligent, yet unwilling, scholar. By portraying himself and the *Panarion* in this way, he was following in the footsteps of a host of earlier authors from the classical world who prefaced their writings with this sort of claim. Scholarship has been witnessing a substantial upsurge of interest in medical, technical, and encyclopaedic literature from the Roman Empire, with more attention now being paid to how authors presented both their fields of knowledge and also their own positions as experts who were qualified to expound on these subjects.[13] Moreover, although the reappraisal has been slower than for these earlier 'pagan' writings, early Christian heresiologies have also started to be examined for their rhetorical qualities and their place in intellectual history. Traditionally they were mined for historical details about various sects, along with quotations from otherwise lost 'heretical' works, but were often dismissed as theologically unsophisticated and distastefully polemical. Scholars such as Averil Cameron, Young Kim, Andrew Jacobs, and Todd Berzon have, however, made compelling arguments for studying them in their own right as sophisticated literary compositions.[14] I have also discussed elsewhere the methods by which Epiphanius foregrounds his heresiological expertise in the *Panarion* through his encyclopaedic understanding and careful subdivision of his subject, as well as his criticisms of other practitioners in the field, just as earlier authors such as Pliny the Elder and Galen had done in their own voluminous works.[15] In this chapter, I am focusing specifically on the prefaces of the *Panarion* and two other heresiologies that followed on from it—Filastrius of Brescia's *Diuersarum hereseon liber* and Augustine of Hippo's *De haeresibus*—exploring how these three authors both employed and expanded upon a range of recognizable rhetorical tools to construct the authority of both themselves and their texts. My aim is not to claim that any of them was drawing directly on any specific classical authors, but rather that their works used techniques that were widespread in ancient technical literature in order to guide their audiences into accepting a particular version of reality.

EPIPHANIUS AND THE RHETORIC OF NECESSITY

Epiphanius' decision to present the *Panarion* as a text offered to Acacius and Paul places it within a long classical tradition for the phrasing of prefaces.

---

[13] Notable examples include Barton (1994); von Staden (1994); Murphy (2004); van der Eijk (2005); König and Whitmarsh (2007); Fögen (2009); Gill et al. (2009); König and Woolf (2013a), (2017).

[14] Cameron (2003), (2008); Kim (2010a), (2010b), (2015a), (2015b); Jacobs (2012), (2013), (2016); Berzon (2016a), (2016b). See also Boyarin (2004), 1–27; Mena (2013); Stefaniw (2013).

[15] Flower (2011), (2018).

The Rhetoric of Heresiological Prefaces   183

Dedicating or addressing a work to a friend or patron is very common in ancient literature, but the opening of the *Panarion* goes much further than this by claiming that this heresiology only exists because of pressure from other people.[16] Before arriving at the work itself, the reader is confronted with Acacius and Paul's request for information, presenting the work as a response to it. Moreover, this letter is itself introduced with the title that claims that Epiphanius was 'persuaded' and almost 'forced' to compose this work. This statement thus acts as a preface to the preface to Epiphanius' two prefaces, conditioning the reader's understanding of both the letter and the *Panarion* before they get to either of them: not only is the presbyters' missive to be read specifically as a request for a complete heresiology, it is also to be treated as merely one example of many such letters received by Epiphanius, all driving him towards this enterprise. Even if it is the case that this title as transmitted in the manuscript tradition is not original, it certainly reflects the rhetoric that Epiphanius himself goes on to employ in his second preface, where he states that an unspecified number of 'scholarly men', including 'the most honoured and most scholarly' Acacius and Paul, 'put pressure on my weakness' and adding that 'I have assembled this work not because I myself greatly desired it'.[17]

Such statements were widespread in classical literature, with many authors claiming to be writing in response to requests or appeals. As Jason König has noted, in the early Roman Empire they were particularly common in didactic works such as technical or compilatory writings on topics such as music, oratory, and medicine.[18] The first-century AD agricultural writer Columella, in introducing the eleventh book of his *De re rustica*, justifies this addition to his planned, ten-book literary scheme by explaining that it was a response to insistent requests for a treatise about gardens.[19] These, he explains, had been directed to him by both the addressee, Publius Silvinus, and also a certain *Augustalis* named Claudius, who 'having been urged on by the words of many learned men, and particularly those concerned with farming, wrung from me an undertaking that I would compose a prose work on the cultivation of gardens'.[20] Tore Janson has also argued that claims to be responding to requests became particularly common during the fourth and fifth centuries, with authors using this rhetoric of compulsion and obedience to depict themselves as acceding unwillingly to demands to share their exceptional

---

[16] Janson (1964) examines Latin prose prefaces and argues, at 116, that dedications become more common in later works. Horace *Odes* 1.1 is also a famous example from a work of poetry, where the dedication is to Maecenas, a close ally of the emperor Augustus.
[17] *Panarion* Proem II 2.5.   [18] König (2009) 43.
[19] Columella, *De re rustica* 11.1.1–2.   [20] Columella, *De re rustica* 11.1.1.

knowledge, whilst simultaneously using the 'rhetoric of modesty' to explain their unworthiness.[21]

Such statements are also particularly prominent in the writings of the second-century doctor Galen, who, like the heresiologists, was certainly not shy about criticizing rivals. For example, his treatise *On His Own Books* opens by stating that the addressee, Bassus, had encouraged him to compose this catalogue, as had the fact that Galen recently encountered two people arguing about whether a particular text was authentically Galenic.[22] Similarly, his *On the Order of His Own Books* is ostensibly written in response to a suggestion from a certain Eugenianus.[23] As König has remarked, claiming to be acceding to a request 'is tied up with a pose of avoiding the appearance of competitiveness and self-advertisement, for example in cases where [Galen] has to be encouraged by his friends and students to write up arguments against his rivals'.[24] These demands by others, as well as the need to set the record straight about his own literary oeuvre, form part of Galen's consistent claim to be forced to write by external factors, rather than his own wishes for publication. In the same way, by presenting his work as the result of pressure from Acacius, Paul, and others, Epiphanius was downplaying any idea that he was keen to promote himself or to attack his rivals, when in fact he was engaged in both these activities. He was adopting the persona of the dispassionate scholar, who wrote what he wrote because others recognized his great learning and sought his advice. Epiphanius, like Galen, was staking a claim to be a disinterested expert, as demonstrated by the widespread and insistent demand for his objective writings.

Furthermore, Galen and Epiphanius both presented their literary compositions as driven by more than just individual appeals for help. Instead, they argued, they were forced to write them by a pressing social need that only they would be able to satisfy. In *On the Order of His Own Books*, Galen states that he is reluctant to write books because people do not understand them properly.[25] Nonetheless, he has been 'compelled', as he says more than once,[26] to write, because people needed to be corrected and properly trained. This concern for the state of society—and his realization of the benefits his work could bring—is also invoked in Galen's *On the Method of Healing*, where he says that it overcame his worries about writing and thus forced him to compose these treatises against his earlier wishes.[27] This stress on the *utilitas* of one's work is also evident elsewhere in ancient technical literature. For

---

[21] Janson (1964) 117–23. This literary motif is also present in the introduction to Origen's commentary on the First Psalm, quoted by Epiphanius at *Panarion* 64.7.1–3. On the 'rhetoric of modesty', see pp.187–8 below.
[22] Galen, *Lib. Prop.* 19.8K. See also *MM* 10.1K. [23] Galen, *Ord. Lib. Prop.* 19.49K.
[24] König (2009) 51.   [25] Galen, *Ord. Lib. Prop.* 19.50–1K.
[26] Galen, *Ord. Lib. Prop.* 19.51K and 19.52K. See König (2009) 57.
[27] Galen, *MM* 10.1–8K; König (2009) 52, 57.

example, Pliny the Elder, in the preface to his *Natural History*, stressed that the text was for *publico bono*, whilst both Vitruvius and Celsus also emphasized the 'usefulness' of their writings.[28] The reality behind this rhetoric is, of course, a matter of debate, but it was nonetheless widespread, and Marco Formisano has also documented its presence across a range of late-antique 'encyclopaedic' works.[29] This idea of a pressing public need is certainly clearly visible in Epiphanius' second preface, where he compares himself to a number of famous naturalists, singling out for special mention Nicander of Colophon, the Hellenistic author of hexameter poems on snakes, scorpions, and other venomous animals, as well as poisons and their antidotes.[30] He then links these texts to his own project, stating that he is 'in the same manner, trying to uncover the roots and beliefs of heresies' so that he can 'frighten and save' people.[31] By portraying heresy as paralleling the dangers of the natural world, he is arguing that his work performs a public service by helping people to avoid or cure its venom.

This combination of disinterest and public service was vital to the persona of the expert heresiologist, just as it was for other technical authors. Although Galen was always keen to prove his enemies wrong, and revelled in recounting anecdotes about his victories over them, as is visible in his *On Prognosis*, he also claimed to be serving a higher cause. He even states in his *On the Order of His Own Books* that people could only benefit from reading his works if they acknowledged that he acted 'without hatred, contentiousness, or irrational affection for any *hairesis*', using the term for a medical 'sect' that would later acquire the meaning 'heresy' for Christians.[32] He was, so he claimed, unlike these other men both because of his superior medical skills and also because he was driven by a desire to uncover and reveal the truth, rather than to stick dogmatically to a party line. Formisano also identifies this trope of the avoidance of *dissimulatio*—which he defines as 'methodological error and bad faith in concealing knowledge out of self-interest or simply neglect'—as another prominent theme in late Latin technical literature, where it is often

---

[28] See, for example, Pliny, *NH* Preface 16, 33, with the excellent analysis of this aspect in Beagon (2013). On Vitruvius' and Celsus' use of this rhetoric, see Callebat (1997) 173–4 and König and Woolf (2013b) 39–40 respectively.

[29] Formisano (2013) esp. 200–4.

[30] *Panarion* Proem II 3.1. His list of other writers on natural history mentioned 'Dioscurides the Wood-Cutter, Pamphilus, King Mithridates, Callisthenes, Philo, Iolaus of Bithynia, Heraclidas of Taranto, Cratenus the Root-Collector, Andrew, Bassus the Tulian, Niceratus, Petronius, Niger and Diodotus'. Dummer (1973) concludes that Epiphanius did not use these earlier works on natural history extensively. In contrast, Zionts (2002), esp. 81–93, believes that Epiphanius was greatly influenced by the zoological and pharmacological information found in Nicander's *Theriaca* and *Alexipharmaca*. On the question of Epiphanius' knowledge of, and alignment with, Nicander, see now Flower (2018).

[31] *Panarion* Proem II 3.2–3.

[32] Galen, *Ord. Lib Prop.* 19.53K. A claim to a similarly disinterested authorial persona can also be found in Tacitus' famous claim, at *Annals* 1.1, to be writing *sine ira et studio*.

associated with claims to *utilitas*.³³ It is clearly visible in the first preface to the *Panarion*, when Epiphanius apologizes for his polemical language in the rest of the work, asking his readers to 'excuse me if perhaps you find that, because of my zeal for combatting the heresies and my desire to ward my readers off from them, I might sometimes speak angrily or call some of them cheats, beggars, or wretches. For it's not my custom to mock or make fun of anyone. It is the need itself for combative words that causes me such sweat for warding off the readers'.³⁴ This claim might seem surprising to many modern readers of the *Panarion*, given Epiphanius' penchant for colourful polemic, but here he claims to be driven not by his own personal animosities, but rather by the nature of his task, which compels him to write in this way to help his audience. The use of such vehement invective is thus justified in the same manner as the writing of the text itself: both are necessary, if unpleasant, activities which Epiphanius embarks upon not through any willingness on his part, but because he, as an expert in heresiology, recognizes that they are required to accomplish his assigned task. Rather than being a reason to question his impartiality, they are transformed into a guarantee of it.

As well as being presented at the very start of the work, this theme is particularly prominent in the much smaller preface to one of Epiphanius' refutations of an individual sect in the main body of the *Panarion*: chapter 77, which deals with Apollinarius of Laodicea, a bishop and contemporary of Epiphanius. Whilst many of the other heresiarchs and groups described in this catalogue would have been widely recognized as heterodox by late fourth-century Christians, Apollinarius' status as a heretic was far from secure at this time. Epiphanius took a leading role in denouncing him and his followers, both in person and through the *Panarion*.³⁵ By assigning the bishop of Laodicea a place within this catalogue of wrong belief, Epiphanius presented him as merely the latest in a long line of enemies of the true faith and so homogenized him with these earlier, less controversial villains. This is a key feature of encyclopaedias: they make their audience receptive to new ideas, such as 'Apollinarius is a heretic', because they contain a lot of information that readers recognize and already accept as true, such as 'Simon Magus is a heretic' or 'Manichaeans are heretics'.³⁶ Yet, Epiphanius also singles Apollinarius out for special treatment. He opens chapter 77 in his usual way, with a link back to the previous chapter, but then he expresses his displeasure at having to describe the 'Apollinarians': 'Immediately after these [the Anomoeans in chapter 76], another belief grew up that was in opposition to the faith, and it is very painful to me in anticipation'.³⁷ He then goes on to explain that it had spread amongst people of high clerical rank and had originated with

---

[33] Formisano (2013) 209.   [34] *Panarion* Proem I 2.3–4.
[35] On these actions, see Pourkier (1992) 43–5; Williams (2009) xvi–xvii; Kim (2015a) 159–72.
[36] See Flower (2011) 78–9, 86, (2018) 260.   [37] *Panarion* 77.1.1.

Apollinarius, who had previously been admired by Epiphanius, Athanasius of Alexandria, and 'all orthodox men'.[38]

After describing his initial disbelief that ideas of this sort could have been espoused by such a venerable figure, he quotes a letter of Athanasius denouncing this heresy and then goes on to open his own refutation of the Apollinarians with these remarks: 'Since I have inserted this letter and not just begun to write against them because of things I heard from them or other people, it has been established clearly to everyone that I have not been making false accusations against any person. Next I will undertake the case against them so that no one anywhere could suppose that I am making false accusations against my brothers. In fact, I still pray that they might straighten out these matters that seem to cause me pain'.[39] Epiphanius' self-justificatory rhetoric thus focuses on how difficult and painful it is for him to have to tackle this heresy.[40] Just as the revered and recently deceased Athanasius had been compelled to turn against his former friend, so Epiphanius is now forced by the facts to do the same thing unwillingly. He introduces Athanasius' letter as evidence not only of Apollinarius' heresy, but also of his own thorough research and noble intentions. He had been careful to find out information from reliable and orthodox sources and here quotes this piece in full before moving on to 'undertake the case against them', as he says in rather a formal and legalistic way.[41] It is not merely that Epiphanius lacks a grudge against Apollinarius: he was actively fond of him, but, as a responsible heresiologist, he has to fulfil his task and avoid any *dissimulatio*, even though it hurts him to do so. Rather than trying to assess the sincerity of what he says, however, it is more fruitful to consider the manner in which he says it. Like Galen and other technical authors, he uses the language of unwillingness and duty to stress the comprehensiveness of his text and also his own status as a dispassionate expert who could be trusted to provide a reliable and salutary guide to his subject, regardless of the social and ecclesiastical standing of his subjects or the personal pain that it might cause him to reveal their errors.

As was mentioned above, in many ancient texts, these claims to be responding to needs and requests are linked with professions of modesty about the authors' abilities and also assertions that, despite a lack of literary polish, their works will nonetheless serve an important purpose.[42] Two of the most famous examples of such rhetoric can be found in the statements about historiographical practice by Thucydides and Tacitus.[43] Similarly, in the preface to his

---

[38] *Panarion* 77.2.1.
[39] *Panarion* 77.14.1–2. This rhetoric of compulsion also recurs at 77.19.6.
[40] These claims are accepted as sincere by Kim (2015a) 162–3.   [41] *Panarion* 77.14.2.
[42] For example, see Beagon (2013) 88 on Pliny the Elder and Harris-McCoy (2008) 106–7 on Vitruvius. For a survey of self-deprecation in Latin prefaces, including in late antiquity, see Janson (1964) 98–100, 124–41.
[43] Thuc. 1.21–2; Tac. *Ann.* 4.32–3.

Natural History, Pliny the Elder describes this monumental achievement as a 'lighter activity' and the product of his 'very mediocre' talent, but states it would still have *utilitas*, despite the fact that it concerns a 'sterile subject'.[44] In the midst of demonstrating his great professional success and important social connections, Galen also describes his treatment of the young emperor Commodus, which 'they say was the greatest feat, but was actually very far from it'.[45] With this apparent display of modesty, Galen actually declares his double superiority in the field of medicine by both his achievement and also his analysis of it: only a truly remarkable man would regard such success as unremarkable. Epiphanius also makes substantial use of it in his second preface to the *Panarion*, including praying for divine help to complete such a monumental task: 'Even as I begin at first to examine this subject, I immediately find myself more than a little distressed, and I am very afraid as I devote myself to a far from insubstantial project. And so I call upon holy God himself and his only-begotten Son Jesus Christ and his Holy Spirit to illuminate my paltry mind and enlighten it with knowledge of these matters.'[46] This is then followed by a comparison with 'pagan' authors, who had invoked the Muses for their own inspiration, as well as repeated references to his own intellectual shortcomings, which make God's help necessary: 'I appeal to the holy Lord of all to bring help to my poverty'; 'I recognise my insufficiency'; 'my limited intellect'.[47] This language continues to be used throughout the *Panarion*, especially in the linking phrases that often conclude individual chapters, where Epiphanius makes statements such as 'proceeding again to the next ones, let us appeal to him [God] as a helper for our poverty and deficiency'.[48] This 'rhetoric of modesty', whereby a writer disavowed their own expertise or downplayed the attractiveness of their work, was therefore another method for avoiding the appearance of arrogance or a desire for contention.[49] For Epiphanius, engaging with this long legacy from classical technical literature helped to establish his *Panarion*, and the field of heresiology, as standing within an intellectual tradition for discussing branches of knowledge. Moreover, he was also able to adopt the persona of the disinterested scholar, for whom the condemnation of figures such as Apollinarius of Laodicea was an unhappy, but necessary burden, whilst presenting his own learning and orthodoxy as widely respected and beyond reproach.

---

[44] Pliny, *NH* Preface 11–16, quoting 12–13.
[45] Galen, *De praecognitione* 12.1–10, quoting 12.1.   [46] *Panarion* Proem II 1.2.
[47] *Panarion* Proem II 1.4, 1.5, 2.1.   [48] *Panarion* 62.8.5.
[49] On the term 'rhetoric of modesty', which can sometimes be found in a superficially paradoxical union with the 'rhetoric of confidence', see van der Eijk (2005) 40; König (2009) 41.

FILASTRIUS AND THE REFLECTION OF SCRIPTURE

Epiphanius' approach was followed in another heresiological text by a pro-Nicene bishop, who also made use of his predecessor's work: the *Diuersarum haereseon liber* of Filastrius of Brescia, probably composed in the 380s or early 390s.[50] Like the *Panarion*, this takes the form of a catalogue of different heretical sects, albeit with much less detail, material, and refutation than Epiphanius provides, instead giving relatively brief accounts of each group and its errors. There are also many more heresies included here than Epiphanius had identified, with 156 appearing in Filastrius' list, as opposed to the 80 counted in the *Panarion*. The two texts are, however, united in their inclusion of 'sects' that predated Christ, with twenty-eight in Filastrius to compare with the twenty in Epiphanius, and both authors also start their accounts of post-Incarnation error with the New Testament figure of Simon Magus. Like Epiphanius, Filastrius also arranged his text roughly chronologically, at least when dealing with named heresies, but he differed from his predecessor in his sense of how this sequence was to be reconstructed. At the very beginning of this text, the first chapter opens with the Ophites, a Gnostic group which Epiphanius placed in his thirty-seventh chapter. For Filastrius, however, they deserve this position of primacy because of the object of their veneration, the Serpent from the Garden of Eden: 'And so this is the number of the heretics from the beginning and origin of the world: first are the Ophites, or Serpentini. They worship the serpent, that is, the snake, saying that this earlier brought to us the beginning of knowledge of good and evil. They are then followed by the Cainites and the Sethians, who worshipped Cain and Seth, the sons of Adam'.[51] Whilst Epiphanius sought to identify the order in which different heresies appeared and the ways in which they were related, for Filastrius, the Ophites, Cainites, and Sethians have to come right at the beginning of the list because the Serpent, Cain, and Seth appeared right at the beginning of Scripture. Even though the sects themselves may not have come into being until much later, biblical time is the system that gives structure and order to this particular text.

This scriptural focus is clearly evident in Filastrius' preface, which is a relatively brief introductory statement, certainly when compared to the more elaborate set of framing documents for the *Panarion*. There is no mention of anyone who had requested the composition of the work, nor is there an explicit dedication. It does, however, open with an explanation for the text's existence:

> I must write about the diverse pestilence of heresies and the various errors which have emerged since the beginning of the world, and have streamed out under the

---

[50] For a brief introduction to this text, its date and its sources, see Heylen (1957) 209–12.
[51] Filastrius 1.1 (ed. Heylen (1957)).

190   *Rhetoric and Religious Identity in Late Antiquity*

Jews, and have sprung forth [*pullulauerint*] since that time when our Lord and saviour Jesus came into the flesh; and I must expound, little by little, their number and acknowledge that not unreasonably was the enemy of the human race compared to a partridge by the holy prophet: although it endures infertility very often, it secretly incubates the eggs of others, as though its own, and still keeps them warm and claims them as its children for however long; when the age of discernment has come to them, then, with false parents lost, recalling the laws of their parents through their own sense, openly observing with their eyes, they do not delay further to follow them.[52]

Filastrius here invokes the 'rhetoric of compulsion' in a manner that is reminiscent of Epiphanius and the other writers discussed above, presenting his task as one that has been forced upon him by outside circumstances, and also sets out the way in which his text will move methodically from Creation, through Jewish history, and then on to the centuries after the Incarnation. Whilst there is also a clear sense here of responding to a vital social need, however, his situation is not presented as identical to either the earlier technical authors or his heresiological forebear: instead, this text is characterized as a direct response to Scripture. The 'holy prophet' mentioned here is revealed later in the preface to be Jeremiah, whose words Filastrius goes on to quote to support his claim that they are coming true in the present age: 'For every day through this saying [*aenigma*] we recognise that the prophecy of the blessed Jeremiah is fulfilled, saying: *The partridge has shouted, and gathers what it has not produced, making riches for himself without wisdom; they will desert him in the middle of his days and he will be unwise in the end*'.[53] The Devil, here presented as having been compared to a deceitful partridge in the Old Testament, is said to have been raising unsuspecting Christians in the nest of heresy, but thankfully they were now coming to their senses and returning to Nicene orthodoxy.

By choosing this particular passage, Filastrius also follows Epiphanius in using parallels with natural history and medicine in his writing. He carefully explains to his readers the behaviour of the partridge in stealing the eggs of other birds, just as the *Panarion* includes its numerous comparisons with a variety of different types of dangerous animal. Not only are heresies said to be a 'pestilence' (*pestilentia*), but the verb *pullulo*, translated here as 'sprung forth', comes from the noun *pullulus*, which can mean either a sprout of a plant or a young bird chick.[54] Similarly, the declaration that 'I must expound, little by little, their number' (*oportet numerumque earum paulatim exponere*) also situates this text within a scientific tradition of carefully distinguishing, cataloguing, and enumerating the range of forms that any particular natural

---

[52] Filastrius Preface 1–2.   [53] Filastrius Preface 3, quoting *Jeremiah* 17.11.
[54] OLD *s.v.* 'pullulo', 'pullulus', with examples of both words from Pliny's *Natural History*.

phenomenon might take.[55] Epiphanius had achieved this by aligning his project explicitly with that of Nicander of Colophon and other ancient authors on these topics, but he also presents a biblical paradigm for the *Panarion*. His claim is that the eighty heresies match the eighty concubines mentioned in *Song of Songs*, whilst the Church was the one bride and dove in the same passage, and he also makes a brief reference to this in his first preface before giving it much greater attention at the end of the text.[56] In Filastrius' portrayal of his text, however, as in his understanding of the history of heresy, attention is focused squarely and exclusively on the pages of Scripture, and he states that he needs to 'acknowledge' (*agnoscere*) the message contained within them. Not only does he possess the relevant ornithological information to understand the reference to a partridge, but he also has the religious and heresiological knowledge to comprehend the *aenigma* of Jeremiah's statement and its prophetic message for his own day: 'For what reason was this comparison announced to us? So that, with the Devil rejected because of his impiety, since he thought that he held the whole earth under his dominion and power, and after that with Christ the true parent seen and recognised by us, with the falsity of the most deceitful parent lost, every man now recognising does not hesitate to follow the footsteps of Christ the true parent.'[57]

Filastrius is, therefore, indebted to a number of the rhetorical techniques of ancient technical literature that are also evident in Epiphanius' *Panarion*. Nonetheless, he chooses to present his textual genealogy in a different manner, making it not merely exclusively Christian, but resolutely biblical. He provides his own exegesis of this passage and sees its fulfilment in the defeat of heresy that is now taking place after a period of danger when the Devil has falsely raised orthodox men as his own.[58] This may be a reference to the action being taken against 'Arian' supporters of Homoian theology by pro-Nicene churchmen, including the Council of Aquileia in 381, orchestrated by Ambrose of Milan and attended by Filastrius himself. His statement that people 'are hearing from the Law and the prophets that Christ is true God, and they are believing and remembering that he has always been with the Father' makes it

---

[55] On Epiphanius' invocation of this idea, see Flower (2018) 254–62.
[56] *Panarion* Proem I 1.3, 35.3.4–8 and 80.10.2–3, using *Song of Songs* 6.8–9. Other aspects of the biblical passage are then expanded upon in the subjoined *De Fide* that follows the eightieth chapter. This is a heavily discussed aspect of Epiphanius' text: see Fraenkel (1962) 184–6; Moutsoulas (1966) 368; Riggi (1967) 7–10; Vallée (1981) 65, 72; Young (1982) 202, (2010) 198–9; Pourkier (1992) 82; Cameron (2003) 475–6; Williams (2009) xxi–xxii; Gilhus (2010) 49–50, (2015) 157; Mena (2013) 260; Smith (2015) 123–4; Berzon (2016a) 92–101, (2016b) 204–16; Manor (2016) 183.
[57] Filastrius Preface 2–3.
[58] The preface also concludes with the optimistic statement that the prophecy of *Psalms* 22.27 (21.27 LXX)—'*All the boundaries of the earth will remember and turn to Christ the Lord*'—is also coming to pass.

clear that 'Arianism' is the main heresy being targeted by Filastrius here.[59] The fifth-century heresiological text known as the *Praedestinatus* also states that Filastrius wrote his work 'when the Arians were condemned', possibly providing further support for its date and context, although the problems and falsehoods of this later work make it impossible to draw any clear conclusions.[60] Regardless of the exact details of its composition, however, these statements in the preface of Filastrius' text assign it a central role within this process of opening the eyes of humanity and bringing them back to Christ as the prophecy predicted. The comparison with Jeremiah's partridge implicitly rejects a hard-line, rigorist approach to former Arians, instead making all men Christian in their origins before they were deceived by the Devil, to whom no one actually belonged by right. They are offered a route to salvation and acceptance if they embrace the version of orthodoxy espoused by Filastrius, recognize the accuracy of the catalogue of heresies that his heresiology carefully enumerates, and accept its status as both a reflection and a fulfilment of the revered text of Scripture.

AUGUSTINE AND THE BURDEN OF KNOWLEDGE

The rhetorical methods for framing heresiological catalogues used by Epiphanius and Filastrius went on to be redeployed and amplified in the late 420s, when Augustine of Hippo wrote his own work on the subject, now known as the *De haeresibus*.[61] Alongside this text, there also survives an exchange of four letters between Quodvultdeus of Carthage and the aged bishop concerning its composition.[62] Quodvultdeus informed Augustine that some clergy in the African capital were not sufficiently educated and so had need of the learned bishop's help. He therefore requested that Augustine write a book to explain 'from when the Christian religion received the name of its promised inheritance, what heresies have existed and exist, what errors they have introduced and do introduce, and what, in opposition to the catholic church, they have believed and do believe concerning faith, the Trinity, baptism, penitence, Christ as man, Christ as God, resurrection, the Old and New Testament, and everything else entirely in which they dissent from truth'.[63] Moreover, the deacon reassured Augustine that he recognized that very many large volumes would be needed to give a full account of all the heresies, and also

---

[59] Filastrius Preface 4.   [60] *Praedestinatus* 1 Title (ed. Gori).
[61] On this text and the circumstances of its composition, see Bardy (1931) 397–8; Müller (1956) 2–6; McClure (1979) 190–2; Inglebert (2001) 450; Shaw (2004) 237–8, (2011) 310–11; Berzon (2016b) 218–45.
[62] Aug. *Epp.* 221–4 (ed. R. van der Plaetse and C. Beukers, CCSL 46, (1969) 273–81).
[63] Aug. *Ep.* 221.2.

that this work must have been done many times before. He therefore requested that, in contrast, this new work be of a different form: 'instead I ask you to briefly, concisely, and succinctly set out the views of each heresy and to append what the Catholic Church believes in opposition, as far as is needed for instruction, so that, if anyone wants to find out about some objection or refutation more copiously, more abundantly, and more plainly, then by this, so to speak, summary produced from all of them he might be carried to expansive and splendid volumes, in which much effort has certainly been expended towards this matter by different people and particularly by your Veneration'.[64]

Augustine replied to Quodvultdeus to explain the difficulty of creating such a work, using as illustrations the works of Filastrius and Epiphanius and noting that the former listed 156 heresies, but the latter described merely 80. According to Augustine, this discrepancy was not to be attributed to any failing of research on Epiphanius' part, since he was the more learned scholar and so would not have missed out anything which Filastrius included.[65] Instead, the problem was much more fundamental, namely a disagreement about the very concept of 'heresy': this, Augustine said, was very difficult to define and so 'we must beware, when we try to count them all, lest we omit some, although they are heresies, or include others, although they are not'.[66] He therefore offered to send a copy of Epiphanius' work to Quodvultdeus for his edification.[67] Undeterred, Quodvultdeus repeated his request in another letter, flattering Augustine that only his own exceptional learning would be sufficient to the task.[68] Augustine therefore eventually relented, although not without telling Quodvultdeus about the various other things that he had promised to write before this one and so asking for more time.[69]

Unlike these earlier authors in the field, Augustine's own presentation of the subject excludes any beliefs or practices that predated the Incarnation, in accordance with Quodvultdeus' request, and instead lists eighty-eight heretical groups, beginning with Simon Magus, as both Epiphanius and Filastrius had done for their coverage of the same period. In his preface, Augustine sets out the rationale and plan for the work, but also simultaneously produces a particular portrait of himself as a scholar who prepares the ground for his rhetoric throughout the work. This preface is addressed to Quodvultdeus and opens by stating that Augustine had, in fact, been considering writing a book

---

[64] Aug. *Ep.* 221.3.   [65] Aug. *Ep.* 222.2.   [66] Aug. *Ep.* 222.2.
[67] As Aug. *De haeresibus* Preface 6 indicates, Augustine was not using the full text of the *Panarion* for his own research, but must instead have only had access to an abridgement of it known as the *Anacephalaeoses*, which was not authentically Epiphanian. On this issue, see Bardy (1931) 401–4; Jannaccone (1952) 23–6; Williams (2009) xxii. For Augustine's rhetoric of competitiveness with Epiphanius and Filastrius in the *De haeresibus*, including the end of the preface, see Flower (2013b), 182–4.
[68] Aug. *Ep.* 223.   [69] Aug. *Ep.* 224.

of this sort for a while, even before receiving the request, but had decided that it was beyond his abilities. Nonetheless, he had finally found himself pushed into this activity by the deacon's repeated pleas: 'But since I concede that no one pressed me with demands as you did, so amongst this very troublesome insistence of yours I gave attention to your name and said 'I will make a start and do what God wants'. For I am confident that God wants this, if he will lead me to the end of this labour with merciful favour so that through the work of my tongue the difficulty of this task might either just be revealed or, with his greater assistance, be removed'.[70] By framing the text in this manner, Augustine clearly distances himself from any initiative or enthusiasm for its creation: he would never have created such a text without Quodvultdeus' persistent and rather irritating requests. This complaint is sometimes taken at face value by modern scholars, with Brent Shaw declaring that 'very much against his will, Augustine was persuaded, albeit with considerable pressure, to produce a typical Mediterranean handbook of heresies at the very end of his life'.[71] Although it is plausible that writing this particular text was not a priority for Augustine at this time, he nonetheless continues the literary convention of employing the rhetoric of modesty and unwillingness at the opening of the preface so that, from the very beginning, the text is presented as something that was extracted from Augustine against his will. The bishop is therefore protected to some extent against criticisms of its quality but more importantly, he is also insulating himself against any potential accusations of arrogant competitiveness or unfairly polemical treatment of individuals and groups.

Moreover, Augustine's statement also includes the claim that he could only complete such a task with God's assistance and approval, thereby following in the footsteps of both Epiphanius and Filastrius in combining the traditional language of necessity with a claim that the completed work would also be the product of divine help and inspiration, and thus have its orthodoxy assured. Augustine even segues into this with a pun on the insistent deacon's name when he states that 'I will make a start and do what God wants (*quod uult deus*)'. He then continues in this vein by claiming that Quodvultdeus was joined by a number of unspecified individuals, just like Epiphanius' largely anonymous group of insistent 'scholarly men', in prevailing upon the bishop: 'you see that it is necessary for me not to be compelled to complete this task by your increasing requests to me as much as to be helped by the pious prayers to God not only by you but also by the other brothers whom you have been able to find as faithful allies in this matter'.[72] He therefore adopts the classical persona of the dispassionate figure of immense erudition, who wrote what he wrote because others recognized his great learning and sought his advice, but

---

[70] Aug. *De haeresibus* Preface 1 (ed. R. van der Plaetse and C. Beukers, CCSL 46, (1969) 283–345).
[71] Shaw (2011) 310.   [72] Aug. *De haeresibus* Preface 2.

he also redefines that process in a manner that goes further than Epiphanius had done in his declarations of the need for divine assistance. Whilst Epiphanius called on God repeatedly to help him after he received requests from others, Augustine here presents the petitions of Quodvultdeus and others as now being redirected towards God in a manner that is said to be more effective than writing to the bishop yet again. Augustine is here aligning his literary composition with the divine will, which allows it to be completed, but he is presenting it as the outcome of not merely his own prayers, but also those of many other true, orthodox Christians. The very existence of the *De haeresibus* is thus made to stand as testimony of God's favour in granting their wishes and bestowing his blessing upon this vitally important weapon against his enemies.

Augustine's emphasis on his lack of personal initiative and the 'rhetoric of compulsion' in his preface also goes further than many other ancient claims to be responding to requests. Rather than giving his own account of the guiding rationale of the *De haeresibus*, he addresses Quodvultdeus directly and states, 'You ask, as is indicated by the letters you sent to me when you first began to seek this from me, that I explain...', before then quoting an extensive chunk from the deacon's original letter outlining the nature of the request.[73] This is then followed by other substantial sections of the letter, including the passage quoted above defining why the work should be relatively brief and praising Augustine as someone who has written extensively in the refutation of heresy.[74] These statements do, of course, illustrate a notable characteristic of this form of preface in ancient literature: their purported addressee is not the only, or even the main, audience for the work. Augustine had no need to tell Quodvultdeus what he had asked for, because he would already know this. Instead, the inclusion of these lengthy, verbatim quotations speaks to other readers, who are reassured by this documentary evidence that Augustine only agreed to write this text in this form because he had been prevailed upon by the petitions of others. They therefore represent an enhanced form of the rhetoric seen in Epiphanius and the examples of technical literature discussed above, with not merely the existence of the text but also the details of its content, concerns, and omissions explained by reference to the specifications provided in Quodvultdeus' request. Furthermore, the letter in which he first approached Augustine about this subject, as well as the three others in the same exchange of correspondence, have been transmitted in manuscripts of the *De haeresibus*, just as the *Letter of Acacius and Paul* has come down to us alongside Epiphanius' *Panarion*. Whether through Augustine's own initiative or that of a later collator, they have therefore come to add yet another layer to

---

[73] Aug. *De haeresibus* Preface 3, quoting the passage from *Ep.* 221.2 that appears on p. 192 above.

[74] Aug. *De haeresibus* Preface 4, quoting *Ep.* 221.3.

this rhetoric, attesting to the veracity of the quotations he uses to frame the *De haeresibus* and so constituting a preface to the preface. They simultaneously guarantee and reinforce the placement of the author within an intellectual and textual tradition that connects him to earlier heresiologists and other writers of ancient technical literature, whilst simultaneously positioning the text itself as a sincere and learned response to the problems of the time and the insufficiencies of earlier works.

CONCLUSION

The three late-antique heresiological catalogues discussed here all used their formal prefaces, as well as other, paratextual prefatory material, as methods by which to position their literary endeavours in ways that were both recognizable and novel. The use of the 'rhetoric of modesty' and the related language of necessity and responding to requests all engaged with the generic commonplaces of classical scientific, medical, and historical texts, establishing a link between heresiology and these familiar forms of writing. Views about orthodoxy and heresy that were potentially controversial and divisive were therefore cast as descriptive accounts of clearly observable phenomena, catalogued by a disinterested expert who wrote not from any personal desire for contention or self-promotion, but because he was compelled by requests or circumstances. It has been argued, most notably by Hervé Inglebert, that heresiology in this period represented a new form of encyclopaedism and a clear departure from classical models of learning. In this interpretation, it becomes part of a larger phenomenon of the religious appropriation and transformation of classical culture, whereby all knowledge was subsumed and made Christian, or else jettisoned as inappropriate.[75] This reading of heresiology, and of the broader intellectual culture of late antiquity, depends on a narrative of the fourth century in which there was 'une réelle tentative de reaction païenne' in the two decades from 360 to 380, which was combatted in turn by the encyclopaedic endeavour of Epiphanius: 'L'histoire des hérésies devenait le prétexte à une redéfinition religieuse du savoir'.[76] Such an interpretation portrays heresiology as part of a cultural war, with battle lines clearly drawn between pagan and Christian.

Instead, however, this chapter argues for a much less combative model, in which engagement with earlier forms of assembling and organizing knowledge did not necessarily involve subordinating and subsuming them.[77]

---

[75] Inglebert (2001) 443–9.   [76] Inglebert (2001) 447, 448.
[77] For other examples of such an approach, see Flower (2011), (2018), as well as Berzon (2016b) for comparisons with ancient ethnographic texts. Jacobs (2016) 132–75 also studies

The Rhetoric of Heresiological Prefaces 197

Heresiologies are, of course, innately concerned with defining Christian identity against a range of alternatives, and often criticize aspects of 'pagan' culture, especially philosophy. In particular, Epiphanius rarely made reference to the great works of classical literature that constituted *paideia* in this period and made a number of hostile statements about them, particularly when criticizing Origen's fall into heresy.[78] Nonetheless, by aligning his project with the natural historical works of Nicander and others, as well as drawing on recognizable literary techniques and tropes from technical literature, he was not undermining or usurping the authority of these existing genres, but rather seeking to enrol heresiology alongside them as a new and secure branch of knowledge.[79] In doing so, however, he combined this modest, scholarly persona with the specifically Christian rhetoric of divine inspiration and assistance to help him overcome his difficulties and complete his great intellectual task. This went much further than ancient invocations of the Muses, pervading the entire text and imbuing it with divinely sanctioned understanding and authority, underlined by the association with *Song of Songs*. This precedent was followed by his two immediate heresiological successors, who both adapted and developed it for their own circumstances: Filastrius employed his own analogy with the natural world, but, in a more extreme manner than the others, shunned any direct comparisons with 'secular' literature to cast his work as both exegesis and fulfilment of Scripture; Augustine, writing a few decades later, used comparisons with earlier heresiologies to frame his *De haeresibus*, combined with a rhetoric of unwillingness that was bolstered by the inclusion of the *ipsissima verba* of Quodvultdeus' request and also a characterization of the text as a divinely granted gift in response to the prayers of his admirers. Their prefaces each represent individual engagements with both the rhetorical norms of ancient technical writing and the distinct concerns of Christian heresiological controversy, allowing their authors to craft religious identities for themselves as expert defenders of orthodoxy against its many enemies.

Epiphanius' works in the context of Roman 'antiquarian' literature, rejecting the notion that there is a tension between 'classical' and 'Christian' knowledge, but nonetheless regarding Epiphanius as wishing to 'demonstrate the power of Christian culture to perfectly contain and display, in tiny bits and morsels, all the knowledge of the world' (175).

[78] Inglebert (2001) 437–8; Kim (2015a) 19.
[79] See also Williams (2009) xxix on Epiphanius' professed rejection of rhetoric, which was itself a very common rhetorical trope in the ancient world.

13

Constructing Identity in the Tomb

The Visual Rhetoric of Early Christian Iconography

Robin M. Jensen

INTRODUCTION

The largest surviving corpora of third- and fourth-century Christian artefacts come primarily from burial contexts and are comprised of wall paintings found in the Christian catacombs of Rome and figurative relief sculptures carved on marble sarcophagi. The latter were fabricated in, and exported from, workshops across the empire, although the largest number of surviving monuments has been found in Rome itself.[1] As most of these objects were destined for private tombs belonging to upper-class or wealthy families, they cannot be regarded as public monuments. Even in the cemeteries apparently owned and managed by church authorities and shared with the more ordinary dead, these monuments were probably intended for select groups of viewers—mainly family members, close friends, and colleagues.

Presumably, the individuals who commissioned the artisans and paid for their work had influence on its design, material, and the general quality of the workmanship. Cost would have been a consideration. Tomb paintings show a range of styles and technical skill. Many sarcophagi probably were custom-made pieces with patrons wielding significant control over the size, material, and subject matter. Less costly monuments likely were pre-fabricated in workshops that sold them partially if not wholly finished to clients with more modest budgets. Some clients would have lined up the work well in advance; others who were in more urgent need may have had to settle for what was available. Thus, it is not easy to say whose decisions—patrons' or artisans'—are reflected in the final products. Yet, the visual motifs that buyers

---

[1] For examples outside of Rome, see Koch (2018).

Robin M. Jensen, *Constructing Identity in the Tomb: The Visual Rhetoric of Early Christian Iconography* In: *Rhetoric and Religious Identity in Late Antiquity.* Edited by: Richard Flower and Morwenna Ludlow, Oxford University Press (2020). © Oxford University Press. DOI: 10.1093/oso/9780198813194.003.00013

either selected or approved indicate something about their identity, values, or the ways they—or the deceased—wished to be represented. Probably it was a collaborative exercise in most instances.

One cannot assume that workshops served only one kind of customer or that there were specialized ateliers that catered mainly to self-identified Christians. Those who worked on the commissions likely were neither conversant with specific religious teachings nor wished to promote one system over another. Nevertheless, beginning in the third century, certain iconographic subjects on these monuments point to Christian affiliation and indicate that they were ordered for Christian rather than polytheist or Jewish patrons. Whilst some fluidity in religious identity must have been likely, and family members could have had varying cultic attachments, depictions of episodes from gospel narratives, like the raising of Lazarus or Jesus changing water to wine, are revealing, even where they appear alongside religiously ambiguous motifs.

Assuming that the workshops served a religiously varied clientele, they would have had to offer a range of religious motifs, although these could be augmented with broadly popular decorative motifs or ambiguous symbols in which viewers might find various meanings. Obviously, New Testament figures were decisively Christian, but as Christians also regarded the Hebrew Scriptures as their sacred texts, images from the Old Testament appear alongside depictions of Jesus or the apostles (Fig. 13.1). In Roman funerary art, Old Testament subjects are typically incorporated into larger programmes that include New Testament iconography, which suggests that these images jointly conveyed a particularly Christian message or significance. This kind of linking had already occurred in the New Testament itself, as in Jesus's reference to Jonah (Matt. 12.38–40) and was a standard mode of textual

Fig. 13.1. Early Christian sarcophagus with scenes from the Old and New Testaments (Sacrifice of Isaac, Jesus healing the blind man, Jesus healing the paralytic, Jesus multiplying loaves and fish, Adam and Eve, Jesus raising the dead). Museo Pio Cristiano, Vatican, early fourth century. Photo credit: Vanni Archive/Art Resource, NY.

interpretation in the early Church. In other words, the incorporation of a biblical figure like Daniel should not be regarded as an indication that the work was done for a Jewish client but rather that the story of Daniel was given a Christian relevance.

The biblical subjects comprised a fairly limited repertoire and consistently recur in both wall paintings and sarcophagus reliefs. Whilst no two paintings or carved programmes are identical, and variances in composition and quality are evident, overall those monuments we typically identify with early Christianity consistently include certain popular characters. Some of these figures appeared earlier than others, with new motifs appearing over time. A discernable trajectory is evident, from a few biblical types in the later third century to a much wider selection of narrative episodes by the early fourth. This growth might be explained by the growing social and financial security of self-identified Christians following the Constantinian peace. Perhaps clients themselves suggested innovations and as artisans agreed and experimented, their catalogue expanded.

Inclusion of certain representative biblical scenes is not the only basis for distinguishing early Christian artworks from pagan or Jewish ones, however. These also show a high degree of stylistic consistency both in terms of how the figures are organized or placed within the pictorial plane, as well as in the ways they function within the overall composition. This shift in technique offers a striking contrast to that found on pagan monuments of the same type and is particularly evident when one compares early to mid-third-century mythological sarcophagi from Rome with their slightly later Christian counterparts of the late third and early fourth century. The Christian sarcophagi not only differ in pictorial content—the usual basis for associating them with Christian clients—they also look dissimilar in ways that may contribute as much to how they communicate their general message as do the subjects they depict. In other words, both the form and content should be considered with respect to the rhetorical value of early Christian iconography. As in oral performance, a speaker's vocal technique conveys her intended meaning as much as her actual words. Visual art likewise uses formal elements of style along with iconography to communicate with its viewers.[2]

Whilst this is applicable to other kinds of early Christian artefacts, a focused study of the sarcophagi makes this especially clear. Fortunately, the corpus of Christian sarcophagi—whether whole or partial—is usefully large. The production of Christian sarcophagi seems to have begun at the end of the third century and continues through the fourth and beyond. More than two thousand examples have survived, allowing a comprehensive study of how Christian pictorial imagery evolved over this period.[3] By comparison, there are over

---

[2] Jensen (2014), (2015).
[3] The standard catalogue for this is Bovini and Brandenburg (1967).

a thousand examples of pagan sarcophagi that have been dated to roughly this same time frame—from the late third through the mid-fourth century.[4] This smaller number reflects the dramatic decrease in distinctively pagan monuments by the middle of the fourth century, undoubtedly due to the rising dominance of Christianity at that time.

Despite their disproportionate numbers, comparing roughly contemporary pagan and Christian examples from Rome allows analysis of their evident differences in iconography and technique, especially as both types served the same purpose (a burial box), had similar size and shape, and were even made in similar or perhaps even the same workshops. In addition, whilst they clearly display different visual content, their figural decoration is placed on the casket on roughly the same, spatially defined fields (e.g., front friezes, ends, and lids). Most significantly, perhaps, each exhibits a high level of internal consistency of both style and content, which makes it somewhat easier to generalize about them and their rhetorical strategies as a group.

ROMAN SARCOPHAGI

Because they are the closest in date, consideration of some mid- to late third-century Roman sarcophagi allows the most useful comparison with early Christian examples. Moreover, excellent, recent scholarly studies have extensively considered the evolution of the style and imagery of these objects, amongst them works by Paul Zanker, Björn Ewald, Janet Huskinson, Stine Birk, Jaś Elsner, Michael Koortbojian, Zahra Newby, and Barbara Borg.[5] Earlier funerary monuments that were produced during the era—often referred to as the Second Sophistic, roughly from the reign of Nero to the first quarter of the third century, when the elite members of the society desired to display their fluency with classical literature—particularly featured references to mythological tales. They featured favourite mythological subjects like Meleager and the Calydonian Boar hunt, or the meetings of Dionysus and Ariadne or Selene visiting the sleeping Endymion (Fig. 13.2).

Whilst such motifs likely would have exhibited the owner's taste or cultural refinement when used for villa wall paintings, luxurious silver platters, or lovely garden statuary, these were specifically for burial coffins. Hence, their imagery would have reflected aspects of their beliefs or attitudes about death or mourning.[6] Heroic depictions of Meleager's boar hunt, probably a reference

---

[4] According to Couzin (2014). There are many earlier pagan sarcophagi, of course.
[5] For example, Elsner (1995); Koortbojian (1995); Newby (2011); Zanker and Ewald (2012); Birk (2013); Huskinson (2015); and Borg (2013).
[6] Zanker and Ewald (2012) 20–1, 103–9 specifically, but generally throughout.

Fig. 13.2. Marble sarcophagus with the myth of Endymion and Selene, mid-second-century CE, Rome. Metropolitan Museum of Art, Fletcher Fund, 1924. Photo credit: Open Access for Scholarly Publication.

Fig. 13.3. Sarcophagus of Quinta Flavia Severina, Musei Capitolini, Rome, 230–40. Wikimedia Creative Commons. Photo credit: Jean-Pol Grandmont.

to the manly virtues of the deceased, were juxtaposed with the scene of his body being returned to his grieving mother. Depictions of devoted mythological couples (e.g., Admetus and Alcestis, Theseus and Ariadne) or the abduction of Persephone, exemplified the ideas of loss, grief, or hopes for reunion in the next world. Erotic or idyllic subjects that featured displays of Bacchic revelries or sea creatures and Nereids gradually became more popular, perhaps alluding to the joys of life or hopes for a blissful afterlife (Fig. 13.3).[7]

Zanker and Ewald's study of the evolution of pagan sarcophagi summarizes certain evident transformations in both the subject matter and style displayed

[7] Zanker and Ewald (2012) 111–38.

Fig. 13.4. Sarcophagus of C. Junius Euphodus and Metilla Acte, depicted in scenes from the myth of Admetus and Alcestis, 161–70, now in the Museo Chiaramonti, Vatican Museum. Wikimedia Creative Commons. Photo credit: Jastrow.

on Roman sarcophagi from during the late second century. They specifically point to the dramatic style that emerged from the 'dissolution of the classical form' and 'compressed compositions' in the late Antonine period and the gradual 'abandonment of mythical images' at the end of the Severan period and through the rest of the third century.[8] This, they argue, could be attributed to 'Romans distancing themselves, at least partially, from the culture of Greek-oriented classical education'.[9] Stylistically, the figures became less proportional and compositions more dense, whilst the themes transitioned away from mythological references to death, heroic activities, and even from sensual pleasures.

The earlier mythological compositions—the hunter/warrior and 'loving couple' types—were sometimes made even more autobiographical by accommodating actual portraits of the deceased and his/her loved ones, whose facial likenesses were given to the mythological characters (Fig. 13.4).[10] Depicting the deceased as the hero of the story allowed the image to be personalized and the myth to convey real-life references to adventures, marital fidelity, bereavement, or optimistic hope for post-mortem reunions. In this way tomb imagery became an enduring memorial of an individual's achievements and intimate relationships. These types were distinctly different from the more straightforward bust portraits of the deceased individual (or married couple) enclosed in a shield (*clipeus*) or circular (tondo) frame (cf. Figs. 13.3, 13.5). Whilst these medallion portraits had existed earlier, they became more common after the middle of the third century.

Around this same time (the mid-third century), new themes emerged and began to dominate. These tended to be less mythological and even non-narrative in character. Amongst them were generic hunting imagery, harvesters and shepherds, scenes of open-air banquets, and personifications of the four seasons (Figs. 13.5, 13.6). Along with these, a different kind of personalized iconography appeared that featured images of seated males holding

---

[8] Zanker and Ewald (2012) 249–51.   [9] Zanker and Ewald (2012) 259.
[10] Newby (2011); Zanker and Ewald (2012) 39–46; Birk (2013) 94–107.

Fig. 13.5. Sarcophagus with Allegory of the Four Seasons, ca. 280, marble, 24 ¾ × 72 × 25 ¾, Chazen Museum of Art, University of Wisconsin-Madison, Max W. Zabel Fund purchase, 69.13.1, used with permission.

Fig. 13.6. Sarcophagus of Julius Achilleus, Museo Nazionale Romano, ca. 270, found in Rome near the Baths of Caracalla. Photo credit: Vanni Archive/Art Resource, NY.

scrolls and accompanied by female muses, family members, or other admirers and represented a significant change in how the dead wanted to be portrayed (Fig. 13.7).[11] These also could be customized as portraits, but instead of inserting the deceased as the protagonists of a story, the departed were shown as they wished to be remembered in life—as respectable and learned heads of families or civic leaders. Such images not only served as visual eulogies, they also extolled the importance of *paideia*, but instead of featuring

[11] Borg (2014) 238.

Fig. 13.7. Sarcophagus said to be of Plotinus, late third to fourth century, Museo Gregoriano Profano, Vatican. Photo credit: Scala/Art Resource.

classical myths that alluded to heroic actions or emotional attachments, they displayed the value of education, cultivated virtues, the value of serenity, and even detachment from distracting passions.[12]

Scholars have suggested that this dramatic turn towards non-mythological iconography indicates a change in religious sensibilities or reflects a new set of values. Could it, as Zanker and Ewald suggest, signal a change in attitude towards classical culture or (alternatively) just a general change of mood—a 'new seriousness in the language of images used in the face of death?'[13] They maintain that the replacement of mythological scenes by images of seasons, harvesting putti, shepherds, and philosophers might have arisen during a time of political and social insecurity or offered 'coping strategies as the traditional concepts of the self faltered'.[14] These authors also propose that this trend towards a certain kind of escapism or an emphasis on retreat into the home or the library might have been prompted by the spread of Christianity, particularly amongst the Roman upper classes.[15] In any case, the surviving evidence indicates that by the middle of the fourth century, sarcophagi with pagan themes or even purely neutral imagery had mostly disappeared in favour of those bearing distinctly Christian motifs.

[12] Ewald (2012).   [13] Zanker and Ewald (2012) 262.
[14] Zanker and Ewald (2012) 263.   [15] Zanker and Ewald (2012) 263, 260.

CHRISTIAN SARCOPHAGI

Even though they had adopted a new (or additional) religious identity or affiliation, Christians carried on many of their traditional burial practices, including the procurement of elaborately carved sarcophagi for the burial of their dead. As on those earlier Roman monuments, both iconographic and formal components conveyed information regarding their owners' wealth, social status, and character or, perhaps more accurately, the ways their friends or family wished to represent and remember them. The iconographic subjects selected for these sarcophagi differed from the earlier Roman examples, however, and as such reflected the distinctively Christian aspects of those owners' affiliation or identity. Moreover, because of their striking similarity to other evidently Christian burial monuments, these aspects were generally shared across their faith community.

Like older pagan sarcophagi, some early Christian examples appear to have been designed to allow placing facial likenesses of the deceased on certain stock figures. Slightly later monuments set standardized portrait medallions on top of, and disconnected from, the rest of the design (cf. Fig. 13.9). Generally, however, most early Christian sarcophagi display few personalizing characteristics (apart from epitaphs) and draw upon a nearly standardized set of iconographic motifs. These motifs, mostly based on biblical narratives from both the Old and New Testaments, seem randomly arranged with little evident attention to composition or quality craftsmanship. Thus, rather than demonstrating a desire to memorialize particular individuals, these objects' design and visual imagery instead display a collection of more or less standard pictorial elements drawn from Christian sacred texts. Markedly, the use of these elements actually represents a significant return to narrative iconography on Roman sarcophagi after its near disappearance on pagan monuments.

So far as we can tell from iconographic evidence alone, identifiably Christian sarcophagi appear around the end of the third century, around (or just after) the time when, as Zanker and Ewald assert, the pagan sarcophagi began to demonstrate a preference for generic pastoral and bucolic settings, or extolling the virtues of reading and philosophical contemplation over the depiction of grand mythological narratives.[16] Initially, a few of these Christian monuments shared many of these common themes with their pagan counterparts, which would make their religious character ambiguous without the addition of clearly Christian motifs. Shepherds, garlands, seated male readers, fishing, and/or harvesting scenes were adapted from this pre-existing imagery and could be attributed Christian significance. For example, a shepherd

---

[16] Zanker and Ewald (2012) 245–60.

Fig. 13.8. Sarcophagus of Sta. Maria Antiqua, Rome (Forum), ca. 290–300. Photo credit: Robin M. Jensen.

bearing a ram over his shoulders could be construed as representing the Christian Good Shepherd (e.g., Figs. 13.8 and 13.12) or simply as a caretaking shepherd protecting his flock.[17] Vintaging or wheat-harvesting scenes could allude to the sacred meal of bread and wine as well as decorative references to the pleasures of country life or the joys of making wine (e.g., Fig. 13.6).

Similarly, Christian monuments frequently included a female praying figure (*orant*) that appears to be borrowed from Roman personifications of *pietas* (cf. Figs. 13.8 and 13.11). In earlier pagan monuments a woman holding a scroll may have been meant to be the feminine counterpart of the learned male reader and apparently emerged at around the same time.[18] Both in painting and sculpture, the Christian *orant* is nearly always shown with both arms raised and her eyes upturned, which implies religious devotion more than erudition. In certain early examples she is juxtaposed with both the seated reader and the shepherd, making up a group that might have been intended to convey the common Roman and Christian virtues of piety, *paideia*, and philanthropy (Fig. 13.8). Without additional visual cues, like the inclusion of a Jonah episode or a depiction of John baptizing Jesus, this group could have been as suitable for a pagan patron as a Christian one.

Thus, in this transitional period, viewers might have discerned a variety of meanings in the imagery, and this could even have been the client's intention. Conventional visual motifs are effectively adapted to convey new messages largely because of their pre-existing resonance. Of course, this also permits viewers to have different perceptions and interpretations and to accommodate

---

[17] Huskinson (2015) 197–8.   [18] Birk (2013) 73–4, 90–1; Huskinson (2015) 198.

patrons whose religious affiliations may have been somewhat fluctuating or adaptable. However, such examples did not continue much beyond the early fourth century. Eventually, the iconographic conversion became nearly complete and the shepherd (for example) more firmly identified with the biblical allegory for Christ (cf. John 10.11). Compositions that simultaneously incorporated subjects like Noah in the ark, Daniel in the lions' den, Jonah emerging from the mouth of the sea creature, or Jesus raising Lazarus were more evidently made for the Christian market. Innovations in the iconographic programmes along with certain unmistakable shifts in style and composition provide evidence of a new kind of visual rhetoric of religious identity. Once distinctively Christian pictorial content and artistic technique began to appear on these costly burial coffins—whether or not still combined with religiously ambiguous or generic motifs—it undoubtedly began to reflect what its adherents discerned as central in the teachings of this new religious movement.

CHRISTIAN ICONOGRAPHIC REPERTOIRE

As noted above, biblical subjects began to appear on Roman sarcophagi at the end of the third century and thereby signal a return to narrative iconography in this medium of Roman art. One of the most visually obvious characteristics of this iconography is its limited catalogue.[19] Most of these objects display a discrete group of regularly recurring motifs. A preponderance of the earliest themes in catacomb painting were drawn from the Old Testament. They included Abraham with Isaac, Jonah (usually shown in a set of sequential episodes), Noah standing in the prayer posture inside an open box-like ark, or Daniel with his lions. The sarcophagi include many of these same subjects but are more prone to depict stories from the New Testament alongside them. Soon a variety of other images are evident, many of them having already been depicted in the paintings found in the Roman catacombs.

Drawn from Old Testament narratives are the disobedience of Adam and Eve, Abraham offering his son Isaac as a sacrifice, Moses striking the rock in the wilderness, Daniel in the lions' den, the three Hebrew youths in the fiery furnace, and Susannah with the Elders. The earliest surviving New Testament subjects on the sarcophagi are Jesus raising Lazarus and John's baptism of Jesus. Soon other images were added, also having parallels in catacomb painting. These include depictions of the magi coming to adore the Christ child, Jesus multiplying loaves and fish, Jesus healing the blind man and the paralytic, Jesus changing water to wine, Jesus with the Samaritan woman, and

[19] Dresken-Weiland (2011) 2010.

Fig. 13.9. Early Christian sarcophagus with various biblical scenes, Museo Pio Cristiano, Vatican, first quarter of the fourth century. Photo credit Scala/Art Resource, NY.

Jesus raising the dead. Non-canonical scriptural images also appear by the middle of the fourth century, including depictions of Peter striking the rock to baptize his Roman jailers. Whereas the image of Moses striking the rock to give water to the Israelites in the desert (Ex 17.6) was more popular in early catacomb painting, the sarcophagi almost unanimously transfer this motif to the apostle Peter, easily identified by his distinctive facial type and accompanying rooster (cf. Fig. 13.9).[20]

Images that one might expect based on their popularity in later Christian art appear to be missing (e.g., the Last Supper and the crucifixion). To modern eyes, even the stock presentations of favourite scenes may seem strange, like the single-file procession of three youthful magi towards Mary and the Christ child, consistently seated in profile. Familiar types are used and reused, even though the literary corpus had far more to offer. In this respect they are like the pagan sarcophagi, which also tended to feature certain stories over others. Yet, as restricted as the Christian narrative subjects may appear to be, they are actually more varied than the subjects commonly found on the pagan sarcophagi. A brief listing of the mythological figures in Stine Birk's catalogue

[20] Dresken-Weiland (2010) 144–6, (2018).

gives about twenty—from Achilles to Venus.[21] By contrast, almost twice as many Christian biblical motifs appear on sarcophagi dated from the late third through to the late fourth century.

VARIOUS INTERPRETATIONS OF THE PROGRAMMES

One of the striking features in early Christian art generally is the popularity of Old Testament themes, especially in the earliest examples. Certain characters, like Adam and Eve, Abraham and Isaac, Jonah, Noah, and Daniel, regularly show up on funerary monuments. Although scholars have sometimes cited this dominance of Hebrew Scripture narratives as evidence of Jewish influence, the fact that Christians regarded the Old Testament as their sacred text along with the New Testament literature is a more plausible explanation.[22] In fact, the choices of Old Testament stories have often been explained as reflecting one of the traditional ways Christians interpreted them, as prefigurations of events from the life of Christ or features of early Christian teaching or practice.[23]

This kind of exegetical strategy links stories from the two Scriptures, often as typological pairs, and according to some scholars, this is the most successful way to interpret the iconography. For example, Abraham's offering of Isaac is a prototype of Jesus's self-sacrifice on the cross and Moses striking the rock is regarded as a foreshadowing of Christian baptism (giving water to the thirsty people). As appealing as this explanation by means of textual parallel is, this exegetical explanation is only partially applicable, as several of the early images have no obvious typological function (e.g., Susannah and the Elders), nor does it account for most of the New Testament scenes that also appear on the sarcophagi, particularly the many images of Jesus healing the infirm or raising the dead (cf. Fig. 13.1). This also challenges a proposal that the iconographic programmes promote Christian identity largely in a negative sense: through a polemic against the veneration of false gods (idolatry) or apologetic assertion of Christianity's superiority to, and rejection of, its Jewish roots.[24]

Some scholars have argued that the subjects depicted on Christian sarcophagi (and catacomb paintings) were drawn from ancient prayers for the dead (*commendatio animae*), which asked God for deliverance as he once rescued heroes like Noah, Isaac, Daniel, and the three Hebrew youths.[25] Whilst these prayers' funereal context makes this an appealing hypothesis, extant texts mainly survive only in ninth-century documents and include figures not generally found in early Christian art (e.g., Lot, Enoch, and David) whilst

---

[21] Birk (2013).   [22] On this question see Jensen (2000) 68–71.
[23] A recent instance in Huskinson (2015) 213–18; also Tkacz (2002).
[24] This interpretation follows Elsner (2014) 338–411.   [25] Tkacz (2002) 109–7.

omitting a few that do (e.g., Jonah or Lazarus). By contrast, certain non-scriptural images, like the representation of diners seated around a semi-circular table, may be depictions of the hoped-for meal in paradise, or perhaps a reference to the funeral meal celebrated in the tomb.

More broadly, scholars often have seen these stock figures generally as alluding to Christian teaching about God's deliverance from personal danger, illness, religious persecution, or—most significantly—death.[26] This explanation applies fairly well to images like the three Hebrew youths in their fiery furnace or Noah surviving the flood but does not suit many others. Moses receiving the Law, the adoration of the magi, Jesus' baptism by John, or Jesus changing water to wine at Cana do not seem to fit the category of salvation narratives nor do they specifically depict divine rescue from the peril or the grave. Reference to the disobedience of Adam and Eve, shown with their tree and serpent, is equally puzzling in this respect. A new type arose around the middle of the fourth century that depicted Christ with his apostles, either teaching or handing over the new law to Peter and Paul, neither of which has obvious associations with death or directly refers to God's plan for individual salvation.

Just as with the Roman mythological sarcophagi, one tends to assume that the decoration of a tomb or coffin should exhibit beliefs about death and expectations for an afterlife. The tomb context is undoubtedly a significant factor guiding their decorative schemes. Nevertheless, the extent to which this iconography differs from that on non-funerary types of Christian artefacts is unclear. Because the preponderance of the surviving evidence comes from a burial milieu, making comparisons is difficult. Small objects like engraved gems or pottery lamps tended to show several of the popular types that regularly appear on sarcophagi (e.g., Jonah, Noah, Adam and Eve, and the Good Shepherd). Fourth-century gold glasses include images of Jesus's miracles (e.g., raising Lazarus, multiplying loaves and fish) and Peter in the guise of Moses striking the rock. Christian wall paintings in contemporary Roman churches might well have featured many of these same images, but this is impossible to know.[27]

Various efforts to find a single, guiding rationale for why a stock collection of biblical narratives was favoured for these funeral monuments may be ultimately futile. Nor is there likely any one right way of interpreting them. Instead it seems more useful to view the iconography as simply a sequence of morally edifying, encouraging, or inspirational stories. Some of the Old Testament figures are exemplars of resistance to idolatry (e.g., Daniel and the three Hebrew youths); others were models of obedience to religious command or trust in God's promises (e.g., Abraham, Noah, and Susannah).

---

[26] Notably Snyder (2003); also Zanker and Ewald (2012) 263–4.
[27] A famous exception is the house church in Dura Europos, although in Syria and not Rome. See also Paulinus of Nola's description of the decoration of his church, *Carm.* 27, 511–95.

Others clearly allude to hope for resurrection from death (e.g., Isaac, Jonah, and Daniel). Depictions of the fall of Adam and Eve might allude to the origins of death itself. New Testament stories that showed Jesus working miracles, healing the sick, and raising the dead displayed his power as well as his compassion; depictions of his adoration by the magi, baptism by John, or entering Jerusalem highlighted his divinity. A few may even be allegorical or typological references to Christian initiatory or sacred meal rituals (e.g., the Samaritan woman at the well, Peter striking the rock, or Jesus' wine and bread miracles).

Whilst individual scenes arguably point to aspects either of Christian teachings about Jesus or right conduct of life, as an accumulation they become a kind of catechetical compendium. They have no evident thematic or chronological order or rationale; Old Testament narratives are mixed in with New Testament subjects. As Zanker and Ewald have argued, despite many attempts, scholars have been at a loss to find some key to their coherence.[28] Perhaps it was simply the case that more was considered to be better and clients paid by the figure and aimed at displaying their piety (or their wealth) by ordering the carvers to include as many as possible.

By the early fourth century, certain other distinctive attributes of the Christian monuments began to appear. Although the most identifying feature of Christian monuments is their incorporation of biblical, especially New Testament content, the Christian sculptural programmes also show certain formal or compositional characteristics that distinguish them from their pagan counterparts. These characteristics also warrant investigation into why they emerge and what they might reflect regarding Christian religious beliefs, practices, and values. Important as subject matter or iconography is for identifying objects with certain religious affiliations or convictions, it is not the only way that objects convey their meaning. Technical aspects of style, craft, or composition are equally essential in a study of visual rhetoric.

PORTRAITS ON CHRISTIAN MONUMENTS

Initially, Christian sarcophagi evidently were designed to allow customization of their iconography by the inclusion of facial likenesses on figures like the *orant* or seated reader. Interestingly, like a few pagan examples, these portraits occasionally were left unfinished, as if the buyers lacked the necessary time to allow the partially completed monument to be customized (e.g., Fig. 13.8).[29] In any case, the shepherd figure was evidently excluded from this kind of portrait.

---

[28] Zanker and Ewald (2012) 264.
[29] Huskinson (1998); Zanker and Ewald (2012) 43; Birk (2013), 199.

Fig. 13.10. Portrait of Catervius and Severina, now in the Cathedral of San Catervo in Tolentino. Photo credit: Mark D. Ellison, used with permission.

Additionally, unlike the pagan sarcophagi, it appears that characters from Christian mythology—for example, Jonah—were never given the facial likeness of the one in the coffin. By the early- to mid-fourth century, portraits of the deceased (as individuals or a couple) were more usually incorporated as busts, commonly enclosed in *clipeus* or half scallop shell (cf. Figs. 13.9, 13.10). Although this form of commemoration had been widely used for pagan monuments in addition to other ways of personalizing the iconography, Christian examples tend to employ this type of portrait feature almost exclusively.[30]

---

[30] Birk (2013) 226. Some exceptions include a wedding scene on a strigillated sarcophagus that eliminates the figures of Juno Pronuba or Concordia; Birk (2013) 228.

214   *Rhetoric and Religious Identity in Late Antiquity*

Normally placed in the centre of the front face of the sarcophagus, these single or—more often—double portraits were not integrated into the rest of the frieze composition. As noted above, they exist apart from the scenes that surround them and, set off by their circular or scalloped frames, seem detached and even unaware of the surrounding figures. Moreover, whilst the facial features of the portraits must have been intended to show some level of individual likeness, minimal efforts to this end were undoubtedly added to a pre-fabricated set of posed busts. Single portraits are less common on the Christian examples. Usually the double portrait depicts a married couple, although examples with two women or two men have been found. Normally, the wife appears to the left of her husband. She wears the matronly veil and turns her face towards him so that she is in three-quarters profile.

In many cases, the wife clasps her husband's right arm with her right hand, so not precisely a depiction of the *dextrarum iunctio* posture so often featured on the Roman sarcophagi that accent the married state (cf. Fig. 13.9). He, by contrast, looks out and to his right and holds a scroll in his left hand. An exception to this appears on the sarcophagus of Catervius and Severina, found in Tolentino, where the couple clasp hands (Fig. 13.10). Here a hand holds a beribboned crown over the heads of the couple evidently implying that their union is one that is not only blessed by God but has an element of sanctity attached to it. This sarcophagus also displays portraits of the couple on the acroteria of the sarcophagus's lid—an addition that is similarly unusual (Fig. 13.12).

Because the *clipeus* or tondo portraits are distinctly set apart from the background imagery of the main frieze, the deceased are not associated with a particular sacred narrative just as they are not presented as one of its actors. Nevertheless, this way of incorporating portraits suggests that adding some sense of personal identity and social conformity, or at least ownership, to these monuments was valued and perhaps even important to those who could afford these kinds of burial boxes. Moreover, these objects frequently featured inscriptions that named the deceased, gave his or her age at death, and in some instances added more biographical details or extensive dedications.[31] By the late fourth century, some examples appear that show small figures of a man and woman kneeling at Christ's feet.

Before that, however, it appears that Christian patrons did not require more than a minimal effort to insert themselves in the biblical narratives as such, or to place themselves in some obvious, privileged personal relationship to Christ. Because of their similarity to one another, these simple *clipeus* portraits reveal little about their models' particular virtues or character. In other words, in contrast to the pagan sarcophagi, Christians apparently chose to include their portraits on their funeral monuments, but not in a manner that would

---

[31] The sarcophagus of Catervius and Severina is a fine example (cf. Fig. 13.12).

COMPOSITIONAL AND STYLISTIC ELEMENTS

The regular recurrence of a stock set of images undoubtedly aids viewers' comprehension, but their discernment also depends on inside knowledge. This is largely because, unlike the mythological sarcophagi, the stories are symbolized by minimal pictorial motifs that do little more than merely point to their sources. For example, Noah stands upright with his hands raised in the prayer posture, alone, and in an open, floating casket. A dove may appear in the image as a second, helpful clue to what the image apparently depicts. No other figures appear (e.g., Noah's wife, children, or animals) and the ark is too small to hold more than one person in any case. Similarly, showing Jesus touching a staff to several jars is the usual way to depict him performing the miracle of changing water to wine and here Jesus's mother is omitted, along with most other details from the story (cf. Figs. 13.9, 13.11). These abbreviated figures are a kind of synecdoche insofar as one detail stands for the whole idea. Thus, viewers must know how to translate this limited visual vocabulary into full Scripture references. The ensembles are visual paradigms rather than illustrations.

Understanding how this works requires a certain level of literacy or at least familiarity with the stories. These images do not replace texts but serve a different kind of communicative function. An ability to identify the figures assumes both basic biblical literacy and familiarity with the monuments' visual vocabulary. In other words, educated viewers not only recognized the motifs, but also understood them. Thus they, like their pagan counterparts, relied upon and demonstrated the owner's *paideia*—or, in this case, Christian erudition. This knowledge might well have been attained through oral forms of discourse (e.g., sermons, catechetical lectures) or through reading, although the former also presumes some experience of exegetical reflection upon the ways the stories point beyond themselves and thus the images are more than mere illustrations of textual narratives.

Exceptions exist. The front panels of a few fourth-century sarcophagi display a single theme: the story of Pharaoh and his army pursing Moses and the Israelites through the Red Sea.[32] The Jonah story is nearly unique in that it often occurs in a series of three or four episodes (Jonah being thrown

---

[32] Koch (2014) 313–15.

Fig. 13.11. Tree sarcophagus, Proconnesian marble, ca. 375 CE; inv. FAN.92.00.2488, Musée départemental Arles antique © J.-L. Maby, L. Roux.

overboard, being swallowed by the fish, being spit up again, and reclining on dry land). Several of these are delightfully rendered with the fish's coiling tail and Jonah's emerging body drawing the viewer's gaze, but even these are normally surrounded by various images from other biblical narratives. Examples of the higher quality monuments have sculpted ends and backs and two full pictorial registers (cf. Fig. 13.9). Many dating to the second half of the fourth century place individual scenes in niches defined by architectural frames or set off by trees, city gates, columns, or other structural elements (Fig. 13.11). Although these types required more expert craftsmen and would have been purchased by more wealthy or elite clients, even these frequently feature lower-quality workmanship or awkwardly rendered figures.[33]

Compared to the iconography on the pagan mythological sarcophagi, which typically show several unified episodes from a single tale, these abbreviated images are more like punctuation marks than pictorial narratives. The characters are often awkwardly rendered, crowded into single or double friezes, overlap one another, and occupy shallow space with little or no background detail. They tend to lack a focal point or main character. The compilation of figures and the fact that they often occupy the same visual plane with little variation of size or posture tends to produce a visual muddle with little space or depth to set them apart. One assumes that the workshops that produced these mediocre objects were able to make more coherently organized and balanced compositions, deeper reliefs, or more naturally proportioned bodies. In this respect, they may remind one of those earlier examples in the late Antonine period, which eschewed classical forms and showed compressed compositions of 'piled up' figures in a 'continuous flow of events'.[34]

---

[33] A notable example is the Junius Bassus sarcophagus, which though highly polished and carefully rendered, includes some awkwardly rendered figures. See Dresken-Weiland (2018).

[34] Zanker and Ewald (2012) 250–1; and discussed above.

Fig. 13.12. Strigillated sarcophagus of Catervius and Severina, now in the Cathedral of San Catervo in Tolentino, Italy, ca. 379. Photo credit: Mark D. Ellison, used with permission.

As on many non-mythological pagan sarcophagi, strigillated panels often filled sections of the front, perhaps a labour-saving (and cost-reducing) device (Fig. 13.12). However, unlike most pagan sarcophagi (with the exception of partially finished bust portraits), some Christian examples were apparently left unfinished, their reliefs merely roughed in. It is difficult for modern scholars to fathom why someone would expend the amount of money these objects must have cost and then leave them incomplete. Perhaps, as in the case of the unfinished portraits, time or funds ran short, or it simply was not critically important to ancient clients.[35]

In general, the assembly of abbreviated figures that frequently appear to march randomly (and even awkwardly) across a sarcophagus' front panel is so striking a change from the composition on earlier pagan mythological sarcophagi that it suggests a particular rhetorical purpose. These sets of images arguably work as a compilation of proof texts rather than a unified narrative of mourning and loss, the memory or anticipation of a blissful afterlife, or commemorate an individual's particular character or virtues. Instead, they rehearse the story of salvation as a kind of visual catechism. They do not follow any particular chronological order, beginning with Adam and Eve and ending with the ascension of Christ, for example, but almost randomly offer one and another character or story to emphasize the divine plan for human deliverance from sin and death. The absence of a focal point serves this purpose, along

[35] Dresken-Weiland (2018).

with the evident lack of linear, chiastic, or other narrative structure. This is yet another new kind of visual rhetoric. Perhaps they could be described as the catechism at a glance. Like beads on a string or a poem with multiple stanzas, its multiplicity is its communicative mode.

CONCLUSION

Even if no two are exactly alike, when considering the corpus of early Christian sarcophagi as a vast collection, their similarities to one another are as striking as their differences from earlier pagan monuments of the same type. These commonalities and differences include groupings of certain stock and abbreviated figures that are uniquely Christian in contrast with the pagan mythological or religiously generic Roman iconographic motifs. Along with this, however, are the compositional and stylistic characteristics of the Christian works that distinguish them from that of their contemporary pagan counterparts.

The content and formal elements of the relief sculpture on Christian sarcophagi are illuminating in themselves, apart from the ways they are different from what came before. They represent a particularly Christian mode of viewing and a Christian type of *paideia*. The fact that, however well sculpted or poorly crafted, these objects consistently use the same pictorial images suggests that their owners tended to emphasize group identity and collectively shared narrative over individual self-expression. In that way, they avoided equating the deceased with mythological heroes or showing their particular virtues by using relatively simple and standard forms for their portraits—when they included them. And although the rationale for the popularity of certain figurative subjects or their selection and arrangement might be variously explained (from exegetical typologies to the content of liturgical prayers), when one considers the whole as a sum of its parts, it seems that the point may simply be the compilation itself. This was a strategy often used in catechetical lectures or early Christian sermons. Creating a verbal or visual crescendo of abbreviated biblical narratives gives both hearers and viewers nearly overwhelming 'proof' of the Christian God's intention to deliver his faithful from death and ultimately raise them up.

14

Renunciation and Ascetic Identity in the *Liber ad Renatum* of Asterius Ansedunensis

Hajnalka Tamas

INTRODUCTION

Late antique asceticism thrived in a variety of forms.[1] From dietary asceticism through renunciation of wealth and property to sexual renunciation and celibacy; from (sub)urban asceticism through seclusion in a monastic environment to anachoretic practices, asceticism represented an attractive *forma mentis* for both higher and lower social strata.[2] Yet, as asceticism took amplitude, this multiplicity of forms, with their fluid mechanisms of distinction, created vagueness and confusion, which at times erupted in instances of abuse—whether factual (ascetics abusing their status for a variety of material gains)[3] or simply argumentative (too radical prerequisites of renunciation, for instance). Radicalization and contestation followed suit. These processes affirmed a plurality of ascetic identities that not only defined ascetic practices against one another, but also engaged to various degrees with broader, Christian, identities. More often than not, it was the ascetic discourse behind the practical outcome that generated controversy. The synod of Gangra, for instance, did not necessarily denounce acts and behaviour considered

---

[1] I would like to thank here the organizers for their kind invitation to participate in the conference and contribute to this volume. Research for this contribution was carried out in the framework of the project *The Monk in Society: Late Antique Asceticism and Social Relations*, funded by the Fritz Thyssen Stiftung für Wissenschaftsförderung (2014–2016).

[2] More recent general works on late antique asceticism include: Elm (1994); Wimbush and Valantasis (1995); De Vogüé (1997); Merkt (2008); Röcke and Weitbrecht (2010); or Molinier (2014).

[3] Renunciation itself could be perceived as an abuse. On how, for instance, relatives of Roman aristocratic ascetics viewed their renunciation of property as abuse, see Curran (2000) 260–320.

unacceptable as such; rather, the theological agenda that informed these practices and their consequences prompted the synodal condemnation.[4]

In the shaping and affirmation of the late antique ascetic ideal, then, the views and legitimation advanced by particular ascetic teachers played an important—and often controversial—role. This contribution will explore one such instance, whereby being an ascetic is the natural state of a human person. This peculiar ascetic anthropology was developed by Asterius Ansedunensis in a little-known, presumably early fifth-century writing, the *Liber ad Renatum monachum*.

In the following, I shall briefly present the background of the *Liber ad Renatum monachum*. Next, I shall present Asterius' defence of asceticism, centred on the holistic renunciation of the world and complete withdrawal from society. This Asterius considers anthropologically inherent: by nature, the human being is called to lead a solitary and self-sufficient life. The third part of this contribution shall analyse the exegetical strategies employed in the *Liber ad Renatum monachum* to substantiate this theological–anthropological view.

ASTERII EPISCOPI ANSEDUNENSIS LIBER AD RENATUM MONACHUM

Structured as a letter written at the request of the (otherwise unknown) ascetic Renatus, the *Liber ad Renatum monachum* is actually a short polemical treatise on true and false asceticism. Asterius first provides the definition of *monachus*, to be understood in its broad sense, that of 'ascetic' (ch. IV.11) Then he illustrates this definition by describing what he considers to be 'true' types of ascetic practice (chapters V–XII). The third and largest part of his work is dedicated to exposing the 'false' ascetics: the vainglorious and short-sighted, who get involved in society and the public space (chapters XIII–XXV); and above all, the syneisakts, ascetic men and women who live together in private houses although they are not blood relatives (chapters XXVI–XXX).

About the author of the *Liber ad Renatum monachum* little is known, except that he was greatly indebted to Jerome. The most important source remains the text itself. The *opusculum* ascribed to Asterius is extant in a single manuscript, dating from the sixteenth century.[5] The *titulus* describes Asterius as *episcopus Ansedunensis*, whereas the index of the manuscript simply qualifies him *diui Hieronymi discipulus*. The codex, therefore, presents Asterius as one of

---

[4] By way of example, the first two canons speak against denying the possibility of salvation for those who are married and those who do not fast (i.e., non-ascetic Christians).

[5] Verona, Bibl. Capitolare CXIII, f. 69r–76v. This contains a series of lesser-known fifth-century texts.

Jerome's intimates and a bishop. This, corroborated with the Hieronymian undertones of the *Liber ad Renatum*, led the handful of scholars who dealt with the *Liber ad Renatum* to identify its author as the once sub-deacon, later bishop Asterius, who at the beginning of the fifth century acted as letter-bearer between Jerome and Augustine. Although this identification is far from certain, the general tone of the work suggests an early fifth-century date.[6]

Asterius was indeed very fond of Jerome. Not only did he quote from Jerome's writings,[7] but he often borrowed his style, his language, and even his exegetical strategies.[8] The most prominent Hieronymian sources on which the *Liber ad Renatum* is modelled are letters 14, 22, 117, and 125 (all containing ascetic recommendations), with copious inspiration drawn from the *Aduersus Iouinianum* as well. Asterius used terms and structures with a distinct Hieronymian ring, such as *agapetarum pestifera uocabula*, *angelica conuersatio*, or *Christum... nudum nudus inquirat*.[9] A curious sailing metaphor in chapter I.3 has a close parallel in the *Aduersus Iouinianum*.[10] The prelude of the *Liber ad Renatum*, as well as its tripartite structure recall letters 117 and 125, respectively.[11] But Asterius was not just a compiler of citations from Jerome. His intimacy with Jerome is manifest in his use of language and rhetoric. Asterius keenly applied the *Latinitas Hieronymiana*, as characteristic junctures show; his blending of Classical heritage (especially Cicero, Virgil, and Ovid) with Scripture and the rhetorical use of Scriptural language betrays the style of Jerome.[12]

---

[6] Jer. *ep.* 102–3; Aug. *ep.* 82 = Jer. *ep.* 116 (here Asterius is styled 'collegam meum', i.e., a bishop). His episcopal see, whether Anthedon, in Palestina, or Ansedunum, in North-Western Italy, remains unknown, for none of the advanced hypotheses is convincing. For a discussion of Asterius' identity and the proposed hypotheses, see Tamas and Van der Sypt (2013) 506–12.

[7] Jakobi (2011) VIII: 'centonem ex Hieronymo consutum'.

[8] Gennaro (1972) XIII–XV.

[9] Aster. *Liber* VII.17 (Jakobi, 7.28–8.1): 'Let Christ the poor be followed by a poorer servant, the naked be sought by a naked'. Cf. Jer. *ep.* 125.20.15 (CSEL 56, 142.8). The expression is rare even for Jerome, occurring only once apart from *ep.* 125 (*Hom. in Lucam de Lazaro et diuite* 242, CChrSL 78); cf. Aug. *Serm.* 95 (PL 38, 584.30).

[10] Jer. *Adv. Iovinian.* 1.3.

[11] The first, probably an invention of Jerome's, presented Asterius with a precedent to write a fictitious letter. In the second, Asterius found the model to arrange his material. Jerome structures letter 125, written to an ascetic named Rusticus, who had sought advice on which ascetic course to follow, in three parts: the definition of asceticism, exposition of the true practices (and, in this case, commendation of monastic asceticism), and cautioning against the false practices. It is possible that Asterius too had invented the plot and modelled his *opusculum* on letter 125, especially since his argumentation is quite generic and it is difficult to imagine a particular situation behind it. In this case, addressee and situation would be nothing more than a rhetorical pretext.

[12] For an analysis of the Hieronymian influences in the prologue of the *Liber ad Renatum* see Grilli (1980) 131–48.

Asterius knew Greek and was familiar with the exegesis of Greek Scriptures. His expert use of the Latin technical languages (nautical and administrative) and his mastery of the Latin Classical heritage show him as a native Latin speaker. He wrote for a Western, Latin audience; his contribution is quite possibly a late echo of the Jovinianist controversy, in the style of Jerome.

At the beginning of the 390s, Jovinian, a former ascetic himself, spoke up against practices of renunciation. One of the cornerstones of his argumentation was Paul's balanced view on marriage and sexuality in 1 Cor 7. Jovinian taught to the elite circles of Rome that virginity and marriage had equal value in the eyes of God; and that fasting was nothing more than a modest partaking of food. In other words, sexual as well as material renunciation was downright pointless. A very moderate asceticism could be, but need not be, practised.[13] The success of Jovinian's teaching can be measured by the bitter attack Jerome, alerted by ascetic-minded friends in Rome, sent from Bethlehem.

The *Aduersus Iouinianum* is a masterful blend of polemics and exegesis. Jerome's declared intention was to refute Jovinian's 'slander' against asceticism, but he took his passionate defence of the primacy of asceticism over married life to the extreme. As a result, the work did not have quite the impact the author had intended. Of course, it did not help that Jerome advertised it as a work written in the space of barely a few days.[14] Even his supporters were sceptical about the content as well as his rhetorical outbursts. Jerome found himself suspected of encratism and even Manichaeism, as he was repeatedly requested to explain himself.[15] His intervention in the Jovinianist affair, however, did succeed in escalating the tension around asceticism. Several veiled replies from prominent ecclesiastical authorities (such as Augustine's *De uirginitate*) as well as less famous writers (the anonymous author of the late-fourth-century *Consultationes Zacchaei et Apollonii*) attempted to calm the situation.[16]

Asterius' *Liber ad Renatum* represents a veritable homage paid to the master from Stridon, style- and content-wise as well. It is the argument of this chapter that Asterius not only reiterated much of Jerome's preference for a virginal and secluded life, but radicalized these views even more, positing that God created the human person as an ascetic and, therefore, man is an ascetic by nature.

---

[13] On Jovinian, see Hunter (2007) 15–205.   [14] Jerome, *Adv. Iovinian.* 1.1.
[15] Jerome, *Ep.* 49.
[16] See Hunter (2007) 243–84. Claussen (1995) has convincingly argued that the balanced view on marriage and asceticism contained in book three of the *Consultationes Zacchaei et Apollonii* was meant to counter both the radical asceticism of the *Aduersus Iouinianum* and the radical rejection of asceticism by Jovinian and others.

TRUE AND FALSE ASCETICISM IN THE *LIBER AD RENATUM MONACHUM*

Given the extent to which Asterius was a Hieronymian epigone, the question to be answered is: does the *Liber ad Renatum* have a modicum of originality, or was Asterius content with simply repeating—rearranging—Jerome's arguments? To find the answer to this question, we ought to examine more closely his theory of asceticism.

The exposition on asceticism and ascetic practices in the *Liber ad Renatum* is structured in three parts that are outlined in a programmatic prologue.[17] These proceed from the general to the particular. The first and shortest part contains the definition of *monachus*, a generic term with which Asterius designates both male and female ascetics (III.8–IV.11). The second outlines the steps that one ought to follow in order to become a veritable *monachus* (IV.12–X.21) and which is the veritable ascetic ideal (XI.22–XII.24). The third, and the most extensive, part examines the libertine usage of the title *monachus*, and denounces the sorts of corrupted ascetic practices to which it is applied (XIII.25–XXX.53).[18] Asterius' attack against the false ascetics culminates in a lengthy critique of the practice of syneisaktism (XXVI.46–XXX.53).

It should be noted from the outset that Asterius steadfastly encouraged solitary asceticism and complete separation from society and the temporal world. Although he does not criticize expressly other forms (such as domestic asceticism or cenobitism), the impression one gathers from the *Liber ad Renatum* is that Asterius equates asceticism with anachoresis. No other ascetic practice can provide sufficient detachment from the affairs of the temporal world. To begin with, according to his definition, the ascetic is 'the person who is content with leading a humble and secret life or a lonely abiding; the monk ought to be silent and desired by others in public spaces rather than be seen'.[19]

And surely, his ensuing presentation of ascetic progression towards achieving *angelica conversatio* is centred on the progressive detachment from everything that might distract the mind from the contemplation of the divine. Ascetics should empty their minds from all the petty things that bind them to this world, in order to achieve complete spiritual freedom (VI.14). 'The more [ascetics] become separated from the world, the closer they get to God', claims Asterius.[20] This begins with bodily detachment: the ascetic has to renounce not only the superfluous, but even the necessary material support

---

[17] Aster. *Liber* II.7 (Jakobi 4.1–10).

[18] For this tripartite programmatic passage and its relation to the rest of the treatise, see Grilli (1980) 131–3; De Vogüé (1997) 160–2.

[19] Aster. *Liber* IV.11 (Jakobi 5.19–22): *Monachus ille est, qui humili secretaque vita uel solitaria est commoratione contentus; monachum quietum esse decet et ab aliis in publico desiderari potius quam uideri.* Cf. De Vogüé (1997) 164.

[20] Aster. *Liber* XI.22 (Jakobi 10.7): *quantoque separantur a mundo, tanto fient proximi deo.*

(VI.15). In Asterius' words, 'whoever aspires to live spiritually should feed on Spirit and faith'.[21] In order, therefore, to appropriate asceticism effectively, one has to become a-pathic, without desires and without feelings (VII.16).

The final and most important step to spiritual freedom is to renounce fellow human beings. Only in this way can the ascetic avoid the mundane responsibilities that go together with relating to other people. For Asterius, these divert the spiritual eye from contemplation (VIII.18–IX.19). A true ascetic should have only his body as companion, for the spirit is safe with a body that is content with little.[22]

It is unsurprising therefore, that Asterius illustrates his teaching with solitary ascetics abiding as far away as possible from even a semblance of civilization: the hermits who live in the wilderness or the desert, or those who dwell in remote caves. The rest of the self-entitled ascetics are, according to Asterius, a bunch of world-lovers who rob the name *monachus* from its essence.[23] False ascetics are addicted to acknowledgement: they seek out the public space (XV.29), they teach in public (XVIII.33–4). They insinuate themselves in the private spheres of others, especially of women, inducing them to sin under the pretext of nightly vigils and conversations (XXII.39–40). Greedily, they mix with the poor so that they might receive alms (XXIII.41); they engage in commerce, pursue functions (XXV.44), and reach to the highest level of the imperial administration (XXV.45). Much like the *Consultationes Zacchaei et Apollonii*, this set of chapters too reminds of the accusations circulating in the Jovinianist controversy, against Jovinian and those who sympathized with his views.[24] But Asterius is not just content to repeat a series of widespread accusations. His vehement attack against these false ascetics is grounded in the absolute incompatibility between the ascetic love of God and the love of fellow humans. Just as the *Consultationes* note that keeping a leg in society (which also stands for material welfare) is dangerous

---

[21] Aster. *Liber* VII.17 (Jakobi 8.3): *Spiritaliter uiuere cupiens spiritu pascatur ac fide*. Cf. Aster. *Liber* XII.23 (Jakobi 10.12–15), on veritable ascetics: 'Therefore we happen to have heard and known of the kinds of dangers such persons delivered themselves to for the sake of the future hope, and in what ways they trampled those things that are reckoned as the goods of this life; for, abnegating themselves to the core, they despised with all their contempt the aids and the consolations of human foresight.' (*Datur itaque audire uel nosse, quibus se huiusmodi pro spe futura periculis dederint et quibus modis uitae istius quae putantur bona calcauerint; penitus enim se abnegantes, subsidia et solacia humanae prouisionis toto fastidio respuerunt*).

[22] Aster. *Liber* IX.19 (Jakobi, 9.3): *Felix hoc uoto, felicior facto: Vnum scire et habere solacium, quo anima in tuto semper est; nam cura corporis, dum paruo contenta est, ut detrimentum non habeat, ita prouocat ad salutem*.

[23] Aster. *Liber* XIV.28 (Jakobi 12.12–17): 'For unfoundedly and merely for the length of a badly performed show—to which they do not hold on in their works—they defame the name into an empty title, and under the pretext of Christianity they bring into the word itself things foreign to virtue.'

[24] *Consult. Zacchaei* III.3.5–8 (SC 402, 178–81).

because it exposes the ascetic to occasions of lapse,[25] so Asterius too maintains that any engagement with society, no matter how minute, carries within the germs of reverting to mundanity—contradicting the essence of asceticism.

False ascetics are legion amongst women too. They use cosmetic devices and licentious gestures to invite the sight;[26] they regularly seek friends and lovers outside of the accepted female ascetic milieu (the household of a relative or the organized community, XXVII.48–9): their very name, *agapetae*, is pestilentious.[27] These women only think they can lead an ascetic life under the shelter of a male ascetic who is not related by blood. In truth, maintains Asterius, both female and male ascetic inevitably end up in a process of spiritual involution (vividly described in XXVIII–XXX), a reverse image of the progressive renunciation undergone by a true ascetic.

Asterius does not hesitate to point out, again, that the rationale behind this involution is privileging one's relationship to others over one's relation to God. In particular, his attitude to society and inter-human relations does not admit compromise. An ascetic cannot live even on the fringes of society; either they leave behind every inclination to relate or they are not ascetics at all.

This view on asceticism has several curious aspects. Firstly, Asterius is not interested at all in ascetic discipline: he barely mentions fasting, prayer, or psalmody; he has little positive to say about vigils, or the reading of Scriptures either. When he does mention vigils and the study of Scripture it is to expose another foul act committed by false monks: these abuse vigils to corrupt women under their guidance, or teach heretical views in the marketplace. Asterius instead defines asceticism exclusively through the lenses of renunciation: what is required from an ascetic is a continuous effort to renounce the world, and especially of one's social relations. More importantly, this effort is sufficient to achieve a contemplative life.

Secondly, the gender inequality of the *Liber ad Renatum* surprises also. Female asceticism is not excluded: Asterius acknowledges that women too are capable of the renunciation he asks. However, he reserves the term *monachus*, meaning ascetic, only for men. For most of the *Liber ad Renatum*, he has in mind a male ascetic. Perhaps this focus is part of the rhetorical setting (the work allegedly offering advice to a male ascetic, Renatus). However, as I shall try to show in the following, the privileging of male asceticism and of renunciation as leading to the contemplative life has deeper roots in Asterius' thought.

---

[25] *Consult. Zacchaei* III.3.11 (SC 402, 182–3).
[26] Aster. *Liber* XXVI.47 (Jakobi 19.13–14): *et dum se uisui omnium subtrahunt, artificiose monstrant, quod uideri non sinunt*. Almost exact parallel in Jer. *ep*. 117.7.
[27] Aster. *Liber* XXX.52 (Jakobi 21.8–9): *Audimus agapetarum pestifera uocabula*.

ASTERIUS' CREATION NARRATIVE: EXEGESIS AND TRANSLATION IN THE SERVICE OF RENUNCIATION

In her influential 1999 book, *Reading Renunciation*, Elizabeth Clark argued that one of the popular ways to substantiate late antique asceticism was to confer an ascetic meaning to Scriptural passages, or to enhance their ascetic implications. This could be achieved by several strategies. Amongst others, Clark mentioned the ascetic exegesis of Gen 3:16–18 (expulsion from the garden of Eden) and Gen 4:1 ('Adam knew his wife Eve').[28] Late antique authors, such as Ambrose or Jerome, argued that sexual intercourse happened as a by-product of the original sin, and, thus, the first man and woman in Eden were, so to speak, sex-free. Therefore, in order to reach the paradisiacal purity of the first humans, Christian men and women should renounce sexuality and, thus, dedicate themselves to an ascetic life. In other words, expositions on the fall narrative were often used as an incentive for sexual renunciation. Related to this strategy was also interpreting Scriptural passages less lenient to an ascetic interpretation from the perspective of other, more 'lenient' passages. In such a way, conglomerates of seemingly unconnected Biblical citations could be invoked to produce overwhelming proof to foster the ascetic ideal. Another strategy commented upon by Clark as 'manifestly advancing the program of renunciation'[29] was the use of express ascetic vocabulary in the translation of certain Scriptural terms that had little or nothing to do with asceticism. Such is the case, for instance, of Jerome's translations of *agenealogetos* as *sine nuptiis* (unmarried) and *sophrosyne* as *castitas* (purity or chastity).[30] In the fourth and the fifth centuries, when asceticism thrived in a variety of practices, which had to be constantly negotiated, and when asceticism was also often contested, these strategies could be very useful to defend it or to promote a particular ascetic practice against others.

In the remainder of my contribution, I shall attempt to show that Asterius was no different in this regard. The peculiarities of his ascetic teaching noted above are connected with his forced exegesis of, primarily, the creation and fall narratives, in order to explain the origins and the essence of asceticism. The following pages, therefore, will discuss how Asterius embedded these strategies into his rhetoric of asceticism, the cornerstone of which is the absolute renunciation of the world, understood primarily as renunciation of social relations.

For Asterius, heremitic asceticism is instilled in the human being. Important to note is that he does not refer to just any type of ascetic practice, but specifically to solitary asceticism. To prove how inherent this is to every

---

[28] Clark (1999) 107–8 (Gen 3:16–18), and 119–20 (Gen 4:1). [29] Clark (1999) 113.
[30] Clark (1999) 113–18.

human person, he traces it back to the moment of creation. God, claims Asterius, created Adam, not just as the first man, but also as the first *monachus*:

> ...when the spiritual fingers of his providence fashioned him [= the man], he constituted him thus: he decreed that man be independent and self-sufficient, needing no help; and he adorned this *monachus*, dearer above all that he had created, and sole guest of the paradise, with the gift of every grace.[31]

In this passage we encounter two of the strategies mentioned above: conferring an ascetic meaning to Scriptural passages/stories; and translating Scriptural terms with a manifestly ascetic vocabulary. The key to understanding the creation of man as Asterius outlined it is *monachus*, in its etymological sense 'he who is alone'. A source for this interpretation is the Septuagint version of Gen 2:18: 'It is not good that the man should be alone'. The Septuagint has μόνον, which Asterius translated as *monachus*.[32] Commenting on Asterius' use of *monachus* as the Latin correspondent for the Greek μόνον, Adalbert de Vogüé remarked that Asterius could have found it in the translations of Symmachus or Aquila.[33] It is possible, though, that he made the connection himself. We know that Asterius was familiar with Greek Scriptures and their exegesis. Elsewhere in the book, he illustrates his skills with an exegetical bit on Ps 101 (102):7–8, 'I am like a lonely bird on the housetop', to which I shall shortly turn. However, regardless of whether he simply took advantage of this existing translation or he chose to render μόνον as *monachus* himself, Asterius certainly had in mind an ascetic meaning for this term. Late antique writers on asceticism, amongst whom a prominent place is taken by Jerome, usually interpreted *monachus* in its etymological sense, 'solitary' or 'lonely',[34] thereby legitimating anachoresis as the highest form of asceticism.[35] Asterius' originality, however, is to trace back this meaning to the creation moment. For him, Adam was the first ascetic—the ascetic par excellence:

> Thus in Adam the premises of asceticism had been consecrated; afterwards, in the course of several ages and through many men of blessed memory the practice and imitation were transmitted unto our age.[36]

---

[31] Aster. *Liber* III.8 (Jakobi 4.17–21): *quem [=hominem] modulantibus spiritalis prouidentiae digitis sacris manibus ita compegit, ut ipsum ex toto sibique sufficientem, nullo egentem subsidio statueret et super cuncta, quae fecerat, cariorem monachum solumque paradisi hospitem omni gratiarum munere decoraret.*
[32] Cf. Morard (1973) 348–54.   [33] De Vogüé (1997) 163.
[34] De Vogüé (1997) 164 quotes Jer. *ep.* 14.6; *Consult. Zacchaei* III.3.17 (SC 402, 186–7).
[35] Ascetic practices were fluid. Their definition and their validity could be negotiated, but they did not stand on equal grounds. Late antique asceticism was hierarchical, and the key factor in this hierarchy was renunciation. The practices which required a higher degree of renunciation were deemed a more faithful keeping of the ascetic ideal.
[36] Aster. *Liber* VI.11 (Jakobi, 5.15–17).

Asterius not only took the term μόνον or *monachus* from Gen 2:18, but he changed the register too. Whereas in Gen 2:18 it has a negative connotation, in the *Liber ad Renatum* it is interpreted positively: God created the first man with the design that he be alone, sufficient to himself (we might add, as far as mundane aspects are concerned). Asterius therefore transformed Adam's uniqueness into a positive natural attribute, albeit the verse refers to it as a negative: 'It is not good that the man should be alone'.

This enables Asterius to regard asceticism as an inherent trait of the human person; being an ascetic is (in) human nature—which means, in light of the rest of the *Liber ad Renatum*, that any aspiration to recover the Adamic state (pre-fall human nature) should end in solitude, self-sufficiency, and having only one's body as company.[37]

To a similar end, Asterius quotes Ps 101 (102):8, both in Greek and in Latin: *Factus sum sicut passer solitarius in tecto*/Ἐγεμόνην ὡς στρουθίον μονάζον ἐπὶ δώματι. His argument is that *monachus*, that is, ascetic, signifies first and foremost solitude.[38] Here, too, he invests μονάζον with an ascetic connotation, identifying it as a technical term. Since the entire vocabulary of *monachus* refers to solitude (as the Latin translation too shows), it only follows that ascetics should shy away from everything that has the potential to disrupt this. And, sure enough, the ensuing criticism of false ascetics exposes precisely how the plethora of social interactions perverts asceticism as (the Adamic, the angelic) state of life.

These exegetical twists, however, do not account for the creation of woman. If self-sufficiency is in the nature of the human being, as Asterius would have, then how should the second part of Gen 2:18 ('I will make him a helper fit for him') be explained? Contrary to what might be expected, Asterius deals with this problem promptly, and uses it to foster his ascetic agenda. His short description on the creation of Eve serves two purposes: on one hand, it further emphasizes that relationality is sinful and corruptive of the Adamic state; on the other hand, it is meant as a prelude to the critique of syneisaktism.

Asterius embraced the view that woman had not been created equal to man. He avoided speaking of Gen 2:18 ('It is not good...'), and gave no reason for the creation of woman. At any rate, he regarded her as more or less a derivate of Adam, certainly his servant and subordinate:

For, borrowed, she took her origin from the very beginnings and from the sample of human substance [taken] from the sleeping man...Nor does she enjoy full rights as companion over the goods and consort over the dominion, but she is made subject to man from whom she received her very name.[39]

---

[37] See n.22.
[38] Aster. *Liber* IV.12 (Jakobi 6.2–7): *monachum solitarium significans* (Jakobi 6.7).
[39] Aster. *Liber* III.9 (Jakobi 5:1–6): *Nam in ipsis exordiis substantiaeque humanae coeptis uiri dormientis mutuatam sumpsit originem et appendix conformati dudum iuuenis pro similitudine*

God intended her to be a comfort (*solacium*) for man, a guardian of his well-being (*custos salutis ac lateris*).[40] Instead, claims Asterius, the primordial relationship between woman and man birthed the first sin and brought about the ruin of both. In fact, when the woman was created, the self-sufficiency of the first man was disrupted. The woman, on her turn, chose to privilege her companionship above everything else, albeit she was conscious of the commandments of the Lord. This voluntary dedication to human relationships (we may surmise, over the relationship with God) represents, for Asterius, the original sin:

> ...knowing all the commandments of the Lord, she took such great care of her companionship that she swept into her ruin the innocent one too: she persuaded a terrible sacrilege and, overcome by a deathly desire, she who had been allotted to comfort dragged the man of life to perpetual death.[41]

According to Asterius, therefore, the moral responsibility for the original sin is the woman's, who went to such great lengths in caring for her relationship that she involved man in her fall. That is why, he cries out, even the premises of companionship (with women) are to be shunned!

Distinguishable behind this interpretation of creation and original sin are the ascetic exegesis of Gen 4:1 and 1 Cor 7:32-5. Sexuality as the consequence of original sin (Gen 4:1) has been often used in ascetic argumentation to support sexual renunciation. Jerome, for instance, argued in the *Aduersus Iouinianum* that Adam and Eve lived in a state of virginity, which was lost with the fall. Asceticism, then, is the attempt to recover this paradisiacal virginal state.[42] Likewise, Paul's reminder that the married are anxious to please their spouse, whereas the unmarried are anxious to please the Lord, is a commonplace of ascetic argumentation. In fact, the entire chapter 7 of 1 Cor is a favourite with ascetic commentators.

The originality of this argument consists in the fact that Asterius referred it to Adam and Eve. Because of the corrupted quality of this first society, interpersonal relationships in general are corrupted. Asterius then constructed his entire anthropology on the renunciation of social relations. Since the natural state of the human being is solitude, and since the societal conduct of the human being carries the germs of sin, the ascetic should first and foremost avoid social contact that disrupts self-sufficiency. False ascetics,

---

subrogatur. Nec tamen in toto potestate fruitur ut bonorum socia consorsque dominii, sed uiro subicitur, a quo et nomen accepit....

[40] Aster. *Liber* III.9 (Jakobi 4.22-23); III.10 (Jakobi 5.8).

[41] Aster. *Liber* III.10 (Jakobi 5.8-12): *egregia interea coniunx, custos salutis ac lateris, et omnia domini conscia praeceptorum, in eo tantum societatis curam seruauit, ut ruina sui etiam conuolueret innocentem: Sacrilegium persuasit immane et desiderio uicta letali, quae solacii causa fuerat attributa, uitalem hominem perpetuam traxit ad mortem.*

[42] Jer. *Adv. Iouinian.* 1.16, 1.29. See Clark (1997) 92.

therefore, are either unable or unwilling to renounce these relations. The fault in every type of false ascetic that he invokes (the greedy, the vainglorious, the addicted to public acknowledgement, the perverter of women, etc.) has at its basis a form of interaction with others. Moreover, syneisakts, who would want to be the image of Adam and Eve, inevitably end up reiterating the original sin. One way or the other, their love for each other gains more importance than their love for God. Asterius thought it safer to escape, to avoid relationality than to risk repeating the same mistake all over again.

CONCLUSION

Asterius blended a series of rather commonplace rhetorical and exegetical elements of late antique ascetic discourse into an original product. He employed the interpretation of *monachus* as solitary; he translated or took advantage of existing translations of the μόνον of Gen 2:18 as *monachus*; he converted μονάζον from Ps 101 (102):8 into a technical, ascetic, term; he used and developed the ascetic exegesis of the creation and fall narratives. Through this (forced) exegetical argumentation he established a theological–anthropological programme that excluded any form of asceticism other than solitary asceticism, understood as renunciation of one's relation to the world and the others.

This, however, is not to state that Asterius did not offer space for organized asceticism. This is true certainly when it comes to women: female asceticism implies by necessity some degree of control, either in its domestic or monastic form. In his definition, Asterius is ready to concede one small point: the life of a true ascetic can be solitary, but it can also be secret. Organized practices are given a minute space, and with the proviso that the ascetic should disengage from interaction by leading a silent and secret life. Yet, given the fundamental role of Asterius' discourse on solitude, it is questionable if he was willing to make allowances for communitarian asceticism, or if he was bound rather to accept *de facto* circumstances. His great master, Jerome, conceded in his later writings that too harsh an anachoresis could damage one's psychological well-being—and recommended for this reason cenobitic communities.[43] Asterius, however, remains intolerant of less committed ascetics.

---

[43] Jer. *ep.* 125 and 130.

15

Christian Literary Identity and Rhetoric about Style

Morwenna Ludlow

My speech and my proclamation were not with plausible words of wisdom...[1]

(1 Cor. 2.4–5)

INTRODUCTION

It has been well established in recent scholarship how 'rhetoric about rhetoric' in antiquity set rhetoric and philosophy against each other.[2] Many writers used this opposition to define their own identity and their artifice obscured the complex and often positive relationship that rhetoric and philosophy had in the ancient world.[3] This chapter will argue that 'rhetoric about literary style' was used in similarly artful acts of self-definition. Just as they employed rhetoric about rhetoric, so early Christian writers used rhetoric about literary style in distinctive ways to define their own identity against each other and in relation to classical antiquity. A better understanding of this rhetoric helps us to understand claims about the nature of Christian speech, especially claims that Christians eschewed such 'plausible' or 'persuasive' words as might be used by skilled rhetoricians. As Paul's words above suggest, questions about techniques of persuasion and sources of human wisdom are closely

---

[1] ἐν πειθοῖ σοφίας.
[2] My thanks to the participants in the colloquia from which this book arises, for their comments on this chapter, especially to Richard Flower and Gillian Clark; also to Wolfram Kinzig and friends in the Oxford-Bonn seminar for fruitful conversation about rhetoric.
[3] Hesk (1999) 201–30; Christian polemic: Vaggione (1993); DelCogliano and Radde-Gallwitz (2011) 44–6.

intertwined: here I focus on those techniques of persuasion which involve the choice of an appropriate literary style.

I will first give an overview of ancient theories of 'style', arguing that the opposition of 'plain' and 'elaborate' obscures a more complex picture. I will then use Basil of Caesarea, Gregory of Nazianzus, and Gregory of Nyssa as examples of the way in which fourth-century Christian writers wrote about literary style. These erudite 'Cappadocians' are far from typical fourth-century Christians; nevertheless, they are a telling example of the way in which praise of Christian plain-talking could co-exist alongside not only the commendation of more sophisticated styles but also the identification of such styles in the Bible.

KINDS OF 'STYLE' (ΧΑΡΑΚΤΗ͂ΡΕΣ, ΊΔ'ΕΑΙ, GENERA DICENDI)

Complexity

Ancient theorists and modern commentators alike are united in agreeing that ancient theories of style are very complex—indeed, one second-century author complains that previous accounts are 'totally muddled'.[4] As a more measured modern commentator puts it, because the various styles emerged as a result of a complex nexus of influences, the styles have 'a distinctive flexibility and latitude of characterization'.[5] One problem, however, is that ancient discussions of style try to convey authority by attempting systematization: the discourse sounds technical, but is frequently quite imprecise.[6] Indeed, different commentators have their own distinctive systems: the famous tri-partite classification of plain, middle, and grand used by Cicero, for example, differs both from an earlier four-fold classification found in Demetrius *On Style* (*c*. second century BCE) and from an alternative three-fold classification of diction used by Dionysius of Halicarnassus (second half of the first century BCE).[7] Hermogenes' complex theory of seven types of style (with twenty sub-types), developed in the second century CE, became very influential in Byzantium.[8]

---

[4] Hermogenes, *On Types of Style* (*Id.*), I:1 (Rabe, 216).
[5] Shuger (1984) 2; Russell (2006) 276: 'The history of these concepts [i.e. types of writing] is extremely complicated and by no means fully known.'
[6] Klock (1987) 15.
[7] Cicero, *Orator* (*Or.*); Demetrius, *On Style* (*Eloc.*); Dionysius, *Demosthenes* (*Dem.*).
[8] Wooten (1987) xvii.

A further difficulty is that the words used in rhetorical treatises or literary criticism for kinds of discourse (χαρακτῆρες, ἰδέαι, *genera dicendi*) do not map easily onto the modern concepts expressed by the English terms 'style' or 'genre'.[9] They cannot refer to 'genres', for ancient theorists frequently stress that the best writers use a variety of styles within one work of a particular kind (e.g. forensic rhetoric); furthermore, the use of the term 'genre' for ancient texts is prone to anachronism.[10] As we will see, the 'styles' do not map neatly even onto particular literary forms: forensic rhetoric was associated with both the slender ('low') and the majestic ('high') styles, comedy with both slender and pleasant styles, tragedy with both pleasant and majestic styles. All three styles can be found in both poetry and prose forms. Furthermore, whilst the English term 'style' generally means '(features pertaining to) the form and mode of expression of a text, as opposed to what is said or expressed', ancient discussions of literary χαρακτῆρες/ἰδέαι/*genera dicendi* relate *both* to 'style' and 'content'.[11] For example, Demetrius' *On Style* systematically discusses the different literary *characters* (χαρακτῆρες) according to their thought (διάνοια), diction (λέξις), and composition (σύνθεσις), all of which are relevant to certain subject matter (πράγματα).[12] Such an understanding leads the author of *On the Sublime* to argue that a text can be sublime as to its subject matter, even if its literary qualities are not very elevated.[13] For these reasons, Donald Russell suggests that the χαρακτῆρες/ἰδέαι/*genera dicendi* 'are best described as tones or qualities of writing, involving the choice not only of words but of subject'.[14] I agree with Russell's argument, but prefer the terms 'moods' or 'sensibilities', because 'tone' or 'quality of writing' might still imply that one is not considering content.

Amid the bewildering evidence, it is tempting for the modern reader to impose her own system. As we shall see below, some scholars have seen a clear system emerging; others agree that, especially for Christians writing in late antiquity, 'there are as yet no generally accepted models that could help us to describe the precise relationship between the prose of these authors and the strata of language of the period they were writing in'.[15] The pattern suggested below attempts to steer a path between the two positions, and will keep flexibility to the fore. I will argue that it is possible to identify three 'moods'

---

[9] Discussions of diction (λέξις) as one of the five classical parts of rhetoric are narrower than discussions of λέξις in works dedicated to the χαρακτῆρες, ἰδέαι, *genera dicendi*: Russell (2006) 275-6.

[10] See, for example, Davis (2002) 111; Rosenmeyer (2006) 421-39.

[11] *The New Shorter OED* (1993); Russell (2006) 277.

[12] Hermogenes studies texts with regard to thought/content (ἔννοια), approach (μέθοδος: assimilate to figures of thought) and style, strictly understood (λέξις): Wooten (1987) xi.

[13] Longinus, *Subl.* 9. Russell (2006) 277.   [14] Russell (2006) 277.

[15] Kinzig (1997) 647.

or 'sensibilities' evoked by texts, identified by three families of literary-critical terms.[16]

Three Styles (χαρακτῆρες/ἰδέαι/genera dicendi)

(i) Slender

The word most commonly used in Greek for the slender style is ἰσχνός (literally: dry, thin, lean, weak, light).[17] Ἰσχνός indicates compositions that are comparatively plain, concise, and spare in their use of imagery, but also ones which are notable for their clarity (τὸ σαφές—often associated with vividness, ἐνάργεια), and precision (ἀκρίβεια—sometimes associated with the quality of purity, flawnessness,[18] or, more negatively, with a fastidious over-attention to detail[19]). The emphasis on clarity and precision means that the slender style is associated with life-like description, but also with the narration of everyday events—as if the slender style held a mirror up to life and reproduced it without distortion.[20] This style's association with everyday subject matter and a somewhat conversational tone[21] meant that the style was sometimes praised as useful and educative[22] and at other times disparaged for being too colloquial or commonplace.[23] The slender style can either teach an audience (through clarity in the court or classroom, or in a letter) or entertain them (through life-like accounts of everyday situations, especially through dialogue). The idea that a slender style can vividly but accurately represent a conversation explains why the slender style was associated both with comedy,[24] dialogue, and letter-writing (which was commonly seen in the ancient world as a conversation committed to paper) and with dialectic.[25] The slender style is thought to be typical of Stoic texts—but, as we shall see, it is *not* the only style associated with philosophy.[26] Nor, as the reference to comedy makes clear, is it connected *only* with philosophy or dialectic. In the sphere of oratory, it was sometimes thought appropriate to forensic speeches.[27]

---

[16] I will focus on Greek terminology (some of which is used by, for example, Cicero and Quintilian), although there are Latin equivalents.
[17] Demetrius, *Eloc.* 190–239; Dionysius, *Dem.* 11, 15; Quintilian, *Inst.* XII.10.58; May (2007) 257.
[18] Dionysius, *Dem.* 11–13 (the 'slender' aspects of Demosthenes' mixed discourse have purity and precision).
[19] Longinus, *Subl.* 33.2, 35.2; Shuger (1984) 17: critiques of being too 'Attic'.
[20] Demetrius, *Eloc.* 209, 227.
[21] Demetrius, *Eloc.* 190, 192, 202, 230; Dionysius, *Dem.* 2, 15.
[22] Especially Quintilian, *Inst.* XII.10.59–60; Cicero, *De optimo genere oratorum* (*Opt. gen.*) 1.3.
[23] Longinus, *Subl.* 32–6.   [24] Shuger (1984) 13–14 on *Rhetorica ad Herennium*.
[25] Demetrius, *Eloc.* 223–4, 227; Shuger (1984) 6 (on Aristotle).
[26] Shuger (1984) 2, 15, 33.   [27] Dionysius, *Dem.* 2, 10; Shuger (1984) 20.

Dionysius and Cicero associate with this style the orator Lysias (445–c.380 BCE) a *logographos* (legal speech-writer) and one of the 'ten Attic orators' who were together regarded as paradigmatic for oratorical style.[28]

(ii) Pleasant

The pleasant style is often denoted by the Greek words ἀνθηρός ('floral') and γλαφυρός (which literally means 'hollowed out' or 'smoothed'; it came to denote literary polish and elegance).[29] It is said to exhibit χάρις (grace or charm) and τὸ ἡδύ (sweetness or pleasantness).[30] Like the slender style, the pleasant style is often associated with clarity (and for Demetrius, relative brevity), although frequently the words denoting clarity also point towards the brightness or even brilliance of the composition.[31] The pleasant style is more complex and uses more carefully worked sentence construction, images, and tropes,[32] with the result that, depending on the writer's perspective, it can be described as delicate, smooth, polished, ornamented—or rich, tasteless, degenerate. It is very frequently associated with a euphonious, smoothly flowing choice of words, and with a lyrical or musical sensibility. Like the slender style, it can be directed in two different ways: to education (where it can achieve subtlety and philosophical finesse) and to entertainment, where it is especially associated with wit and playfulness. The pleasant style is therefore thought to belong both to philosophy (Plato especially is cited as a model of the pleasant style, but so also is Aristotle) and to comedy.[33] When the style is associated with charm and grace it is connected with lyric poetry, especially that of Sappho, and with rhetorical forms such as the marriage-speech; the pared-down and more life-like tragedy of Euripides could also be said to demonstrate the pleasant style.[34] The common denominator here seems to be the sense that the pleasant style can influence or persuade the audience through its aesthetic qualities: it achieves the 'leading of the soul' (ψυχαγωγία).[35] There is more emphasis on emotion, whilst the plain style

---

[28] Dionysius, *Dem.* 2, 9; Longinus, *Subl.* 32–6; Shuger (1984) 17, 22–5, 29. Lysias as an example of a more polished, witty style: Demetrius, *Eloc.* 186–9, 259.

[29] Russell (2006) 276. For a fuller discussion of the characteristics of this style, see Ludlow (2018).

[30] Demetrius, *Eloc.* 127–31; Dionysius, *Dem.* 4–5, 11–13; Quintilian, *Inst.* XII.10.59–60, 64.

[31] Demetrius, *Eloc.* 137–8.

[32] Demetrius, *Eloc.* 139–62, 176–85; Shuger (1984) 16 (citing Cicero, *Brutus* (*Brut.*) 301–20) and 25–6 (on Dionysius).

[33] Plato: Demetrius, *Eloc.* 183–5: 'Plato's works glide smoothly along'; Dionysius, *Dem.* 3, 5–6, 15; Shuger (1984) 31 (on Longinus). Aristotle: Demetrius, *Eloc.* 128, 154; Shuger (1984) 15–19 (on Cicero), 26 (on Dionyius). Comedy: Demetrius, *Eloc.* 142–3, 152–3, 159, 161–9.

[34] Sappho: Demetrius, *Eloc.* 132, 140–2, 148–9 (also used as an example of sublimity: Longinus, *Subl.* 10.1); Euripides: Shuger (1984) 10–12, 36.

[35] ψυχαγωγία: Plato, *Phaedrus* 261a. Shuger (1984) 35.

has more emphasis on reason—although this disjunction should not be overplayed, because Plato was regarded as an exemplar of the pleasant style. With regard to oratory, this style is sometimes associated with epideictic and with the works of Isocrates.[36]

(iii) Majestic or sublime[37]

The majestic style is often denoted by Greek words indicating greatness (e.g. μεγαλοπρεπής—magnificent, μεγαλοφυής—of noble nature, μεγαληγορία—'great-talking', μεγαλοφωνία—'grandiloquence', and their cognates).[38] Other terms indicate bulk (ὄγκος, ἁδρός)[39] or height (especially ὑψηλός—sublime).[40] The style is used to talk about weighty matters, such as the gods, the natural world, or investigations into human nature.[41] Emotion is used alongside argument to persuade an audience (in forensic and deliberative rhetoric) or in narrative or drama to affect them (in epic, history, and tragedy). The authors often associated with this style are Aeschylus, Thucydides, and sometimes Demosthenes.[42] Compared to the pleasant style's use of relatively restrained emotion (delight and charm) the majestic style is generally associated with more intense, if not violent, emotions.[43] But these emotions are within the bounds of dignity (σεμνότης), otherwise the style becomes inappropriate.

Although there is an intensification of emotional force from the slender to the pleasant and then to the majestic style, there is not a corresponding increasing complexity of sentence structure, nor necessarily a greater sophistication of imagery. For Cicero, the majestic style was like archaic art—sketchy and unsophisticated, yet very effective in its overall impact—whilst the pleasant style was more like later classical painting—detailed and with bright colours.[44] Dionysius called the majestic style 'striking, elaborate, obscure, and terrifying' with 'an intense intellectual and emotional excitement which startles the mind, inducing tension, and violent emotion'.[45] These qualities are

---

[36] Isocrates: Dionysius, *Dem.* 3.
[37] Here I elide two categories in Demetrius' analysis: the forceful and the grand.
[38] μεγαλοπρεπής: Demetrius, *Eloc.* 37, 39; Dionysius, *Thucydides* (*Thuc.*) 23. μεγαλοφυής: Longinus, *Subl.* 9.1, 13.2, 34.4, 36.4. μεγαληγορία: Dionysius, *Thucydides*, 27; Demetrius, *Eloc.* 29; Longinus, *Subl.* 8.4.
[39] ὄγκος: Demetrius, *Eloc.* 77, 120, 247; Longinus, *Subl.* 8.3, 39.3. ἁδρός: Quintilian, *Inst.* XII.10.58-9.
[40] Passim in Longinus, *Subl.*   [41] Demetrius, *Eloc.* 75-6; Dionysius, *Dem.* 1-2.
[42] Aeschylus: Aristophanes, *Frogs*, passim; Demetrius, *Eloc.* 267. Thucydides: Demetrius, *Eloc.* 39, 44, 48, 112; Dionysius, *Dem.* 1, 9, 15.
[43] Shuger (1984) 9 (on Aristophanes' estimation of Aeschylus); Demetrius, *Eloc.* 99 (terror, awe); Cicero, *Brut.* 55.203 (the orator evokes tragic emotions); Quintilian, *Inst.* VI.11.16-19; Dionysius, *Dem.* 2.
[44] Shuger (1984) 15-16.   [45] Shuger (1984) 24.

communicated through a style that uses short phrases, asymmetry, and surprising juxtapositions: in other words, the sentence structure is *less* complex and less highly worked than that of the pleasant style.[46] So, it is tempting, but unsatisfactory to map the styles as points on a universally accepted ascending scale. Indeed, although the terms 'grand', 'majestic', or 'sublime' suggest that this style was the highest or best, as some ancient theorists such as Longinus argued, others clearly preferred a middle style because it reached a wider audience.[47]

The Appropriate—τὸ πρέπον

In sum, these χαρακτῆρες, ἰδέαι, or *genera dicendi* relate to three fairly distinct 'moods' or 'sensibilities'. They are used to evoke spareness, precision, and clarity; or elegance, brilliance, and charm; or high emotion and sublimity. The mood or sensibility evoked was identified by ancient authors with certain typical key terms—like ἰσχνός, ἐναργεία; γλαφυρός, χάρις, ἡδύ; μεγαληγορία, ὄγκος, ὑψηλός—which became buzzwords applied to both style *and* subject matter. Crucially these moods were directly related to certain kinds of emotional effect: the astonishment provoked by the majestic, the pleasant luring of the elegant style, and the satisfaction brought by the clarity of the slender style. Two or more different moods could be evident in a single text, but each was especially appropriate to and could therefore evoke certain contexts and certain kinds of subject matter. Ancient audiences educated in the classics would have had an instinctive sensitivity to them and would have been able to 'tune in' to them by picking up on certain indicators almost subconsciously (just as experienced modern readers quickly grasp that an author is working with the conventions of gothic horror or the campus novel). Ancient Christian authors educated in the classics would have shared this instinctive sensitivity.

For these reasons, scholars such as Innes and Russell have argued that 'the fundamental criterion [of style] is propriety, τὸ πρέπον: certain subjects fit certain styles, and violation of this is normally a fault...Since the choice of style depends on appropriate context, all the styles are equally valid...'[48] Since understandings of mood were assumed to be universal and instinctive, 'breaches of etiquette, such as a low word in a solemn context, [were greeted] with horror and disgust'.[49] This concern with propriety or fit suggests that many ancient theorists were in effect identifying various virtues, rather than levels of style: like Aristotelian ethical virtues, each excellence of style is to be

---

[46] Shuger (1984) 25.   [47] Dionysius, *Dem.* 15.
[48] Innes (1995) 324 (citing Demetrius, Aristophanes, and Cicero); cf. Russell (2001) 10-11.
[49] Russell (2006) 278.

used as appropriate to context.[50] This helps with understanding what theorists have to say about combining styles. It is common (especially in Latin writers) to associate the slender style with imparting information ('teach'), the pleasant with pleasing or conciliating ('delight'), and the grand with appealing to the emotions ('move').[51] It might be tempting, then, to associate them respectively with forensic, epideictic, and political rhetoric; in fact, however, rhetorical theorists frequently praise the flexible use of different styles as appropriate throughout a single work. For example, Hermogenes admires Demosthenes precisely because 'he was always combining styles everywhere', so that his deliberative speeches contained elements of judicial and epideictic rhetoric too.[52] Dionysius of Halicarnassus argues that especially Demosthenes, but also Isocrates and Plato exemplify the best style which is not 'middle' in the sense of in between, but in the sense of being a mix of the plain and grand styles.[53] Quintilian is equally positive about the value of mixing styles:

> Eloquence therefore takes many forms; but it is very foolish to ask which of them the orator should take as his standard. Every variety which is correct has its use, and what is commonly called a 'style' (*genus dicendi*) is not something that *belongs* to the orator. He will use *all* 'styles', as circumstances demand, and as required not only by the Cause as a whole but by its various parts... He will make many changes of tone (*multa mutabit*) to accord with differences of persons, places, and circumstances.[54]

The excellence of an orator then lies in being able to use specific styles as appropriate, for in that way he will reach his audience. Dionysius specifically argues that a mix of styles is best because it appeals to a broad audience: those who attend the assemblies and law-courts are neither hyper-intellectuals with minds like Thucydides (the master of grandiloquent style); nor are they simpletons who do not understand what a well-composed speech is. 'They are a collection of men who work on the land and the sea, and common tradesmen, whose sympathies are most readily won with a *comparatively* straightforward and ordinary style of oratory.'[55]

The Rhetorical Deployment of Literary Terms

Such advice points us back to the inherent complexity and fluidity of ancient concepts of 'style': if the fundamental rule is 'be appropriate', then there could

---

[50] Wooten (1987) xvii (on Theophrastus and Hermogenes). The relation between kinds and virtues of style is not clear-cut: Russell (2006) 276–7.
[51] Quintilian, *Inst.* XII.10.59.   [52] Hermogenes, *Id.* I.1.
[53] Dionysius, *Dem.* 3–6, 9, 15–17.
[54] Quintilian, *Inst.* XII.10.69–71. See also: Cicero, *Brut.* 185; *Orator* 69; *Opt. gen.* I.3.
[55] ἁπλούστερον καὶ κοινότερον διαλεγόμενος: Dionysius, *Dem.* 15. My emphasis.

in principle be as many styles as kinds of context or subject matter. Most critics, however, (ancient and modern) have grouped them in some way or other, although they are divided on how this should be done. Donald Russell argues that, 'most often we hear of three 'styles': ἁδρός ('grand'), ἰσχνός ('thin'), and some kind of intermediate—either a desirable mean between the two extremes or a distinct 'ornamental' or 'smooth' style (γλαφυρός, ἀνθηρός)'.[56] An earlier strong tendency in modern scholarship, however, was to assume a fundamental *two*-fold theory of ancient style. For example, G. L. Hendrickson (writing in 1905) concluded:

> it becomes clear that our styles (whether three or more) represent a fundamental two-fold analysis, so that the pre-eminence awarded to the grand style is merely recognition of its original character as artistic prose, in contrast to language purely as a vehicle of thought.[57]

He argues that whilst previous modern scholars considered plain, rational prose (especially as used in philosophy) to be superior to artistic, emotional prose (in rhetoric), this is not how the matter was seen in the ancient world.[58]

Hendrickson's argument, published in 1905, was influenced by Eduard Norden's 1898 division of Greek prose into plain and 'artistic prose' (*Kunstprosa*):[59] together their viewpoint dominated German-speaking and Anglophone scholarship respectively. Although hugely influential, Norden's and Hendrickson's position did not, however, completely wipe out scholarly antipathy to 'artistic' Greek prose. There remained a continuing suspicion of 'Asianist' style and the rhetoric emanating from the 'Second Sophistic', due to the way in which some ancient authors opposed this to plain, clear, Attic prose.[60] This tendency is very evident in early twentieth-century patristic scholars who denied, criticized, or were puzzled by certain early Christian writers' lapses into what they clearly consider to be decadent prose style.[61] One line of argument is that elaborate speech is an exception to the rule of Christian simple speech—the *sermo piscatorius* of Peter and the early disciples, which was inherited by later fathers.[62] Others have argued that the use of more elaborate style was unconscious or due to the power of cultural influences: thus, Gregory of Nyssa was supposedly unable to resist the effects of his rhetorical training, whilst the more robust Basil was able to overcome them.[63]

---

[56] Russell (2006) 276; cf. Innes (1995) 325.

[57] Hendrickson (1905) 289. Shuger rejects his elision of the 'grand' and 'middle' styles, but herself stresses a 'plain-and-middle' versus 'grand' binary opposition in order to argue for 'the actual pre-eminence of the grand style', by showing its 'range and intellectual seriousness': Shuger (1984) 2.

[58] Hendrickson (1905) 289–90.   [59] Norden (1898).

[60] See Whitmarsh (2001) and (2005).

[61] A trend excellently described in relation to Chrysostom by Mitchell (2002) 23–6.

[62] Kinzig (1997) 639, with references.

[63] Aubineau (1971) 93; comparison with Basil: Méridier (1906) 6.

Such estimations are reinforced by the fact that (as we shall see below) ancient writers sometimes themselves drew apparently sharp contrasts between, for example, good plain style and fancy but useless prose. The question is how these should be read. As Tim Whitmarsh has argued, '[t]he authors of technical treatises were not simply *transcribing* universally accepted cultural norms into written forms, but attempting to *prescribe*, authoritatively, their own partisan views of what constituted correct practice'.[64] Many scholarly claims about ancient comments on style, however, read them as descriptive analyses, rather than as the rhetorical efforts of authors positioning themselves in a competition about excellence and moral probity. The very nature of the notion of 'the appropriate' left plenty of scope for argument. One result of the argument was that the three-fold *genera dicendi* were collapsed for rhetorical effect into binary oppositions—especially in debates about 'plain' Atticism and 'elaborate' Asianism.[65]

In any age, acts of competitive literary (self-)definition lead naturally to the creation of binaries. In the ancient world, advocates of a slender style contrasted themselves with inappropriately decorative and decadently emotional styles. Those espousing sublimity accused any other style of being trivial. Proponents of the pleasant style defended it against elaborate pomposity and—on another occasion—could boast of the appropriately graceful use of ornament, compared to an opponent's bare aridity. But scraping beneath the surface we can see that these binaries were also based on comparison—'this is better than that'—as Dionysius' advocacy of 'a comparatively straightforward and ordinary style of oratory' shows. Thus, despite the blunt way they were often presented, the binaries were comparative, not absolute and this is a further reason why they should not be read as comprising a *theory* of style.

Whitmarsh is careful to show that such rhetorical positioning occurs within a particular socio-political context. Whilst Whitmarsh has analysed Greek writers in the Roman Empire, others have made a similar point with regard to Latin poets in relation to their Greek antecedents: thus Gregson Davis notes the fluid relationship between 'the ancient theory of levels or "characters" of style' and 'normative literary kinds (epic, lyric etc.)'. As a result generic boundaries 'are a rhetorical artefact: they constitute a conventional point of reference that poets use in order to define their own unique artistic space. Crucial to these acts of self-definition are rhetorical strategies that foreground the issue of stylistic decorum.'[66]

For scholars of early Christianity, this raises the question: should we not understand *Christian* acts of literary self-positioning with regard to style as rhetorically heightened discourse which emerges from a specific socio-political

[64] Whitmarsh (2005) 41; my emphasis. [65] Whitmarsh (2005) 53–4.
[66] Davis (2002) 111.

context?[67] In what follows I will argue that Christian authors shared the same kinds of concerns about 'stylistic decorum' as their non-Christian contemporaries and forbears. If the fundamental rule of good style is 'be appropriate' and at least three literary sensibilities can be identified, we can understand Christians' use of binary oppositions as the deliberate rhetorical simplification of more complex literary theory. Instead of reading Christian literary self-positioning in relation to a blunt opposition of 'plain' and 'elaborate' (often assimilated by scholars to 'Christianity' versus 'Hellenism'), we can see it as a *comparative* exercise, continually seeking to validate good Christian writing as the more (or most) appropriate in relation to a particular theme or context.

THE CAPPADOCIANS: BASIL OF CAESAREA, GREGORY OF NAZIANZUS, AND GREGORY OF NYSSA

The Bible and Literary Style

It is a commonplace in modern scholarly writing on Late Antique attitudes to the Christian Bible that not only was it written in (or translated into) *koine* Greek, but it was regarded by both Christians and others as displaying a simple, plain, or even bad style.[68] Following Eduard Norden, some scholars have pointed out that a few Christian writers bucked the trend to assert that the Bible did have good literary qualities,[69] but this exception has been applied mainly to the poetic books of the Old Testament.[70] However, even a relatively cursory acquaintance with the Cappadocians' biblical hermeneutics allows us to add considerably more nuance and texture to this view, if one is aware both of the concept of mood or sensibility set out in the first half of this chapter and of the way in which the articulation of these sensibilities was subject to its own rhetoric. By looking for the literary buzzwords I identified in the first part of my chapter, we can see that Basil and the two Gregories identify instances of plain, pleasant, and magnificent sensibilities in the Bible. However, they do not consider these completely distinct realms of discourse. Rather, their use of comparative vocabulary shows that they frequently analyse literary features of a text in order to judge how appropriate they are.

---

[67] Others have made this point emphatically with regard to Christian use of rhetoric in general (see especially Averil Cameron (1991)).

[68] Kinzig (1997) 634–6 gives ample examples.

[69] Norden (1898) 526: some writers took the other route—that is 'to refer to an allegedly artistic perfection of Holy Scripture' ('sich auf eine angeblich künstlerische Vollendung der h. Schrift zu berufen'). Cf. Kinzig (1997) 635–6.

[70] Socrates' comments on Paul in *HE* 3.16.23–6: Kinzig (1997) 635–6.

(i) The 'simplicity of faith'

Basil's and Gregory of Nyssa's texts against Eunomius of Cyzicus include significant polemic, not least against his literary style.[71] Eunomius and his writing are criticized using terms associated specifically with the majestic style: he is guilty of ὑπερβολή (meaning both moral excess and literary hyperbole) and Basil imagines him claiming sublimity in a parody of the sublime style: '"I have ascended to the very pinnacle of virtue, transcended earthly matters, and transferred my entire way of life to heaven!"'[72] Gregory of Nyssa implies (in terms closely echoing ancient literary criticism) that Eunomius aspires to Demosthenic magnificence, but fails: he achieves emotional excess, rather than intensity and his prose is heavy or distended. His logic is muddled: if he persuades it is not through argument and his claim to precision (ἀκρίβεια—a feature of the 'slender' style) is specious.[73] Mostly, the Cappadocians compare Eunomius' bombast with their own clarity, but at times they implicitly or explicitly contrast his prose with that of the Bible. For example, in the same pages where he criticizes Eunomius' swollen style, Basil states that David 'plainly' (φανερῶς) confesses that the knowledge of God is inaccessible and the Apostle (Paul) 'clearly' (σαφῶς) condemns those who are swollen with pride.[74]

The Cappadocians also contrast Eunomius' arrogance with the 'simplicity of the faith'[75] and this notion of faith is found frequently elsewhere: in Oration 32, Gregory of Nazianzus stresses that faith can be grasped by all; likewise, Gregory of Nyssa argues that 'the word of *sound faith* (Tit. 1.13, 2.2) conveys its strength in simplicity to those who welcome the God-inspired utterances with a good disposition. It has no need of subtle interpretation to assist its truth.'[76] Basil characterizes the cosmology of Genesis 1.1 as 'the simplicity of faith' compared to the 'demonstrations of reason'—that is, classical philosophy.[77] Sometimes, they suggest the simplicity of faith is matched by a simple Christian style: Nazianzen argues that the faith is not just for 'sophisticates and those with a flair for language and logic'; better, in fact, is the man 'poor in words and understanding, who uses simple expressions and clings to them as

---

[71] For example, Cassin (2008) and (2012); Ludlow (2014a); DelCogliano and Radde-Gallwitz (2011) 39–46.

[72] Basil, *Eun.* I.3. ὑπερβολή and the magnificent style: Demetrius, *Eloc.* 52.

[73] Ludlow (2014a) 455–9.

[74] Basil, *Eun.* I.12; I.3 (citing 1 Tim. 3.6). Norden and later commentators cite a passage in Nyssen's *Contra Eunomium* as evidence of a contrast between Eunomius' elaborate and Paul's plain style; the critical edition reveals that 'Paul' is a minority reading and the passage probably refers to Basil! Gregory of Nyssa, *Eun.* I.1.18 (GNO I.27:23); Norden (1898) 501; Kinzig (1997) 635 n.4.

[75] For example, Basil, *Eun.* I.1 and 4; Gregory of Nyssa, *Eun.* III.1.85 (GNO II.33); see also: Basil, *Spir.* 9.22; *Ep.* 258.2; Gregory of Nyssa, *Ep.* 5.9; *Thaum.* PG46.901.27; Gregory of Nazianzus, *De vita sua* 602.

[76] Gregory of Nazianzus, *Or.* 32.26; Gregory of Nyssa, *Ep.* 24.1, 4.   [77] Basil, *hex.* I.10.

to a flimsy raft in his effort to survive'.[78] But, read in its context, this is advice to his addressees, not a description of biblical style. Indeed, whilst the Cappadocians are quick to assert that the essential message of the gospel is simple to grasp, they seem to avoid asserting that the Bible itself has a simple or plain style. One reason for their hesitation is their belief that in many places Scripture teaches through puzzles (ἐν αἰνίγμασι: Sirach 39.3; cf ἐν αἰνίγματι 1 Cor. 13.2): even though the message may be simple, it is not always presented in a simple way.[79] This, of course, is the basis of allegorical or spiritual exegesis, which is practised by all three, but in different ways and to different extents. Gregory of Nazianzus' mnemonic poems provide a different kind of evidence: the metrical lists of books of the Bible, plagues, the ten commandments, the parables and miracles in the Gospels, and so on, are self-evidently ways of simplifying texts which are complex, at least from the perspective of narrative.[80]

In sum, although the Cappadocians do praise unadorned style, they usually do so in contrast to Eunomius' or others' intellectual pretensions: that is, they are clearly drawing a rhetorical contrast between more and less elaborate prose and—crucially—are condemning *inappropriately* elaborate prose. When it comes to the Bible, they do not comment specifically on whether it is finely wrought prose or not: they think that its fundamental message is simple, even though it is presented through a complex variety of narratives and often in enigmatic ways.

(ii) Majestic or sublime

We noted above that literary criticism uses words beginning with μεγαλο- to signal sublime discourse. The Cappadocians are clearly aware of this terminology: for example, Basil says that Aeschylus 'lamented with mighty voice' (μεγαλοφώνως ὠδύρατο).[81] Nyssen's devastating critique of Eunomius' style reveals that he was aware of the terms used to describe the majestic prose that Eunomius was vainly trying to emulate.[82] In playful mode, Gregory of Nazianzus mocks Basil's magnificent and tragic style; but he and Nyssen also use the same terminology (μεγαλοφωνία and cognates) for sincere praise of Basil's powerful rhetoric.[83]

---

[78] Gregory of Nazianzus, *Or.* 32.26.
[79] Of many examples, see Gregory of Nyssa Cant, Pref. GNO 6.REF.REF; Hom. 11, GNO 6.324.18. Gregory of Nazianzus *Or.* 28.20.
[80] Gregory of Nazianzus, *Poems on Scripture* (ed. and tr. Dunkle (2012)); and Dunkle's introduction, 17, 20–3.
[81] Basil, *Ep.* 74 (ed./tr. Deferrari (1928) vol. II 72–3); cf. Gregory of Nazianzus' parody of Hesiod: *Or.* 4.115.
[82] Gregory of Nyssa, *Eun* I.551; II.409; cf. Basil *Eun.* 2:14; Ludlow (2014a).
[83] Gregory of Nazianzus, *Epp.* 5.4.3; 46.5.4; *Or.* 43:68; Gregory of Nyssa, *Bas* 2.3; cf. *Op hom*, Pref. (PG44:125.50).

But do the Cappadocians use this kind of language when discussing the Bible? They certainly use epithets beginning μεγαλο- to denote various authors, especially Paul and John the Evangelist. In his Homily on John 1, Basil claims that 'every utterance (φωνή) of the Gospels is nobler (μεγαλοφυεστέρα) than the other teachings of the Spirit' and John is the most 'resounding' (μεγαλοφωνότατος) of the evangelists: his utterances are 'greater (μείζονα) than every ear [can bear] and higher than every thought (πάσης δὲ διανοίας ὑψηλότερα)'.[84] For Gregory of Nyssa, John is ὁ ὑψηλὸς Ἰωάννης.[85] Just as Demosthenes was associated with a 'flash of lightning or a thunderbolt', so Basil associates the hugeness of John's utterances with his name, son of thunder (ὁ υἱὸς τῆς βροντῆς: cf. Mark 3:17) and Gregory says that John has a thundering voice (ἡ βρονταία φωνή).[86] For Gregory of Nyssa, the apostle Paul possesses 'ἀποστολικῆς μεγαλοφωνίας'; Basil's comments on Rom. 11.33 (which Paul 'shouts out': ἐξεβόησε) suggests he agrees.[87] Nazianzen singles out Isaiah as 'the most grandiloquent of the prophets' (τῷ μεγαλοφωνοτάτῳ τῶν προφητῶν) and praises the 'most grandiloquent David' (τοῦ μεγαλοφωνοτάτου Δαβίδ), who rouses one's conscience 'just like a herald of great voice booming an important proclamation' (τις μεγαλοφωνότατος κῆρυξ ἀπὸ ὑψηλοῦ καὶ πανδήμου κηρύγματος).[88]

The Cappadocians use a similar range of language to describe certain passages or books of the Bible. Evoking both Ps. 54.7 and the winged soul in Plato's *Phaedrus*, Gregory of Nyssa writes of the Lord's Prayer: 'Who will give me those wings [of a dove] that my mind may wing its way up to the heights (τῷ ὕψει) of those noble words (τῆς τῶν ῥημάτων μεγαλοφυΐας)?'[89] He emphasizes that Christian teaching in general and the contents of Scripture in particular are 'noble' (μεγαλοφυής—a word used by Longinus to denote the sublime or magnificent sensibility).[90] For Gregory, the Lord's Prayer evokes sublimity and the Psalms and Ecclesiastes contain sublime thoughts (τὰ ὑψηλὰ νοήματα).[91]

In particular, the Cappadocians emphasize the emotional impact of a magnificent sensibility. For example, Basil says that the thought of Genesis

---

[84] Basil, *In Joh. 1*, PG31.472.25.
[85] 'Sublime John': Gregory of Nyssa, *Eun.* III.1.13; 1.36; 6.40; 8.40; 9.38. See also: Basil, *Eun.* II.27; Gregory of Nyssa, *Eun.* II.2.23; III.9.16.
[86] Longinus, *Subl.* 12.4. Basil, *In Joh. 1*, PG31.472.26; Gregory of Nyssa, *Eun.* III.2.16 cf. Gregory of Nazianzus: both 'sons of thunder' had μεγαλοφωνία: *Or*.18.24; 43.76.
[87] Gregory of Nyssa, *Eun.* III.1.108; cf. III.3.39 and III.10.9; Basil, *Eun.* I.12.
[88] Gregory Nazianzus, *Or.* 4.1 (cf. Basil, *Eun.* 1.12); *Or.* 19.4; *Or.* 14.21.
[89] Gregory of Nyssa, *Or dom* II GNO VII/2.22.21–2.
[90] Longinus, *Subl.* 9.1; 13.2; 34.4 (of Demosthenes); 36.4.; Gregory of Nyssa *Eun.* I.587; *Beat* GNO VII/2.122.11; *Or dom* GNO VII/2.61.9–14; *Cant* GNO VI.165.4; cf. Basil, *hom. in Ps.* PG29.281.14 (tr. Way (1981) 93).
[91] Gregory of Nyssa, *Inscr* GNO V.25–6 (tr. Heine (1995), I.1.5 and 6, p.84), GNO V.29–30, 33 (tr. Heine (1995), I.3.17 and 23, pp.87–8, 91); *Eccl* GNO V.277.3; *Or dom* GNO VII/2.22.16–23.11.

1.1 demonstrates astonishing profundity (βάθος): 'If such is the forecourt of the sanctuary, if the portico of the temple is so grand and magnificent (σεμνὰ καὶ ὑπέρογκα), if the splendour of its beauty (τῇ ὑπερβολῇ τοῦ κάλλους) thus dazzles (περιαστράπτοντα) the eyes of the soul, what will be the holy of holies?'[92] In the famous opening of his sixth homily on the beatitudes, Gregory of Nyssa writes of the spiritual vertigo caused by the Lord's sublime voice (ἐκ τῆς ὑψηλῆς τοῦ Κυρίου φωνῆς).[93] For Basil, the proof of John's sublimity is that even those outside the faith are amazed by it.[94]

It is possible that the Cappadocians knew of Longinus' use of Genesis 1.3 as an example of sublimity which lies in a concept or 'bare idea itself' (ψιλὴ ἔννοια), more than in the way it is expressed.[95] In any case, it is perhaps not surprising to find the Cappadocians praising the sublime *content* of the Bible, as distinct from other features that might pertain to a majestic sensibility. However, although they have less to say about vocabulary or sentence structure in the Bible, there are hints that they believed the *expression* of certain ideas to be majestic or sublime. Thus Basil comments on the sublime delivery of God's words at Jesus' baptism, 'this is my beloved Son' (Matt 3.17): 'the God of majesty thundered from above with a mighty voice of testimony'.[96] Gregory of Nyssa attributes sublimity to the diction of Isa 40.12: 'Do you observe the magnificent language of the one who describes the ineffable power (μεγαλοφυΐαν τοῦ τὴν ἄφραστον διαγράφοντος δύναμιν)? ... The prophetic word has with such eloquence (ἐν ταῖς τοιαύταις μεγαληγορίαις) described [it] ...'[97] He also praises the way in which the ascending order of the text contributes to the sublimity of the Psalms.[98] The Cappadocians do not attribute a complex and highly worked sentence structure to the magnificent sensibility but, as we have seen, nor did ancient literary critics. Magnificence was often associated with archaic, impressionistic, somewhat uneven prose and it would be reasonable to see such a style in the Greek of the LXX and the NT.

The Cappadocians' repeated assertion that human thoughts can never encapsulate God's transcendent nature somewhat undercuts their affirmation

---

[92] Basil, *hex.* I.1 and 2; II.2.

[93] Gregory of Nyssa, *Beat* VI.1, GNO VII/2.136-7, especially 137.10, 24-5 for his soul's dizziness (ἰλιγγιᾷ, τὸν ἴλιγγον). Cf. Basil, *Eun* I.12 (tr. Radde-Gallwitz (2011) 109): Paul's words reflect his being dizzied 'by the vastness of what he contemplated'.

[94] For example, Basil, *In Joh. 1*, PG31.472 (θαυμάσαντας, ἐθαύμασε, καταπλαγῆναι, etc.); cf. Gregory of Nazianzus' reaction to attempting to put theology into words: *Poemata Arcana* 6.27-46.

[95] Heath (1999).

[96] ὁ δὲ Θεὸς τῆς δόξης τῇ μεγαλοφωνίᾳ τῆς μαρτυρίας ἄνωθεν ἐπεβρόντησε. Basil, *hom in Ps.* PG29.289.44 (tr. Way (1981) 200); he connects the μεγαλοφωνία of God's voice with thunder, another mark of the sublime: Basil, *hom in Ps.* PG29.292.21 (tr. Way (1981) 201); cf. Gregory of Nazianzus on the loudness and magnificence of Jesus' words at the raising of Lazarus: *Or.* 40.33.

[97] Gregory of Nyssa, *Beat* VII.1, GNO VII/2.150.22-5.

[98] Gregory of Nyssa, *Inscr* GNO V.159 (tr. Heine (1995) II.15 (244)).

of Scripture's sublimity. Commenting on Eccl 1.8, 'Words are too weak to express heavenly things', Gregory of Nyssa writes that 'every lofty expression and grandiloquence is a sort of speechlessness and silence (πᾶσα ὑψηγορία τε καὶ μεγαλοφωνία ἀφασία τίς ἐστι καὶ σιωπή)', compared to God.[99] Similarly, Isaiah's eloquence captures a part of the divine activity, but not its source, and although Paul inundates the reader with his eloquence it is like a mere dewdrop compared to the true Word of God.[100] Nevertheless, all these statements reiterate the idea that this discourse still evokes a magnificent sensibility —indeed, this is how it leads its audience upwards to God.[101] In sum, Scripture's magnificence is comparative, not absolute.

Indeed, much of what the Cappadocians wrote about magnificence is comparative (or superlative). The Gospels' discourse is 'nobler (μεγαλοφυεστέρα)' than that of the rest of the Bible; John, Paul, or Isaiah are 'the most grandiloquent'. Eunomius attempts a more sublime style than Basil (but fails). Thus, the Cappadocians are identifying the presence of a magnificent literary sensibility to varying degrees, but none of these claims is absolute. It might seem contradictory for Gregory of Nyssa to claim in one text that Basil's written style is plain (which allows the pure unadulterated truth to shine out beautifully)[102] and in another that Basil's sublime discourse matches the sublime ordering of the universe recounted in Genesis.[103] But both claims depend on an implicit comparison heightened for rhetorical effect: Basil's discourse is both clearer than Eunomius' and more sublime than many of his contemporaries'.

(iii) Pleasant

As we saw above, the pleasant sensibility is denoted in ancient literary criticism in terms that suggest decoration, polish, brilliance, and clarity; it brings charm, sweetness, or pleasure to the audience and has the power to lead the soul. The Cappadocians seem to be familiar with this range of vocabulary. For example, Gregory of Nyssa mocks Eunomius' attempt at a polished 'Attic' style:

> [He] so delicately fashions (ἁβρύνει) his own writing with brilliant style (τῇ λαμπρότητι τῆς ἑρμηνείας)... adorning his account with this speech surpassing fair (ἐν τῇ περιττῇ ταύτῃ καλλιεπείᾳ τὴν συγγραφὴν ἀγλαΐζων), as immediately to

---

[99] Gregory of Nyssa, *Eccl* 293.20.
[100] Gregory of Nyssa, *Beat* VII.1 (GNO VII/2.50.22-7); *Cant* Hom. 11 (GNO VI.326.11-17).
[101] For example, Gregory of Nyssa, *Eun* II.242.
[102] Gregory of Nyssa, *Eun* I.1.18: 'Basil, true servant of the Word, adorned only by the truth, thought it shameful to clothe speech (= the word) in ornamentation, and taught us to aim at the truth alone.'
[103] Gregory of Nyssa, *Op hom*, Pref. (PG44:125.50): τὴν ὑψηλὴν τοῦ παντὸς διακόσμησιν; τὸ ὑψηλὸν στόμα.

seize the hearer with delight (ἡδονῇ) at the words. [Gregory quotes Eunomius.] See the flowers of ancient Attica! How sparkles in the work's composing an easy brilliance of style! With what elegance and variety (γλαφυρῶς καὶ ποικίλως) is its verbal beauty wreathed (περιανθίζεται)![104]

Just as Eunomius tries and fails to emulate magnificent and pleasant speech, so Basil is praised for his success at both. Thus Gregory of Nazianzus remembers not only his sublimity, but also the charm, pleasure, and delight (χάρις, ἡδονή, τρυφή) he gave to his congregations.[105] The Cappadocians appear to associate such qualities especially with letter-writing: a typical example is Basil's thanks for a letter which brought sweetness and charm (ἡδὺ, χάριν).[106]

Gregory of Nyssa seems to associate the pleasant style with particular topics (especially weddings, gardens, and pastoral themes).[107] Thus, for example, he reminds his readers that a preacher must speak in a manner fitting the occasion (προσφυῶς τοῖς πράγμασιν), just as a rhetor would also use fitting and polished (γλαφυρῶν) words.[108] Basil and especially Gregory of Nazianzus focus more on positioning the pleasant style as a moderate mode of discourse. An early letter from Basil advises that ascetics in his community 'observe good measure in both speaking and listening' (μέτρα ὁρίζοντα λόγῳ καὶ ἀκουῇ), using words associated with the pleasant style to describe this middle way: γλυκὺν, τὸ ἡδύ.[109] Gregory of Nazianzus' advice to letter-writers has a similar tone. Good letters have three main virtues: brevity, clarity, and grace (ἡ χάρις). They must be of a length appropriate to the occasion and topic, and more like a conversation than a formal speech. Should this seem somewhat plain, Gregory reminds his reader that they should not be lacking in adornment (ἀκαλλώπιστα) or they will be dry and graceless (ξηρὰ καὶ ἀχάριστα). One can use various figures by which prose is sweetened (καταγλυκαίνεται), but not to self-indulgent excess. The crucial thing about this style of letter (like Dionysius' mixed style) is that it convinces both the simple and the educated reader.[110]

With regard to Scripture, it is very clear that the Cappadocians thought that at least some of the poetic works of the Old Testament evoked a pleasant sensibility. Throughout his commentary on the Song of Songs, Gregory uses language associated with the pleasant style to describe the words of Scripture. Most boldly, he suggests the words of the lover/the Word himself evoke this style in order to lead the soul on to higher things:

The Word (ὁ λόγος) thus speaks with elegance in its account (ἀβρύνεται τῇ ὑπογραφῇ) of springtime's beauty, both casting out gloom and dwelling fondly

---

[104] Gregory of Nyssa, *Eun* I.1.481–2. [105] Gregory of Nyssa, *Or.* 43.66.
[106] Basil, *Ep.* 100 (tr. Deferrari (1928) vol. II, 183). [107] Ludlow (2018), (2014b).
[108] Gregory of Nyssa, *Sanct Pasch*, GNO IX.247.11–12; 17–18.
[109] Basil, *Ep.* 2 (tr. Deferrari (1926) Vol. I, 19). [110] Gregory of Nazianzus, *Ep.* 51.4–5.

upon accounts of things that afford more pleasure (τοῖς γλυκυτέροις διηγήμασιν). It is best, though, I think, that our understanding not come to rest in the account of these sweet things (τῇ τῶν γλαφυρῶν τούτων ὑπογραφῇ) but rather journey by their help toward the mysteries that these oracles reveal, so that the treasure of the ideas hidden in the words may be brought to light.[111]

The pleasant style would seem appropriate to the subject matter of the Song— love, gardens, and pastoral themes. Similarly, there are hints that Gregory thinks that those parts of Ecclesiastes that describe gardens and beautiful things have this sensibility.[112] It may be for a similar reason that Basil associates parts of the creation narrative with a pleasant sensibility. Whilst the account of the first day evokes sublimity, that of the second and successive days 'pleases and delights all the friends of truth'; thus Basil can write of the 'grace of Scripture' (τὴν χάριν τῶν γεγραμμένων) and the 'charm of truth (τὸ ἐκ τῆς ἀληθείας ἡδὺ) which the Psalmist expresses so emphatically when he says, "How sweet (γλυκέα) are thy words unto my taste, yea, sweeter than honey to my mouth"'.[113]

The Psalms, on the other hand, are pleasant, not because of their subject matter, but because of their effect. According to Basil, the Holy Spirit mixed 'the delight of melody ... with the doctrines' like 'wise physicians who, when giving the fastidious rather bitter things to drink, frequently smear the cup with honey'; for Gregory, David had, as it were 'poured the pleasantness of honey over sublime teachings'.[114] They denote the pleasantness of the Psalms with various words which resonate with terms used in literary criticism about the pleasant style: ἡδονή, τὸ τερπνόν, τὸ προσηνες, τὸ λεῖον, κόσμος, χάρις, τέρψις, γλύκειος.[115] There are some differences of emphasis: Basil justifies the mode of the Psalms by repeated insistence on the *usefulness* of their teachings,[116] whilst Gregory suggests that the apparently frivolous musical mode is justified because it makes palatable a content which is sublime (τῶν ὑψηλῶν δογμάτων).[117] He also explains that the Psalms are not like lyric poems in the classical Greek tradition,[118] especially because, although the Psalms use tone, they are chanted rather than sung. David, Gregory argues, used a 'simple and unelaborate' chant (ἀκατάσκευόν τε καὶ ἀνεπιτήδευτον). Therefore, in both Basil's repeated insistence on usefulness and in Gregory's careful attempts to distance the Psalms from inappropriate modes of music, one can see teachers who are well-educated in the literary sensibilities of the day educating their

---

[111] Gregory of Nyssa, Cant Hom. V (GNO VI 146,13–147,5).
[112] Gregory of Nyssa, Eccl GNO V.331–4.3.   [113] Basil, hex, III.1.
[114] Basil, hom. in Ps. 1.1; Gregory of Nyssa Inscr GNO V.33 (tr. Heine (1995) III:23, p.91).
[115] Gregory of Nyssa, Inscr GNO V.33 (tr. Heine (1995) III:23, p.91).
[116] Basil, hom. in Ps. 1.2.
[117] Gregory of Nyssa, Inscr GNO V.34 (tr. Heine (1995) III:25, p.92); cf. Basil's references to 'promises of glory, an unveiling of mysteries': Basil, hom. in Ps. 1.2.
[118] Inscr GNO V.34 (tr. Heine (1995) III:25, p.92).

audience in how to place the Psalms in relation to them: the Psalms give pleasure, but they are a moderate and appropriate form of discourse—appropriate even (perhaps especially) for women and children.[119]

CONCLUSIONS

The scholarly debate about early Christian literary 'style' has tended to assume a contrast between plain and elaborate discourse, with a particular focus on carefully worked figures and sentence composition. However, this was not everything that was meant by literary $\chi\alpha\rho\alpha\kappa\tau\hat{\eta}\rho\epsilon s/i\delta\epsilon\alpha\iota$/*genera dicendi*. Following scholars such as Russell and Innes, I have posited three 'styles', and have suggested they are best understood as moods or sensibilities, each with their appropriate subject matter ($\pi\rho\acute{\alpha}\gamma\mu\alpha\tau\alpha$), ideas ($\delta\iota\acute{\alpha}\nu o\iota\alpha$), language ($\lambda\acute{\epsilon}\xi\iota s$), and composition ($\sigma\upsilon\nu\theta\epsilon\sigma\iota s$). Furthermore, I have argued that the opposition of plain and elaborate discourse in ancient sources is a rhetorical opposition used in literary self-positioning. One finds this rhetoric both in arguments about 'Atticism' from the first century BCE onwards and in contrasts between the *sermo piscatorius* of the Gospels and elaborate 'Hellenist' discourse. We have seen it displayed in the Cappadocians' rhetorical positioning of their own style as plainer and clearer than that of Eunomius.

But this rhetorical binary of (good) plain speech versus (bad) elaborate speech is not the sum of the Cappadocians' concept of literary style. There is clear evidence that they were not only aware of, but trained to observe and use, all three sensibilities or *genera dicendi* noted above. Not only do they use these categories to critique their contemporaries, but they identify passages of the Bible—in both Old and New Testaments—as examples of the pleasant and the majestic styles. They appear more hesitant to declare biblical prose as slender or plain, although they declare that the faith itself (the $\delta\iota\acute{\alpha}\nu o\iota\alpha$ of Scripture) is simple for all to grasp. Once released from an overemphasis on sentence construction ($\sigma\upsilon\nu\theta\epsilon\sigma\iota s$) in one's understanding of 'style', the modern reader can see these early Christian literary critics noting places where biblical texts use ideas, figures, and images which fit the pleasant or majestic sensibilities and describing how they effectively evoke the appropriate emotions. For the Cappadocians, at least, then, there is very little evidence that they thought there was a clear distinction between an 'elaborate' discourse of the classical greats and a 'plain and simple' biblical discourse. In whatever they read, they identified the mood and judged whether appropriate means had been used to evoke it.

---

[119] The psalms are an ornament to women: Basil, *hom. in Ps.* 1.2.

An understanding of ancient literary 'styles' as broad sensibilities and a recognition of the role of rhetorical literary positioning has helped us work towards a more nuanced appreciation of what the Cappadocians have to say about literary 'style' and the Bible. It is likely that similar research on, for example, Origen, John Chrysostom, and Theodoret would also pay dividends. Scholarly claims about the fathers' attitude to plain biblical discourse have been based on a relatively small corpus of quotations that have tended to be studied outside their rhetorical context. Although such oppositions appear to oppose the Bible and classical culture, in fact the plain–elaborate opposition is itself part of a broader rhetoric about style in classical and late antiquity, which sits across more complex theories of style. Future research could fruitfully investigate whether other writers than the Cappadocians apply these more nuanced concepts of sensibility and the appropriate to the biblical text. It might also be valuable to ask what is at stake in modern scholars' perpetuation of the rhetoric of 'plain' Christian versus 'elaborate' classical style.

Bibliography

Abrahamyan, A. G. 1944. *Anania Širakac'u matenagrut'ynuě*. Yerevan.
Adler, W. 1992. 'Eusebius' Chronicle and its Legacy', in H. A. Attridge and G. Hata, eds., *Eusebius, Christianity, and Judaism*, Leiden, 467–91.
Adler, W. 2006. 'Eusebius' Critique of Africanus', in M. Wallraff, ed., *Julius Africanus und die christliche Weltchronik*, Berlin, 148–57.
Adler, W. and P. Tuffin, 2002. *The Chronography of George Synkellos. A Byzantine Chronicle of Universal History from the Creation*. Oxford.
Alt, K. 1996. 'Porphyrios als Helfer in griechischen Nöten. Brief an Markella Kap. 4', in R. Faber and B. Seidensticker, eds., *Worte, Bilder, Töne. Studien zur Antike und Antikerezeption*, Würzburg, 201–10.
Amherdt, D. 2004. *Ausone et Paulin de Nole: correspondance: introduction, texte latin, traduction et notes*, Saphenia 9, Bern.
Amherdt, D. 2006. 'Ausone: rhétorique et christianisme', in E. Amato, ed., *Approches de la troisième sophistique: hommages à Jacques Schamp*, Collection Latomus 296, Bruxelles, 378–88.
Andrei, O. 2006. 'Dalle chronographiai di Giulio Africano alla Synagoge di "Ippolito", Un dibattito sulla scrittura cristiana del tempo', in M. Wallraff, ed., *Julius Africanus und die christliche Weltchronik*, Berlin, 113–45.
Andrei, O. 2015. 'Giuliano: Da apostate a l'Apostata (Sul buon uso dell'apostasia)', in A. Marcone, ed., *L'imperatore Giuliano: Realtà storica e rappresentazione*, Milan, 252–83.
Armisen-Marchetti, M. 2018. *Arnobe, Contre les gentils, Livre II*, Paris.
Arnold, C. C. 1982. 'Introduction', in C. Perelman, *The Realm of Rhetoric*, trans. W. Kluback, Notre Dame, IN, vii–xx.
Asad, T. 1993. *Genealogies of Religion: Discipline and Reasons of Power in Christianity and Islam*, Baltimore, MD.
Asim, J. 2007. *The N Word: Who Can Say It, Who Shouldn't, and Why*, New York.
Aslan, R. 2010. *Beyond Fundamentalism: Confronting Religious Extremism in the Age of Globalization*, New York.
Assmann, J. 2008. 'Communicative and Cultural Memory', in A. Erll and A. Nünning, eds., *Cultural Memory Studies. An International and Interdisciplinary Handbook*, Berlin, 109–18.
Aubineau, M. 1971. *Grégoire de Nysse. Traité de La Virginité*, Sources Chrétiennes 119, Paris.
Austin, J. 1962. *How To Do Things With Words*, Cambridge, MA.
Ayres, L. 2004. *Nicaea and its Legacy: An Approach to Fourth-Century Trinitarian Theology*, Oxford.
Baker-Brian, N. and S. Tougher, eds., 2012. *Emperor and Author: The Writings of Julian the Apostate*, Swansea.

Baker-Brian, N. J. 2016. 'A New Religion? The Emergence of Manichaeism in Late Antiquity', in J. Lössl and N. J. Baker-Brian, eds., *A Companion to Religion in Late Antiquity*, Malden, MA, 319–43.

Bardy, G. 1931. 'Le "De Haeresibus" et ses sources', *Miscellanea Agostiniana* 2: 397–16.

Barlow, C. W., ed., 1950. *Martini Opera: Canons of the Council of Ancyra in Canones ex orientalium partum synodis a Martino episcopo ordinata et collecta. In Martini episcopi Bracarensis Opera omnia*. New Haven, CT.

Barnes, T. D. 1978. 'A Correspondent of Iamblichus', *Greek, Roman and Byzantine Studies* 19: 99–106.

Barton, T. S. 1994. *Power and Knowledge: Astrology, Physiognomics and Medicine under the Roman Empire*, Ann Arbor, MI.

Battifol, P. 1895. 'Un historiographe anonyme arien du IVe siècle', *Römische Quartalschrift* 9: 93–7.

Bausi, A. and A. Camplani, 2013. 'New Ethiopic Documents for the History of Christian Egypt', *Zeitschrift für antikes Christentum* 17: 215–47.

Bausi, A. and A. Camplani, 2016. 'The History of the Episcopate of Alexandria (HEpA): Editio Minor of the Fragments Preserved in the Aksumite Collection and in the Codex Veronensis LX (58)', *Adamantius* 22: 249–02.

Beagon, M. 1992. *The Elder Pliny on the Human Animal: Natural History Book 7*, Oxford.

Beagon, M. 1994. 'The Curious Eye of the Elder Pliny', in R. K. Gibson and R. Morello, eds., *Pliny the Elder: Themes and Contexts*, Leiden, 71–88.

Beagon, M. 2007. 'Situating Nature's Wonders in Pliny's *Natural History*', *Bulletin of the Institute of Classical Studies* 50: 19–40.

Beagon, M. 2013. '*Labores pro bono publico*: The Burdensome Mission of Pliny's *Natural History*', in J. König and G. Woolf, eds., *Encyclopaedism from Antiquity to the Renaissance*, Cambridge, 84–107.

Beard, M. 1994. 'The Roman and the Foreign: The Cult of the "Great Mother" in Imperial Rome', in N. Thomas and C. Humphrey, eds., *Shamanism, History, and the State*, Ann Arbor, MI, 164–90.

Beatrice, P. F. 1990. 'Le croix et les idoles d'après l'apologie d'Athanase contre les païens', in A. Gonzalez, ed., *Cristianesimo y aculturacion en tiempo del Imperio Romano*, Murcia, 159–77.

Beatrice, P. F. 1993. 'Antistes philosophiae: Ein Christenfiendlicher Propagandist am Hofe Diokletians nach dem Zeugnis des Laktanz', *Augustinianum* 33: 31–47.

Becker, M. 2016. *Porphyrios: Gegen die Christen (Contra Christianos). Fragmente, Testimonien und dubia mit Einleitung, Übersetzung und Anmerkungen*, Berlin.

BeDuhn, J. 2015a. 'Parallels between Coptic and Iranian Kephalaia: Goundesh and the King of Touran', in I. Gardner, J. BeDuhn, and P. C. Dilley, eds., *Mani at the Court of the Persian Kings: Studies on the Chester Beatty Kephalaia Codex*, Leiden, 52–74.

BeDuhn, J. 2015b. 'Mani and the Crystallization of the Concept of Religion in Third Century Iran', in I. Gardner, J. BeDuhn, and P. C. Dilley, eds., *Mani at the Court of the Persian Kings. Studies on the Chester Beatty Kephalaia Codex*, Leiden, 247–75.

Belanger, C. 2014. 'Solinus' *Macrobians*: A Roman Literary Account of the Axumite Empire', in K. Brodersen, ed., *Solinus: New Studies*, Heidelberg, 96–118.

Belayche, N. 2009. '*Ritus et cultus* ou *superstitio*? Comment les lois du *Code Théodosien* (IX & XVI) de Constantin à Théodose parlent des pratiques religieuses traditionnelles', in S. Crogiez-Pétrequin and P. Jaillette, eds., *Le Code Théodosien. Diversité des approches et nouvelles perspectives*, Collection de l'École Française de Rome 412, Rome, 191–208.

Bell, D. N., tr., 1983. *The Life of Shenoute, by Besa*. Cistercian Studies Series 73, Kalamazoo, MI.

Berzon, T. S. 2016a. 'Known Knowns and Known Unknowns: Epiphanius of Salamis and the Limits of Heresiology', *Harvard Theological Review* 109: 75–101.

Berzon, T. S. 2016b. *Classifying Christians: Ethnography, Heresiology, and the Limits of Knowledge in Late Antiquity*, Berkeley, CA.

Bidez, J. 2004. *Julian: Lettres et fragments*, 5th edn, Paris.

Bidez, J. and F. Winkelmann, 1972. *Philostorgius. Kirchengeschichte mit dem Leben des Lucian von Antiochien und den Fragmenten eines arianischen Historiographen*, Berlin.

Birk, S. 2013. *Depicting the Dead: Self-Representation and Commemoration on Roman Sarcophagi with Portraits*, Aarhus.

Blaudeau, P. 2006. *Alexandrie et Constantinople, 451–491: de l'histoire à la géo-ecclésiologie*, Bibliothèque des écoles françaises d'Athènes et de Rome 327, Rome.

Boin, D. 2010. 'A Hall for Hercules at Ostia and a Farewell to the "Pagan Revival"', *American Journal of Archaeology* 114: 253–66.

Boin, D. 2013a. 'A Late Antique Statuary Collection at Ostia's Sanctuary of Magna Mater: A Case Study on the Visibility of Late Roman Religion', *Papers of the British School at Rome* 81: 47–77.

Boin, D. 2013b. *Ostia in Late Antiquity*, Cambridge.

Boin, D. 2014. 'Hellenistic "Judaism" and the Social Origins of the "Pagan–Christian" Debate', *Journal of Early Christian Studies* 22: 167–96.

Boin, D. 2015. *Coming Out Christian in the Roman World: How the Followers of Jesus Made a Place in Caesar's Empire*, New York.

Boin, D. 2018. *A Social and Cultural History of Late Antiquity*, Malden, MA.

Bonner, G. 1984. 'The Extinction of Paganism and the Church Historian', *Journal of Ecclesiastical History* 35: 339–57.

Borg, B. 2013. *Crisis and Ambition: Tombs and Burial Customs in Third-Century AD Rome*, Oxford Studies in Ancient Culture and Representation, Oxford.

Borg, B. 2014. 'Rhetoric and Art in Third-Century Rome', in J. Elsner and M. Meyer, eds., *Art and Rhetoric in Roman Culture*, Cambridge, 235–55.

Borgeaud, P. 2004. *Mother of the Gods. From Cybele to the Virgin Mary*, trans. L. Hochroth, Baltimore, MD and London.

Bouffartigue, J. 1991. 'Julien ou l'hellénisme décomposé', in S. Said, ed., *ΕΛΛΗΝΙΣΜΟΣ: Quelques jalons pour une histoire de l'identité Grecque*, Leiden, 251–66.

Bouffartigue, J. 2005. 'L'authenticité de la lettre 84 de l'empereur Julien', *Revue de Philologie* 79: 231–42.

Boulding, M., ed., 1997. *The Works of Saint Augustine: A Translation for the Twenty-First Century. 1, 1, The Confessions*, New York.

Boulding, M., tr., 2004. *The Works of Saint Augustine: A Translation for the Twenty-First Century. 3, 19, Exposition of the Psalms*, New York.

Bovini, G. and H. Brandenburg, 1967. *Repertorium der christlich-antiken Sarkophage, Vol. I, Rom und Ostia*, Wiesbaden.
Bowden, H. 2010. *Mystery Cults in the Ancient World*, London.
Bowersock, G. W. 1978. *Julian the Apostate*, Cambridge, MA.
Bowersock, G. W. 1986. 'Symmachus and Ausonius', in F. Paschoud, ed., *Colloque genevois sur Symmaque, à l'occasion du mille-six-centième anniversaire du conflit de l'autel de la Victoire*, Paris, 1–15.
Bowersock, G. W. 1990. *Hellenism in Late Antiquity*, Ann Arbor, MI.
Boyarin, D. 2004. *Border Lines: The Partition of Judaeo-Christianity*, Philadelphia, PA.
Boyarin, D. 2008. 'The Christian Invention of Judaism: The Theodosian Empire and the Rabbinic Refusal of Religion', in H. de Vries, ed., *Religion: Beyond a Concept*, New York, 150–77.
Brakke, D. 2008. 'From Temple to Cell, from Gods to Demons: Pagan Temples in the Monastic Topography of Fourth-Century Egypt', in J. Hahn, U. Gotter, and S. Emmel, eds., *From Temple to Church: Destruction and Renewal of Local Cultic Topography in Late Antiquity*, Religions in the Graeco-Roman World 163, Leiden, 92–113.
Braun, R. 1978. 'Julien et le christianisme', in R. Braun and J. Richer, eds., *L'empereur Julien: De l'histoire à la légende (331–1715)*, Paris, 159–88.
Bremmer, J. N. 2000. 'La confrontation entre l'apôtre Pierre et Simon le magicien', in A. Moreau and J.-C. Turpin, eds., *La magie 1. Du monde babylonien au monde hellénistique*, Montpellier, 219–31.
Bremmer, J. N. 2002. 'Magic in the *Apocryphal Acts of the Apostles*', in J. N. Bremmer and J. R. Veenstra, eds., *The Metamorphosis of Magic from Late Antiquity to the Early Modern Period*, Leuven, 51–70.
Brennecke, H. C. 1988. *Studien zur Geschichte der Homöer: Der Osten bis zum Ende der homöischen Reichskirche*, Beiträge zur historischen Theologie 73, Tübingen.
Breyfogle, T. 1995. 'Magic, Women, and Heresy in the Late Empire: The Case of the Priscillianists', in M. Meyer and P. Mirecki, eds., *Ancient Magic and Ritual Power*, Religions in the Graeco-Roman World 129, Leiden, 435–54.
Broadhead, E. K. 2010. *Jewish Ways of Following Jesus: Redrawing the Religious Map of Antiquity*, Wissenschaftliche Untersuchungen Zum Neuen Testament 266, Tübingen.
Brooks, E. W., ed., 1910. *Eliae metropolitae Nisibeni opus chronologicum, Vol. 1*, Corpus Scriptorum Christianorum Orientalium 62: Scriptores Syri 21, Paris.
Brottier, L. 2004. 'Jean Chrysostome: un pasteur face à des demi-chrétiens', in B. Cabouret, P.-L. Gatier, and C. Saliou, eds., *Antioche de Syrie: histoire, images et traces de la ville antique*, Topoi Orient Occident, Supplément 5, Lyon, 439–57.
Brottier, L. 2005. *L'appel des "demi-chrétiens" à la "vie angélique": Jean Chrysostome prédicateur: entre idéal monastique et réalité mondaine*, Paris.
Brown, P. 1967. *Augustine of Hippo*, Berkeley, CA.
Brown, P. 1992. *Power and Persuasion in Late Antiquity: Towards a Christian Empire*, Madison, WI.
Brown, P. 1996. *The Rise of Western Christendom: Triumph and Diversity AD 200–1000*, Oxford.

Brown, P. 1997. 'So Debate: The World of Late Antiquity Revisited', *Symbolae Osloenses* 72: 5–30.

Brown, P. 2012. *Through the Eye of a Needle: Wealth, the Fall of Rome, and the Making of Christianity in the West, 350–550 AD*, Princeton, NJ.

Brubaker, R. 2002. 'Ethnicity without Groups', *Archives Européennes de Sociologie* 43.2: 163–89.

Brubaker, R. 2004. *Ethnicity without Groups*, Cambridge, MA.

Brubaker, R., M. Feischmidt, J. Fox, and L. Grancea, 2006. *Nationalist Politics and Everyday Ethnicity in a Transylvanian Town*, Princeton, NJ.

Bruggisser, P. 1996. 'Pierre de Labriolle (1874–1940) et la perception du christianisme d'Ausone face aux orientations de la recherche actuelle', in I. Lewandowski and L. Mrozewicz, eds., *L'image de l'antiquité chez les auteurs postérieurs*, Poznań, 113–38.

Bryce, H. and H. Campbell, 1886. 'Arnobius, *Against the Heathen*', in *Ante-Nicene Fathers, Vol. 6*, Buffalo, NY, 413–39.

Burgess, R. W. 2002. 'Jerome Explained: An Introduction to his *Chronicle* and a Guide to its Use', *American Historical Bulletin* 16: 1–32.

Burgess, R. W. and M. Kulikowski, 2013. *Mosaics of Time: The Latin Chronicle Traditions from the First Century BC to the Sixth Century AD. Vol. I: A Historical Introduction to the Chronicle Genre from its Origins to the High Middle Ages*, Studies in the Early Middle Ages 33, Turnhout.

Burgess, R. W. and W. Witakowski, 1999. *Studies in Eusebian and Post-Eusebian Chronography*, Historia Einzelschriften 135, Stuttgart.

Burke, P. J. 2003. 'Relationships among Multiple Identities', in P. J. Burke, T. J. Owens, R. Serpe, and P. A. Thoits, eds., *Advances in Identity Theory and Research*, New York, 195–214.

Burke, P. J. and J. E. Stets, 2009. *Identity Theory*, Oxford.

Burns, D. M. 2014. *Apocalypse of the Alien God: Platonism and the Exile of Sethian Gnosticism*, Philadelphia, PA.

Burrus, V. 2009. 'Carnal Excess: Flesh at the Limits of Imagination', *Journal of Early Christian Studies* 17: 247–65.

Callebat, L. 1997. 'Encyclopédie et architecture: le *De Architectura* de Vitruve', in J. Bouffartigue and F. Mélonio, eds., *L'enterprise encyclopédique*, Nanterre, 169–80.

Cameron, Alan, 2011. *The Last Pagans of Rome*, Oxford.

Cameron, Averil, 1991. *Christianity and the Rhetoric of Empire: The Development of Christian Discourse*, Berkeley, CA.

Cameron, Averil, 1998. 'Education and Literary Culture', in A. Cameron and P. Garnsey, eds., *The Cambridge Ancient History, Vol. XIII: The Late Empire: A.D. 337–425*, Cambridge, 665–707.

Cameron, Averil, 2003. 'How to Read Heresiology', *Journal of Medieval and Early Modern Studies* 33: 471–92 (repr. in D. B. Martin and P. Cox Miller, eds., 2005. *The Cultural Turn in Late Ancient Studies: Gender, Asceticism and Historiography*. Durham, NC, 193–212).

Cameron, Averil, 2008. 'The Violence of Orthodoxy', in E. Iricinschi and H. M. Zellentin, eds., *Heresy and Identity in Late Antiquity*, Tübingen, 102–14.

Cameron, Averil, 2014. *Dialoguing in Late Antiquity*, Cambridge, MA.

Cameron, M. 2012. 'Augustine and Scripture', in M. Vessey, ed., *A Companion to Augustine*, Oxford, 200–14.
Camplani, A. 2015. 'The Religious Identity of Alexandria in Some Ecclesiastical Histories of Late Antique Egypt', in P. Blaudeau and P. Van Nuffelen, eds., *L'historiographie tardo-antique et la transmission des savoirs*, Millennium-Studien 55, Berlin, 85–119.
Caner, D. F. 1997. 'The Practice and Prohibition of Self-Castration in Early Christianity', *Vigiliae Christianae* 51: 396–415.
Carlig, N. 2013. 'Recherches sur la forme, la mise en page et le contenu des papyrus scolaires grecs et latins chrétiens d'Égypte', *Studi di egittologia e di papirologia* 10: 55–98.
Casella, M. 2010. *Storie di ordinaria corruzione. Libanio, orazioni LVI, LVII, XLVI*, Messina.
Cassin, M. 2008. '"Plumer Isocrate": L'usage polémique du vocabulaire comique chez Grégoire de Nysse', *Revue des Études Grecques* 121.2: 783–96.
Cassin, M. 2012. *L'écriture de la controverse chez Grégoire de Nysse: polémique littéraire et exégèse dans le Contre Eunome*, Paris.
Cavallo, G. 2001. 'L'altra lettura. Tra nuovi libri e nuovi testi', *Antiquité Tardive* 9: 131–8.
Chabot, J.-B., ed., 1927. *Incerti auctoris Chronicon pseudo-dionysianum vulgo dictum*, Corpus Scriptorum Christianorum Orientalium 91: Scriptores Syri 43, Paris.
Chadwick, H. 1955. *Sentences of Sextus*, Cambridge.
Chadwick, H. 1993. *The Early Church*, rev. edn, London.
Champeaux, J. 2007. *Arnobe, Contre les gentils, Livre III*, Paris.
Champeaux, J. 2018. *Arnobe: le combat Contre les païens. Religion, mythologie et polémique au IIIe siècle ap. J.-C.*, Turnhout.
Chaniotis, A. 2008. 'Priests as Ritual Experts in the Greek World', in B. Dignas and K. Trampedach, eds., *Practitioners of the Divine*, Washington, DC, 17–34.
Charles-Saget, A. 1993. 'La théurgie, nouvelle figure de l'*ergon* dans la vie philosophique', in H. J. Blumenthal and E. G. Clark, eds., *The Divine Iamblichus*, London, 107–15.
Charlet, J.-L. 1984–1989. 'Théologie, politique et rhétorique: la célébration poétique de Pâques à la cour de Valentinien et d'Honorius, d'après Ausone (*Versus paschales*) et Claudien (*De Saluatore*)', in *La poesia tardoantica: tra retorica, teologia e politica: atti del v Corso della Scuola superiore di archeologia e civiltà medievali presso il Centro di cultura scientifica 'E. Majorana', Erice (Trapani) 6–12 dicembre 1981*, Messina, 259–87.
Chin, C. 2008. *Grammar and Christianity in the Late Roman World*, Philadelphia, PA.
Claes, M. and A. Dupont, 2017. 'Augustine's Sermons and Disability', in C. Laes, ed., *Disability in Antiquity*, London, 328–41.
Clark, E. A. 1997. 'Reading Asceticism: Exegetical Strategies in the Early Christian Rhetoric of Renunciation', *Biblical Interpretation* 5.1: 82–104.
Clark, E. A. 1999. *Reading Renunciation: Asceticism and Scripture in Early Christianity*, Princeton, NJ.
Clark, E. A. 2004. 'Creating Foundations, Creating Authorities: Reading Practices and Christian Identities', in J. Frishman, W. Otten, and G. Rouwhorst, eds., *Religious Identity and the Problem of Historical Foundation: The Foundational Character of Authoritative Sources in the History of Christianity and Judaism*, Leiden, 553–72.

Clark, G. 2000. *Porphyry: On Abstinence from Killing Animals*, Ithaca, NY.
Clark, G. 2007a. 'City of Books: Augustine and the World as Text', in W. E. Klingshirn, ed., *The Early Christian Book*, Washington, DC, 117-38.
Clark, G. 2007b. 'Augustine's Porphyry and the Universal Way of Salvation', in G. Karamanolis and A. Sheppard, eds., *Studies on Porphyry*, London, 127-40.
Clark, G. 2008. 'Can We Talk? Augustine and the Possibility of Dialogue', in S. Goldhill, ed., *The End of Dialogue*, Cambridge, 117-34.
Clarke, E., J. Dillon, and J. Hershbell, eds., 2003. *Iamblichus: On the Mysteries*, Atlanta, GA.
Clarke, G. W., ed., 1984-1989. *The Letters of St. Cyprian of Carthage*, 4 vols, New York.
Claussen, M. A. 1995. 'Pagan Rebellion and Christian Apologetics in Fourth-Century Rome: *The Consultationes Zacchaei et Apollonii*', *Journal of Ecclesiastical History* 46: 589-614.
Conduché, C., J.-B. Guillaumin, E. Marquis, J. Regnault-Larrieu, P. Petitmengin, and A. Salamon, 2013. 'Le de cursu temporum d'Hilarianus et sa réfutation (CPL 2280 et 2281). Une querelle chronologique à la fin de l'Antiquité', *Recherches augustiniennes et patristiques* 37: 131-267.
Conte, G. B. 1994. *Genres and Readers*, tr. G. W. Most, Baltimore, MD.
Conti, S. 2004. *Die Inschriften Kaiser Julians*, Stuttgart.
Conybeare, F. C. 1904. 'Dialogus de Christi die natali. Ex lingua armena latine reddidit', *Zeitschrift für die neutestamentliche Wissenschaft* 5: 327-34.
Corcoran, S. 2000. *Empire of the Tetrarchs: Imperial Pronouncements and Government, AD 284-324*, Oxford.
Corke-Webster, J. 2017. 'Trouble in Pontus: The Pliny-Trajan Correspondence on the Christians Reconsidered', *Transactions of the American Philological Association* 147: 371-411.
Courcelle, P. 1953. 'Les sages de Porphyre et les *viri novi* d'Arnobe', *Revue des études latines* 31: 257-71.
Courcelle, P. 1968. *Recherches sur les Confessions de saint Augustin*, 2nd edn, Paris.
Couzin, R. 2014. 'The Christian Sarcophagus Population of Rome', *Journal of Roman Archaeology* 27: 275-303.
Cremer, F. W. 1969. *Die Chaldäischen Orakel und Iamblich de Mysteriis*, Meisenheim am Glan.
Cribiore, R. 1996. *Writing, Teachers and Students in Graeco-Roman Egypt*, Atlanta, GA.
Cribiore, R. 2001. *Gymnastics of the Mind: Greek Education in Hellenistic and Roman Egypt*, Princeton, NJ.
Cribiore, R. 2007. *The School of Libanius in Late Antique Antioch*, Princeton, NJ.
Cribiore, R. 2009. 'The Value of a Good Education: Libanius and Public Authority', in P. Rousseau, ed., *A Companion to Late Antiquity*, Chichester, 233-45.
Cribiore, R. 2013. *Libanius the Sophist: Rhetoric, Reality, and Religion in the Fourth Century*, Ithaca, NY.
Croke, B. 2010. 'Reinventing Constantinople: Theodosius I's Imprint on the Imperial City', in S. McGill, C. Sogno, and E. Watts, eds., *From the Tetrarchs to the Theodosians: Later Roman History and Culture 284-450 CE*, Cambridge, 241-64.
Crone, P. 2012. 'Buddhism as Ancient Iranian Paganism', in T. Bernheimer and A. Silverstein, eds., *Late Antiquity: Eastern Perspectives*, Exeter, 25-41.

Croom, A. 2013. 'How To Do Things With Slurs: Studies in the Way of Derogatory Words', *Language & Communication* 33: 177–204.

Curran, J. 2000. *Pagan City and Christian Capital: Rome in the Fourth Century*, Oxford.

Davis, G. 2002. 'Ait Phaselus: The Caricature of Stylistic Genre (Genus Dicendi) in Catullus Carm. 4', *Materiali e Discussioni per l'analisi dei Testi Classici* 48: 111–43.

Debié, M. 2015. *L'écriture de l'histoire en Syriaque: transmissions interculturelles et constructions identitaires entre hellénisme et islam: avec des répertoires des textes historiographiques en annexe*, Late Antique History and Religion 12, Leuven.

de Jong, A. 2008. '*A Quodam Persa Exstiterunt*. Re-Orienting Manichaean Origins', in A. Houtman, A. de Jong, and M. Misset-van der Weg, eds., *Empsychoi Logoi. Religious Innovations in Antiquity: Studies in Honour of Pieter Willem van der Horst*, Leiden, 81–106.

de Jong, A. 2014. 'The *Cologne Mani Codex* and the Life of Zarathustra', in G. Herman, ed., *Jews, Christians and Zoroastrians: Religious Dynamics in a Sasanian Context*, Piscataway, NJ, 129–47.

DelCogliano, M. 2011. 'The Promotion of the Constantinian Agenda in Eusebius of Caesarea's On the Feast of Pascha', in S. Inowlocki and C. Zamagni, eds., *Reconsidering Eusebius: Collected Papers on Literary, Historical, and Theological Issues*, Leiden, 39–68.

DelCogliano, M. and A. Radde-Gallwitz, tr., 2011. *Basil, Against Eunomius*, Washington, DC.

DePalma Digeser, E. 1998. 'Lactantius, Porphyry, and the Debate over Religious Toleration', *Journal of Roman Studies* 88: 129–46.

de Vogüé, A. 1997. *Histoire littéraire du mouvement monastique* I/5, Paris.

Dilley, P. 2015a. 'Mani's Wisdom at the Court of the Persian Kings: The Genre and Context of the Chester Beatty *Kephalaia*', in I. Gardner, J. BeDuhn, and P. Dilley, eds., *Mani at the Court of the Persian Kings. Studies on the Chester Beatty Kephalaia Codex*, Leiden, 15–51.

Dilley, P. 2015b. 'Also Schrieb Zarathustra. Mani as Interpreter of the "Law of Zarades"', in I. Gardner, J. BeDuhn, and P. Dilley, eds., *Mani at the Court of the Persian Kings. Studies on the Chester Beatty Kephalaia Codex*, Leiden, 102–35.

Dodds, E. R. 1951. *The Greeks and the Irrational*, Berkeley, CA.

Doody, A. 2010. *Pliny's Encyclopedia: The Reception of the Natural History*, Cambridge.

Drake, H. 1996. 'Lions into Lambs: Explaining Early Christian Intolerance', *Past and Present* 153: 3–36.

Drake, H. 2011. 'Intolerance, Religious Violence, and Political Legitimacy in Late Antiquity', *Journal of the American Academy of Religion* 79: 193–235.

Dresken-Weiland, J. 2010. *Bild, Grab und Wort: Untersuchungen zu Jenseitsvorstellungen von Christen des 3. und 4. Jahrhunderts*, Regensburg.

Dresken-Weiland, J. 2011. 'Bilder im Grab und ihre Debeutung im Kontext der Christianisierung der frühchristlichen Welt', *Antiquité Tardive* 19: 63–78.

Dresken-Weiland, J. 2018. 'Christian Sarcophagi from Rome', in R. M. Jensen and M. Ellison, eds., *The Routledge Handbook to Early Christian Art*, London, 39–55.

Dubuisson, D. 2003. *The Western Construction of Religion*, Baltimore, MD.

Dulaurier, E. 1859. *Recherches sur la chronologie arménienne technique et historique*, Paris.

Bibliography

Dumézil, B. 2005. *Les racines chrétiennes de l'Europe. Conversion et liberté dans les royaumes barbares Ve-VIIIe siècle*, Paris.
Dummer, J. 1973. 'Ein naturwissenschaftliches Handbuch als Quelle für Epiphanius von Constantia', *Klio* 55: 289-99.
Dyck, A. R. 2010. 'Cicero's Abridgment of his Speeches for Publication', in M. Horster and C. Reitz, eds., *Condensing Texts—Condensed Texts*, Wiesbaden, 369-74.
Dyson, R. W. tr. 1998. *Augustine. The City of God against the Pagans*, Cambridge.
Edwards, M. 1999. 'The Flowering of Latin Apologetic: Lactantius and Arnobius', in M. Edwards, M. Goodman, and S. Price, eds., in association with C. Rowland, *Apologetics in the Roman Empire: Pagans, Jews, and Christians*, Oxford, 197-221.
Edwards, M. 2003. *Constantine and Christendom*, Liverpool.
Edwards, M. 2015. *Religions of the Constantinian Empire*, Oxford.
Eijk, P. van der, 2005. *Medicine and Philosophy in Classical Antiquity: Doctors and Philosophers on Nature, Soul, Health and Disease*, Cambridge.
Elm, S. 1994. *Virgins of God: The Making of Asceticism in Late Antiquity*, Oxford.
Elm, S. 2012. *Sons of Hellenism: Fathers of the Church: Emperor Julian, Gregory of Nazianzus, and the Vision of Rome*, Transformation of the Classical Heritage 49, Berkeley, CA.
Elm, S. 2013. 'What the Bishop Wore to the Synod: John Chrysostom, Origenism, and the Politics of Fashion at Constantinople', *Adamantius* 19: 156-69.
Elm, S. 2015. 'When Augustine Spoke of Babylon, What Did He See?', in B. Vinken, ed., *Translatio Babylonis: Unsere orientalische Moderne*, Munich, 29-42.
Elm, S. 2017a. 'Signs under the Skin: Flogging Eternal Rome', in I. Därmann and T. Macho, eds., *Unter die Haut. Tätowierungen als Logo-und Piktogramme*, Munich, 51-75.
Elm, S. 2017b. 'New Romans: Salvian of Marseilles on *The Government of God*', *Journal of Early Christian Studies* 25: 1-27.
Elm, S. 2017c. 'Sold to Sin through *origo*: Augustine of Hippo on Slavery and Freedom', *Studia Patristica* 98: 1-21.
Elm, S. 2018. 'Dressing Moses: Reading Gregory of Nyssa's *Life of Moses* Literally', in M. Edwards and A. Marmodoro, eds., *Exploring Gregory of Nyssa. Philosophical, Theological, and Historical Studies*, Oxford, 49-73.
Elsner, J. 1995. *Art and the Roman Viewer: The Transformation of Art from the Pagan World to Christianity*, Cambridge.
Elsner, J. 2014. 'Rational, Passionate, and Appetitive: The Psychology of Rhetoric and the Transformation of Visual Culture from Non-Christian to Christian Sarcophagi in the Roman World', in J. Elsner and M. Meyer, eds., *Art and Rhetoric in Roman Culture*, Cambridge, 316-49.
Engels, D. and P. Van Nuffelen, 2014. 'Religion and Competition in Antiquity: An Introduction', in D. Engels and P. Van Nuffelen, eds., *Religion and Competition in Antiquity*, Brussels, 9-44.
Engemann, J. 1975. 'Zur Verbreitung der magischen Übelabwehr in der nichtchristlichen und christlichen Spätantike', *Jahrbuch für Antike und Christentum* 18: 22-48.
Errington, M. 2006. *Roman Imperial Policy from Julian to Theodosius*, Chapel Hill, NC.

Escribano Paño, M. V. 2010. 'Heretical Texts and *Maleficium* in the *Codex Theodosianus* (*CTh* 16.5.34)', in R. L. Gordon and F. Marco Simón, eds., *Magical Practice in the Latin West*, Leiden, 105–38.

Evans Grubbs, J. 1989. 'Abduction Marriage in Antiquity: A Law of Constantine (*CTh* 9.24.1) and its social context', *Journal of Roman Studies* 79: 59–83.

Evans Grubbs, J. 1995. *Law and Family in Late Antiquity: The Emperor Constantine's Marriage Legislation*, Oxford.

Ewald, B. 2012. 'Paradigms of Personhood and Regimes of Representation: Some Notes on the Transformation of Roman Sarcophagi', *RES. Anthropology and Aesthetics* 61/62: 41–64.

Fear, A. T. 1996. 'Cybele and Christ', in E. N. Lane, ed., *Cybele, Attis and Related Cults. Essays in Memory of M. J. Vermaseren*, Leiden, 37–50.

Feeney, D. 2007. *Caesar's Calendar: Ancient Times and the Beginning of History*, Berkeley, CA.

Ferguson, T. 2005. *The Past is Prologue: The Revolution of Nicene Historiography*, Supplements to Vigiliae Christianae 75, Leiden.

Flint, V. I. J., ed., 1999. *Witchcraft and Magic in Europe: Ancient Greece and Rome. Athlone History of Witchcraft and Magic in Europe 2*. London.

Flower, R. 2011. 'Genealogies of Unbelief: Epiphanius of Salamis and Heresiological Authority', in C. M. Kelly, R. Flower, and M. S. Williams, eds., *Unclassical Traditions, Vol. II: Perspectives from East and West in Late Antiquity*, Cambridge Classical Journal Supplementary Vol. 35, Cambridge, 70–87.

Flower, R. 2013a. *Emperors and Bishops in Late Roman Invective*, Cambridge.

Flower, R. 2013b. 'The Insanity of Heretics Must Be Restrained: Heresiology in the Theodosian Code', in C. Kelly, ed., *Theodosius II: Rethinking the Roman Empire in Late Antiquity*. Cambridge, 172–94.

Flower, R. 2018. 'Medicalizing Heresy: Doctors and Patients in Epiphanius of Salamis', *Journal of Late Antiquity* 11: 251–73.

Fögen, M. T. 1993. *Die Enteignung der Wahrsager. Studien zum kaiserlichen Wissensmonopol in der Spätantike*, Frankfurt am Main.

Fögen, T. 2009. *Wissen, Kommunikation und Selbstdarstellung: Zur Struktur und Charakteristik römischer Fachtexte der frühen Kaiserzeit*, München.

Forbes, C. A. 1970. *Firmicus Maternus: The Error of the Pagan Religions*, New York and Ramsey, NJ.

Formisano, M. 2013. 'Late Latin Encyclopaedism: Towards a New Paradigm of Practical Knowledge', in J. König and G. Woolf, eds., *Encyclopaedism from Antiquity to the Renaissance*, Cambridge, 197–215.

Förster, H. 2007. *Die Anfänge von Weihnachten und Epiphanias: eine Anfrage an die Entstehungshypothesen*, Studien und Texte zu Antike und Christentum 46, Tübingen.

Fowden, G. 1983. *The Egyptian Hermes*, Princeton, NJ.

Fowden, G. 2005. 'Late Polytheism: The World-View', in A. K. Bowman, P. Garnsey, and Averil Cameron, eds., *The Cambridge Ancient History, Vol. XII: The Crisis of Empire, A.D. 193–337*, Cambridge, 521–37.

Fox, J. E. and C. Miller-Idriss, 2008. 'Everyday Nationhood', *Ethnicities* 8.4: 536–63.

Fraenkel, P. 1962. 'Histoire sainte et hérésie chez Saint Épiphane de Salamine: d'après le Tome I du *Panarion*', *Revue de Théologie et de Philosophie* 12: 175–91.

Fragu, F. 2010. *Arnobe, Contre les Gentils, Livres VI–VII*, Paris.
Frakes, R. M. 2011. *Compiling the Collatio Legum Mosaicarum et Romanarum in Late Antiquity*, Oxford.
Frankfurter, D. 1997. 'Ritual Expertise in Roman Egypt', in P. Schäfer and H. G. Kippenberg, eds., *Envisioning Magic*, Leiden, 115–35.
Frankfurter, D. 2002. 'Dynamics of Ritual Expertise in Antiquity and Beyond: Towards a New Taxonomy of "Magicians"', in P. Mirecki and M. Meyer, eds., *Magic and Ritual in the Ancient World*, Leiden, 159–78.
Frankfurter, D. 2005. 'Beyond Magic and Superstition', in V. Burrus, ed., *A People's History of Christianity, Vol. 2: Late Ancient Christianity*, Minneapolis, MN, 255–84.
Frankfurter, D. 2008. 'Iconoclasm and Christianization in Late Antique Egypt: Christian Treatments of Space and Image', in J. Hahn, S. Emmel, and U. Götter, eds., *From Temple to Church: Destruction and Renewal of Local Cultic Topography in Late Antiquity*, Leiden, 135–59.
Frankfurter, D. 2015. 'Review of Nongbri 2013', *Journal of Early Christian Studies* 23: 632–4.
Freund, S. 2017. '*Contra religionem nomenque Christianorum*. Die Gegner des Christentums in den *Divinae institutiones* des Laktanz', in M. Becker and I. Männlein-Robert, eds., *Die Christen als Bedrohung? Text, Kontext und Wirkung von Porphyrios' Contra Christianos*, Stuttgart, 237–60.
Fulkerson, G. 1985. 'Augustine's Attitude toward Rhetoric in "De Doctrina Christiana": The Significance of 2.37.55', *Rhetoric Society Quarterly* 15.2–3: 108–11.
Funk, W.-P. 2002. *Manichäische Handschriften der staatlichen Museen zu Berlin, Bd. I, Kephalaia I. Zweite Hälfte*, Lieferung 15/16, Stuttgart.
Funk, W.-P., 2009. 'Mani's Account of Other Religions According to the Coptic *Synaxeis* Codex', in J. D. BeDuhn, ed., *New Light on Manichaeism. Papers from the Sixth International Congress on Manichaeism*, Leiden, 115–27.
Gadamer, H.-G. 2006. *Wahrheit und Methode. Grundzüge einer philosophischen Hermeneutik*, Gesammelte Werke Hans-Georg Gadamer 1–2, Tübingen.
Gaddis, M. and R. Price, 2005. *The Acts of the Council of Chalcedon*, Translated Texts for Historians 45, Liverpool.
Gager, J. G. 1972. *Moses in Greco-Roman Paganism*, Nashville, TN.
Gardner, I. and S. N. C. Lieu, eds., 2004. *Manichaean Texts from the Roman Empire*, Cambridge.
Gardner, I., J. BeDuhn, and P. C. Dilley, eds., 2015. *Mani at the Court of the Persian Kings. Studies on the Chester Beatty Kephalaia Codex*, Leiden.
Gardner, I., J. BeDuhn, and P. C. Dilley, eds., 2018. *The Chapters of the Wisdom of My Lord Mani*, Leiden.
Garland, R. 1995. *Eye of the Beholder: Deformity and Disability in the Graeco-Roman World*, Ithaca, NY.
Gaudemet, J. 1969. 'La première mesure législative de Valentinien III', *Iura* 20: 129–47.
Geffcken, J. 1978. *The Last Days of Greco-Roman Paganism*, tr. S. MacCormack, Amsterdam.
Gennaro, S., ed., 1972. *Scriptores 'Illyrici' minores*, CCSL 85, Turnhout.
Germino, E., 2009. 'La legislazione dell'Imperatore Giuliano: primi appunti per una palingenesi', *Antiquité Tardive* 17: 159–74.

Germino, E. 2012. 'I; *Codex Theodosianus*: un codice Cristiano?', in L. De Giovanni, ed., *Società e diritto nella Tarda Antichità* (Studi e testi di *KOINΩNIA*, n.s. 3), Naples, 11–43.

Gevaert, B. and C. Laes, 2013. 'What's in a Monster? Pliny the Elder, Teratology and Bodily Disability', in B. Gevaert and C. Laes, eds., *Disabilities in Roman Antiquity*, Leiden, 211–30.

Giardina, A. 2001. 'Conclusioni', *Antiquité Tardive* 9: 289–95.

Gifford, E. H., tr., 1903. *Eusebius. Preparation for the Gospel*. Oxford.

Gilhus, I. 2010. 'Bischof Epiphanius von Salamis und der "Medizinschrank gegen Ketzer"', in T. Hägg, ed., *Kirche und Ketzer: Wege und Abwege des Christentums*, Köln, 41–55.

Gilhus, I. 2015. 'The Construction of Heresy and the Creation of Identity: Epiphanius of Salamis and his Medicine-Chest against Heretics', *Numen* 62: 152–68.

Gill, C., T. Whitmarsh, and J. Wilkins, eds., 2009. *Galen and the World of Knowledge*, Cambridge.

Giversen, S. 1986. *The Manichaean Coptic Papyri in the Chester Beatty Library, Vol. 1, Kephalaia*, Geneva.

Godrej, F. 2011. 'Spaces for Counter-Narratives: The Phenomenology of Reclamation', *Frontiers: A Journal of Women Studies* 32: 111–33.

Goff, B. E. 1991. 'The Sign of the Fall: The Scars of Orestes and Odysseus', *Classical Antiquity* 10: 259–67.

Goffman, E. 1967. *Interaction Ritual: Essays on Face-to-Face Behavior*, New York.

Goldhill, S. 2008. 'Introduction. Why Don't Christians Do Dialogue?', in S. Goldhill, ed., *The End of Dialogue in Antiquity*, Cambridge, 1–11.

Gordon, R. 1999. 'Imagining Greek and Roman Magic', in V. I. J. Flint, ed., *Witchcraft and Magic in Europe: Ancient Greece and Rome, Athlone History of Witchcraft and Magic in Europe 2*, London, 161–269.

Gordon, R., 2008. 'Superstitio, Superstition and Religious Repression in the Late Roman Republic and Principate (100BCE–300CE)', in S. A. Smith and A. Knight, eds., *The Religion of Fools: Superstition Past and Present, Past and Present Supplement 3*, Oxford, 72–94.

Gordon, R. and F. Marco Simón, 2010. 'Introduction', in R. L. Gordon and F. Marco Simón, eds., *Magical Practice in the Latin West*, Leiden, 1–49.

Goulet, R. 2004. 'Hypothèses récentes sur le traité de Porphyre Contre les chrétiens', in M. Narcy and É. Rebillard, eds., *Hellénisme et Christianisme*, Villeneuve-d'Ascq, 61–109.

Graf, F. 2000. 'Une histoire magique', in A. Moreau and J.-C. Turpin, eds., *La magie 1. Du monde babylonien au monde hellénistique*, Montpellier, 41–60.

Graf, F. 2002. 'Augustine and Magic', in J. N. Bremmer and J. R. Veenstra, eds., *The Metamorphosis of Magic from Late Antiquity to the Early Modern Period*, Leuven, 87–103.

Grafton, A. and M. Williams, 2006. *Christianity and the Transformation of the Book: Origen, Eusebius, and the Library at Caesarea*, Cambridge, MA.

Grant, R. 1966. *Gnosticism and Early Christianity*, 2nd rev. edn, New York.

Green, R. P. H. 1991. *The Works of Ausonius*, Oxford.

Green, R. P. H. 1993. 'The Christianity of Ausonius', in E. A. Livingston, ed., *Papers Presented at the Eleventh International Conference on Patristic Studies Held in Oxford 1991. Latin Fathers (Other than Augustine and His Opponents), Nachleben of the Fathers*, Studia Patristica 28, Leuven, 39–48.

Green, R. P. H. 1995. *Augustine: De Doctrina Christiana*, Oxford.

Greenwood, D. N. 2017. 'Constantinian Influence upon Julian's Pagan Church', *Journal of Ecclesiastical History* 68: 1–21.

Grilli, A. 1980. 'Il proemio d'Asterio Ad Renatum monachum', in *Scripta Philologa 2*, Istituto di Filologia Classica, Milan, 131–48.

Guignebert, C. 1923. 'Les demi-chrétiens et leur place dans l'Eglise antique', *Revue de l'histoire des religions* 88: 65–102.

Gustafson, W. M. 1997. 'Penal Tattooing in Late Antiquity', *Classical Antiquity* 16: 79–105.

Gwatkin, H. M. 1882. *Studies of Arianism: Chiefly Referring to the Character and Chronology of the Reaction Which Followed the Council of Nicæa*, Cambridge.

Gwynn, D. M. 2007. *The Eusebians: The Polemic of Athanasius of Alexandria and the Construction of the 'Arian Controversy'*, Oxford.

Haake, M. 2008. 'Philosopher and Priest: The Image of the Intellectual and the Social Practice of the Elites in the Eastern Roman Empire (First–Third Centuries AD)', in B. Dignas and K. Trampedach, eds., *Practitioners of the Divine*, Washington, DC, 145–65.

Hadot, P. 1971. *Marius Victorinus: recherches sur sa vie et ses œuvres*, Paris.

Hagendahl, H. 1967. *Augustine and the Latin Classics*, 2 vols, Studia Graeca et Latina Gothoburgensia 20, Göteborg.

Handelman, D. 1977. 'The Organization of Ethnicity', *Ethnic Groups* 1: 187–200.

Harkins, P. W. 1979. *Discourses against Judaizing Christians*, Fathers of the Church 68, Washington, DC.

Harries, J. 2012. 'Julian the Lawgiver', in N. Baker-Brian and S. Tougher, eds., *Emperor and Author: The Writings of Julian the Apostate*, Swansea, 121–36.

Harris-McCoy, D. 2008. *Varieties of Encyclopedism in the Early Roman Empire: Vitruvius, Pliny the Elder, Artemidorus*. PhD dissertation, University of Pennsylvania.

Harrison, C. 2002. 'The Rhetoric of Scripture and Preaching: Classical Decadence or Christian Aesthetic?', in R. Dodaro and G. Lawless, eds., *Augustine and his Critics: Essays in Honour of Gerald Bonner*, London, 214–30.

Hartmann, U. 2017. 'Auf der Suche nach Platons *Politeia*? Neuplatoniker an den Kaiserhöfen der Tetrarchen und Constantins', in M. Becker and I. Männlein-Robert, eds., *Die Christen als Bedrohung: Text, Kontext, und Wirkung von Porphyrios' Contra Christianos*, Stuttgart, 207–36.

Hartney, A. 2004. 'Transformation of the City: John Chrysostom's Oratory in the Homiletic Form', in M. Edwards and C. Reid, eds., *Oratory in Action*, Manchester, 83–98.

Heath, M. 1999. 'Echoes of Longinus in Gregory of Nyssa', *Vigiliae Christianae* 53: 395–400.

Heath, M. 2004. *Menander: A Rhetor in Context*, Oxford.

Hen, Y. 2015. 'The Early Medieval West', in D. J. Collins, ed., *The Cambridge History of Witchcraft and Magic*, Cambridge, 183–206.

Hendrickson, G. L. 1905. 'The Origin and Meaning of the Ancient Characters of Style', *The American Journal of Philology* 26.3: 249–376.

Henrichs, A. 2008. 'What is a Greek Priest?', in B. Dignas and K. Trampedach, eds., *Practitioners of the Divine*, Washington, DC, 1–14.

Herzog, R. and G. Nauroy, eds., 1993. *Nouvelle histoire de la littérature latine. 5, Restauration et renouveau: la littérature latine de 284 à 374 après J.-C.*, Turnhout.

Hesk, J. 1999. 'The Rhetoric of Anti-Rhetoric in Athenian Oratory', in S. Goldhill and R. Osborne, eds., *Performance Culture and Athenian Democracy*, Cambridge, 201–30.

Heylen, F. 1957. *Filastrii episcopi Brixiensis diversarum hereseon liber*, CCSL 9, Turnhout, 209–324.

Holl, K., ed., 1915. *Epiphanius I: Ancoratus und Panarion haer. 1–33*, GCS 25, Leipzig.

Holl, K., M. Bergermann, and C.-F. Collatz, 2013. *Epiphanius I: Ancoratus und Panarion haer. 1–33*, 2nd edn, GCS n.f. 10/1, Berlin.

Honoré, A. M. 1986. 'The Making of the Theodosian Code', *Zeitschrift der Savigny-Stiftung für Rechtsgeschichte* 103: 161–89.

Horster, M. and C. Reitz, eds., 2003. *Antike Fachschriftsteller: Literarischer Diskurs und sozialer Kontext*, Stuttgart.

Horster, M. and C. Reitz, eds., 2010. *Condensing Texts—Condensed Texts*, Stuttgart.

Humphries, M. 1997. '*In nomine patris*: Constantine the Great and Constantius II in Christological Polemic', *Historia* 46: 448–64.

Humphries, M. 2008. 'Rufinus's Eusebius: Translation, Continuation, and Edition in the Latin *Ecclesiastical History*', *Journal of Early Christian Studies* 16: 143–64.

Humphries, M. 2012. 'Valentinian III and the City of Rome (AD 425–55): Patronage, Politics, and Power', in L. Grig and G. Kelly, eds., *Two Romes: Rome and Constantinople in Late Antiquity*, New York, 161–82.

Humphries, M. 2018. 'Christianity and Paganism in the Roman Empire, 250–450 CE', in N. Baker-Brian and J. Lössl, eds., *A Companion to Religion in Late Antiquity*, Malden, MA and Chichester, 61–80.

Hunt, D. 1993. 'Christianising the Roman Empire: The Evidence of the Code', in J. Harries and I. Wood, eds., *The Theodosian Code*, London, 143–58.

Hunt, D. 2012. 'The Christian Context of Julian's *Against the Galileans*', in N. Baker-Brian and S. Tougher, eds., *Emperor and Author: The Writings of Julian the Apostate*, Swansea, 251–61.

Hunter, D. G. 2007. *Marriage, Celibacy and Heresy in Ancient Christianity: The Jovinianist Controversy*, Oxford.

Hunter, D. G. 2012. 'Augustine on the Body', in M. Vessey, ed., *A Companion to Augustine*, Oxford, 353–64.

Hurtado, L. W. 2006. *The Earliest Christian Artefacts: Manuscripts and Christian Origins*, Grand Rapids, MI.

Huskinson, J. 1998. 'Unfinished Portrait Heads on Later Roman Sarcophagi: Some New Perspectives', *Papers of the British School at Rome* 66: 129–38.

Huskinson, J. 2015. *Roman Strigillated Sarcophagi: Art and Social History*, Oxford.

Huttner, U. 2011. 'Kalender und religiöse Identität: Ostern in Hierapolis', *Zeitschrift für antikes Christentum* 15: 272–90.

Inglebert, H. 2001. *Interpretatio christiana: les mutations des savoirs (cosmographie, géographie, éthnographie, histoire) dans l'antiquité chrétienne (30-630 après J.-C.)*, Collection des études augustiniennes, Sér. Antiquité 166, Paris.
Inglebert, H. 2014. *Le monde, l'histoire: essai sur les histoires universelles*, Paris.
Innes, D. 1995. *Aristotle, Poetics; Longinus, On the Sublime; Demetrius, On Style*, Cambridge, MA.
Jacobs, A. 2000. 'Writing Demetrias: Ascetic Logic in Ancient Christianity', *Church History* 69: 719-48.
Jacobs, A. 2012. 'Matters (Un-)Becoming: Conversions in Epiphanius of Salamis', *Church History* 81: 27-47.
Jacobs, A. 2013. 'Epiphanius of Salamis and the Antiquarian's Bible', *Journal of Early Christian Studies* 21: 437-64.
Jacobs, A. 2016. *Epiphanius of Cyprus: A Cultural Biography of Late Antiquity*, Oakland, CA.
Jager, E. 2000. *The Book of the Heart*, Chicago, IL.
Jakobi, R., ed., 2011. *Asterius: Liber ad Renatum monachum*, Berlin.
Jannaccone, S. 1952. *La dottrina eresiologica di S. Agostino: studio di storia letteraria e religiosa a proposito del trattato De Haeresibus*, Raccolta di studi di letteratura cristiana antica 20, Catania.
Janowitz, N. 2001. *Magic in the Roman World*, London.
Janowitz, N. 2002. *Icons of Power: Ritual Practices in Late Antiquity*, University Park, PA.
Jansen, L. 2014. 'Introduction: Approaches to Roman Paratextuality', in L. Jansen, ed., *The Roman Paratext: Frame, Texts, Readers*, Cambridge, 1-18.
Janson, T. 1964. *Latin Prose Prefaces: Studies in Literary Conventions*, Stockholm.
Jay, P. 1985. *L'exégèse de saint Jérôme d'après son Commentaire sur Isaïe*, Paris.
Jensen, R. M. 2000. *Understanding Early Christian Art*, London.
Jensen, R. M. 2014. 'Verso una vera arte cristiana: Evidenze stilistiche e iconografiche dell'adattamento Cristiano dell'arte figurative tardo antica', in D. Guastini, ed. and tr., *Genealogia delle immagini cristiane*, Firenze, 39-59.
Jensen, R. M. 2015. 'Compiling Narratives: The Rhetorical Strategies of Early Christian Art', *Journal of Early Christian Studies* 23: 1-26.
Johnson, A. P. 2006. *Ethnicity and Argument in Eusebius' Praeparatio Evangelica*, Oxford.
Johnson, A. P. 2010. 'Rethinking the Authenticity of Porphyry, *contra Christianos*, fr. 1', *Studia Patristica* 46: 53-8.
Johnson, A. P. 2011. 'Porphyry's Hellenism', in S. Morlet, ed., *Le traité de Porphyre contre les chrétiens*, Paris, 165-81.
Johnson, A. P. 2012a. 'Philosophy, Hellenicity, Law: Porphyry on Origen, Again', *Journal of Hellenic Studies* 132: 55-69.
Johnson, A. P. 2012b. 'Hellenism and Its Discontents', in S. F. Johnson, ed., *The Oxford Handbook on Late Antiquity*, Oxford, 437-66.
Johnson, A. P. 2013. *Religion and Identity in Porphyry of Tyre: The Limits of Hellenism in Late Antiquity*, Cambridge.
Johnson, A. P. 2014a. 'Ethnicity: Greeks, Jews and Christians', in J. McInerny, ed., *The Blackwell Companion to Ethnicity in the Ancient Mediterranean*, Oxford, 376-89.

Johnson, A. P. 2014b. *Eusebius*, London.
Johnson, A. P. 2017. 'The Implications of a Minimalist Approach to Porphyry's Fragments', in M. Becker and I. Männlein-Robert, eds., *Die Christen als Bedrohung: Text, Kontext, und Wirkung von Porphyrios' Contra Christianos*, Stuttgart, 41–58.
Johnson, A. P. forthcoming. 'Being Greek in the Age of Constantine'.
Jones, A. H. M., J. R. Martindale, and J. Morris, 1971. *The Prosopography of the Later Roman Empire* I, (Abbreviated as *PLRE* I). Cambridge.
Jones, C. P. 2014. *Between Pagan and Christian*, Cambridge, MA.
Jordan, D. R. 1988. 'New *Defixiones* from Carthage', in J. H. Humphrey, ed., *The Circus and a Byzantine Cemetery at Carthage, Vol. 1*, Ann Arbor, MI, 117–34.
Jordan, D. R. 1994. 'Magica Graeca Parvula', *Zeitschrift für Papyrologie und Epigraphik* 100: 325–35.
Joslyn-Siemiatkoski, D. 2009. *Christian Memories of the Maccabean Martyrs*, New York.
Jürgasch, T. 2015. 'Christians and the Invention of Paganism in the Late Roman Empire', in M. Salzman, M. Sághy, and R. Lizzi Testa, eds., *Pagans and Christians in Late Antique Rome*, Cambridge, 115–38.
Kahlos, M. 2004. 'Incerti In Between: Moments of Transition and Dialogue in Christian Polemics in the Fourth and Fifth Centuries', *La Parola Del Passato* 59: 5–24.
Kahlos, M. 2005. 'Pompa Diaboli: The Grey Area of Urban Festivals in the Fourth and Fifth Centuries', in C. Deroux, ed., *Studies in Latin Literature and Roman History 12*, Collection Latomus 287, Bruxelles, 467–83.
Kahlos, M. 2006a. '*Perniciosa ista inanium dulcedo litterarum*—The Perils of Charming Literature in Fourth and Fifth Century Texts', *Maia* 58.1: 53–67.
Kahlos, M. 2006b. 'In-between Figures in Christian Literature', in M. Edwards, F. Young, and P. Parvis, eds., *Papers Presented at the Fourteenth International Conference on Patristic Studies Held in Oxford 2003*, Studia Patristica 40, Leuven, 215–20.
Kahlos, M. 2007a. 'Comissationes et Ebrietates: Church Leaders against Banqueting at Martyria and at Tombs', in O. Merisalo and R. Vainio, eds., *Ad Itum Liberum: Essays in Honour of Anne Helttula*, Jyväskylä, 13–23.
Kahlos, M. 2007b. *Debate and Dialogue: Christian and Pagan Cultures c. 360–430*, Aldershot.
Kahlos, M. 2015. 'Magic and the Early Church', in D. J. Collins, ed., *The Cambridge History of Witchcraft and Magic*, Cambridge, 148–82.
Kahlos, M. 2016. 'Meddling in the Middle? Urban Celebrations, Ecclesiastical Leaders, and the Roman Emperor in Late Antiquity', in J. Day, R. Hakola, M. Kahlos, and U. Tervahauta, eds., *Spaces in Late Antiquity—Cultural, Theological and Archaeological Perspectives*, London, 11–31.
Kaldellis, A. 2004. *Procopius of Caesarea: Tyranny, History, and Philosophy at the End of Antiquity*, Philadelphia, PA.
Kaldellis, A. 2008. *Hellenism in Byzantium: The Transformations of Greek Identity and the Reception of the Classical Tradition*, New York.
Kelley, N. 2007. 'Deformity and Disability in Greece and Rome', in H. Avalos, S. J. Melcher, and J. Schipper, eds., *This Abled Body: Rethinking Disabilities in Biblical Studies*, Atlanta, GA, 31–45.

Kim, L. 2017. 'Atticism and Asianism', in D. S. Richter and W. A. Johnson, eds., *The Oxford Handbook of the Second Sophistic*, Oxford, 41–66.

Kim, Y. R. 2010a. 'Reading the *Panarion* as Collective Biography: The Heresiarch as Unholy Man', *Vigiliae Christianae* 64: 382–413.

Kim, Y. R. 2010b. 'Bad Bishops Corrupt Good Emperors: Ecclesiastical Authority and the Rhetoric of Heresy in the *Panarion* of Epiphanius of Salamis', *Studia Patristica* 47: 161–6.

Kim, Y. R. 2015a. *Epiphanius of Salamis: Imagining an Orthodox World*, Ann Arbor, MI.

Kim, Y. R. 2015b. 'The Transformation of Heresiology in the *Panarion* of Epiphanius of Salamis', in G. Greatrex and H. Elton, eds., *Shifting Genres in Late Antiquity*, Farnham, 53–65.

Kinzig, W. 1997. 'The Greek Christian Writers', in S. E. Porter, ed., *Handbook of Classical Rhetoric in the Hellenistic Period, 330 B.C.–A.D. 400*, Leiden, 633–70.

Klijn, A. F. J. and G. J. Reinink, 1973. *Patristic Evidence for Jewish–Christian Sects*, Supplements to Novum Testamentum 36, Leiden.

Klimkeit, H.-J. 1993. *Gnosis on the Silk Road. Gnostic Texts from Central Asia*, San Francisco, CA.

Klingshirn, W. E. 2003. 'Isidore of Seville's Taxonomy of Magicians and Diviners', *Traditio* 58: 59–90.

Klock, C. 1987. *Untersuchungen zu Stil und Rhythmus bei Gregor von Nyssa: ein Beitrag zum Rhetorikverständnis der griechischen Väter*, Frankfurt am Main.

Koch, G. 2014. *Frühchristliche Sarkophage*, Munich.

Koch, G. 2018. 'Sarcophagi from Outside of Rome', in R. M. Jensen and M. Ellison, eds., *The Routledge Handbook to Early Christian Art*, London, 56–72.

Kofsky, A. 2002. *Eusebius of Caesarea against Paganism*, Leiden.

König, J. 2009. 'Conventions of Prefatory Self-presentation in Galen's *On the Order of My Own Books*', in C. Gill, T. Whitmarsh, and J. Wilkins, eds., *Galen and the World of Knowledge*, Cambridge, 35–58.

König, J. and T. Whitmarsh, eds., 2007. *Ordering Knowledge in the Roman Empire*, Cambridge.

König, J. and G. Woolf, eds., 2013a. *Encyclopaedism from Antiquity to the Renaissance*, Cambridge.

König, J. and G. Woolf, 2013b. 'Encyclopaedism in the Roman Empire', in J. König and G. Woolf, eds., *Encyclopaedism from Antiquity to the Renaissance*, Cambridge, 23–63.

König, J. and G. Woolf, eds., 2017. *Authority and Expertise in Ancient Scientific Culture*, Cambridge.

Koortbojian, M. 1995. *Myth, Meaning, and Memory on Roman Sarcophagi*, Berkeley, CA.

Kotansky, R. 2002. 'An Early Christian Gold *Lamella* for Headache', in P. Mirecki and M. Meyer, eds., *Magic and Ritual in the Ancient World*, Leiden, 37–46.

Kötter, J.-M. and C. Scardino, 2017. *Gallische Chroniken*, Kleine und fragmentarische Historiker der Spätantike G, 7/8, Paderborn.

Kuefler, M. 2001. *The Manly Eunuch. Masculinity, Gender Ambiguity, and Christian Ideology in Late Antiquity*, Chicago, IL and London.

Labhardt, A. 1960. 'Curiositas. Notes sur l'histoire d'un mot et d'une notion', *Museum Helveticum* 17: 204–24.

Labhardt, A. 1996–2002. 'Curiositas', in C. Mayer, ed., *Augustinus-Lexikon* 2, Basel, 187–95.

Labriolle, P. de 1910. *Un épisode de la fin du paganisme, la correspondance d'Ausone et de Paulin de Nole, avec une étude critique, des notes et un appendice sur la question du christianisme d'Ausone*, Paris.

Lambert, P.-Y. 2010. 'Celtic Loricae and Ancient Magical Charms', in R. L. Gordon and F. Marco Simón, eds., *Magical Practice in the Latin West*, Leiden, 629–48.

Lancellotti, M. G. 2002. *Attis between Myth and History: King, Priest and God*, Leiden.

Langlois, P. 1969. 'Les poèmes chrétiens et le christianisme d'Ausone', *Revue de philologie, de littérature et d'histoire anciennes* 43: 39–58.

Laplanche, F. 1999. 'De Loisy à Guignebert', in Y.-M. Hilaire, ed., *De Renan à Marrou: l'histoire du christianisme et les progrès de la méthode historique (1863–1968)*, Histoire et civilisations, Villeneuve-d'Ascq, 57–72.

Le Bonniec, H. 1982. *Arnobe, Contre les Gentils, Livre I*, Paris.

Leith, D. 2009. 'Question-types in Medical Catechisms on Papyrus', in L. Taub and A. Doody, eds., *Authorial Voices in Greco-Roman Technical Writing*, Trier, 107–23.

Lenski, N. 2016. *Constantine and the Cities*, Philadelphia, PA.

Liebeschuetz, J. H. W. G., tr., 2005. *Ambrose of Milan: Political Letters and Speeches; Letters, Book Ten, including the Oration on the Death of Theodosius I; Letters Outside the Collection (Epistulae extra collectionem); Letter 30 to Magnus Maximus; The Oration on the Death of Valentinian II*. Translated Texts for Historians 43, Liverpool.

Liebeschuetz, J. H. W. G. 2012. 'Julian's *Hymn to the Mother of the Gods*: The Revival and Justification of Traditional Religion', in N. Baker-Brian and S. Tougher, eds., *Emperor and Author: The Writings of Julian the Apostate*, Swansea, 213–27.

Lietzmann, H. 1904. *Apollinaris von Laodicea und seine Schule*, Tübingen.

Lieu, S. N. C. 2006. '"My Church is Superior...": Mani's Missionary Statement in Coptic and Middle Persian', in L. Painchaud, and P.-H. Poirier, eds., *Coptica, Gnostica, Manichaica: Mélanges Offerts à Wolf-Peter Funk*, Leuven, 519–28.

Lim, R. 1995. *Public Disputation, Power and Social Order in Late Antiquity*, Berkeley, CA.

Lincoln, B. 2012. *Gods and Demons, Priests and Scholars: Critical Explorations in the History of Religions*, Chicago, IL and London.

Lizzi Testa, R. 2009. 'The Late Antique Bishop: Image and Reality', in P. Rousseau, ed., *A Companion to Late Antiquity*, Chichester, 52–38.

Long, J. 2012. 'Afterword: Studying Julian the Author', in N. Baker-Brian and S. Tougher, eds., *Emperor and Author: The Writings of Julian the Apostate*, Swansea, 323–38.

Lössl, J. 1999. 'Dolor, dolere', in C. Mayer, ed., *Augustinus-Lexikon* 2.3–4, Basel, 581–91.

Luck, G. 1999. 'Witches and Sorcerers in Classical Literature', in V. Flint, R. Gordon, G. Luck, and D. Ogden, eds., *Witchcraft and Magic in Europe: Ancient Greece and Rome*, London, 93–158.

Ludlow, M. 2014a. 'Contra Eunomium III 10—Who is Eunomius?', in J. Leemans and M. Cassin, eds., *Gregory of Nyssa: Contra Eunomium III: An English translation with commentary and supporting studies: Proceedings of the 12th International Colloquium on Gregory of Nyssa (Leuven, 14–17 September 2010)*, Vigiliae Christianae supplement 124, Leuven, 442–74.

Ludlow, M. 2014b. 'Useful and Beautiful: A Reading of Gregory of Nyssa's *On Virginity* and a Proposal for Understanding Early Christian Literature', *Irish Theological Quarterly* 79.3: 219–40.

Ludlow, M. 2018. 'The Rhetoric of Landscape in Gregory of Nyssa's Homilies on the Song of Songs: Logos, Beauty and the "Middle Style"', in G. Maspero, M. Brugarolas, and I. Vigorelli, eds., *Gregory of Nyssa: 'In Canticum Canticorum': Analytical and Supporting Studies. Proceedings of the 13th International Colloquium on Gregory of Nyssa (Rome, 17–20 September 2014)*, Vigiliae Christianae Supplement 150, Leiden, 288–311.

MacCormack S. 2001. 'The Virtue of Work: An Augustinian Transformation', *Antiquité Tardive* 9: 74–98.

MacKenzie, D. N. 1998. 'Ērān, Ērānšahr', *Encyclopaedia Iranica* 8.5: 534. Available at: http://www.iranicaonline.org/articles/eran-eransah (accessed January 2019).

MacMullen, R. 1981. *Paganism in the Roman Empire*, New Haven, CT.

MacMullen, R. 1986. 'What Difference did Christianity Make?', *Historia* 35: 322–43.

MacMullen, R. 1989. 'The Preacher's Audience (AD 350–400)', *Journal of Theological Studies* 40.2: 503–11.

MacMullen, R. 1990. *Changes in the Roman Empire*, Princeton, NJ.

Magoulias, H. J. 1967. 'The Lives of Byzantine Saints as Sources of Data for the History of Magic in the Sixth and Seventh Centuries AD', *Byzantion* 37: 228–69.

Manganaro, G. 1963. 'Nuovi documenti magici della Sicilia orientale', *Rendiconti della Classe di Scienze morali, storiche e filologiche dell'Accademia dei Lincei* 18: 57–74.

Manor, T. S. 2016. *Epiphanius' Alogi and the Johannine Controversy: A Reassessment of Early Ecclesial Opposition to the Johannine Corpus*, Vigiliae Christianae Supplement 135, Leiden.

Marasco, G. 2005. *Filostorgio: cultura, fede e politica in uno storico ecclesiastico del V secolo*, Studia ephemeridis 'Augustinianum' 92, Rome.

Marchesi, C. 1953. *Arnobii Adversus Nationes Libri VII*, Turin.

Marcone, A. 2012. 'The Forging of an Hellenic Orthodoxy: Julian's Speeches against the Cynics', in N. Baker-Brian and S. Tougher, eds., *Emperor and Author: The Writings of Julian the Apostate*, Swansea, 239–50.

Markus, R. A. 1970. *Saeculum. History and Society in the Theology of St. Augustine*, Cambridge.

Markus, R. A. 1990. *The End of Ancient Christianity*, Cambridge.

Markus, R. A. 1996. *Signs and Meanings. World and Text in Ancient Christianity*, Liverpool.

Marx-Wolf, H. 2016. *Spiritual Taxonomies and Ritual Authority*, Philadelphia, PA.

Mason, S. 2007. 'Jews, Judaeans, Judaizing, Judaism: Problems of Categorization in Ancient History', *Journal for the Study of Judaism* 38: 460–71.

Masterson, M. 2014. 'Authoritative Obscenity in Iamblichus and Arnobius', *Journal of Early Christian Studies* 22: 373–98.

Matthews, J. 1989. *The Roman Empire of Ammianus*, London.

Matthews, J. 2000. *Laying Down the Law: A Study of the Theodosian Code*, New Haven, CT.

May, J. M. 2007. 'Cicero as Rhetorician', in W. J. Dominik and J. Hall, eds., *A Companion to Roman Rhetoric*, Malden, MA, 250–63.
Mayer, W. and P. Allen, 2000. *John Chrysostom*, The Early Church Fathers, London.
Mazzarino, S. 1988. *L'impero romano*, 3rd edn, Bari.
Mazzarino, S. 1989. *Storia sociale del vescovo Ambrogio*, Rome.
McCabe, A. 2007. *A Byzantine Encyclopaedia of Horse Medicine: The Sources, Compilation, and Transmission of the Hippiatrica*, Oxford.
McClure, J. 1979. 'Handbooks against Heresy in the West, from the Late Fourth to the Late Sixth Centuries', *Journal of Theological Studies* 30: 186–97.
McCracken, G. E. 1949. *Arnobius of Sicca, The Case against the Pagans*, 2 vols, Cork.
McDonald, M. F. 1964. *Lactantius: Divine Institutes, Books I–VII*, Washington, DC.
McLynn, N. B. 1994. *Ambrose of Milan: Church and Court in a Christian Capital*, Berkeley, CA.
McLynn, N. B. 2009. 'Pagans in a Christian Empire', in P. Rousseau, ed., *A Companion to Late Antiquity*, Chichester, 572–87.
McRae, D. 2016. *Legible Religion: Books, Gods, and Rituals in Roman Culture*, Cambridge, MA.
Meier, M. 2002. 'Zur Neukonzeption chronologisch-eschatologischer Modelle im oströmischen Reich des 6. Jh. n. Chr. Ein Beitrag zur Mentalitätsgeschichte der Spätantike', in W. Geerlings, ed., *Der Kalender. Aspekte einer Geschichte*, Paderborn, 151–81.
Meltzer, E. 1999. 'Old Coptic Texts of Ritual Power', in M. W. Meyer, R. Smith, and N. Kelsey, eds., *Ancient Christian Magic: Coptic Texts of Ritual Power*, Princeton, NJ, 13–25.
Mena, P. 2013. 'Insatiable Appetites: Epiphanius of Salamis and the Making of the Heretical Villain', *Studia Patristica* 67: 257–63.
Meredith, A. 1980. 'Porphyry and Julian against the Christians', in *Aufstieg und Niedergang der römischen Welt* 2.23.2, 1119–49, Berlin and New York.
Méridier, L. 1906. *L'Influence de la seconde sophistique sur l'oeuvre de Grégoire de Nysse*, Paris.
Merkt, A., ed., 2008. *Das frühe christliche Mönchtum: Quellen und Dokumente von den Anfängen bis Benedikt*, Darmstadt.
Meyer, M. W. and P. A. Mirecki, eds., 1995. 'Introduction', in *Ancient Magic and Ritual Power*. Religions in the Graeco-Roman World 129, Leiden, 1–10.
Meyer, M. and R. Smith, 1999. 'Introduction', in M. Meyer, R. Smith, and N. Kelsey, eds., *Ancient Christian Magic. Coptic Texts of Ritual Power*, Princeton, NJ, 1–9.
Miles, M. R. 2012. 'From Rape to Resurrection: Sin, Sexual Difference, and Politics', in J. Wetzel, ed., *Augustine's City of God: A Critical Guide*, Cambridge, 75–91.
Millar, F. 2006. *A Greek Roman Empire: Power and Belief under Theodosius II (408–450)*, Berkeley, CA.
Mitchell, M. M. 2002. *The Heavenly Trumpet: John Chrysostom and the Art of Pauline Interpretation*, Louisville, KY.
Mitchell, S. 2014. *A History of the Later Roman Empire AD 284–641*, 2nd edn, Chichester.
Moffatt, A. 1972. 'The Occasion of St Basil's Address to Young Men', *Antichthon* 6: 83–6.

Molinier, J.-L. 2014. *Solitude et communion, IVe –VIe siècle*, Paris.
Morard, F.-E. 1973. 'Monachos, moine. Histoire du terme grec jusqu'au IV siècle', *Freiburger Zeitschrift für Philosophie und Theologie* 20: 348–54.
Moreschini, C. 1995. *Esegesi, parafrasi e compilazione in età tardoantica*, Naples.
Morlet, S. 2010. *La Démonstration évangélique d'Eusèbe de Césarée. Etude sur l'apologétique chrétienne à l'époque de Constantin*, Paris.
Morlet, S. 2011. 'Eusebius' Polemic Against Porphyry: A Reassessment', in S. Inowlocki and C. Zamagni, eds., *Reconsidering Eusebius*, Leiden, 119–50.
Morony, M. 2005. 'History and Identity in the Syrian Churches', in J. J. Van Ginkel, T. M. Van Lint, and H. L. Murre-Van den Berg, eds., *Redefining Christian Identity: Cultural Interaction in the Middle East since the Rise of Islam*, Leuven, 1–33.
Mosshammer, A. A. 1984. *Georgius Syncellus. Ecloga chronographica*, Leipzig.
Mosshammer, A. A. 2008. *The Easter Computus and the Origins of the Christian Era*, Oxford.
Mosshammer, A. A. 2017. *The Prologues on Easter of Theophilus of Alexandria and [Cyril]*, New York.
Moutsoulas, E. 1966. 'Der Begriff "Häresie" bei Epiphanius von Salamis', *Studia Patristica* 7: 362–71.
Muehlberger, E. 2013. *Angels in Late Ancient Christianity*, Oxford.
Muhlberger, S. 1981. *The Fifth-Century Chroniclers: Prosper, Hydatius, and the Gallic Chronicler of 452*, Leeds.
Müller, C. 1993. *Geschichtsbewußtsein bei Augustinus. Ontologische, anthropologische und universalgeschichtlich/heilsgeschichtliche Elemente einer augustinischen 'Geschichtstheorie'*, Würzburg.
Müller, L. G. 1956. *The De Haeresibus of Saint Augustine: A Translation with an Introduction and Commentary*, The Catholic University of America Patristic Studies 90, Washington, DC.
Murdoch, A. 2003. *The Last Pagan: Julian the Apostate and the Death of the Ancient World*, Stroud.
Murphy, T. 2004. *Pliny the Elder's Natural History: The Empire in the Encyclopedia*, Oxford.
Muscolino, G. 2008–2009. *Porfirio: Il Contra Christianos. Per una nuova edizione dei frammenti*, Doctoral thesis, Salerno.
Naas, V. 2002. *Le projet encyclopédique de Pline l'Ancien*, Rome.
Naas, V. 2011. 'Imperialism, *mirabilia* and Knowledge', in R. Gibson and R. Morello, eds., *Pliny the Elder: Themes and Contexts*, Leiden, 57–70.
Nau, F. 1915–1917. 'Une liste de chronographes', *Revue de l'Orient chrétien* 10: 101–3.
Nesselrath, T. 2013. *Kaiser Julian und die Repaganisierung des Reiches: Konzept und Vorbilder*, Münster.
Neusner, J. 1989. 'Science and Magic, Miracle and Magic in Formative Judaism: The System and the Difference', in J. Neusner, E. S. Frerichs, and P. V. M. Flesher, eds., *Religion, Science, and Magic: In Concert and in Conflict*, New York, 61–81.
Neville, G. 1977. *St John Chrysostom: Six Books on the Priesthood*, New York.
Newby, Z. 2011. 'In the Guise of Gods and Heroes: Portrait Heads on Roman Mythological Sarcophagi', in J. Elsner and J. Huskinson, eds., *Life, Death, and Representation: Some New Work on Roman Sarcophagi*, New York, 189–227.

Nieto, F. J. F. 2010. 'A Visigothic Charm from Asturias and the Classical Tradition of Phylacteries Against Hail', in R. L. Gordon and F. Marco Simón, eds., *Magical Practice in the Latin West*, Leiden, 551–99.

Nock, A. D. 1926. *Sallustius, Concerning the Gods and the Universe*, Cambridge.

Nongbri, B. 2008. 'Dislodging "Embedded" Religion: A Brief Note on a Scholarly Trope', *Numen* 55: 440–60.

Nongbri, B. 2013. *Before Religion. A History of a Modern Concept*, New Haven, CT.

Norden, E. 1898. *Die antike Kunstprosa vom VI. Jahrhundert v. Chr. bis in die Zeit der Renaissance*, Leipzig.

Norman, A. F. 1969. *Libanius. Selected Orations, Vol. I: Julianic Orations*, Cambridge, MA.

O'Brien Wicker, K., tr., 1987. *To Marcella: Porphyry the Philosopher*. Society of Biblical Literature, Texts and Translations 28. Atlanta, GA.

O'Daly, G. 1999. *Augustine's City of God. A Reader's Guide*, Oxford.

O'Donnell, J. J. 1979. 'The Demise of Paganism', *Traditio* 35: 45–88.

O'Donnell, J. J. 1992. *Augustine, Confessions*, 3 vols, Oxford.

O'Donnell, J. J. 2005. *Augustine: A New Biography*, New York.

Odorico, P. 2014. 'Dans le cahier des chroniqueurs. Le cas d'Eustathe d'Antioche', in J. Signes Codoñer and I. Pérez Martin, eds., *Textual Transmission in Byzantium: Between Textual Criticism and Quellenforschung*, Turnhout, 373–89.

Ogden, D. 1999. 'Binding Spells: Curse Tablets and Voodoo Dolls in the Greek and Roman Worlds', in V. Flint, R. Gordon, G. Luck, and D. Ogden, eds., *Witchcraft and Magic in Europe. Ancient Greece and Rome*, London, 1–90.

Oréal, E. 2012. 'Communication', in H. D. Saffrey and A.-Ph. Segonds, eds., *Porphyre. Lettre à Anébon l'Égyptien*, Paris, xxxii–xxxvi.

Paniagua, D. 2014. '*Iisdem fere verbis Solini saepe sunt sententias mutati*: Solinus and Late Antique Literature from Ambrose to Augustine—an Old Assumption Reexamined', in K. Brodersen, ed., *Solinus: New Studies*, Heidelberg, 119–40.

Papaconstantinou, A. and D. Schwartz, eds., 2015. *Conversion in Late Antiquity: Christianity, Islam, and Beyond*, London.

Parker, G. 2008. *The Making of Roman India*, Cambridge.

Paulsen, D. L. 1990. 'Early Christian Belief in a Corporeal Deity: Origen and Augustine as Reluctant Witnesses', *Harvard Theological Review* 83: 105–16.

Pecere, O. and A. Stramaglia, eds., 1996. *La letteratura di consumo nel mondo greco-latino*, Cassino.

Pedersen, N. A. 2006. *Manichaean Homilies. With a Number of Hitherto Unpublished Fragments*, Turnhout.

Penella, R. J., tr., 2000. *The Private Orations of Themistius*, Berkeley, CA.

Penella, R. J., tr., 2007. *Man and the Word: The Orations of Himerius*, Berkeley, CA.

Perelman, C. 1982. *The Realm of Rhetoric*, trans. W. Kluback, Notre Dame, IN.

Pettipiece, T. 2009a. *Pentadic Redaction in the Manichaean Kephalaia*, Leiden.

Pettipiece, T. 2009b. 'The Buddha in Early Christian Literature', *Millennium* 6: 133–43.

Pettipiece, T. 2013. 'Coptic Answers to Manichaean Questions: The Erotapokritic Nature of the Kephalaia', in M.-P. Bussières, ed., *La littérature des questions et réponses dans l'antiquité profane et chrétienne: de l'enseignement à l'exégèse*, Turnhout, 51–61.

Piganiol, A. and A. Chastagnol, 1972. *L'empire Chrétien, 325–395*, 2nd edn, Paris.

Pizzolato, L. and C. Somenzi, 2005. *I setti fratelli Maccabei nella Chiesa antica d'Occidente*, Milan.
Pohl, W., C. Gantner, and R. E. Payne, eds., 2012. *Visions of Community in the Post-Roman World: The West, Byzantium and the Islamic World, 300–1100*, Farnham.
Posner, D. 2015. 'Montaigne, Julian, and "Others": The Quest for Peaceful Coexistence in Public Space', in M. Schuck and J. Crowley-Buck, eds., *Democracy, Culture, Catholicism: Voices from Four Continents*, New York, 71–82.
Pourkier, A. 1992. *L'hérésiologie chez Épiphane de Salamine*, Paris.
Price, S. R. F. 2004. 'Religious Personnel: Greece', in S. I. Johnston, ed., *Religions of the Ancient World*, Cambridge, 302–5.
Pummer, R. 2002. *Early Christian Authors on Samaritans and Samaritanism: Texts, Translations, and Commentary*, Texte und Studien zum antiken Judentum 92, Tübingen.
Rahman, J. 2015. 'Missing the Target: Group Practices that Launch and Deflect Slurs', *Language Sciences* 52: 70–81.
Rauhala, M. 2011. 'Devotion and Deviance: The Cult of Cybele and the Others Within', in M. Kahlos, ed., *The Faces of the Other: Religious Rivalry and Ethnic Encounters in the Later Roman World*, Turnhout, 51–82.
Rebillard, É. 2012. *Christians and Their Many Identities in Late Antiquity, North Africa, 200–450 CE*, Ithaca, NY.
Rebillard, É. 2013. *Transformations of Religious Practices in Late Antiquity*, Farnham.
Rebillard, É. and J. Rupke, eds., 2015. *Group Identity and Religious Individuality in Late Antiquity*, Washington, DC.
Reeves, J. C. 2011. *Prolegomena to a History of Islamicate Manichaeism*, Sheffield.
Reidy, J. J. 2015. 'Eusebius of Emesa and the "Continuatio Antiochiensis Eusebii"', *Journal of Ecclesiastical History* 66: 471–87.
Remus, H. 1999. '"Magic", Method, Madness', *Method and Theory in the Study of Religion* 11: 258–98.
Richard, M. and J. A. Munitiz, eds., 2006. *Anastasii Sinaitae Quaestiones et Responsiones*, Corpus Christianorum Series Graeca 59, Turnhout.
Richter, D. S. and W. A. Johnson, eds., 2017. *The Oxford Handbook of the Second Sophistic*, Oxford.
Ricks, S. D. 1995. 'The Magician as Outsider in the Hebrew Bible and the New Testament', in M. Meyer and P. Mirecki, eds., *Ancient Magic and Ritual Power*, Leiden, 131–43.
Ricoeur, P. 1991. *Temps et récit*, 3 vols, Paris.
Riedweg, C. 2005. 'Porphyrios über Christus und die Christen: *De Philosophia ex Oraculis Haurienda* und *Adversus Christianos* im Vergleich', in A. Wlosok, ed., *L'Apologétique chrétienne gréco-latine à l'époque prénicénienne*, Entretiens sur l'antiquité classique 51, Genève, 151–203.
Riggi, C. 1967. 'Il termine "hairesis" nell'accezione di Epifanio di Salamina (*Panarion*, t. I; *De fide*)', *Salesianum* 29: 3–27.
Riggi, C. 1968. 'Il cristianesimo di Ausonio', *Salesianum* 30: 642–95.
Ritner, R. K. 1995. 'The Religious, Social, and Legal Parameters of Traditional Egyptian Magic', in M. W. Meyer and P. A. Mirecki, eds., *Ancient Magic and Ritual Power*, Religions in the Graeco-Roman World 129, Leiden, 43–60.

Robert, L. 1948. 'Epigrammes relatives à des gouverneurs', *Hellenica* 4: 35–114.
Robinson, J. M. 2013. *The Manichaean Codices of Medinet Madi*, Eugene, OR.
Rochefort, G. 1960. *Saloustios, Des dieux et du monde*, Paris.
Rochefort, G. 2003. *L'Empereur Julien, Oeuvres Complètes* 2.1, *Discours de Julien Empereur (VI–IX)*, Paris.
Röcke, W. and J. Weitbrecht, eds., 2010. *Askese und Identität in Spätantike, Mittelalter und Früher Neuzeit*, Transformationen der Antike 14, Berlin.
Roebuck, V. J., tr. 2010. *The Dhammapada*, London.
Rolfe, J. C. 1940. *Ammianus Marcellinus. History, Vol. II: Books 20–26*, London and Cambridge, MA.
Roller, L. E. 1999. *In Search of God the Mother: The Cult of Anatolian Cybele*, Berkeley, CA.
Romer, F. E. 2014. 'Reading the Myth(s) of Empire: Paradoxography and Geographic Writing in the *Collectanea*', in K. Brodersen, ed., *Solinus: New Studies*, Heidelberg, 75–89.
Rosen, K. 2006. *Julian: Kaiser, Gott und Christenhasser*, Stuttgart.
Rosenmeyer, T. G. 2006. 'Ancient Literary Genres: A Mirage?', in A. Laird, ed., *Ancient Literary Criticism*, Oxford, 421–39.
Rougé, J., R. Delmaire, and F. Richard, 2005. *Les lois religieuses des empereurs romains de Constantin à Théodose II (312–438)* 1 *Code théodosien: Livre XVI*, Sources chrétiennes 497, Paris.
Rougé, J., R. Delmaire, O. Huck, F. Richard, and L. Guichard, 2009. *Les lois religieuses des empereurs romains de Constantin à Théodose II (312–438)* 2 *Code théodosien I–XV, Code justinien, Constitutions sirmondiennes*, Sources chrétiennes 531, Paris.
Rousseau, P., ed., 2009. *A Companion to Late Antiquity*, Malden, MA.
Rouwhorst, G. 2005. 'The Emergence of the Cult of the Maccabean Martyrs in Late Antique Christianity', in J. Leemans, ed., *More than a Memory: The Discourse of Martyrdom and the Construction of Christian Identity in the History of Christianity*, Leuven, 81–96.
Rubin, Z. 2002. '*Res Gestae Divi Saporis*: Greek and Middle Iranian in a Document of Sasanian Anti-Roman Propaganda', in J. N. Adams, M. Janse, and S. Swain, eds., *Bilingualism in Ancient Society. Language Contact and the Written Text*, Oxford, 267–97.
Russell, D. A., ed. and tr., 2001. *Quintilian: The Orator's Education*, 4 vols, Cambridge, MA.
Russell, D. A. 2006. 'Rhetoric and Criticism', in A. Laird, ed., *Ancient Literary Criticism*, Oxford, 267–83.
Rutgers, L. V. 2009. *Making Myths: Jews in Early Christian Identity Formation*, Leuven.
Saffrey, H. D. 1971. 'Abamon, pseudonyme de Jamblique', in R. B. Palmer and R. G. Hamerton-Kelly, eds., *Philomathes: Studies and Essays in the Humanities in Memory of Philip Merlan*, The Hague, 227–39.
Saffrey, H. D. and A.-Ph. Segonds, eds. and trs., 2012. *Porphyre. Lettre à Anébon l'Égyptien*, Paris.
Salazar, C. 2000. *The Treatment of War Wounds in Graeco-Roman Antiquity*, Leiden.
Salway, B. 2013. 'The Publication and Application of the Theodosian Code', *MEFRA* 125.2. Available at: http://journals.openedition.org/mefra/1754 (accessed 7 December 2018).

Salzman, M., R. Lizzi Testa, and M. Sághy, eds., 2015. *Pagans and Christians in Late Antique Rome: Interpreting the Evidence*, New York.
Salzman, M. R. 1987. 'Superstitio in the *Codex Theodosianus* and the Persecution of Pagans', *Vigiliae Christianae* 41: 172–88.
Salzman, M. R. 1990. *On Roman Time: The Codex-Calendar of 354 and the Rhythms of Urban Life in Late Antiquity*, Berkeley, CA.
Salzman, M. R. 1993. 'The Evidence for the Conversion of the Roman Empire to Christianity in Book 16 of the *Theodosian Code*', *Historia* 42: 362–78.
Sandwell, I. 2007. *Religious Identity in Late Antiquity: Greeks, Jews, and Christians in Antioch*, Cambridge.
Sargisean, P. 1904. *Ananun Žamanakagrut'iwn*, Venice.
Sawalaneanc', T. 1870. *Tearn Mixayēli Patriark'i Asorwoy Žamanakagrut'iwn*, Jerusalem.
Schlapbach, K. 2014. 'Solinus' *Collectanea rerum memorabilium* and Augustine's *curiosa historia*', in K. Brodersen, ed., *Solinus: New Studies*, Heidelberg, 141–56.
Schmidt, T. C. 2015. 'Calculating December 25 as the Birth of Jesus in Hippolytus' Canon and Chronicon', *Vigiliae Christianae* 69: 542–63.
Schott, J. M. 2008. *Christianity, Empire, and the Making of Religion in Late Antiquity*, Philadelphia, PA.
Schott, J. M. 2009. 'Philosophies of Language, Theories of Translation, and Imperial Intellectual Production: The Cases of Porphyry, Iamblichus, and Eusebius', *Church History* 78: 855–61.
Schwartz, S. 2001. *Imperialism and Jewish Society, 200 B.C.E. to 640 C.E.*, Princeton, NJ.
Scrofani, G. 2010. *La religione impure: La riforma di Giuliano Imperatore*, Brescia.
Sen, A. 2006. *Identity and Violence: The Illusion of Destiny*, New York.
Shaw, B. D. 2004. 'Who were the Circumcellions?', in A. H. Merrills, ed., *Vandals, Romans and Berbers: New Perspectives on Late Antique North Africa*, Aldershot, 227–58.
Shaw, B. D. 2011. *Sacred Violence: African Christians and Sectarian Hatred in the Age of Augustine*, Cambridge.
Shaw, G. 1995. 'Theurgy: Rituals of Unification in the Neoplatonism of Iamblichus', *Traditio* 41: 1–28.
Shepardson, C. 2014. *Controlling Contested Places: Late Antique Antioch and the Spatial Politics of Religious Controversy*, Berkeley, CA.
Shuger, D. K. 1984. 'The Grand Style and the "Genera Dicendi" in Ancient Rhetoric', *Traditio* 40: 1–42.
Shumate, N. 1996. *Crisis and Conversion in Apuleius' Metamorphoses*, Ann Arbor, MI.
Siémons, J.-L. 1988. *Theosophia in Neo-Platonic and Christian Literature*, London.
Simmons, M. B. 1995. *Arnobius of Sicca, Religious Conflict and Competition in the Age of Diocletian*, Oxford.
Simon, M. 1964. *Verus Israel: étude sur les relations entre chrétiens et Juifs dans l'empire romain (135–425)*, 2nd edn, Bibliothèque des Ecoles françaises d'Athènes et de Rome 156, Paris.
Skjaervø, P. O. 2011. 'Kartīr', *Encyclopaedia Iranica* 15.6: 608–28. Available at: http://www.iranicaonline.org/articles/kartir#pt2 (accessed January 2019).

Smith, A. 1993. 'Iamblichus' Views on the Relationship of Philosophy to Religion in *De Mysteriis*', in H. J. Blumenthal and E. G. Clark, eds., *The Divine Iamblichus*, London, 74–86.

Smith, G. S. 2015. *Guilt by Association: Heresy Catalogues in Early Christianity*, Oxford.

Smith, J. Z. 1995. 'Trading Places', in M. Meyer and P. Mirecki, eds., *Ancient Magic and Ritual Power*, Leiden, 13–27.

Smith, R. 1995. *Julian's Gods: Religion and Philosophy in the Thought and Action of Julian the Apostate*, London.

Snyder, G. 2003. *Ante-Pacem: Archaeological Evidence of Church Life before Constantine*, Macon, GA.

Sogno, C. 2012. '*Curiositas mihi recusat*. A Playful Defense of "Low" Biography against "High" History', in D. Brakke, D. Deliyannis, and E. Watts, eds., *Shifting Cultural Frontiers in Late Antiquity*, Farnham, 73–84.

Soler, E. 2006. *Le sacré et le salut à Antioche au IVe siècle ap. J.-C.: pratiques festives et comportements religieux dans le processus de christianisation de la cité*, Bibliothèque archéologique et historique/Institut français du Proche-Orient 176, Beyrouth.

Soler, E. 2010. 'Les "demi-chrétiens" d'Antioche: la pédagogie de l'exclusivisme chrétien et ses ressorts dans la prédication chrysostomienne', in H. Inglebert, S. Destephen, and B. Dumézil, eds., *Le problème de la christianisation du monde antique*, Paris, 281–91.

Somers, M. R. 1994. 'The Narrative Constitution of Identity', *Theory and Society* 23: 605–49.

Spears, A. 1998. 'African-American Language Use: Ideology and So-Called Obscenity', in S. Mufwene, J. Rickford, G. Bailey, and J. Baugh, eds., *African American English: Structure, History, and Use*, New York, 226–50.

Spiegel, G. M. 1990. 'History, Historicism, and the Social Logic of Texts in the Middle Ages', *Speculum* 65: 59–86.

Stark, R. 1997. *The Rise of Christianity: How the Obscure, Marginal Jesus Movement Became the Dominant Religious Force in the Western World in a Few Centuries*, San Francisco, CA.

Stefaniw, B. 2013. 'Straight Reading: Shame and the Normal in Epiphanius's Polemic Against Origen', *Journal of Early Christian Studies* 21: 413–35.

Stein, M. 2016. *Manichaica Latina. Band 4: Manichaei Thesaurus*, Opladen.

Stenger, J. R. 2014. 'Libanius and the "Game" of Hellenism', in L. Van Hoof, ed., *Libanius: A Critical Introduction*, Cambridge, 268–92.

Stern, S. 2001. *Calendar and Community: A History of the Jewish Calendar, Second Century BCE–Tenth Century CE*, Oxford.

Stolte, B. H. 2002. 'Magic and Byzantine Law in the Seventh Century', in J. N. Bremmer and J. R. Veenstra, eds., *The Metamorphosis of Magic from Late Antiquity to the Early Modern Period*, Leuven, 105–15.

Stowers, S. 2008. 'The Ontology of Religion', in W. Braun and R. T. McCutcheon, eds., *Introducing Religion*, London, 434–49.

Stratton, K. B. 2007. *Naming the Witch: Magic, Ideology, and Stereotype in the Ancient World*, New York.

Stratton, K. B. 2015. 'Early Greco-Roman Antiquity', in D. J. Collins, ed., *The Cambridge History of Witchcraft and Magic*, Cambridge, 83–112.

Strobel, A. 1977. *Ursprung und Geschichte des frühchristlichen Osterkalenders*, Berlin.
Strobel, A. 1984. *Texte zur Geschichte des frühchristlichen Osterkalenders*, Liturgiewissenschaftliche Quellen und Forschungen 64, Münster.
Stroumsa, G. 1993. 'Le radicalisme religieux du premier christianisme: contexte et implications', in A. Le Boulluec and E. Patlagean, eds., *Les retours aux Écritures: fondamentalismes présents et passés*, Louvain, 357–82.
Studer, B. 1996. 'La *cognitio historialis* di Porfirio nel De civitate Dei', in E. Cantarelli, ed., *Il De civitate Dei: l'opera, le interpretazioni, l'influsso*, Rome, 51–65.
Sundermann, W. 1981. *Mitteliranische manichäische Texte kirchengeschichtlichen Inhalts*, Berlin.
Sundermann, W. 1986. 'Mani, India and the Manichaean Religion', *South Asian Studies* 2: 11–19.
Sundermann, W. 1992. 'Iranische Kephalaiatexte?', in G. Wiessner and H.-J. Klimkeit, eds., *Studia Manichaica II. Internationaler Kongress zum Manichäismus*, Wiesbaden, 305–18.
Sundermann, W. 2009. 'Mani', *Encyclopaedia Iranica*. Available at: http://www.iranicaonline.org/articles/mani-founder-manicheism(accessed January 2019).
Swetnam-Burland, M. 2011. '"Egyptian" Priests in Roman Italy', in E. Gruen, ed., *Cultural Identity in the Ancient Mediterranean*, Los Angeles, CA, 336–53.
Tamas, H. and L. Van der Sypt, 2013. 'Asceticism and Syneisaktism in Asterius' *Liber ad Renatum monachum*', *Zeitschrift für antikes Christentum* 17.3: 504–25.
Tanaseanu-Döbler, I. 2010. 'Weise oder Scharlatane? Chaldaeerbilder der griechischrömischen Kaiserzeit und die *Chaldaeischen Orakel*', in H. Seng and M. Tardieu, eds., *Die Chaldaeischen Orakel: Kontext, Interpretation, Rezeption*, Heidelberg, 19–42.
Tanaseanu-Döbler, I. 2013. *Theurgy in Late Antiquity: The Invention of a Ritual Tradition*, Göttingen.
Tardieu, M. 1988. 'La Diffusion du Bouddhisme dans l'Empire Kouchan, l'Iran et la Chine, d'après un Kephalaion Manichéen Inédit', *Studia Iranica* 17: 153–82.
Tardieu, M. 2008. *Manichaeism*, with an Introduction by P. Mirecki; trans. by M. B. DeBevoise, Urbana and Chicago, IL.
Teitler, H. 2017. *The Last Pagan Emperor: Julian the Apostate and the War against Christianity*, Oxford.
Teske, R. J., ed., 2007. *The Works of Saint Augustine: A Translation for the Twenty-First Century. 1, 20, Answer to Faustus, a Manichean*, New York.
Tkacz, C. B. 2002. *The Key to the Brescia Casket: Typology and the Early Christian Imagination*, Paris.
Tougher, S. 2007. *Julian the Apostate*, Edinburgh.
Tougher, S. 2018. 'Julian Augustus on Augustus: Octavian in the *Caesars*', in P. Goodman, ed., *Afterlives of Augustus, AD 14–2014*, Cambridge, 87–102.
Toulouse, S. 2005. 'La théosophie de Porphyre et sa conception du sacrifice intérieur', in G. Stella, ed., *La cuisine et l'autel*, Turnhout, 329–41.
Trebilco, P. 2012. *Self-Designations and Group Identity in the New Testament*, New York.
Trentin, L. 2011. 'Deformity in the Roman Imperial Court', *Greece and Rome* 58: 195–208.
Trombley, F. R. 1985. 'Paganism in the Greek World at the End of Antiquity: The Case of Rural Anatolia and Greece', *Harvard Theological Review* 78: 327–52.

Trombley, F. R. 1993. *Hellenic Religion and Christianization, c. 370–529, Vol. I*, Leiden.
Trombley, F. R. 2012. *Hellenic Religion and Christianization, c. 370–529*, 2 vols, Leiden.
Turcan, R. 1982. *Firmicus Maternus, L'Erreur des Religions Paiennes*, Paris.
Turcan, R. 1996a. 'Attis Platonicus', in E. N. Lane, ed., *Cybele, Attis and Related Cults: Essays in Memory of M. J. Vermaseren*, Leiden, 387–403.
Turcan, R. 1996b. *The Cults of the Roman Empire*, trans. A. Nevill, Oxford.
Turpin, W. 1985. 'The Law Codes and Late Roman Law', *Revue internationale des droits de l'Antiquité* 32: 339–53.
Upson-Saia, K. 2011. 'Resurrecting Deformity: Augustine on Wounded and Scarred Bodies in the Heavenly Realm', in D. Schumm and M. Stoltzfus, eds., *Disability in Judaism, Christianity, and Islam*, New York, 93–112.
Vaggione, R. P. 1993. 'Of Monks and Lounge Lizards: "Arians", Polemics and Asceticism in the Roman East', in M. R. Barnes and D. H. Williams, eds., *Arianism after Arius: Essays on the Development of the Fourth Century Trinitarian Conflicts*, Edinburgh, 182–213.
Vallée, G. 1981. *A Study in Anti-Gnostic Polemics: Irenaeus, Hippolytus, and Epiphanius*, Waterloo, ON.
Van Bladel, K. 2009. *The Arabic Hermes. From Pagan Sage to Prophet of Science*, Oxford.
Van Dam, R., tr., 1988. *Gregory of Tours. Glory of the Martyrs*. Translated Texts for Historians 4, Liverpool.
Van Dam, R. 1993. *Saints and Their Miracles in Late Antique Gaul*. Princeton, NJ.
Van der Horst, P. W. 1982. 'The Way of Life of the Egyptian Priests according to Chaeremon', in M. S. H. G. Heerma van Voss, J. K. Hoensch, G. Mussies, E. van der Plas, and B. P. Velde, eds., *Studies in Egyptian Religion Dedicated to Prof. Jan Zandee*, Leiden, 61–71.
Van der Horst, P. W. 1984. *Chaeremon. Egyptian Priest and Stoic Philosopher. The Fragments Collected and Translated with Explanatory Notes*, Leiden.
Van Ginkel, J. J. 2006. 'The Perception and Presentation of the Arab Conquest in Syriac Historiography: How did the Changing Social Position of the Syrian Orthodox Community Influence the Account of their Historiographers?', in E. Grypeou, M. Swanson, and D. Thomas, eds., *The Encounter of Eastern Christianity with Early Islam*, Leiden, 171–84.
Van Hoof, L., ed., 2014. *Libanius: A Critical Introduction*, Cambridge.
Van Hoof, L. 2017. 'The Omnimoda Historia of Nummius Aemilianus Dexter: A Latin Translation of Eusebius' Chronography?', *Vigiliae Christianae* 71: 199–204.
Van Hoof, L., P. Manafis, and P. Van Nuffelen, 2017. 'Philo of Carpasia: Ecclesiastical History', *Revue d'Histoire Ecclésiastique* 112: 35–52.
Van Liefferinge, C. 1999. *La Théurgie: Des Oracles Chaldaïques à Proclus*, Liège.
Van Liefferinge, C. 2001. ' "Ethniques" et "Hellènes", Quelques réflexiones sur la portée nationale du paganisme', in E. Delruelle and V. Pirenne-Delforge, eds., *Kēpoi: de la religion à la philosophie: mélanges offerts à André Motte*, Kernos Supplement 11, Liège, 247–55.
Van Nuffelen, P. 2002a. 'Deux fausses lettres de Julien l'Apostat (La lettre aux Juifs, *Ep.* 51 [Wright], et la lettre à Arsacius, *Ep.* 84 [Bidez])', *Vigiliae Christianae* 56: 131–50.

Van Nuffelen, P. 2002b. 'La tête de l'"histoire acéphale"', *Klio* 84: 125–40.
Van Nuffelen, P. 2002c. 'Gélase de Césarée, un compilateur du cinquième siècle', *Byzantinische Zeitschrift* 95: 263–82.
Van Nuffelen, P. 2004. *Un héritage de paix et de piété. Étude sur les histoires ecclésiastiques de Socrate et de Sozomène*, Orientalia Lovanensia Analecta 142, Leuven.
Van Nuffelen, P. 2014. 'Not the Last Pagan: Libanius between Elite Rhetoric and Religion', in L. Van Hoof, ed., *Libanius: A Critical Introduction*, Cambridge, 293–314.
Van Nuffelen, P. 2019. 'Review of Wallraff, Stutz, and Marinides 2017', *Journal of Ecclesiastical History* 70: 148–9.
Van Nuffelen, P. forthcoming. 'Considérations sur l'anonyme homéen', in E. Amato, ed., *Les historiens grecs à l'état fragmentaire dans l'Antiquité tardive*, Rennes.
Van Nuffelen, P. and L. Van Hoof, 2020. 'Clavis historicorum antiquitatis posterioris (300–800)—Introduction', in P. Van Nuffelen and L. Van Hoof, eds., *Clavis Historicorum Antiquitatis Posterioris: An Inventory of Late Antique Historiography (A.D. 300–800)*, Brepols, i–lxxxii.
Van Oort, J. 1991. *Jerusalem and Babylon. A Study into Augustine's City of God and the Sources of his Doctrine of the Two Cities*, Leiden.
Velásquez, S. I. 2010. 'Between Orthodox Belief and "Superstition" in Visigothic Hispania', in R. L. Gordon and F. Marco Simón, eds., *Magical Practice in the Latin West*, Leiden, 601–27.
Vermaseren, M. J. 1977. *Cybele and Attis: The Myth and the Cult*, London.
Vessey, M. 2005. 'History, Fiction, and Figuralism in Book 8 of Augustine's Confessions', in D. B. Martin and P. Cox Miller, eds., *The Cultural Turn in Late Ancient Studies: Gender, Asceticism, and Historiography*, Durham, NC, 237–57.
Vessey, M. 2010. 'Reinventing History: Jerome's Chronicle and the Writing of the Post-Roman West', in S. McGill, C. Sogno, and E. Watts, eds., *From the Tetrarchs to the Theodosians: Later Roman History and Culture 284–450 CE*, Cambridge, 265–89.
Vessey, M. 2012. 'History of the Book: Augustine's *City of God* and Post-Roman Cultural Memory', in J. Wetzel, ed., *Augustine's City of God: A Critical Guide*, Cambridge, 14–32.
Vessey, M. 2014. 'Fashions for Varro in Late Antiquity and Christian Ways with Books', in C. Harrison, C. Humfress, and I. Sandwell, eds., *Being Christian in Late Antiquity: A Festschrift for Gillian Clark*, Oxford, 253–77.
Volgers, A. and C. Zamagni, eds., 2004. *Erotapokriseis: Early Christian Question-and-Answer Literature in Context*, Leuven.
Von Harnack, A. 1916. *Porphyrios, 'Gegen die Christen', 15 Bucher: Zeugnisse, Fragmente und Referate*, Berlin.
Von Martels, Z. 2014. 'Turning the Tables on Solinus' Critics: The Unity of Content and Form of the *Polyhistor*', in K. Brodersen, ed., *Solinus: New Studies*, Heidelberg, 10–23.
Von Staden, H. 1994. 'Author and Authority: Celsus and the Construction of a Scientific Self', in M. E. Vázquez Buján, ed., *Tradición e innovación de la medicina latina de la antigüedad y de la alta edad media: actas del IV coloquio internacional sobre "los textos médicos latinos antiguos"*, Santiago de Compostela, 103–17.

von Wilamowitz-Moellendorf, U. 1900. 'Ein Bruchstück aus der Schrift des Porphyrius gegen die Christen', *Zeitschrift für die neutestamentliche Wissenschaft* 1: 101–5.

Wallraff, M. 2009. 'Magie und Religion in den Kestoi des Julius Africanus', in M. Wallraff and L. Mecella, eds., *Die Kestoi des Julius Africanus und ihre Überlieferung*, Texte und Untersuchungen zur Geschichte der Altchristlichen Literatur 165, Berlin, 39–52.

Wallraff, M., J. Stutz, and N. Marinides, 2017. *Gelasius of Caesarea. Ecclesiastical History. The Extant Fragments: With an Appendix Containing the Fragments from Dogmatic Writings*, Die griechischen christlichen Schriftsteller der ersten Jahrhunderte NF 25, Berlin.

Watts, E. 2015. *The Final Pagan Generation*, Berkeley, CA.

Weedon, C. 2004. *Culture and Identity: Narratives of Difference and Belonging*, Maidenhead.

Whitebrook, M. 2001. *Identity, Narrative, and Politics*, London.

Whitmarsh, T. 2001. *Greek Literature and the Roman Empire: The Politics of Imitation*, Oxford.

Whitmarsh, T. 2005. *The Second Sophistic*, Oxford.

Whitmarsh, T. 2007. 'Prose Literature and the Severan Dynasty', in S. Swain, S. Harrison, and J. Elsner, eds., *Severan Culture*, Cambridge, 29–51.

Whitmarsh, T. 2017. 'Greece: Hellenistic and Early Imperial Continuities', in D. S. Richter and W. A. Johnson, eds., *The Oxford Handbook of the Second Sophistic*, Oxford, 11–24.

Wild, C. 2011. 'Jenseits von Gut und Böse. Baudelaire und die Moralistik', in V. Kapp and D. Scholl, eds., *Literatur und Moral. Schriften zur Literaturwissenschaft*, Berlin, 469–86.

Wilken, R. L. 1983. *John Chrysostom and the Jews: Rhetoric and Reality in the Late Fourth Century*, Transformation of the Classical Heritage 4, Berkeley, CA.

Williams, F. 2009. *The Panarion of Epiphanius of Salamis: Book I (Sects 1–46)*, 2nd edn, Leiden.

Wilson, N. G., ed., 1975. *Saint Basil on Greek Literature*, London.

Wimbush, V. L. and R. Valantasis, eds., 1995. *Asceticism*, Oxford.

Wischmeyer, W. 1998. 'Magische Texte. Vorüberlegungen und Materialen zum Verständnis christlicher spätantiker Texte', in J. van Oort and D. Wyrwa, eds., *Heiden und Christen im 5. Jahrhundert*, Leuven, 88–122.

Wood, P. 2010. *'We have No King but Christ': Christian Political Thought in Greater Syria on the Eve of the Arab Conquest (c. 400–585)*, Oxford.

Wooten, C. W., tr., 1987. *Hermogenes' 'On Types of Style'*, Chapel Hill, NC.

Wright, W. C. 1913. *The Works of the Emperor Julian, Vol. 1*, London and New York.

Wright, W. C. 1923. *The Works of the Emperor Julian, Vol. 3*, London and New York.

Wright, W. C. 1961. *Eunapius and Philostratus. Lives of the (Philosophers and) Sophists*, Loeb Classical Library 134, Cambridge, MA.

Young, F. M. 1982. 'Did Epiphanius Know What He Meant By Heresy?', *Studia Patristica* 17: 199–205.

Young, F. M. 2010. *From Nicaea to Chalcedon: A Guide to the Literature and its Background*, 2nd edn, London.

Zanker, P. and B. Ewald, 2012. *Living with Myths: The Imagery of Roman Sarcophagi*, tr. J. Slater, Oxford.

Ziadé, R. 2007. *Les martyrs Maccabées: de l'histoire juive au culte Chrétien (Les homélies de Grégoire de Nazianze et de Jean Chrysostome)*, Leiden.

Zionts, R. A. 2002. *A Critical Examination of Epiphanius' Panarion in Terms of Jewish-Christian Groups and Nicander of Colophon*, Ph.D thesis, Pennsylvania State University.

Zöpfl, F. 1927. *Der Kommentar des Pseudo-Eustathius zum Hexaemeron*, Münster.

Index

Abamon (pseudonym of Iamblichus) 35–6
Abraham (patriarch) 90, 91, 139, 163, 169, 173–4, 178, 208, 210–11
Acdestis 72–3
Achilles (Homeric hero) 210
Acts of Thomas 119, 136
Adam (patriarch) 6, 11, 83, 91, 95–6, 163–5, 174, 178, 189, 199, 208, 210–12, 217, 226–30
Adimantus (Manichaean teacher) 20
Aeschylus 236, 243
Africa 91
Agdamia (city in Phrygia) 101
Agdistis, *see* Acdestis
Agdus (rock) 72
Alexander (individual criticised by Libanius) 104
Alexander III (king of Macedon) 119
Alexander Polyhistor 174
Alexandria 9, 54n.27, 161, 164, 174–6
Ambrose of Milan 140, 156, 191, 226
Ammianus Marcellinus 52–4, 150, 153
Amphilochius of Iconium 101
Anastasius of Sinai 138–9
Anatolius (author of a paschal cycle) 169
Ancyra, Council of (314) 140
Andreas (chronicler) 9, 161–3, 169–174, 176–8
Anebo (supposed Egyptian priest) 34–5, 45
angels/archangels 134, 139, 228
Annianus (chronicler) 9, 161–3, 173–7
Anomoeanism 19, 186
Anonymous Arian historiographer (= Anonymous Homoean historian, supposed author of *Continuatio Eusebii antiochiensis*) 164–5
Antioch in Pisidia 101
Antioch on the Orontes 6, 19–20, 103–106, 108
Antoninus Pius (Roman emperor) 149
Apocryphal Acts of the Apostles 136
Apollinarius of Laodicea 186–7
Apollo 45, 111n.67
Apollonius of Tyana 132
Apostolic Constitutions 140
Aquila (Biblical translator) 227
Aquileia, Council of (381) 191
Arcadius (Roman emperor) 156
Ardashir (Persian king) 119

Ariadne 201–2
Arianism 20, 161, 165–8, 191; *see also* Anomoeanism, Homoianism
Aristotle 235, 237
Arnobius of Sicca 5, 29, 67, 69–76, 80, 132
Arsacius (purported correspondent of Julian) 51, 54–5
Asia Minor 51
Asianism (in style) 239–40
Assyrians 35–6
Asterius Ansedunensis 10–11, 220–30
Athanasius of Alexandria 29, 164, 166, 169, 173, 176, 187
Athens/Athenians 79, 114
Attalus (king of Pergamum) 67
Attic style, Atticism 235, 239, 240, 246–7, 249
Attis 67–9, 71–82
Augustine of Hippo 3, 5–6, 7, 9–10, 17, 18, 20–1, 22, 25–6, 40n.65, 42, 68, 83–98, 99–100, 106, 109–113, 132–8, 140, 182, 192–5, 197, 221–2
Ausonius (Roman author and imperial official) 3, 15, 17, 18, 22, 26–7, 162, 178

Babylon 86, 90, 96–8
Bacchic celebrations 202
Balaam (biblical figure) 139
baptism 17–18, 21
Bardaisan (religious teacher) 121
Bardaisanites 117
Basil of Caesarea 11, 101, 110, 232, 239, 241–9
Bethlehem 222
bodhisattva 124–5
Braga, Council of (572) 141
Buddha 119, 121, 125; see also *bodhisattva*

Cainites ('gnostic' sect) 189
Calama (city in North Africa) 25
calendar, arguments about 170–3
Cappadocian Fathers, *see* Basil of Caesarea; Gregory of Nazianzus; Gregory of Nyssa
Carthage 67, 78, 83, 92
castration 67–9, 72–9
Celsus (first-century AD encyclopaedic author) 185
Celsus (Platonist philosopher and critic of Christianity) 131

Index

Cervonius (proconsul of Achaea) 103
Chaeremon (Stoic philosopher) 40
Chalcedon, Council of (451) 149
Chaldeans 31, 35–6, 40, 45, 174–6
China 119
Christmas 173–4
Cicero 87, 113, 221, 232, 234–8
Claudia (Roman priestess) 78
Claudius (Roman emperor) 68
Clement of Alexandria 40n.69
Cluj (Romanian town) 23
Codex-Calendar of Philocalus/354 68
Codex Theodosianus 145–59
Collatio Mosaicarum et Romanarum Legum (= *Comparison of Roman and Mosaic Laws*) 151–2
Columella (Roman agricultural author) 183
Commodus (Roman emperor) 188
Constans (Roman emperor) 70, 151
Constantine I (Roman emperor) 8, 18–19, 50, 53, 55, 69–71, 136n.39, 140, 146–52, 154–8, 163, 168, 171, 174, 178
Constantinople 63, 70, 101, 108, 145, 147–9, 152, 155–8
Constantinople, Council of (360) 156
Constantinople, Council of (381) 156
Constantius II (Roman emperor) 70, 150, 155–6, 165
Continuatio continuationis 9
Continuatio Eusebii antiochiensis 9
Crispus (son of Constantine I) 69
Cybele, *see* Magna Mater
Cyprian of Carthage 16
Cyril of Jerusalem 168

daemons/demons 31, 40, 45, 63, 131, 135, 137, 139–40
Daisan (river) 121
Daniel (prophet) 200, 208, 210–12
David (king) 210, 242, 244, 248
Decius (Roman emperor) 16
Delphi 78, 111n.67
devil 134, 135n.33, 136, 190–2
Demosthenes 236, 238, 242, 244
Demetrius (author of *On Style*) 232–7, 242
Dexter (historian) 162
Diocletian (Roman emperor) 33, 149, 151
Dionysius of Halicarnassus 232, 234n.17, 235–8, 240, 247
Dionysus 201
Donatism 157
Dura Europos 61

Easter 9, 77, 81–2, 169–173, 175, 177–8
Ebion 20

Eden 226
Egypt/Egyptians 31, 34–40, 43n.95, 45, 101, 119, 133n.20, 137–9, 175
Eleusinian Mysteries 79, 81
encratism 222
En-Dor, the witch of 139
Endymion 201–2
Enoch (biblical figure) 163, 174, 210
Epiphanius of Salamis 9–10, 162, 180–97
Essenes 41
Ethiopians 91
Eucharist 77
Eunomius of Cyzicus 242–3, 246–7, 249
Euripides 235
Eusebius of Caesarea 4, 8–9, 20, 29–30, 33n.19, 36–8, 45–6, 49, 55, 62, 69n.15, 75n.38, 90, 131, 149, 158, 161–178
Eusebius (student of Libanius) 106
Evagrius Ponticus 139
Eve 199, 208, 210–12, 217, 226, 228–30

Faustus (Manichaean bishop) 20–21
Festus (proconsul of Asia, 372–8) 102
Filastrius of Brescia 9–10, 182, 189–94, 197, 182
Firmicus Maternus 5, 30n.9, 67, 69–71, 75–7, 80–1
Franks 160

Gabriel (archangel) 139
Galen (second-century AD doctor) 9, 182, 184–5, 187–8
Galerius (Roman emperor) 60, 151
Galli (priests of Magna Mater) 67, 69, 72, 74
Gallus, *see* Attis
Gandhara 118
Gangra, Synod of 219
Gaul 138
Gaza 128–9, 137
Gelasius of Caesarea 164, 177
goat 73–4
Gondeisos (waterway in Khuzestan) 121
Goths 94
Goundesh (Persian sage) 116, 120–4
Gratian (Roman emperor) 180–1
Gregory of Nazianzus 11, 50, 52–4, 62, 63, 103, 166, 232, 242–5, 247
Gregory of Nyssa 11, 232, 239, 242–8
Gregory of Tours 7, 137, 140

Hadrian (Roman emperor) 149
Hannibal (Carthaginian general) 74
Hebrews 46
Helena (Roman empress) 140, 149
Heliconius (historian) 162

Index

Heliodorus (provincial governor and erstwhile seller of fish-pickle) 103
Helios 54n.27, 71, 74, 76–7
Hellenism 3, 4, 28–47, 48–9, 51–62, 241, 249
Heraclius (Cynic) 80
Hermogenes (writer on literary style) 232–3, 238
Hermogenes (proconsul of Achaea) 103
Hilaria (festival) 78–9
Hilarianus (chronographer) 162–3, 175n.68, 177–8
Hilarion (monk) 128–9, 131, 136–7, 142
Himerius (rhetorician) 103
Hippo Zaritus 93
Hippolytus of Rome 163, 170, 174, 178
Hispania 138–9
Homer 108

Ia (daughter of Midas) 72
Iamblichus (philosopher) 4, 29–30, 34–6, 38, 43–6, 49
incerti 22
India/Indians 7, 40, 119, 120–1, 124–5
Iodasphes (Persian sage) 124–6
Isaac (patriarch) 199, 208, 210, 212
Isaiah (prophet) 246
Isocrates (orator) 236, 238
Italy 91

Jacob (patriarch) 139
Jeremiah (prophet) 190
Jerome 10–11, 20, 90, 128–9, 133n.20, 136–7, 142, 161–2, 166, 178, 220–3, 226–7, 229–30
John the Baptist 207–8, 211–12
John Chrysostom 5, 6, 7, 16–17, 19–20, 26n.78, 100–101, 105–109, 111–2, 134–6, 250
John of Ephesus 160
John the Evangelist 244–6
John Lydus 68
John Malalas 161, 178
John Philoponus 42
Jonah (biblical figure) 199, 207–8, 210–13, 215–16
Jovinian/Jovinianist controversy 10, 222, 224
Judaism 9, 19–21, 34, 37, 41, 46, 55–6, 153, 155–6, 161, 167–173, 177, 190, 199–200, 210
Julia Domna (Roman empress) 119n.48
Julian (Roman emperor) 3, 4–5, 29n.5, 32n.18, 48–64, 67–71, 77–82, 101, 110, 147, 150, 151n.39, 153, 155, 161, 165–7
Julian calendar 171

Julius Africanus (chronographer) 162–3, 174
Julius Constantius (father of Julian) 70
Jupiter 71–3
Justin martyr 29n.5, 132

Kartīr the *mobed* 125
Kirdīr, son of Artabana (Sassanian dignitary) 125–6
Korybantes 43

Lactantius (rhetorician) 29, 69
Laodicea, Council of (c. 380) 138–9
Lazarus (Jesus' friend) 199, 208, 211
Libanius (rhetorician and professor) 5, 6, 26n.78, 53, 100–108, 111–2
Liber (god) 72, 76
Libya 175
Lollianus Mavortius (consul, 355) 70
Longinus (author of *On the Sublime*) 233–7, 244–5
Lot (nephew of Abraham) 210
Lysias (one of the ten Attic orators) 235

Maccabean revolt 50, 55–7, 61
Magi 39, 41, 45, 208–9, 211–12
Magna Mater 5, 43, 67–82, 133–4
Magnus Maximus (Roman usurper) 155
Mani 7, 20, 115–27
Manichaeanism 3, 5, 6–7, 20–21, 114–27, 132, 151, 153, 186, 222
Marcella (wife of Porphyry) 33, 43
Marcian (Roman emperor) 149
Marnas (deity venerated in Gaza) 128–9
Marius Victorinus (rhetorician and professor) 18, 22
Martialis (third-century Spanish bishop) 16, 18
Martin of Braga 139
Martin of Tours 137
martyrdom 17, 60–61, 102
Mary, mother of Jesus 209
Masoukeos (Persian sage) 120, 123–4
Medinet Madi 115, 118
Megalensia (festival) 67
Meleager, myth of 201
Meletius of Antioch 168
Metrodorus 162–3, 178
Michael (archangel) 139
Michael Psellos 35
Midas (king of Pessinus) 72
Milan 156
'Milan', 'Edict' 'of' (313) 52
Moses (prophet)) 131, 138–9, 208–11, 215, 222
Muses 188, 197, 204

Nana (daughter of Sangarius) 72
Naqš-e Rostam 125

Nectarius (correspondent of Augustine) 25–6
Neoplatonism 5, 68, 71, 77–81; see also Platonism
Nereids 202
Nestorius of Constantinople 158
Nicaea, Council of (325) 9
Nicander of Colophon 9, 185, 191, 197
Nicomedia 33, 101
Nimrod (biblical figure) 96–7
Nisibis 166
Noah (patriarch) 6, 83, 90, 91, 96, 208, 210–11, 215
North Africa 151, 153

Olympius (governor of Cappadocia Secunda) 103
Ophites ('gnostic' group) 189
Optimus (bishop and pupil of Libanius) 101
Origen (Christian scholar) 20, 33–4, 131, 133, 250
Osiris 76
Ovid 221

Pabakos (Manichaean catechumen) 123
paideia 2, 10, 33, 99–113, 204, 207, 215, 218
Palladas (poet) 29n.5
Panodorus (compiler of chronography or chronicle) 162–3, 173–4, 179
Paschal Chronicle 161, 164–9
Passover 171–3
Paul (apostle) 211, 222, 229, 231, 241–2, 244–6
Paulinus of Nola 18, 26
Persephone 202
Persia/Persians 7, 38–9, 41, 116–27
Pessinus 67, 72–3, 75–6
Peter (apostle) 209, 211–12, 239
Phaethon 74
Philo of Alexandria 171
Philo of Carpasia 164, 177
Philostorgius (ecclesiastical historian) 149, 164, 168
Philostratus (sophist) 109, 119n.48, 132, 136n.38
Phoenicians 37
Phrygia 72–5, 77
Plato 46, 109, 112, 235–6, 238, 244
Platonism 29, 43; see also Neoplatonism
Pliny the Elder 6, 9, 85, 87, 91–3, 97, 182, 185, 187n.42, 188, 190n.54
Pliny the Younger 151
Plotinus (philosopher) 205
Polyphemus (cyclops) 87
pomegranates 72, 81

Porphyry of Tyre 4, 28–47, 49, 69, 75n.38, 80, 86–8, 91–2
Proclus (philosopher) 35
Proserpina 76
Pulcheria (Roman empress) 149

Qainan, son of Arphaxsad 170
Quintilian (grammarian) 104–105, 111–2, 238
Quodvultdeus of Carthage 192–5, 197

Raphael (archangel) 139
Ravenna 147
religio 150, 155
Rimini, Council of (359) 156
Rome 67, 68, 74–5, 77, 85–6, 90, 92, 94–5, 97, 104, 198, 222
Rufinus (ecclesiastical historian) 164

Sabazios 43
Sabinus the Arian (possibly the same person as Sabinus of Heracleia) 163
Sallust (historian) 87
Samaritan woman (conversed with Jesus according to John 4) 208, 212
Samaritans 171, 173
Sangarius (king or river) 72
Salutius (Praetorian Prefect) 81
Sappho 235
Second Sophistic 2, 56, 109
Selene 201–2
semi-Christian 3, 15–22, 26, 32
Serdica, Council of (343) 169
Servius (Roman grammarian) 22
Sethians ('gnostic' sect) 189
Severus (pupil of Libanius) 100
Shadrach, Meshach and Abednego (three Hebrew youths in the fiery furnace) 208, 210–11
Shapur (king of Touran) 120
Shapur I (Persian king) 116–7, 119–20, 124–6
Shenoute of Atripe 137
shepherd, image of 203, 205–8, 211–12
Simon Magus (heresiarch) 186, 189, 193
Simplicianus (Milanese presbyter) 18
Sirmondian Constitutions 152
Socrates (ecclesiastical historian) 8, 109, 149, 158, 164, 168, 171, 178
Sol, see Helios
Solinus (encyclopaedic author) 6, 92–3
Solomon (king) 139
Sozomen (ecclesiastical historian) 8, 54, 106, 149, 168, 171
Sulpicius Severus (composer of narrative chronicle in Latin) 162–3, 179

Index

superstitio 8, 54, 136n.37, 150–2
Susannah (biblical figure) 208, 210–11
Symmachus (biblical translator) 20, 227
Symmachus (pagan senator) 22
syneisaktism 220, 223, 228, 230
Syrians 38
Syro-Mesopotamia 118

Tacitus 187
Talmud 115
taurobolium 68
Tertullian (Christian author) 38n.55, 61, 68
tetrarchic period/law codes 148
Theoderic the Great (Ostrogothic king) 141
Theodoret (ecclesiastical historian) 149, 250
Theodosian Code (Codex Theodosianus) 8, 145–59
Theodosius I (Roman emperor) 156–7
Theodosius II (Roman emperor) 8, 145–59
Theodotion (biblical translator) 20
Theophanes, Chronicle of 164–7
Theophilus of Alexandria 9, 164, 175–7
theosophia/theosophoi 39–46
Theseus 202
Thessalonica 155

Thucydides 187, 236, 238
Timotheus (author of a text about Magna Mater) 71, 73
Timothy the Apollinarian 164
Tisamenus (*consularis* of Syria) 103n.26
Trajan (Roman emperor) 151
Troglodytes 34
Trullo, Council of (691) 141

Uriel (archangel) 139

Valens (Roman emperor) 155, 180–1
Valentinian I (Roman emperor) 180–1
Valentinian II (Roman emperor) 156–7
Valentinian III (Roman emperor) 146–8, 152–8
Valerius (pontifex) 72
Varro (Roman scholar) 87, 90, 91
Vatican Hill 68
Venus 210
Vergil 87, 113, 221
Vitruvius (Roman author on architecture) 185, 187n.42

Zeus 78
Zoroaster 119, 123